795

Medieval Academy Rep
9

D1284414

Medieval Academy Reprints for Teaching

EDITORIAL BOARD

Jeremy duQ. Adams
Judson Allen
Robert L. Benson
Christopher Kleinhenz
Hilary S. Marshall
David Staines
Prudence Tracy

JOHN GOWER
EDITED BY RUSSELL A. PECK

Confessio Amantis

Published by University of Toronto Press
Toronto Buffalo London
in association with the Medieval Academy of America

PREFACE

In his own day Gower's reputation as poet and moral spokes-
man was secure beyond doubt. He was even the first English poet
to enjoy international recognition, his *Confessio Amantis* having
been translated into both Spanish and Portuguese early in the fif-
teenth century. For more than two hundred years he was yoked
with Chaucer as the heart of the English tradition of poetry. Lyd-
gate and the Scottish poets praised and imitated his poems; in the
Renaissance he was honored not only by Shakespeare, but also by
Ben Jonson, who cites Gower more than any other author in his
English Grammar. Nor can it justly be said that his reputation
outstripped his true merit. True it is that these various men of
letters honored Gower for different qualities—Lydgate and the
Scottish poets for his narrative skill and technical innovations,
Jonson for his correctness, and Shakespeare as a repository of an-
cient and hallowed truth. But the variety of tributes is testimony
to Gower's variety of abilities.

Modern critics have tended to look on Gower as a man of his
times, to praise him for his earnest involvement in the affairs of
his day, but to deny him longevity of significance. Indeed, no
English poet embodies as many qualities which we in retrospect
would identify as crucial to medieval sensibility—keen social con-
science, love of authority and tradition, philosophical pessimism;
a fetish for analogy, encyclopedic lore, symmetry, and order, as
well as aphorism, proverb, and sententiae; delight in stories almost
for their own sake and pleasure in variety of narrative forms (alle-
gory, fable, folklore, and biblical, classical, and historical modes);
pleasure in wit, ludicrous incongruities, and the bizarre and gro-
tesque. But these characteristics in no way deny him a voice in
our own time. His words of wisdom and pleasure may offer a

v

restorative for the twentieth century as well as for Chaucer's renaissance and Shakespeare's renaissance.

In choosing the Middle English selections for this edition, I have tried to maintain four criteria. First, I have attempted to include enough of the frame story to give readers an accurate estimate of the over-all shape of the poem in order that they might appreciate its argument as well as its *genre*. Second, I have included all tales which seem to me to be particularly pertinent to advancing the argument. I have also tried to include representative examples of the wide variety of narrative forms and subjects which the poem encompasses and which demonstrate the scope of story matter which the medieval audience delighted in. Finally, for the benefit of students of medieval literature who like to make comparisons, I have included all the tales which Chaucer tells or alludes to.

The text of my Middle English selections is based on Professor G. C. Macaulay's standard edition of the poem, first published in two volumes in 1900 by the Early English Text Society, and later included as volumes two and three in *The Works of John Gower,* 4 volumes (Oxford, 1901). An editor of the *Confessio Amantis,* unlike an editor of Chaucer's *Canterbury Tales,* is not confronted with the impossible task of choosing between several different but equally authoritative manuscripts. Although an unusually large number of manuscripts of Gower's poem have survived (forty-nine by the most recent count), the Fairfax 3 manuscript of the Bodleian Library is the most authoritative, and it is on the Fairfax manuscript that Professor Macaulay based his edition. I have checked his work against the manuscript and found it to be admirably accurate. His few emendations are indicated in his footnotes and are generally made with the authority of other good manuscripts. The manuscript is written in a very good hand of the end of the fourteenth century. Moreover it has been carefully edited and corrected by the principal amanuensis. These revisions are sufficiently extensive and detailed to suggest that Gower himself must have supervised them.

There is some punctuation in the Fairfax manuscript; Professor Macaulay has usually followed it when it occurs internally within lines, though he takes greater liberties with end-of-line punctuation. The manuscript also employs an elaborate scheme which seems to be Gower's own for capitalization of particular substantives. Such capitalization has been carefully maintained in this edition. So too the indentations of verse paragraphs, which are represented in the manuscript by illuminated capital letters.

My indebtedness to Professor Macaulay and Miss Zelma Leonhard in my discussions of sources in the footnotes and to Professor John H. Fisher for biographical details is gratefully acknowledged. I also wish to thank Professors Stanley Kahrl and Robert Hinman, for discussing various editorial decisions with me; Professors Alfred Geier and Frederick W. Locke, for their assistance in translating Gower's Latin; and Leonard Tennenhouse and Monica McAlpine, for a variety of assistances.

Russell A. Peck

Kingston-upon-Hull
November, 1967

CONTENTS

ix

INTRODUCTION

Scripture veteris capiunt exempla futuri,
Nam dabit experta res magis esse fidem.
[Writings of antiquity contain examples for the future,
For a thing known by experience will afford greater faith.]
—*Vox Clamantis*

Gower's *Confessio Amantis* is one of several Middle English poems
which may be classified as poems of consolation. The model be-
hind this genre is Boethius's *Consolation of Philosophy.* The like-
nesses of the group, which includes poems such as *Pearl* and
Chaucer's *Book of the Duchess,* lie in both subject matter and plot
structure. In each the primary subject is the narrator's restless state
of mind; the plot is his search for repose. The skeletal structure of
the plot normally follows four main steps: (1) There will be an
opening description of the narrator's spiritual inertia. His psycho-
logical turmoil will be presented as an illness, usually in the form
of a death-wish of some sort. He will probably express a desire for
help, but at the same time acknowledge that he does not know
where to find it. (2) The distracted narrator will perform a posi-
tive action which will precipitate a change of scene, whereupon
new characters will appear who will be projections of different
fragments of himself or his environment. The new setting is the
realm of the mind in which the quest will take place. (3) The
argument of the poem will be conducted through dialogue between
the narrator and the new characters. This is the most elastic part
of the genre, and it is here and in the conclusion that the author
will exercise the most originality as he chooses particular devices
suitable to the intention of his poem. But regardless of the device,

whether it be a hart hunt, a walk beside a river coming from Paradise, or a confession, the argument will most likely begin with questions of identity, such as "What are you?" "Who are you?" or "What is the trouble with your soul?" It will then progress through a series of partial revelations which will be presented dramatically and will probably be reminiscent of Boethius's baring of his wound in order that Philosophy might apply the appropriate medicine. (4) The analysis and therapy will end with a tense moment in which the disturbed persona will waver, then achieve a final revelation which will bring about his return, usually to home.

The *Confessio Amantis* is organized along the lines which I have outlined, though Gower will, as we shall see, exercise a great deal of ingenuity in working within them. His most radical change is the introduction of a complex social analogue which he presents through exposition and which at first seems quite separate from the romance plot. Such a scheme is highly ambitious, and in its daring perhaps even admirable. Gower attempts to conjoin social criticism presented in a nonfictional mode with fiction. At least the effect is to leave no doubt in the reader's mind about Gower's convictions regarding the validity of his argument and, as we find ourselves dealing with England as well as the Lover, it may even magnify our views of mankind. Since this side of the poem is likely to give readers of the *Confessio* the greatest difficulty, I shall attempt to relate my analysis of the romance plot to the exposition on England as often as I can in this short space, though I shall by no means be able to deal with that problem adequately.

The romance plot of the *Confessio* begins as the narrator, having told us of his "woful care," "wofull day," and "wofull chance" at the hands of Fortune, sets out walking one day in May. Everything around him seems happy and gay, but he is miserable. He is unhappy because,

I was further fro my love
Than Erthe is fro the hevene above.
[I.105–106]

He wanders into a wood, not to appreciate the music of the birds, he says, but to weep, wish, and complain to himself. He throws himself to the ground and wishes he were dead. Then he awakens from his pain and, filled with self-pity, he cries out to Cupid and Venus, who suddenly appear before him and transfix his heart on love's fiery dart.

This opening description and event define the narrator's dilemma and thus establish the main considerations of the plot. Amans has committed a crime against Nature. In his love fantasy he has set himself apart from the mutual pleasures of her domain. He has no interest in the beauty of May or the harmonies of the birds; his singular concern is pampering his secretive emotions. In such an unnatural stance he is indeed, to turn his comparison around, farther from heaven in his love than earth is. Lying prostrate in the wood, performing antics most strange to Nature's creatures, he is the epitome of alienation. The piercing of his heart by Cupid's dart clinches his loss of natural freedom. He is captive to his cupidity, and many lines will pass before he returns home from this spiritual exile.

When Venus first addresses Amans, she asks him questions of identity: "What art thou, Sone?" (I.154,160). Amans replies, "A Caitif that lith hiere: / What wolde ye, my Ladi diere?" (I. 161–162). The question is reminiscent of Boethius's *Consolation*, where Philosophy asked, "What are you?" of that narrator. The right answer is, of course, "A man." But in his infatuation Amans has forgotten what a man should be. He asks to be cured of his affliction, but Venus says:

"Tell thi maladie:
What is thi Sor of which thou pleignest?
Ne hyd it noght, for if thou feignest,
I can do the no medicine."
[I.164–167]

Again her request reminds us of Philosophy's request that Boethius bare his wound by reiterating his illness. But Venus is no Philosophy. Her intention is quite the opposite, her demands a parody of Philosophy's. Her motives are defensive and courtly, based on suspicion rather than mutuality. She has learned how to deal with "faitours." In her world nobody trusts anybody. Let Amans explain his intentions.

To develop the argument of his poem Gower uses the device of confession. It is a felicitous choice, as C. S. Lewis has observed, because of the possibilities for variety and dramatic effects which it offers. But Gower did not choose the device for literary reasons alone. Confession, as he understood it, is an act of self-discovery. It is for him what psychoanalysis is for us. It begins with a review of experience in an effort to find out why it is that we are the way we are, in order that we may ultimately reintegrate our minds and emotions. "You have forgotten what you are," Philosophy tells Boethius: Amans's problem is precisely the same. He is guilty of faulty self-definition. Having lost his natural orientation he is not only far from his heart's desire, but even uncertain of what that desire is. Venus sends him to a confessor named Genius, who will become his attendant spirit. To Genius he appeals:

I prai the let me noght mistime
Mi schrifte, for I am destourbed
In al myn herte, and so contourbed,
That I ne may my wittes gete,
So schal I moche thing foryete:
Bot if thou wolt my schrifte oppose
Fro point to point, thanne I suppose,
Ther schal nothing be left behinde.
Bot now my wittes ben so blinde,
That I ne can miselven teche.

[I.220–229]

At least his intention is good, and that is no small matter. Indeed, by the end of the poem there will be nothing left behind: Genius, "with his wordes debonaire," will search out the circumstances of Amans's soul, and through his questions redefine man in his natural and historical environments so that Amans may remember what he is and forget what he is not.

To appreciate what goes on in the re-education of the Lover, we will require some background information on the confessor himself. Gower develops his character Genius from two well-known medieval counterparts, one in Alanus de Insulis's *De Planctu Naturae,* and the other in Jean de Meun's *Roman de la Rose.* In these two antecedents Genius represents a combination of natural reason, ingenuity (what we would call "creativity"), and procreativity. He is subservient to Nature, and Nature, being God's creation, is essentially good. That she is subject to time and mortality is not her fault, but rather man's, who, in sinning, acts "unnaturally." Genius looks after Nature's mortal creatures; he is pleased when each finds satisfaction proper to its created purpose. So too in Gower, where Genius's primary means for judging behavior is to decide whether an act is natural or "unkynde." He is a most felicitous choice for Gower's theme of man's crimes against Nature. It is to Genius that Amans must turn for penance, since in his idleness "genius" is what has been lost. Genius, with his "lust and lore," will help Amans to recreate a balanced view of himself.

Gower presents Genius as Venus's priest, but this does not, we must remind ourselves, make him subservient to her or even entirely sympathetic with her motives. In Alanus, Venus and her son Cupid help Genius to fulfill his office of replenishing Nature (that is to say, the sexual urge for singular pleasure which Venus and Cupid represent does help Nature to reproduce her kind). So too Gower's Genius enjoys the assistance of Venus and the god of love. For that we may assume he is grateful. But, nevertheless, he objects scornfully to their selfish demands which turn natural love into unnatural fantasies or mutually exclusive and unfruitful games. In fact, from the beginning of the poem it is clear that his interests are greater than Venus's and that he will speak of more things than love, at least love as cupidinous Amans has come to define the term. In order to help Amans see beyond his infatuation, Genius will as the poem progresses ultimately instruct him in all the humanities. The climax of his argument is Book VII, in which he explains the education of a king, a lesson which Amans must learn if he is to reclaim and rule the lost kingdom of his soul.

Genius knows that love which is founded on mutuality, on what both Gower and Chaucer call "common profit," is the only love which is consistently satisfactory and fruitful. Although Genius's understanding of higher love is limited, he can appreciate it as history has revealed it, just as Jean de Meun's Genius appreciates without fully understanding the *beau parc* of the good shepherd with its *fontaine de vie* toward the end of *Roman de la Rose*. Most certainly he can see from his natural vantage point that the love of Cupid is inconstant and that that of Venus usually ends in mockery. That Venus would send Amans to Genius is understandable, however, in that she owes her very existence to the phenomenon of nature over which Genius has jurisdiction.

In short, we should understand Amans's confession to Genius as a reappreciation of Nature. As such it involves a twofold process, both a turning outside himself to discover objectively man's use and misuse of his creative energies throughout history and a turning within himself to rediscover his own neglected creative ability. Genius is the keeper of the past as well as the present. This feature of his office explains both his method of consoling Amans with examples from the past and his encouragement of Amans to be a good lover now. As keeper of the past he helps Amans to sort out the nightmare of mankind's history so that Amans may sort out his own. To do this he questions, illustrates, and compares events of antiquity with events in Amans's personal love. His illustrations are not simply moral examples. They are the stories of mankind—the wisdom and error of the past since its beginning. They are presented simply, essentially without commentary or explanation. They are evoked to stand before Amans for the sake of his "remembrance."

As Boethius and Augustine so clearly emphasize, confession is remembering. Memory provides the key to Amans's restoration. It is his means of reclaiming his forgotten, natural self in order that he may be released from its fantastic substitute. The *Confessio* begins by asserting that lore of the past has been left behind for us to draw it into "remembrance" (Prol. 69, 93); by so doing we begin not only to perceive the agencies by which men have corrupted themselves but also begin to rediscover the meaning of "common profit." Repeatedly Genius emphasizes that the tales he tells are to be held in remembrance, and Amans again and again asks to be questioned so that he might recall what he has forgotten. This process of forgetting, confessing, and remembering is neatly epitomized in the account of Nebuchadnezzar's dream at the end of Book I. In a vision Nebuchadnezzar saw what his fate would be if he continued in his vainglorious pride. He called Daniel to him who explained what the dream meant. But the king forgot; he let the counsel "passe out of his mynde." The consequence of his forgetfulness is loss of manhood. He is turned into an ox and for seven years eats grass, drinks from the slough, and sleeps among the bushes, until finally he remembers what he has lost and prays for forgiveness. He makes a covenant with God and vows to follow humility, at which point, in the twinkling of an eye, just as he reformed his mind so too his body is reformed to that of a man. Needless to say, when he returned to his throne he remembered to reform his behavior as king also. Only his vain glory he forgot: "Evere afterward out of memoire / He let it passe" (I.3038).

Gower presents memory as the Lover's means of drawing the loose ends of his distracted self together. It enables him to see himself wholly. The antithesis to memory and unified vision is "divisioun." Gower uses the metaphor of division extensively to depict the circumstances of fourteenth-century England as well as those of Amans. Sin, which is a forgetting, is "moder of divisioun" (Prol. 1030), and division is "moder of confusioun" (Prol. 852). To forget one's ordained purpose is to disintegrate into pointless fragments. Gower's favorite emblem for disintegration, an emblem he used in *Vox Clamantis* as well as in the *Confessio,* he also found in the book of Daniel, which describes Nebuchadnezzar's dream of the monster of time with its head of gold, chest of silver, belly of brass, and legs and feet of steel and clay which is crumbling into powder (Prol. 585 ff.). (The emblem was considered important enough to provide the opening illumination in the Fairfax manuscript of the poem, which begins with a representation of Nebuchadnezzar asleep, the monster standing over him.) Significantly the monster is in the shape of a man for, as Gower explains, the corruption of time is the consequence of man's severance from God: "Al this wo is cause of man," who is himself "the lasse world" (Prol. 905 ff.). Beyond time sits

The hyhe almyhti pourveance,
In whos eterne remembrance
Fro ferst was every thing present.
[Prol. 585–587]

As men become increasingly forgetful they become further divided from God and eternal memory. Gower comments on the divided feet of the monster which represent the later days and sees epitomized there the wars and civil strife of his own day as well as the Church, divided by schism and crumbling into factions such as Lollardy. The more men ignore common profit to seek singular ends, the more they hate each other and turn against each other.

By analogy, these times of division apply to "the lasse world," Amans, as well. Through metaphors of division Gower links the romance plot with the Prologue. Amans too is a state at war with itself, unable to arrive at a treaty suitable to the demands of its many factions. He is, as we have seen, his own worst enemy. Toward the end of his confession, Genius will compare him to a burning stick which is reducing itself to ashes.

Intimately related to Gower's views on memory and division are his views on poetry. He concludes his discussion of Nebuchadnezzar's monster of time with the story of Arion. Arion is the bard whose song was so sweet that it restored peace wherever it was heard:

of so good mesure
He song, that he the bestes wilde
Made of his note tame and milde,
The Hinde in pes with the Leoun,

The Wolf in pes with the Moltoun,
The Hare in pees stod with the Hound;
And every man upon this ground
Which Arion that time herde,
Als wel the lord as the schepherde,
He broghte hem alle in good acord;
So that the comun with the lord,
The lord with the comun also,
He sette in love bothe tuo
And putte awey malencolie.
[Prol. 1056–1069]

The poet is society's rememberer who sees with a unified vision to charm men out of their melancholy and "divisioun." He orders chaos and with his recreation teaches men to laugh, not hate (Prol. 1071). Gower must surely have seen his own purpose in the example. His poem, like the music of Arion, or like the songs of Apollonius and his daughter Thaise in Book VIII, would provide therapy in troubled times. We shall see, in fact, that before the poem is over even Amans, with a smile, turns poet.

The progress of Amans's confession may be measured by the expository sections of the poem. These sections have often been labeled digressive, but I suspect that Gower saw them to be dramatically appropriate as well as central to his theme. They appear to be carefully arranged to link the Prologue and Epilogue with the romance plot. Each is longer and more complex than that which proceeded it, as if to imply that Amans, in coming out of his lethargy, is capable of benefitting from larger areas of experience. (Cf. Boethius's *Consolation,* where Philosophy gives increasingly difficult arguments as the narrator recovers.) The first is the shortest (III.2251–2360). It occurs in the book on Wrath and concerns the difficulty of justifying war of any kind. Considering Amans's inner turmoil this is certainly the place to begin. Moreover, although he is at war with himself up to the very end, he does learn from the discussion, and later argues quite persuasively against killing. The passage also recalls the story of Arion and aptly links it to the prayer for peace in the Epilogue, where the exposition and romance plot become one.

The remaining three expository sections pertain to the three estates described in the Prologue: the estate of rulers, the estate of the church, and the estate of the commons. The first of these discussions (IV.2363–2700) occurs in the book on Sloth and applies to the third estate. It explains why men must labor and outlines the inventors and originators of the various professions. The next (V.729–1970) is the history of religions and pertains to the second estate. Gower apparently placed his discussion of religion in this book because he saw avarice to be the vice which more than any other was ruining the church. The last expository section (Book VII) is the longest and most complex. It pertains to the first estate and is the account of King Alexander's education. The topics are dealt with in reverse order from those in the Prologue, perhaps to suggest a working outward from disorder toward right order as Amans relearns proper governance.

Amans's search for repose is, of course, analogous to England's search for peace and just administration. To regain his psychological homeland he must reclaim within himself each of the three estates. First he must reclaim his "commons," that is to say, his emotions which labor helps to regulate. The discussion on labor dwells mainly on alchemy and the writings of great men of letters. Amans does not take well to Genius's suggestion that he should study Ovid if he wants advice on dealing with his passion. He says he will heed no suggestions about giving up his lady. In the conclusion, after a long labor of penance, he changes his attitude, however, and it is Ovid and the other men of letters who aid him in his final metamorphosis. Then a transformation as remarkable as any of alchemy takes place, as we shall see, when Venus fixes up his kidneys (seat of the passions).

The discussion pertaining to the second estate is more involved. Significantly Amans himself asks for instruction in the history of religions. His training begins with an outline of the pagan gods, then of Judaism, and then of Christianity. The sequence delineates the steps toward true revelation. That most of the exposition deals with the pagan deities is understandable if we keep in mind that the pagan world is simply the mutable world in which men spend most of their time. The tone of this portion of the poem is light, as Gower enjoys the incongruity of having Genius mock his accomplices. For Amans to discover objectively the ridiculousness of the pagan gods would be a crucial step toward recognizing the ridiculousness of his own pagan behavior as he attempts to do homage to Venus. But the lesson does not soak in yet. Only in the Epilogue, after he has recognized the old man in himself, does he get beyond pagan behavior to reinstate intelligently his second estate.

The instruction of Amans in the first estate provides the climax to the exposition. Again Amans himself, out of curiosity, requests the discussion. He has become sufficiently engaged in what Genius has to say to forget momentarily his infatuation. To put Book VII aside as an unforgivable digression, as many critics have done, is to do Gower an injustice. It is one of the most essential stages in the poem's plot. Its opening account of the universe defines the boundaries of the domain which Amans should be king over by natural right, and the discussion of man defines the natural being which Amans has forgotten. The ethical generalizations on Truth, Liberality, Justice, Pity, and Chastity define positive means for dealing with cupidity once Amans has realized what cupidity is. They provide the means through which man cares for his soul. As Genius notes at the end of the poem:

For conseil passeth alle thing
To him which thenkth to ben a king;
And every man for his partie
A kingdom hath to justefie,
That is to sein his oghne dom.
If he misreule that kingdom,
He lest himself, and that is more
Than if he loste Schip and Ore
And al the worldes good withal:
For what man that in special

Hath noght himself, he hath noght elles,
Nomor the perles than the schelles.

[VIII.2109–2120]

Rather than digressing, Book VII completes the moral landscape
for the conclusion to the argument.

Like the expository sections of the *Confessio,* the conclusion
to the poem has afforded readers a great deal of difficulty. Book
VIII poses four separate problems: (1) the discussion of incest;
(2) the Tale of Apollonius; (3) the concluding sequence of the
romance itself; and (4) the Epilogue.

As Book VIII begins the reader is confronted with the ques-
tion of why Gower does not deal with the seventh sin (lechery)
as he dealt with the other six. In Book I Genius had said he would
exorcise Amans of all seven sins, but now, instead of discussing
lechery and her various servants (*Mirour de l'Omme* names five:
fornicioun, stupre, avolterie, incest, and *foldelit*), he speaks briefly
of the laws governing marriage, then discusses incest, and that is
all. C. S. Lewis has suggested that Genius cannot speak of the sins
of Venus since he is her priest. It is true that in Book V Genius
tried to avoid talking about Venus when he described the Greek
gods, but when he was specifically called upon to do so he showed
little inhibition and minced no words. There may be other reasons
as well.

First, a technical problem. In treating other sins, Genius had
discussed each as a category of behavior and then (usually) had
applied each to love. Thus many of the preceding tales deal with
lechery. By Book VIII Genius has already told stories about forni-
cation, adultery, and infatuation of various sorts. He has also told
tales of incest. Why then would he single out incest as his final
moral category for discussion? The answer may lie in the peculiar
relationship of that vice to the illness of Amans.

Medieval writers commonly associated self-love and singular
profit with incest. In *Roman de la Rose,* for example, the dreamer's
self-indulgence, at first defined by Guillaume de Lorris as Nar-
cissism, is enlarged upon by Jean de Meun in the Pygmalion story

where the narcissistic lover falls so greatly in love with his image that consummation occurs, the progeny of which continues in incestuous love when Cinyrus and Myrrha beget Adonis. The term *incest* comes from Latin *in-* (not) *castus* (chaste); it commonly designated unnatural spiritual, as well as sexual, union. Its antidote, in the *Mirour,* at least, is Continence. Of all sins it preeminently typifies crime against family and thus against community. It is implied, then, in the selfishness of all sins. In fact, the word the Latin Fathers generally used for sin—*cupiditas*—originates in the myth of Cupid, who incestuously loved his mother as if he were blind, the after effect being indeed loss of his wits. But the best illustration of this attitude towards incest may be found in Gower's own *Mirour de l'Omme.* That poem begins with an allegorical geneology of Sin. She and all her unnatural brood are the products of incest. Born of Satan's selfish love, Sin is seduced by her father. She gives birth to Death, who in turn incestuously loves his mother, the get of this couple being the seven sins. Satan then takes his grandchildren and begets on them thirty-five subspecies of Sin. These are no true marriages: all are unnatural and motivated by singular profit. Instead of creating harmony they bring division of what should not be divided. We are reminded of the formula in the Prologue to the *Confessio,* where Sin is mother of division, and division the mother of confusion.

Such an interpretation of incest is supported in the text of the *Confessio* itself. At the end of Book VII, after Genius finishes telling of the instruction of kings, Amans says his heart is still restless. He wonders if something pertaining to love has been "foryete or left behind" (VII.5425). Genius acknowledges that one thing remains "thi schrifte forto make plein," and that is to speak "of love which is unavised" (VII.5433). After a Latin epigram condemning the treachery of Venus's love, he summarizes the creation story, the fall of Lucifer, and the generations of man from Adam. His point is to explain how marriage laws developed and to show where men should place their love. Rather than isolating incest as a particular species of lechery Genius seems mainly concerned with exploring connotations. He speaks of "unavised" love, "mistimed" love, "unkynde" love, and in the epigram to the story of Apollonius he speaks of excessive and immoderate love, though never does he specifically use the word *incest*. Although Genius is ostensibly talking about incest, and although Amans understands him only in its narrower sense, all of his generalizations seem designed to encourage the reader to look on this sin as an epitome of the selfish and unnatural qualities of cupidinous love in general. Two circumlocutions stand out particularly in this regard: Genius objects to men who passionately "taken wher thei take may" (VIII.152) and, again, to a man who knows no good "bot takth what thing comth next to honde" (VIII.163). Here the focus is clearly on nearsighted love. After he has told the story of Apollonius, Genius observes that instead of taking whatever love is close at hand, men should "Tak love where it·mai noght faile" (VIII.2086). His point seems to be that Amans should stop feeding morosely on his emotions and look to something more important.

The story of Apollonius dramatizes the idea superbly. Antiochus is the man who indulges himself myopically, taking where he may what is near at hand. But the effects are terrible. He becomes worse than a beast:

The wylde fader thus devoureth
His oghne fleissh, which non socoureth.
[VIII.309–310]

Having abandoned his natural office of father, he corrupts his other office, that of king, and adjusts laws to satisfy his "fol desire." To avoid dealing with his inner anarchy he becomes a tyrant, slays his daughter's natural suitors and puts their heads on the town gates. Sin breeds sin: "with al his Pride" he slothfully ignores his natural responsibilities ("Him thoghte that it was no Sinne"), lecherously gluts himself on his own flesh, enviously hides his daughter from other men, and then even becomes a murderer "full of rancour and of ire." Ultimately he becomes too "unkynde," and God strikes him down with lightning.

Apollonius, on the other hand, shows what it means "to love in good manere." He fulfills admirably Genius's five points of policy which should govern a king's behavior. He adheres to Truth, accepting responsibilities and fulfilling promises. He exemplifies Liberality in providing wheat for the starving people of Tharse and in properly rewarding the physician Cerymon for saving his wife. He understands the importance of Justice and brings wicked Dionise and Strangulio to trial according to the laws of their own land. He has Pity on the people of Tharse, first in giving them food and then in respecting their laws and judgment when their king has offended him. And he adheres to Chastity, not only in the winning of his wife and in the care of himself and her memory after her supposed death, but also in the care of his daughter. He is confronted with a situation like that which confronted Antiochus. When Thaise sings to him to woo him from his melancholy, he feels strong love for her. But he does not impose on her. Rather than taking what is near at hand and thus losing his daughter, as Antiochus did, he recovers his daughter by loving chastely. Diana rewards him for his chastity by enabling him to recover his wife. He in no way behaves *incaste*.

Apollonius's story is admirably suited to the conclusion of the *Confessio*. In addition to exemplifying good kingship and condemning incontinence, its plot provides a model for Amans at the end of his quest. Apollonius is a lover in exile who also is trying to regain his homeland. Fortune is a most bitter enemy, pursuing him with storms and assassins, stripping him of friends and possessions. She denies him his identity at every turn, making him a prince without a country, a husband without a wife, and a father without a child. Even so he maintains his integrity. Although driven to the brink of despair, so far in fact that like Saul he strikes out, he recovers with the aid of his daughter. Thaise is his good seed. Like her father she too is victimized by Fortune, narrowly escaping murder only to end up in a brothel. But she, like her father, remembers her skill in music and science to save herself and also advance the community. Both she and Apollonius have learned to maintain their spiritual estates. The tale thus ends on a note of joy after woe: Apollonius finally achieves a happy homecoming. No more exile for him. He becomes king of all the lands he attended, and governs them "of on assent."

Amans's homecoming differs from Apollonius's in that his exile is a spiritual exile. He has learned from Genius's examples, but at the same time he has not learned. He misses the point of Apollonius's story, though he does now ask directly for advice. He is at least that much closer to Truth. He speaks plainly: "What shall I do?" Genius tells him to seek love which may not fail; let trifles be. He calls Amans's love sinful and says he should free himself before it is too late:

Yit is it time to withdrawe,
And set thin herte under that lawe,
The which of reson is governed
And noght of will. And to be lerned,
Ensamples thou hast many on
Of now and ek of time gon,
That every lust is bot a while;
And who that wole himself beguile,
He may the rathere be deceived.
[VIII.2133–2141]

But he insists that Amans must make the decision himself; he can only show the way. He then poses his last question, the ultimate question of Christian humanism: "Now ches if thou wolt live or deie" (VIII.2148).

But Amans is simply not ready to make that choice. Although the preliminary questions have been asked and illustrated, their meaning has not yet come home. Again he dodges to protect his emotions. His defense is the characteristic "but you don't understand" of lovers:

Mi wo to you is bot a game,
That fielen noght of that I fiele.
[VIII.2152–2153]

He wants sympathy. Yet at the same time he begins to realize rationally that Genius's advice makes sense. As he starts using reason the point of view of the poem shifts. Instead of dialogue and debate between Genius and Amans, we now have first person narration. The effect is to make the debate seem to be going on within Amans, while at the same time he seems to be looking down at himself:

Tho was betwen mi Prest and me
Debat and gret perplexete:
Mi resoun understod him wel,
And knew it was soth everydel
That he hath seid, bot noght forthi
Mi will hath nothing set therby.
For techinge of so wis a port
Is unto love of no desport;
Yit myhte nevere man beholde
Reson, wher love was withholde,
Thei be noght of o governance.
[VIII.2189–2199]

In this divided state of mind Amans begs Genius to present his supplication to Venus. Genius agrees. Then Amans, quite objectively, tells how he sat upon a green and wrote with tears instead of ink his appeal. The appeal itself is clearly by a man "noght of o governance": one voice pleads to Nature for release from love's cruelty and the other pleads to Venus for satisfaction. Yet the effect of his writing is to formalize his dissatisfaction so that he can cope with it. The complaint stands sharply in contrast to his emotional outburst in Book I when Venus first appeared. Although Reason does not yet hold sway, she is at least present. His analysis of his malady is accurate, and although his desires are still at odds with his analysis, he is beginning, in these twelve stanzas of rhyme royal, to impose order on them.

The effect of Amans's prayer is immediate. Venus appears less than a mile away. Again she asks, this time in mockery, who he is. "John Gower," he responds. The point here is not to let the world know who wrote the poem. Rather it marks a new beginning. Amans has come a long way from "a Caitif that lith hiere." His homeland has been identified; what remains is the repossession. Venus acknowledges the schizophrenic intention of Amans's "bille," but offers no help. She leaves the dispute to Amans and Nature. Amans must reconcile himself with Nature or be refused any consolation. Gower cleverly has Amans recount her words in retrospect as he ponders her whimsical rejection of his appeal. It is he who acknowledges, now with keen awareness, that "olde grisel is no fole" (VIII.2407). Her only counsel is "remembre wel hou thou art old" (VIII.2439). That acknowledgment causes Amans to faint, which brings him to the final step in his re-education.

In his swoon Amans envisions a parliament of lovers. These lovers are those whose stories Genius has just told. They pass in review before him—first those caught up in the heat of their desire, then those betrayed by love who are in sorrow. In contrast he sees the four constant women whose example of goodness the whole world remembers. This vision designates Amans's recognition of the moral implications of what he has learned. In this act of remembrance he incorporates the meaning of the past into himself. The scene shifts from the recollection of the examples from history to the historians themselves. Old Age approaches Venus, accompanied by his train of lovers—David, Aristotle, Virgil, Plato, "Sortes," and Ovid. These authors of the past pray for Amans's release. It is their prayer which is answered: Cupid removes the fiery dart. The wisdom of antiquity answers the needs of the present, once the present understands through its own experience. It is a matter of community regained.

The rest is simple. As Amans comes out of his trance Venus places an ointment on his heart, his temples, and his kidneys, implying the restitution of his three estates (the kingdom of his soul, the sanctuary of his intelligence, and the residence of his passions). She also gives him a mirror that he might recognize the old man he has become. This time he does not swoon. He looks directly at himself, reason returns, and he is made "sobre and hol ynowh." Venus laughs at him and asks him what love was. Amans cannot answer: "Be my trouthe, I knew him noght." His fantasy has gone so far from him that it is as if Cupid had never been.

Genius gives Amans absolution—a "peire of bedes," with the motto *por reposer,* and Venus tells him to return to his books, where moral virtue dwells. Then she returns to the stars. Amans is on his own. For a brief but telling moment he stands in amazement: has all his labor, all his lust come to this—an old man and some beads? Then, like Troilus at the end of his romance, he smiles at it all. The smile is the final clue to his release. In that moment,

Homward a softe pas y wente,
Wher that with al myn hol entente
Uppon the point that y am schryve
I thenke bidde whil y live.
[VIII.2967–2970]

The reiteration is complete: Amans has become "John Gower," poet.

The concluding prayer for the State of England, which I have been referring to as the Epilogue, grows naturally out of the romance plot, as Gower, almost brilliantly it seems to me, fuses his larger social theme with Amans's story. This prayer for England's welfare stands in striking contrast to the infatuated pleas of Amans before he was shriven. Having regained his sense of kingdom he prays, now as poet, for common profit, right use of memory and good governance.

For if men takyn remembrance
What is to live in unite,
Ther ys no staat in his degree
That noughte to desire pes.
[VIII.2988–2991]

CHRONOLOGY OF GOWER'S LIFE AND WORKS

ca. 1330   John Gower is born, probably in Kent or Yorkshire, into a family of considerable prominence and means, which held land in Kent, Yorkshire, Norfolk, and Suffolk; kin to Sir Robert Gower.

ca. 1345   *Geoffrey Chaucer born.*

1365   Gower purchases Aldingdon Septvauns, an estate in Kent. The purchase was later contested by the crown, but in 1368 Gower's claim is adjudged just. During this decade of his life Gower appears to have prospered, perhaps in some legal or civil office.

1368   Gower acquires a manor of Kentwell in Suffolk which formerly had belonged to Sir Robert Gower.

1373   Gower disposes of the manors of Aldingdon and Kentwell.

ca. 1376–1379   Gower writes *Mirour de l'Omme,* an allegory of about 32,000 octosyllabic lines composed in twelve-line stanzas. He appears not to have had the poem recopied, since only one fragmentary manuscript of the poem is known to exist. It may be that Gower wrote the work for his own pleasure in what turned out to be a trial run for his two greater poems, both of which draw on it. Although the poem is in French, Gower later changed its title to *Speculum Hominis,* then to *Speculum Meditantis,* so that it might correspond to the Latin titles of his other works.

    The *Mirour* is a commentary on the dilemma of fallen man. Its structure is panoramic, like a triptych which tells allegorically the genealogy of sin and the corruption of the time world, then offers a catalogue of vices and virtues which neatly classifies the errors of man and the remedies open to him, and finally presents an exaltation of the Virgin Mary, who offers frenzied man a realizable hope for extrication from the bewildering world.

1377   *King Edward III dies; the regency for Richard II, age 10, is established.*

ca. 1377 Gower takes up residence at St. Mary Overeys Priory, where he spends most of the rest of his life. Tradition claims that in this year Gower financed repair and restoration of the priory, which had burned a century and a half earlier. The priory had its own scriptorium, where Gower apparently supervised the copying of his poems.

1377–1381 In about 1377 Gower begins work on *Vox Clamantis,* a moral essay of seven books written in Latin elegiac verse. The title is prophetic and comes from the gospel account of John the Baptist who comes as the voice crying in the wilderness. The tone throughout is apocalyptic. Gower seems to have begun composition with what is now Book II and to have completed the poem shortly after the Peasant's Revolt, adding at that time the allegorical dream vision which constitutes Book I. Eighteen years later, after the ascension of Henry IV to the throne, he added the Tripartite Chronicle to the poem.

Book II announces the poem's title and defines man's loss of eminence in the universe: Fortune is not to blame; the fault of man's alienation lies in himself. Books III and IV offer a bold diatribe against the corrupt clergy and religious orders. Book V is an attack on knighthood, which has also failed. Book VI attacks those who have corrupted the laws themselves—lawyers, judges, and the king. Book VII summarizes man's desperate condition by recounting Nebuchadnezzar's vision of the degeneration of the time world. Book I, written last, provides a brilliant dramatization of the consequences of irresponsible behavior of the upper echelons of society. By means of dream fable, Gower depicts the nightmarish world of a society gone berserk, where even the common men, in whom Gower elsewhere has great faith, turn themselves into animals ravaging each other. Book I ends with an emblem of chaos in which common profit has been totally obliterated. In a dramatically memorable scene, the narrator, unwillingly caught up in his narrative, finds himself isolated in a wilderness, afraid of all men about him, who seem surely bent on his destruction. This book should not be understood simply as an attack on the commons in revolt against hierarchy, but rather as a dramatic statement of the consequences of a whole society in disintegration, the causes of which Gower analyzes in the remaining books. To Gower the Peasants' Revolt must have seemed veritable proof of the validity of his prophetic attack on corrupt religious and civil authorities.

1378 Chaucer gives power of attorney to John Gower and Richard Forester while he travels abroad on the continent.

1382 Gower is granted manors of Feltwell in Norfolk and Moulton in Suffolk, which he rents to Thomas Blakelake, parson, for £160 per annum.

ca. 1385 Chaucer dedicates *Troilus and Criseyde* to "moral Gower" and "philosophical Strode." (The term "moral" should be understood to include that which pertains to the mores of society, as well as ethics.)

ca. 1386 Gower begins work on *Confessio Amantis;* Chaucer begins work on the *Legend of Good Women.*

1389 Richard II declares himself monarch of full age, free of tutelage.

1390 Gower completes the first recension of the *Confessio Amantis* which he dedicates to the young King Richard, who had encouraged him to write the poem, and to his friend Geoffrey Chaucer. Thirty-one of the forty-nine known manuscripts of the poem follow this recension. It was popular because of the account of the king's commissioning of the poem and because of the dedication to Chaucer.

1390–1392 Gower revises *Confessio Amantis.* During this period he reworks Books V, VI, and VII of the poem, adding new material (see note 25 to Book V and notes 15 and 23 to Book VII) and rearranging the old, in addition to revising the conclusion of the poem to exclude praises of King Richard. To the Prologue he adds a dedication to Henry of Lancaster. (See note 2 to the Prologue.)

1393 The third recension of *Confessio Amantis* is issued, now dedicated to Henry of Lancaster, Count of Derby. In return, Henry presents Gower with an ornamental collar. The third recension of the poem drops the passages which the second recension had added to the middle books and rewrites again the Prologue and conclusion to the poem. The Fairfax manuscript is the principal manuscript of this group, and although it is a relatively small group, it represents Gower's final and most careful revision of the poem.

1394–1397 Gower composes various lesser Latin poems, including "Carmen Super Multiplici Viciorum Pestilencia," "O Deus Immense," and "De Lucis Scrutino."

1397 Gower writes a sequence of eighteen French ballades entitled *Traitié*. Each ballade is of three stanzas in rhyme royal, without envoy; the eighteenth ballade has a fourth stanza which functions as envoy to the whole sequence.

1398 Gower marries Agnes Groundolf. This may have been his second marriage. If so, the first marriage must have been of his younger days, some years prior to his residence at St. Mary Overeys. The marriage to Agnes Groundolf may have been a matter of convenience in order that someone might care for the aging poet who was, according to tradition, on the verge of blindness.

1399 Richard II is deposed by act of Parliament; Henry of Lancaster becomes King Henry IV. Five weeks after his coronation Henry grants Gower two pipes per annum of Gascony wine.

1399–1400 Gower dedicates and presents *Cinkante Balades* to King Henry. He also writes at this time his so-called laureate poems ("Rex celi deus," "H. aquile pullus," "O recolende"), praising the king in whom he placed such high hope, and also his last English poem, "In Praise of Peace." This latter poem may have been written after the poet had become blind.

1400 Geoffrey Chaucer dies.

1408 John Gower dies and is buried in St. Mary Overeys Priory Church. He now lies in Southwark Cathedral.

THE LANGUAGE OF GOWER

The *Confessio Amantis* is written in the language familiar to students of Chaucer. That language, the literary dialect of cultivated Londoners of the late fourteenth century, has been described more fully than any other Middle English dialect. Since excellent descriptions of the dialect are readily available to students an attempt will not be made here to give a full account of Gower's Middle English. My remarks will be limited to the basic aspects of pronunciation and grammar and those orthographic and idiomatic features of his poem which set it apart linguistically from Chaucer's poetry. Symbols of the International Phonetic Alphabet, shown in the table below, will be used to convey the appropriate sound:

Symbol	Key Word	Symbol	Key Word
$/\alpha/$	father	$/b/$	bishop
$/æ/$	hat	$/d/$	doom
$/e/$	fate	$/f/$	fear
$/\varepsilon/$	help	$/g/$	grim
$/i/$	feet	$/h/$	hell
$/\textsc{i}/$	fit	$/j/$	yield
$/o/$	old	$/k/$	kind
$/\textipa{O}/$	hot	$/l/$	law
$/u/$	food	$/m/$	maiden
$/\textsc{u}/$	full	$/n/$	new
$/\Lambda/$	but	$/\eta/$	sing
$/\textschwa/$	above	$/p/$	pit
$/\alpha\textsc{i}/$	mind	$/r/$	rest
$/\alpha\textsc{u}/$	hound	$/s/$	save
$/\textipa{O}\textsc{i}/$	boy	$/\int/$	ship

Symbol	Key Word	Symbol	Key Word
/ɪu/	virt*ue*	/t/	*t*rust
/œ/	French p*eu*	/θ/	*th*in
/ð/	*th*en	/tʃ/	*ch*oice
/v/	*v*ice	/ʒ/	vi*s*ion
/w/	*w*ish	/dʒ/	*j*udge
/z/	*z*odiac	/ɝ/	vi*r*tue
/x/	German ni*ch*t	/ɚ/	love*r*

The principal differences between the orthography of the *Confessio Amantis* and the *Canterbury Tales* may be attributed to the greater influence of French and Kentish spelling conventions on Gower's poem. Gower apparently regarded *ie* as a digraph for /e/. He (or his amanuensis) may have learned the convention from Kentish or from Anglo-Norman French, where the diphthong /ie/ had become /e/ though the *ie* spelling had been maintained. So one finds *chiere, hiere, hiede, siek,* and the like in the *Confessio,* where the student of Chaucer would expect *chere* (*cheere*), *here* (*heere*), *hede* (*heed*), *sek* (*seek*). Although Gower's scribe also uses *chere, here, hede,* and *sek* in addition to the *ie* forms, he will not hesitate to rhyme the one with the other, as in *the dede: wommanhiede* (VII.4887–4888). He also uses the Anglo-Norman French digraph *oe* where Chaucer uses *e* or *o,* as in *poeple, proeved, moerdre,* and *coevere.* Gower probably pronounced the sound as /e/ or /o/ as did Chaucer, though he may have pronounced it /œ/, as the vowel in French *peu* or German *hören.*

In the *Confessio* one also encounters spellings which reflect Romance etymology instead of actual pronunciation, such as *doubte* (which rhymes with *aboute*), *deceipte* (which rhymes with *conceite*), and *pleigne* (which rhymes with *peine*).

In Chaucer one encounters a few Kentish phonemes, but in Gower they are frequent, especially Kentish *e* from Old English *y* where we would expect *i.* So we find in Gower *ferst, senne, hell, pet,* and so forth where we would normally find *first, sinne, hil,* and *pit* in Chaucer. Gower also uses *i* occasionally in all these instances, but we also find the Southern u for i, as in *hulles* or *puttes* for hills or pits, though this is infrequent. Finally, we find the Kentish *-ende* participial ending in the *Confessio*, where Chaucer normally uses *-inge*, though the latter form is also common in Gower.

Middle English consonants have essentially the same phonetic value that our equivalents have. With the exception of the etymological consonants in accordance with French spelling conventions, all of Gower's Middle English consonants are apparently pronounced. *Kniht*, for example, would be pronounced /knɪxt/, with /x/ being a sound like *ch* in German *buch*, a sound for which Gower uses the symbol *h* where Chaucer uses *gh*. *Folk* would be pronounced /fɔlk/; *king* /kiŋg/, the *ng* being pronounced like the *ng* in finger; and *ryhtwisnesse* /rɪxtwisnɛsːə/. Gower commonly uses *s* and *c* interchangeably for /s/ (another instance of French influence), as in *pourchase:pourchace; distresse:distresce*. Normally *s* and *th* are not voiced, though they may have been voiced if they occurred between vowels in a word. Gower's *ch* is consistently pronounced /tʃ/, as in modern English *church*. He uses the digraph *gg* to indicate the affricative /dʒ/, as in *jugge* /dʒʊdʒə/. His *r* is thought to have been strongly trilled with the tip of the tongue. He frequently doubles consonants at the end of words such as *all, wedd, bedd*, perhaps to indicate shortness of vowel, though he is not consistent here.

To generalize about the vowels of Gower's dialect is more difficult simply because Middle English, like modern English, has more vowel sounds than its orthography has vowel symbols. Gower wrote before the great vowel shift. Thus, the simplest means of inferring how he pronounced tense vowels is to work backwards. The following simplified scheme may be helpful in arriving at a rough approximation of Gower's pronunciation of vowels in stressed syllables. (For a more refined discussion see Helge Kökeritz, *A Guide to Chaucer's Pronunciation*, Holt, Rinehart and Winston: New York, 1962.) In unstressed syllables the differentiation between corresponding vowels would have been less distinctly realized:

Gower's Spelling	*Approximately Equivalent Sounds*
a	$/\alpha/$ regardless of whether we pronounce the modern equivalent $/\alpha/$, $/æ/$, or $/e/$; if unstressed it would have been $/ə/$, as in $/əbovə/$.
e	$/e/$ if the modern equivalent is $/i/$ and spelled *ee*, as in *seem;* between $/æ/$ and $/e/$ if the modern equivalent is pronounced $/i/$ or $/ɛ/$ and spelled *ea*, as in *sea* and *dead;* $/ɛ/$ if the modern equivalent is spelled *e* and pronounced $/ɛ/$, as in *help*. If the digraph *ie* is used the sound in Middle English is $/e/$.
i (y)	$/i/$ if the modern equivalent is $/\alpha i/$ and spelled *i* or *y*, as in *write* or *why;* $/ɪ/$ if the modern equivalent is $/ɪ/$, as in *sit*.
o	$/o/$ if the modern equivalent is spelled *oo* and pronounced $/u/$, $/ʊ/$, or $/ʌ/$, as in *root, foot,* and *blood;* $/ɔ/$ if the modern equivalent is $/o/$, as in *holy;* $/ɔu/$ if the modern equivalent is $/ɔ/$, as in *thought;* $/ʊ/$ if the modern equivalent is $/ʌ/$, as in *sun;* $/ɔ/$ if the modern equivalent is $/\alpha/$, as in *ox*.
u	$/ʊ/$ if the modern equivalent is $/ʌ/$, as in *under;* $/ɪu/$ if the modern vowel is $/ju/$ or $/u/$, as in *virtue* or *rude*.
ou (ow)	$/u/$, another instance of French orthography. If it is followed by *n*, Gower sometimes rhymes it with $/o/$, as in *question:suggestioun; Lamedon:Jasoun*.
ai, ay, ei, ey	Between $/e/$ and $/\alpha i/$, perhaps the diphthong $/æi/$.
eu (ew)	$/iu/$ or $/ɛu/$.
oe	$/œ/$ or $/e/$ or $/o/$.
oi (oy)	$/ɔi/$.

Unlike Chaucer, Gower does not, except in a few scattered instances, double the vowel to indicate length. The one principal exception is the word *goode,* where the vowel is always doubled, probably to differentiate the word from *God*.

Because of Gower's smooth and skillfully controlled metrical line, students should have little trouble understanding where the stress falls in individual words. Middle English stress is essentially like that of modern English, with stress falling normally on the first syllable or base of the word. The main differences occur in polysyllabic words recently borrowed from French, especially those ending with Old French suffixes such as *-age* (*brocágĕ, avantágĕ*); *-oure* (*coloúrĕ, honoúrĕ*); *-esse* (*gentilléscĕ, worthinéssĕ*); *-ure* (*natúrĕ, creatúrĕ*); *-ance* (*creáncĕ, penáncĕ*); *-ioun* (*discréciouǹ, desputêisoùn*); *-aire* (*adversáirĕ, contráirĕ*), as opposed to Chaucer's *-arie;* and *-oire* (*históire, memóire*), as opposed to Chaucer's *-orie* (a further instance of the greater French influence in Gower). Normally these suffixes would receive secondary stress, though in some instances they may even bear primary stress.

INFLECTIONS

NOUNS

By Gower's day the Old English declensions had disappeared, leaving only a few more inflections than we now have. The noun had essentially only two endings, an *-es* for plural (as in *boƙes*), and an *-es* for genitive (as in *this worthi ƙinges wif*). The main difference between Middle English and modern English noun inflections is simply the number of exceptions to these two principal forms. Modern English has a few unchanged plurals, but they were more common in Middle English and included words like *hors, mile, monthe, wynter,* and *thing.* Middle English also had a greater number of *-en* plurals than we have, words like *yhen* and *ton* (eyes and toes), as well as our *oxen, children,* and *brethren.* A few Middle English genitives are formed by adding *-e* (which may be traced back to Old English gen. fem. sing. or to weak declension endings), as in *myn herte rote* or *the cherche ƙeie;* other genitives have no inflection at all, especially nouns of relationship like *fader, moder, dowhter* (as in *his fader soule, his dowhter speche,* or *this ladi wit*), or words which normally end in *-s.*

One encounters final *-e* on nouns in many prepositional constructions, apparently with some sense of the Old English dative singular (*to wedde, to wyve, fro the lande*), though the *-e* is not necessarily pronounced. As one might expect from a trilingual author, some Latin inflection creeps into the *Confessio*, especially with proper names (for example, to *Ephesim, peine of Tantaly, were named Centauri, in Cancro, to axe Esionam, Phebum to love hath so constreyned*), and one also finds more French feminine forms (*capiteine, chamberere, citizeine, cousine*) than one meets in Chaucer.

Gower sometimes contracts nouns which begin with a vowel with their definite article to achieve metrical regularity, as in *their* (the air), *thyle* (the isle), *thilke* (the same), *thymage* (the image), and the like, and occasionally he contracts a negative with its noun, as in *noman* (no man). Since contractions such as these may be confusing to readers at first, I have noted the first few occurrences in marginal glosses on the text in addition to describing them here.

ADJECTIVES

In Old English, adjectives were declined according to two declensions, the strong declension being used with unaccompanied nouns and the weak declension being used with nouns which were defined by the declined article, a demonstrative, or a possessive pronoun. By Gower's day the distinction was essentially gone. All endings of the weak declension have been reduced to final *-e* and are thus undistinguishable from adjectives which end in *e* regardless of declension. To complicate matters further, the final *-e* may very well have disappeared from speech; moreover, there are many exceptions and irregularities to what seem to be the rules guiding writers of the late fourteenth century. Nevertheless, there is enough consistency, especially among native monosyllabic adjectives, to necessitate a description. The two kinds of adjectives, those ending in a consonant and those ending in *e*, seem to be declined as follows:

Strong Declension

Singular	plein	simple
Plural	pleine	simple

Weak Declension

Singular	pleine	simple
Plural	pleine	simple

Gower normally uses the weak form when the noun is defined by the article, demonstrative, possessive pronoun, or genitive noun; also if the noun it accompanies is in the vocative, or if it is used itself as a noun, or if it modifies a proper noun. There are predictable exceptions to these rules: if the adjective occurs after its noun it will probably be uninflected; if the adjective is of more than one syllable it will not be inflected unless the accent falls on the last syllable, in which case there might be a final -*e*. To this last qualification an exception is superlative adjectives to which Gower will regularly (almost always) add final -*e*.

PRONOUNS

The personal pronouns have the following forms which Gower consistently follows:

Singular

First Person		*Second Person*	*Third Person*		
Nom.	I	thou, thow	he	sche	it
Gen.	my, min	thy, thin	his	hir(e)	his
Obj.	me	the(e)	him	hir(e)	it (him)

Plural

Nom.	we	ye	they
Gen.	oure	youre	her(e)
Obj.	ous	you	hem

These forms should be memorized.

Gower regularly uses both *that* and *which* as relative pronouns. *Whom* and *whos* both occur, but only rarely; *who* has not yet become established as a relative. In several instances Gower uses *the* with *which, whom,* or *whos,* where we would use who(m) or whose, as in *a beste the whom no reson mihte areste.* Gower's demonstrative pronouns are those of Chaucer: *this, that: thes(e), tho.* He will use *miself, himself, hirself,* and *hemself* regularly as reflexive pronouns in addition to the dative of reference which will function as an intensifier sometimes with reflexive force, as in *Ther ben lovers that feignen hem an humble port* (There are lovers who feign humble bearing for themselves), where the *hem* (for themselves) is not essential to the syntax as an object would be, but rather intensifies the involvement of the referent in the action.

ADVERBS

Gower's adverbs commonly end in *-ly, -liche,* and *-e.* The latter forms are frequent. He also uses *-es* and *-en,* as in *ones, twyes, hennes, abouten.*

VERBS

Like all Germanic languages, Middle English has two conjugations of verbs. The strong conjugation, in which past tense and past participle are formed by a change of vowel in the stem, included fewer verbs than it had in Old English, though it was still a more prominent conjugation than it is today, in that several of Gower's strong verbs (*help, halp, holpen; schape, schop, schapen; wexe, wax, woxe,* and so forth) have since become regular by analogy with the more common weak conjugation. The weak conjugation forms past tense and past participle simply by adding a dental stop (*t* or *d*) to the stem (*amended, lente*).

For Gower, both conjugations have a plural form which is usually *-n* in both past and present tenses, as well as a third person singular present indicative form which is usually *-th.* Gower will often syncopate the *-th* ending to deny it syllabic value in order to maintain regular meter, as in *that on sleth.* In his narration of the tales Gower commonly maintains past tense in strong verbs but shifts to present tense with weak verbs. Professor Macaulay points out that this practice is too consistent to be accidental and suggests that Gower's motive is to avoid surplus of unstressed syllables which the *-ede* endings of the past tense of the weak verb imposes

(II.cxvi). That thesis is hampered, however, by the fact that frequently the present tense ending which replaces the past is given syllabic value, and that frequently, when the past ending is used, the final *-e* is not even spelled, let alone sounded. Moreover, in some instances where the past tense of the weak verb does occur, it is syncopated for purposes of meter, as in *she beclipte hire lord,* where presumably the final *-e* on both *beclipte* and *hire* is not sounded. Clearly more is involved than simple use of historical present, for Gower moves back and forth between tenses even within particular contexts. But what the logic is (if any) behind Gower's choice of narrative tense is not clear to me.

Gower uses verbal contractions and prefixes which are no longer natural in English. He will attach *n-* to negate verbs beginning with a vowel (*naproche,* for "not approach"; *nabeith,* for "buys not"), and he will substitute *n* for *w* in *wot, wiste,* and *wille* so that they become *not* (know not), *nyste* (knew not), and *nylle* (will not). He also contracts *to* with the base to form an infinitive, as in *tabate* (to abate), *tacompte* (to account), *teschue* (to eschew). Moreover, Gower often uses Old English prefixes to intensify the aspect of the verb, especially *to-* and *for-,* as in *tobete* (beaten to pieces), *tobroke* (broken to pieces), *tohewe* (hewn to bits), *tosprad* (spread about), *toswal* (swelled up greatly); *forsmite* (smitten to death), *forstormed* (driven by severe storms), *forwakid* (weary of lack of sleep), *forwept* (wornout with weeping), to mention only a few.

Formation of the infinitive in the *Confessio* is not yet what we would consider to be regular. Normally it occurs with *for to,* as in *forto speke of tyme ago,* or with *to* alone, as in *to teche it forth.* Occasionally one encounters an *-en* ending on the infinitive, as in *to holden up the rihte lawe,* though never if the *to* is contracted, and occasionally one finds naked infinitives where we would require *to,* as in *in this wyse I thenke trete.* Gower's present participle is normally formed with *-ende,* as we have observed in our discussion of Kentish influences. The ending sometimes receives stress. The *y-* prefix for past participle is exceedingly rare in Gower.

PREPOSITIONS, ARTICLES, AND CONJUNCTIONS

Although prepositions had grown in number and in special-
ization of meaning since Old English, three prepositions (of, in,
and on) were used much more loosely than we allow today, often
being interchangeable. Although Gower uses many fewer idioms
than Chaucer does, nevertheless, he does use some involving prepo-
sitions which seem foreign to us. *Of that* occurs where we would
use *since* or *because,* as in *of that men sen hem so divided* (since
men see them so divided). He also uses prepositions as verbal
directives in the manner which became so common during the
Renaissance (*touchende of, speke of*), but he sometimes puts the
prepositional directive (adverb) before the verb in a manner
reminiscent of earlier English usage of prefixes to qualify the
aspect of the verb (*the point the king of tolde*).

Gower's use of definite and indefinite articles also seems
strikingly modern, though he occasionally omits either where we
would require them, or supplies either where we would not. He
uses the indefinite article to mean one, though not often.

Gower sometimes uses *and* where we would require *but* or
if, and he will sometimes introduce both halves of comparisons
with *or,* where we would use only one conjunction between the
clauses. Such idioms are characteristic of late fourteenth-century
English. His most unusual use of coordinating conjunctions is his
placement of *and* and sometimes *but* in the midst of the conjoined
clause instead of at the juncture of the two clauses: *Constance and
every wiht compleigneth* (and every one mourns for Constance);
Of love and he so maistred is (and he so mastered is by love);
And to Lucrece anon he lepte, / The blodi swerd and pulleth oute
(and he lept quickly to Lucrece and pulls out the bloody sword).
The construction is exceedingly common in the *Confessio.*

SELECTED BIBLIOGRAPHY
OF CRITICISM

Coffman, George R. "John Gower in his Most Significant Role," *Elizabethan Studies & other Essays in Honor of George F. Reynolds.* Univ. of Colo. Stud., Ser. B, II (1945), 52–61.

———. "John Gower, Mentor for Royalty: Richard II," *PMLA,* LXIX (1954), 953–964.

Fisher, John H. *John Gower.* New York, 1964.

Fison, Peter. "The Poet in John Gower," *Essays in Criticism,* VIII (1958), 16–26.

Fox, George. *Mediaeval Sciences in the Works of John Gower.* Princeton, 1931.

Leonhard, Zelma B. *Classical Mythology in the Confessio Amantis.* Dissertation, Northwestern University, 1944.

Lewis, C. S. *Allegory of Love.* Oxford, 1936.

Macaulay, G. C., ed. *Works of John Gower.* 4 vols. Oxford, 1901.

Murphy, James J. "John Gower's *Confessio Amantis* and the First Discussion of Rhetoric in the English Language," *PQ,* XLI (1962), 401–411.

Pearsall, Derek. "Gower's Narrative Art," *PMLA,* LXXXI (1966), 475–484.

Schueler, Donald G. "Some Comments on the Structure of John Gower's *Confessio Amantis,*" ed. Rima Drell Reck. *Explorations of Literature*: LSU Studies, No. 18 (Baton Rouge, 1966), pp. 15–24.

Stockton, Eric, trans. *The Major Latin Works of John Gower.* Seattle, 1962.

Wickert, Maria. *Studien zu John Gower.* Cologne, 1953.

CONFESSIO AMANTIS

Enter Gower

To sing a song that old was sung,
From ashes ancient Gower is come,
Assuming man's infirmities
To glad your ear and please your eyes.
It hath been sung at festivals,
On ember-eves and holy-ales;
And lords and ladies in their lives
Have read it for restoratives.
The purchase is to make men glorious,
Et bonum quo antiquius, eo melius.
If you, born in these latter times
When wit's more ripe, accept my rhymes
And that to hear an old man sing
May to your wishes pleasure bring,
I life would wish, and that I might
Waste it for you, like taper light.

.   .   .

I tell you what mine authors say.

—WM. SHAKESPEARE

PROLOGUS

Torpor, ebes sensus, scola parua labor minimusque
   Causant quo minimus ipse minora canam:
Qua tamen Engisti lingua canit Insula Bruti
   Anglica Carmente metra iuuante loquar.
Ossibus ergo carens que conterit ossa loquelis
   Absit, et interpres stet procul oro malus.[1]

Of hem that writen ous tofore	[them/before us]
The bokes duelle, and we therfore	[remain]
Ben tawht of that was write tho:	[then]
Forthi good is that we also	[therefore]
In oure tyme among ous hiere	
Do wryte of newe som matiere,	
Essampled of these olde wyse	[modeled on/wise books]
So that it myhte in such a wyse,	[manner]
Whan we ben dede and elleswhere,	[dead]
10 Beleve to the worldes eere	[be left behind/ear]
In tyme comende after this.	[coming]
Bot for men sein, and soth it is,	[since men say/true]
That who that al of wisdom writ	[writes only of wisdom]
It dulleth ofte a mannes wit	
To him that schal it aldai rede,	[all day]
For thilke cause, if that ye rede,	[th'same/choose]
I wolde go the middel weie	
And wryte a bok betwen the tweie,	[two]
Somwhat of lust, somwhat of lore,	
20 That of the lasse or of the more	[less]

I

Som man mai lyke of that I wryte:
And for that fewe men endite   [since/compose]
In oure englissh, I thenke make   [plan to make]
A bok for Engelondes sake,
The yer sextenthe of kyng Richard.[2]
What schal befalle hierafterward
God wot, for now upon this tyde   [time]
Men se the world on every syde
In sondry wyse so diversed,
30   That it welnyh stant al reversed,
As forto speke of tyme ago.   [compared to]
The cause whi it changeth so
It needeth nought to specifie,
The thing so open is at ÿe   [eye]
That every man it mai beholde:
And natheles be daies olde,
Whan that the bokes weren levere,   [more dear]
Wrytinge was beloved evere
Of hem that weren vertuous;
40   For hier in erthe amonges ous,
If noman write hou that it stode,
The pris of hem that weren goode   [prize]
Scholde, as who seith, a gret partie   [as one may say]
Be lost: so for to magnifie
The worthi princes that tho were,   [once (then)]
The bokes schewen hiere and there,
Wherof the world ensampled is;
And tho that deden thanne amis   [those/did]
Thurgh tirannie and crualte,
50   Right as thei stoden in degre,   [just as]
So was the wrytinge of here werk.   [their]
Thus I, which am a burel clerk,   [common]
Purpose forto wryte a bok
After the world that whilom tok   [once took place]
Long tyme in olde daies passed:
Bot for men sein it is now lassed,   [see/lessened]

In worse plit than it was tho, [then]
I thenke forto touche also
The world which neweth every dai,
60 So as I can, so as I mai.
Thogh I seknesse have upon honde [sickness]
And longe have had,[3] yit woll I fonde [try]
To wryte and do my bisinesse,
That in som part, so as I gesse,
The wyse man mai ben avised.
For this prologe is so assised [composed]
That it to wisdom al belongeth:
What wysman that it underfongeth, [undertakes]
He schal drawe into remembrance
70 The fortune of this worldes chance,
The which noman in his persone
Mai knowe, bot the god al one.
Whan the prologe is so despended,
This bok schal afterward ben ended
Of love, which doth many a wonder
And many a wys man hath put under.
And in this wyse I thenke trete [way]
Towardes hem that now be grete,
Betwen the vertu and the vice
80 Which longeth unto this office.[4]
Bot for my wittes ben to smale
To tellen every man his tale,
This bok, upon amendment
To stonde at his commandement,
With whom myn herte is of accord,
I sende unto myn oghne lord,
Which of Lancastre is Henri named:
The hyhe god him hath proclamed
Ful of knyhthode and alle grace.
90 So woll I now this werk embrace
With hol trust and with hol believe;
God grante I mot it wel achieve. [may]

THE STATE

    🏾 If I schal drawe in to my mynde[5]
    The tyme passed, thanne I fynde
    The world stod thanne in al his welthe:
    Tho was the lif of man in helthe,   [then]
    Tho was plente, tho was richesse,
    Tho was the fortune of prouesse,
    Tho was knyhthode in pris be name,   [of value]
100 Wherof the wyde worldes fame
    Write in Cronique is yit withholde;
    Justice of lawe tho was holde,
    The privilege of regalie   [royalty]
    Was sauf, and al the baronie
    Worschiped was in his astat;
    The citees knewen no debat,
    The poeple stod in obeissance
    Under the reule of governance,
    And pes, which ryhtwisnesse keste,   [kissed]
110 With charite tho stod in reste:
    Of mannes herte the corage
    Was schewed thanne in the visage;
    The word was lich to the conceite
    Withoute semblant of deceite:
    Tho was ther unenvied love,
    Tho was the vertu sett above
    And vice was put under fote.
    Now stant the crop under the rote,   [root]
    The world is changed overal,
120 And therof most in special
    That love is falle into discord.
    And that I take to record
    Of every lond for his partie
    The comun vois, which mai noght lie;
    Noght upon on, bot upon alle

It is that men now clepe and calle,
And sein the regnes ben divided,
In stede of love is hate guided,
The werre wol no pes purchace,
130   And lawe hath take hire double face,
So that justice out of the weie
With ryhtwisnesse is gon aweie:
And thus to loke on every halve,
Men sen the sor withoute salve,
Which al the world hath overtake.
Ther is no regne of alle outtake,   [excepted]
For every climat hath his diel   [share]
After the tornynge of the whiel,
Which blinde fortune overthroweth;
140   Wherof the certain noman knoweth:
The hevene wot what is to done,   [knows]
Bot we that duelle under the mone   [moon]
Stonde in this world upon a weer,   [doubt]
And namely bot the pouer   [power]
Of hem that ben the worldes guides
With good consail on alle sides
Be kept upriht in such a wyse,
That hate breke noght thassise   [jurisdiction]
Of love, which is al the chief
150   To kepe a regne out of meschief.
For alle resoun wolde this,
That unto him which the heved is   [head]
The membres buxom scholden bowe,   [obedient]
And he scholde ek her trowthe allowe,
With al his herte and make hem chiere,
For good consail is good to hiere.
Althogh a man be wys himselve,
Yit is the wisdom more of tuelve;
And if thei stoden bothe in on,   [one]
160   To hope it were thanne anon
That god his grace wolde sende

To make of thilke werre an ende,
Which every day now groweth newe:
And that is gretly forto rewe
In special for Cristes sake,
Which wolde his oghne lif forsake   [own]
Among the men to yeve pes.[6]   [give peace]
But now men tellen natheles
That love is fro the world departed,
170 So stant the pes unevene parted
With hem that liven now adaies.
Bot forto loke at alle assaies,   [at all angles]
To him that wolde resoun seche
After the comun worldes speche
It is to wondre of thilke werre,   [war]
In which non wot who hath the werre;   [worse]
For every lond himself deceyveth   [itself]
And of desese his part receyveth,
And yet ne take men no kepe.   [heed]
180 Bot thilke lord which al may kepe,   [th'same]
To whom no consail may ben hid,
Upon the world which is betid,
Amende that wherof men pleigne   [complain]
With trewe hertes and with pleine,
And reconcile love ayeyn,
As he which is king sovereign
Of al the worldes governaunce,
And of his hyhe porveaunce
Afferme pes betwen the londes
190 And take her cause into hise hondes,
So that the world may stonde appesed
And his godhede also be plesed.

THE CHURCH

To thenke upon the daies olde,[7]
The lif of clerkes to beholde,

Men sein how that thei weren tho   [see]
Ensample and reule of alle tho
Whiche of wisdom the vertu soughten.
Unto the god ferst thei besoughten
As to the substaunce of her Scole,   [their]
200   That thei ne scholden noght befole
Her wit upon none erthly werkes,
Which were ayein thestat of clerkes,
And that thei myhten fle the vice
Which Simon hath in his office,[8]
Wherof he takth the gold in honde.
For thilke tyme I understonde
The Lumbard made non eschange[9]
The bisschopriches forto change,
Ne yet a lettre for to sende
210   For dignite ne for Provende,   [prebend]
Or cured or withoute cure.
The cherche keye in aventure
Of armes and of brygantaille   [brigands]
Stod nothing thanne upon bataille;
To fyhte or for to make cheste   [contentious strife]
It thoghte hem thanne noght honeste;
Bot of simplesce and pacience
Thei maden thanne no defence: [prohibition]
The Court of worldly regalie
220   To hem was thanne no baillie;   [possession]
The vein honour was noght desired,
Which hath the proude herte fyred;
Humilite was tho withholde,
And Pride was a vice holde.   [held]
Of holy cherche the largesse
Yaf thanne and dede gret almesse   [gave]
To povere men that hadden nede:
Thei were ek chaste in word and dede,
Wherof the poeple ensample tok;
230   Her lust was al upon the bok,

Or forto preche or forto preie,
To wisse men the ryhte weie
Of suche as stode of trowthe unliered.   [untaught]
Lo, thus was Petres barge stiered
Of hem that thilke tyme were,
And thus cam ferst to mannes Ere   [ear]
The feith of Crist and alle goode
Thurgh hem that thanne weren goode
And sobre and chaste and large and wyse.
240 Bot now men sein is otherwise,
Simon the cause hath undertake,
The worldes swerd on honde is take;
And that is wonder natheles,
Whan Crist him self hath bode pes   [proclaimed peace]
And set it in his testament,
How now that holy cherche is went,
Of that here lawe positif [10]
Hath set to make werre and strif
For worldes good, which may noght laste.
250 God wot the cause to the laste   [knows]
Of every right and wrong also;
But whil the lawe is reuled so
That clerkes to the werre entende,
I not how that thei scholde amende   [know not]
The woful world in othre thinges,
To make pes betwen the kynges
After the lawe of charite,
Which is the propre duete
Belongende unto the presthode.
260 Bot as it thenkth to the manhode,
The hevene is ferr, the world is nyh,
And veine gloire is ek so slyh,
Which coveitise hath now withholde,
That thei non other thing beholde,
Bot only that thei myhten winne
And thus the werres thei beginne,

Wherof the holi cherche is taxed,
That in the point as it is axed
The disme goth to the bataille,[11]   [tithe (L *decima,* 'tenth')]
270   As thogh Crist myhte noght availe
To don hem riht be other weie.
In to the swerd the cherche keie   [key]
Is torned, and the holy bede   [prayer]
Into cursinge, and every stede   [place]
Which scholde stonde upon the feith
And to this cause an Ere leyth,
Astoned is of the querele.
That scholde be the worldes hele   [what/health]
Is now, men sein, the pestilence   [plague]
280   Which hath exiled pacience
Fro the clergie in special:
And that is schewed overal,
In eny thing whan thei ben grieved.
Bot if Gregoire be believed,[12]
As it is in the bokes write,
He doth ous somdel forto wite   [helps us know in part]
The cause of thilke prelacie,
Wher god is noght of compaignie:
For every werk as it is founded
290   Schal stonde or elles be confounded;
Who that only for Cristes sake
Desireth cure forto take,   [curacy]
And noght for pride of thilke astat,
To bere a name of a prelat,
He schal be resoun do profit
In holy cherche upon the plit
That he hath set his conscience;
Bot in the worldes reverence
Ther ben of suche manie glade,
300   Whan thei to thilke astat ben made,
Noght for the merite of the charge,
Bot for thei wolde hemself descharge

Of poverte and become grete;
And thus for Pompe and for beyete   [property]
The Scribe and ek the Pharisee
Of Moïses upon the See
In the chaiere on hyh ben set;
Wherof the feith is ofte let,
Which is betaken hem to kepe.   [given]
310   In Cristes cause alday thei slepe,
Bot of the world is noght foryete;
For wel is him that now may gete
Office in Court to ben honoured.
The stronge coffre hath al devoured
Under the keye of avarice
The tresor of the benefice,
Wherof the povere schulden clothe
And ete and drinke and house bothe;
The charite goth al unknowe,
320   For thei no grein of Pite sowe:
And slouthe kepeth the libraire
Which longeth to the Saintuaire;
To studie upon the worldes lore
Sufficeth now withoute more;
Delicacie his swete toth
Hath fostred so that it fordoth   [destroys]
Of abstinence al that ther is.
And forto loken over this,
If Ethna brenne in the clergie,[13]
330   Al openly to mannes ÿe
At Avynoun thexperience[14]
Therof hath yove an evidence,   [given]
Of that men sen hem so divided.   [see them]
And yit the cause is noght decided;
Bot it is seid and evere schal,
Betwen tuo Stoles lyth the fal,   [stools]
Whan that men wenen best to sitte: [think]
In holy cherche of such a slitte

Is for to rewe un to ous alle;
340 God grante it mote wel befalle   [may]
Towardes him which hath the trowthe.
Bot ofte is sen that mochel slowthe,   [sloth]
Whan men ben drunken of the cuppe,
Doth mochel harm, whan fyr is uppe,
Bot if somwho the flamme stanche;   [unless]
And so to speke upon this branche,
Which proud Envie hath mad to springe,
Of Scisme, causeth forto bringe
This newe Secte of Lollardie,
350 And also many an heresie
Among the clerkes in hemselve.
It were betre dike and delve
And stonde upon the ryhte feith,
Than knowe al that the bible seith
And erre as somme clerkes do.
Upon the hond to were a Schoo
And sette upon the fot a Glove
Acordeth noght to the behove
Of resonable mannes us: [usage]
360 If men behielden the vertus
That Crist in Erthe taghte here,
Thei scholden noght in such manere,
Among hem that ben holden wise,
The Papacie so desguise
Upon diverse eleccioun,
Which stant after thaffeccioun
Of sondry londes al aboute:
Bot whan god wole, it schal were oute,   [wear]
For trowthe mot stonde ate laste.   [must]
370 Bot yet thei argumenten faste
Upon the Pope and his astat,
Wherof thei falle in gret debat;
This clerk seith yee, that other nay,
And thus thei dryve forth the day,

And ech of hem himself amendeth
Of worldes good, bot non entendeth
To that which comun profit were.
Thei sein that god is myhti there,
And schal ordeine what he wile,
380 Ther make thei non other skile
Where is the peril of the feith,
Bot every clerk his herte leith
To kepe his world in special,
And of the cause general,
Which unto holy cherche longeth,   [belongs]
Is non of hem that underfongeth   [undertakes]
To schapen eny resistence:
And thus the riht hath no defence,
Bot ther I love, ther I holde.

390 Lo, thus tobroke is Cristes folde,   [broken to pieces]
Wherof the flock withoute guide
Devoured is on every side,
In lacke of hem that ben unware
Schepherdes, whiche her wit beware   [their/spend]
Upon the world in other halve.   [half]
The scharpe pricke in stede of salve
Thei usen now, wherof the hele   [health]
Thei hurte of that thei scholden hele;
And what Schep that is full of wulle [wool]
400 Upon his back, thei toose and pulle, [shear]
Whil ther is eny thing to pile: [plunder]
And thogh ther be non other skile   [reason]
Bot only for thei wolden wynne,
Thei leve noght, whan thei begynne,
Upon her acte to procede,   [their]
Which is no good schepherdes dede.   [deed]
And upon this also men sein,
That fro the leese which is plein   [shelter (OE *hleo*)/open]
Into the breres thei forcacche   [drive out]
410 Her Orf, for that thei wolden lacche [cattle/seize]

With such duresce, and so bereve
That schal upon the thornes leve
Of wulle, which the brere hath tore; [briar]
Wherof the Schep ben al totore [torn to pieces]
Of that the hierdes make hem lese. [lose]
Lo, how thei feignen chalk for chese,
For though thei speke and teche wel,
Thei don hemself therof no del: [part]
For if the wolf come in the weie,
420 Her gostly Staf is thanne aweie, [their spiritual]
Wherof thei scholde her flock defende;
Bot if the povere Schep offende
In eny thing, thogh it by lyte [little]
They ben al redy forto smyte;
And thus, how evere that thei tale, [reckon]
The strokes falle upon the smale,
And upon othre that ben grete
Hem lacketh herte forto bete.
So that under the clerkes lawe
430 Men sen the Merel al mysdrawe, [lot (OF *merel*, 'token, coin')]

I wol noght seie in general, [say]
For ther ben somme in special
In whom that alle vertu duelleth,
And tho ben, as thapostel telleth, [those are]
That god of his eleccioun
Hath cleped to perfeccioun [named]
In the manere as Aaron was:
Thei ben nothing in thilke cas
Of Simon, which the foldes gate
440 Hath lete, and goth in othergate, [abandoned]
Bot thei gon in the rihte weie.
Ther ben also somme, as men seie,
That folwen Simon ate hieles, [heels]
Whos carte goth upon the whieles
Of coveitise and worldes Pride,

And holy cherche goth beside,
Which scheweth outward a visage
Of that is noght in the corage.   [heart]
For if men loke in holy cherche,
450 Betwen the word and that thei werche
Ther is a full gret difference:
Thei prechen ous in audience
That noman schal his soule empeire,
For al is bot a chirie feire   [cherry fair]
This worldes good, so as thei telle;
Also thei sein ther is an helle,
Which unto mannes sinne is due,
And bidden ous therfore eschue
That wikkid is, and do the goode.
460 Who that here wordes understode,   [their]
It thenkth thei wolden do the same;
Bot yet betwen ernest and game
Ful ofte it torneth other wise.
With holy tales thei devise
How meritoire is thilke dede
Of charite, to clothe and fede
The povere folk and forto parte
The worldes good, bot thei departe
Ne thenken noght fro that thei have.
470 Also thei sein, good is to save
With penance and with abstinence
Of chastite the continence;
Bot pleinly forto speke of that,
I not how thilke body fat,   [know not]
Which thei with deynte metes kepe
And leyn it softe forto slepe,
Whan it hath elles al his wille,
With chastite schal stonde stille:
And natheles I can noght seie,
480 In aunter if that I misseye.   [on the chance I may say
                                                      wrong]

Touchende of this, how evere it stonde,
I here and wol noght understonde,
For therof have I noght to done:
Bot he that made ferst the Mone,
The hyhe god, of his goodnesse,
If ther be cause, he it redresce.
Bot what as eny man accuse,
This mai reson of trowthe excuse;
The vice of hem that ben ungoode
490 Is no reproef unto the goode:
For every man hise oghne werkes
Schal bere, and thus as of the clerkes
The goode men ben to comende,
And alle these othre god amende:
For thei ben to the worldes ÿe
The Mirour of ensamplerie,
To reulen and to taken hiede
Betwen the men and the godhiede.

THE COMMONS

🕂 Now forto speke of the comune,[15]   [commons]
500 It is to drede of that fortune
Which hath befalle in sondri londes:
Bot often for defalte of bondes
Al sodeinliche, er it be wist,
A Tonne, whanne his lye arist,   [tun/its]
Tobrekth and renneth al aboute,
Which elles scholde noght gon oute;
And ek fulofte a litel Skar
Upon a Banke, er men be war,
Let in the Strem, which with gret peine,
510 If evere man it schal restreigne.
Wher lawe lacketh, errour groweth,
He is noght wys who that ne troweth,   [believes]

For it hath proeved ofte er this;
And thus the comun clamour is
In every lond wher poeple dwelleth,
And eche in his compleignte telleth
How that the world is al miswent,
And ther upon his jugement
Yifth every man in sondry wise. [gives]
520 Bot what man wolde himself avise, [consider]
His conscience and noght misuse,
He may wel ate ferste excuse
His god, which ever stant in on: [stands united]
In him ther is defalte non,
So moste it stonde upon ousselve [ourselves]
Nought only upon ten ne twelve,
Bot plenerliche upon ous alle, [fully]
For man is cause of that schal falle.
        And natheles yet som men wryte
530 And sein that fortune is to wyte, [blame]
And som men holde oppinion
That it is constellacion,
Which causeth al that a man doth:
God wot of bothe which is soth. [knows/true]
The world as of his propre kynde [its own nature]
Was evere untrewe, and as the blynde
Improprelich he demeth fame,
He blameth that is noght to blame
And preiseth that is noght to preise:
540 Thus whan he schal the thinges peise, [weigh]
Ther is deceipte in his balance,
And al is that the variance
Of ous, that scholde ous betre avise; [beware]
For after that we falle and rise,
The world arist and falth withal,
So that the man is overal
His oghne cause of wel and wo.
That we fortune clepe so

Out of the man himself it groweth;
550 And who that other wise troweth, [believes]
Behold the poeple of Irael: [Israel]
For evere whil thei deden wel,
Fortune was hem debonaire,
And whan thei deden the contraire,
Fortune was contrariende.
So that it proeveth wel at ende
Why that the world is wonderfull
And may no while stonde full,
Though that it seme wel besein;
560 For every worldes thing is vein,
And evere goth the whiel aboute,
And evere stant a man in doute,
Fortune stant no while stille,
So hath ther noman al his wille.
Als fer as evere a man may knowe,
Ther lasteth nothing bot a throwe; [short time]
The world stant evere upon debat,
So may be seker non astat, [certain]
Now hier now ther, now to now fro,
570 Now up now down, this world goth so,
And evere hath don and evere schal:
Wherof I finde in special
A tale writen in the Bible,
Which moste nedes be credible;
And that as in conclusioun
Seith that upon divisioun
Stant, why no worldes thing mai laste,
Til it be drive to the laste. [end]
And fro the ferste regne of·alle
580 Into this day, hou so befalle,
Of that the regnes be muable [changing]
The man himself hath be coupable, [culpable]
Which of his propre governance
Fortuneth al the worldes chance.

NEBUCHADNEZZAR'S DREAM

❀ The hyhe almyhti pourveance,[16]   [foresight]
In whos eterne remembrance
Fro ferst was every thing present,
He hath his prophecie sent,
In such a wise as thou schalt hiere,
590 To Daniel of this matiere,
Hou that this world schal torne and wende,
Till it be falle to his ende;
Wherof the tale telle I schal,
In which it is betokned al.

   As Nabugodonosor slepte,
A swevene him tok, the which he kepte
Til on the morwe he was arise,
For he therof was sore agrise.   [terrified (OE *agrisan*)]
To Daniel his drem he tolde,
600 And preide him faire that he wolde
Arede what it tokne may;   [explain/signify]
And seide: "Abedde wher I lay,
Me thoghte I syh upon a Stage
Wher stod a wonder strange ymage.
His hed with al the necke also
Thei were of fin gold bothe tuo;
His brest, his schuldres and his armes
Were al of selver, bot the tharmes,   [intestines]
The wombe and al doun to the kne,   [belly]
610 Of bras thei were upon to se;
The legges were al mad of Stiel,
So were his feet also somdiel,   [in part]
And somdiel part to hem was take
Of Erthe which men Pottes make;
The fieble meynd was with the stronge,   [mingled]
So myhte it wel noght stonde longe.
And tho me thoghte that I sih

A gret ston from an hull on hyh   [hill]
Fel doun of sodein aventure
620 Upon the feet of this figure,
With which Ston al tobroke was
Gold, Selver, Erthe, Stiel and Bras,
That al was in to pouldre broght,
And so forth torned into noght."
    This was the swevene which he hadde,   [dream]
That Daniel anon aradde,   [explained]
And seide him that figure strange
Betokneth how the world schal change
And waxe lasse worth and lasse,   [less]
630 Til it to noght al overpasse.
The necke and hed, that weren golde,
He seide how that betokne scholde
A worthi world, a noble, a riche,
To which non after schal be liche.   [like]
Of Selver that was overforth
Schal ben a world of lasse worth;
And after that the wombe of Bras
Tokne of a werse world it was.
The Stiel which he syh afterward   [saw]
640 A world betokneth more hard:
Bot yet the werste of everydel
Is last, whan that of Erthe and Stiel
He syh the feet departed so,
For that betokneth mochel wo.
Whan that the world divided is,
It moste algate fare amis,   [assuredly]
For Erthe which is meynd with Stiel   [alloyed]
Togedre may noght laste wiel,   [well]
Bot if that on that other waste;
650 So mot it nedes faile in haste.
The Ston, which fro the hully Stage   [mountain]
He syh doun falle on that ymage,
And hath it into pouldre broke,   [powder]

That swevene hath Daniel unloke, [dream]
And seide how that is goddes myht,
Which whan men wene most upryht [think]
To stonde, schal hem overcaste.
And that is of this world the laste,
And thanne a newe schal beginne,
660 Fro which a man schal nevere twinne; [divide]
Or al to peine or al to pes
That world schal lasten endeles.
    Lo thus expondeth Daniel
The kynges swevene faire and wel
In Babiloyne the Cite,
Wher that the wiseste of Caldee
Ne cowthen wite what it mente; [had not wit to know]
Bot he tolde al the hol entente,
As in partie it is befalle.
670 Of gold the ferste regne of alle
Was in that kinges time tho,
And laste manye daies so,
Therwhiles that the Monarchie
Of al the world in that partie
To Babiloyne was soubgit;
And hield him stille in such a plit,
Til that the world began diverse:
And that was whan the king of Perse,
Which Cirus hyhte, ayein the pes [peace]
680 Forth with his Sone Cambises
Of Babiloine al that Empire,
Ryht as thei wolde hemself desire,
Put under in subjeccioun
And tok it in possessioun,
And slayn was Baltazar the king,
Which loste his regne and al his thing.
And thus whan thei it hadde wonne,
The world of Selver was begonne
And that of gold was passed oute:

690 And in this wise it goth aboute
In to the Regne of Darius;
And thanne it fell to Perse thus,
That Alisaundre put hem under,
Which wroghte of armes many a wonder,
So that the Monarchie lefte
With Grecs, and here astat uplefte,
And Persiens gon under fote,
So soffre thei that nedes mote.
And tho the world began of Bras,
700 And that of selver ended was;
Bot for the time thus it laste,
Til it befell that ate laste
This king, whan that his day was come,
With strengthe of deth was overcome.
And natheles yet er he dyde,
He schop his Regnes to divide   [appointed (shaped)]
To knyhtes whiche him hadde served,
And after that thei have deserved
Yaf the conquestes that he wan;   [gave/won]
710 Wherof gret werre tho began
Among hem that the Regnes hadde,
Thurgh proud Envie which hem ladde,
Til it befell ayein hem thus:
The noble Cesar Julius,
Which tho was king of Rome lond,
With gret bataille and with strong hond
Al Grece, Perse and ek Caldee
Wan and put under, so that he
720 Noght al only of thorient
Bot al the Marche of thoccident   [region]
Governeth under his empire,
As he that was hol lord and Sire,
And hield thurgh his chivalerie
Of al this world the Monarchie,
And was the ferste of that honour

Which tok the name of Emperour.
　　Wher Rome thanne wolde assaille,
Ther myhte nothing contrevaille,
Bot every contre most obeie:
730　Tho goth the Regne of Bras aweie,
And comen is the world of Stiel,
And stod above upon the whiel.
As Stiel is hardest in his kynde
Above alle othre that men finde
Of Metals, such was Rome tho
The myhtieste, and laste so
Long time amonges the Romeins
Til thei become so vileins,　　　　　　　　　[villainous]
That the fals Emperour Leo
740　With Constantin his Sone also
The patrimoine and the richesse,
Which to Silvestre in pure almesse
The ferste Constantinus lefte,
Fro holy cherche thei berefte.
Bot Adrian, which Pope was,
And syh the meschief of this cas,
Goth in to France forto pleigne,
And preith the grete Charlemeine,[17]
For Cristes sake and Soule hele
750　That he wol take the querele
Of holy cherche in his defence.
And Charles for the reverence
Of god the cause hath undertake,
And with his host the weie take
Over the Montz of Lombardie;
Of Rome and al the tirandie
With blodi swerd he overcom,
And the Cite with strengthe nom;　　　　　[took]
In such a wise and there he wroghte,
760　That holy cherche ayein he broghte
Into franchise, and doth restore

The Popes lost, and yaf him more: [gave]
And thus whan he his god hath served,
He tok, as he wel hath deserved,
The Diademe and was coroned.
Of Rome and thus was abandoned
Thempire, which cam nevere ayein
Into the hond of no Romein;
Bot a long time it stod so stille
770 Under the Frensche kynges wille,
Til that fortune hir whiel so ladde,
That afterward Lombardz it hadde,
Noght be the swerd, bot be soffrance
Of him that tho was kyng of France,
Which Karle Calvus cleped was;
And he resigneth in this cas
Thempire of Rome unto Lowis
His Cousin, which a Lombard is.
And so hit laste into the yeer
780 Of Albert and of Berenger;
Bot thanne upon dissencioun
Thei felle, and in divisioun
Among hemself that were grete,   [themselves]
So that thei loste the beyete   [possession]
Of worschipe and of worldes pes.   [peace]
Bot in proverbe natheles
Men sein, ful selden is that welthe
Can soffre his oghnė astat in helthe;
And that was on the Lombardz sene,
790 Such comun strif was hem betwene
Thurgh coveitise and thurgh Envie,
That every man drowh his partie,
Which myhte leden eny route,   [mob]
Withinne Burgh and ek withoute:
The comun ryht hath no felawe,
So that the governance of lawe
Was lost, and for necessite,

Of that thei stode in such degre
Al only thurgh divisioun,
800 Hem nedeth in conclusioun
Of strange londes help beside.
    And thus for thei hemself divide
And stonden out of reule unevene,
Of Alemaine Princes sevene
Thei chose in this condicioun,
That upon here eleccioun   [their]
Thempire of Rome scholde stonde.
And thus thei lefte it out of honde
For lacke of grace, and it forsoke,
810 That Alemans upon hem toke:
And to confermen here astat,
Of that thei founden in debat
Thei token the possessioun
After the composicioun
Among hemself, and therupon
Thei made an Emperour anon,
Whos name as the Cronique telleth
Was Othes; and so forth it duelleth,
Fro thilke day yit unto this
820 Thempire of Rome hath ben and is
To thalemans. And in this wise,
As ye tofore have herd divise
How Daniel the swevene expondeth
Of that ymage, on whom he foundeth
The world which after scholde falle,
Come is the laste tokne of alle;
Upon the feet of Erthe and Stiel
So stant this world now everydiel
Departed; which began riht tho,
830 Whan Rome was divided so:
And that is forto rewe sore,
For alway siththe more and more   [since]
The world empeireth every day.   [grows worse]

Wherof the sothe schewe may,   [truth]
At Rome ferst if we beginne:
The wall and al the Cit withinne
Stant in ruine and in decas,   [ruin (L *decasus*)]
The feld is wher the Paleis was,   [field]
The toun is wast; and overthat,   [waste]
840   If we beholde thilke astat
      Which whilom was of the Romeins,
      Of knyhthode and of Citezeins,
      To peise now with that beforn,   [weigh (compare)]
      The chaf is take for the corn,
      As forto speke of Romes myht:
      Unethes stant ther oght upryht   [scarcely/anything]
      Of worschipe or of worldes good,
      As it before tyme stod.
      And why the worschipe is aweie,
850   If that a man the sothe seie,   [speaks the truth]
      The cause hath ben divisioun,
      Which moder of confusioun
      Is wher sche cometh overal,
      Noght only of the temporal
      Bot of the spiritual also.
      The dede proeveth it is so,
      And hath do many day er this,
      Thurgh venym which that medled is
      In holy cherche of erthly thing:
860   For Crist himself makth knowleching
      That noman may togedre serve
      God and the world, bot if he swerve   [unless]
      Froward that on and stonde unstable;   [one]
      And Cristes word may noght be fable.
      The thing so open is at ÿe,
      It nedeth noght to specefie
      Or speke oght more in this matiere;
      Bot in this wise a man mai lere   [manner/learn]
      Hou that the world is gon aboute,

870 The which welnyh is wered oute,   [worn]
    After the forme of that figure
    Which Daniel in his scripture
    Expondeth, as tofore is told.
    Of Bras, of Selver and of Gold
    The world is passed and agon,
    And now upon his olde ton   [toes]
    It stant of brutel Erthe and Stiel,   [brittle (untrustworthy)]
    The whiche acorden nevere a diel;   [not at all]
    So mot it nedes swerve aside
880 As thing the which men sen divide.
        Thapostel writ unto ous alle[18]
    And seith that upon ous is falle
    Thende of the world; so may we knowe,
    This ymage is nyh overthrowe,
    Be which this world was signified,
    That whilom was so magnefied,
    And now is old and fieble and vil,   [vile]
    Full of meschief and of peril,
    And stant divided ek also
890 Lich to the feet that were so,
    As I tolde of the Statue above.
    And this men sen, thurgh lacke of love
    Where as the lond divided is,
    It mot algate fare amis: [must necessarily]
    And now to loke on every side,
    A man may se the world divide,
    The werres ben so general   [wars]
    Among the cristene overal,
    That every man now secheth wreche,   [vengeance]
900 And yet these clerkes alday preche
    And sein, good dede may non be
    Which stant noght upon charite:
    I not hou charite may stonde,   [don't know]
    Wher dedly werre is take on honde.
    Bot al this wo is cause of man,

The which that wit and reson can,
And that in tokne and in witnesse
That ilke ymage bar liknesse
Of man and of non other beste.   [creature]
910 For ferst unto the mannes heste   [command]
Was every creature ordeined,
Bot afterward it was restreigned:
Whan that he fell, thei fellen eke,   [also]
Whan he wax sek, thei woxen seke;   [sick]
For as the man hath passioun
Of seknesse, in comparisoun
So soffren othre creatures.
Lo, ferst the hevenly figures,
The Sonne and Mone eclipsen bothe,
920 And ben with mannes senne wrothe;   [sin/made angry]
The purest Eir for Senne alofte
Hath ben and is corrupt fulofte,
Right now the hyhe wyndes blowe,
And anon after thei ben lowe,
Now clowdy and now clier it is:
So may it proeven wel be this,
A mannes Senne is forto hate,
Which makth the welkne to debate.   [heavens]
And forto se the proprete
930 Of every thyng in his degree,
Benethe forth among ous hiere
Al stant aliche in this matiere:
The See now ebbeth, now it floweth,
The lond now welketh, now it groweth,   [withers]
Now be the Trees with leves grene,
Now thei be bare and nothing sene,
Now be the lusti somer floures,
Now be the stormy wynter shoures,
Now be the daies, now the nyhtes,
940 So stant ther nothing al upryhtes,
Now it is lyht, now it is derk;

And thus stant al the worldes werk
After the disposicioun
Of man and his condicioun.
Forthi Gregoire in his Moral [19]
Seith that a man in special
The lasse world is properly: [smaller (microcosmic)]
And that he proeveth redely;
For man of Soule resonable
950   Is to an Angel resemblable,
And lich to beste he hath fielinge,
And lich to Trees he hath growinge;
The Stones ben and so is he:
Thus of his propre qualite
The man, as telleth the clergie,
Is as a world in his partie,
And whan this litel world mistorneth,
The grete world al overtorneth.
The Lond, the See, the firmament,
960   Thei axen alle jugement
Ayein the man and make him werre: [make war against him]
Therwhile himself stant out of herre,   [out of order (ME *herre*,
                                             'hinges')]

The remenant wol noght acorde:
And in this wise, as I recorde,
The man is cause of alle wo,
Why this world is divided so.
      Division, the gospell seith
On hous upon another leith,
Til that the Regne al overthrowe:
970   And thus may every man wel knowe,
Division aboven alle
Is thing which makth the world to falle,
And evere hath do sith it began.
It may ferst proeve upon a man;
The which, for his complexioun
Is mad upon divisioun

Of cold, of hot, of moist, of drye,
He mot be verray kynde dye:[20]
For the contraire of his astat
980 Stant evermore is such debat,
Til that o part be overcome,
Ther may no final pes be nome. [taken]
Bot other wise, if a man were
Mad al togedre of o matiere [one]
Withouten interrupcioun, [separation of parts]
Ther scholde no corrupcioun
Engendre upon that unite:
Bot for ther is diversite
Withinne himself, he may noght laste,
990 That he ne deieth ate laste.
Bot in a man yit over this
Full gret divisioun ther is,
Thurgh which that he is evere in strif,
Whil that him lasteth eny lif:
The bodi and the Soule also
Among hem ben divided so,
That what thing that the body hateth
The soule loveth and debateth;
Bot natheles fulofte is sene
1000 Of werre which is hem betwene
The fieble hath wonne the victoire.
And who so drawth into memoire
What hath befalle of old and newe,
He may that werre sore rewe,
Which ferst began in Paradis:
For ther was proeved what it is,
And what desese there it wroghte;
For thilke werre tho forth broghte
The vice of alle dedly Sinne,
1010 Thurgh which division cam inne
Among the men in erthe hiere,
And was the cause and the matiere

Why god the grete flodes sende,
Of al the world and made an ende
Bot Noë with his felaschipe,
Which only weren saulf be Schipe. [safe]
And over that thurgh Senne it com [besides]
That Nembrot such emprise nom, [took]
Whan he the Tour Babel on heihte
1020 Let make, as he that wolde feihte [fight]
Ayein the hihe goddes myht,
Wherof divided anon ryht
Was the langage in such entente,
Ther wiste non what other mente, [knew]
So that thei myhten noght procede.
And thus it stant of every dede,
Wher Senne takth the cause on honde,
It may upriht noght longe stonde;
For Senne of his condicioun
1030 Is moder of divisioun [mother]
And tokne whan the world schal faile.
For so seith Crist withoute faile,
That nyh upon the worldes ende
Pes and acord awey schol wende
And alle charite schal cesse
Among the men and hate encresce;
And whan these toknes ben befalle,
Al sodeinly the Ston schal falle,
As Daniel it hath beknowe,
1040 Which al this world schal overthrowe,
And every man schal thanne arise
To Joie or elles to Juise, [justice]
Wher that he schal for evere dwelle,
Or straght to hevene or straght to helle.
In hevene is pes and al acord,
Bot helle is full of such descord
That ther may be no loveday:
Forthi good is, whil a man may,

Echon to sette pes with other
1050 And loven as his oghne brother;
So may he winne worldes welthe
And afterward his soule helthe.
    Bot wolde god that now were on
An other such as Arion,[21]
Which hadde an harpe of such temprure,
And therto of so good mesure
He song, that he the bestes wilde
Made of his note tame and milde,
The Hinde in pes with the Leoun,
1060 The Wolf in pes with the Moltoun,   [sheep]
The Hare in pees stod with the Hound;
And every man upon this ground
Which Arion that time herde,
Als wel the lord as the schepherde,
He broghte hem alle in good acord;
So that the comun with the lord,
And lord with the comun also,
He sette in love bothe tuo
And putte awey malencolie.
1070 That was a lusti melodie,
Whan every man with other low;   [laughed]
And if ther were such on now,
Which cowthe harpe as he tho dede,
He myhte availe in many a stede   [place]
To make pes wher now is hate;
For whan men thenken to debate,
I not what other thing is good.
Bot wher that wisdom waxeth wod,   [mad]
And reson torneth into rage,
1080 So that mesure upon oultrage   [outrage]
Hath set his world, it is to drede;
For that bringth in the comun drede.
Which stant at every mannes Dore:
Bot whan the scharpnesse of the spore   [spur]

The horse side smit to sore,
It grieveth ofte. And now nomore,
As forto speke of this matiere,
Which non bot only god may stiere.   [guide]

Explicit Prologus

INCIPIT LIBER PRIMUS

Naturatus amor nature legibus orbem
  Subdit, et vnanimes concitat esse feras:
Huius enim mundi Princeps amor esse videtur,
  Cuius eget diues, pauper et omnis ope.
Sunt in agone pares amor et fortuna, que cecas
  Plebis ad insidias vertit vterque rotas.
Est amor egra salus, vexata quies, pius error,
  Bellica pax, vulnus dulce, suaue malum.[1]

I may noght strecche up to the hevene
Min hand, ne setten al in evene
This world, which evere is in balance:
It stant noght in my sufficance   [ability]
So grete thinges to compasse,
Bot I mot lete it overpasse
And treten upon othre thinges.
Forthi the Stile of my writinges
Fro this day forth I thenke change
10 And speke of thing is noght so strange,   [foreign]
Which every kinde hath upon honde,
And wherupon the world mot stonde,
And hath don sithen it began,   [since]
And schal whil ther is any man;
And that is love, of which I mene
To trete, as after schal be sene.
In which ther can noman him reule,
For loves lawe is out of reule,
That of tomoche or of tolite   [too much/too little]

33

20 Welnyh is every man to wyte, [blame]
And natheles ther is noman [moreover (in truth)]
In al this world so wys, that can
Of love tempre the mesure,
Bot as it falth in aventure: [falls/chance]
For wit ne strengthe may noght helpe,
And he which elles wolde him yelpe [otherwise/boast]
Is rathest throwen under fote, [most quickly]
Ther can no wiht therof do bote. [man/be of help]
For yet was nevere such covine, [conspiracy]
30 That couthe ordeine a medicine [knew how to concoct]
To thing which god in lawe of kinde
Hath set, for ther may noman finde
The rihte salve of such a Sor.
It hath and schal ben everemor
That love is maister wher he wile,
Ther can no lif make other skile; [no creature can do otherwise]
For wher as evere him lest to sette, [wherever he chooses to sit]
Ther is no myht which him may lette. [power/stop him]
Bot what schal fallen ate laste,
40 The sothe can no wisdom caste, [wiseman/forecaste]
Bot as it falleth upon chance;
For if ther evere was balance
Which of fortune stant governed,
I may wel lieve as I am lerned [believe/told]
That love hath that balance on honde,
Which wol no reson understonde.
For love is blind and may noght se,
Forthi may no certeinete
Be set upon his jugement,
50 Bot as the whiel aboute went [goes]
He yifth his graces undeserved, [gives]
And fro that man which hath him served
Fulofte he takth aweye his fees, [wages]
As he that pleieth ate Dees, [dice]

And therupon what schal befalle
He not, til that the chance falle,   [knows not]
Wher he schal lese or he schal winne.   [lose]
And thus fulofte men beginne,
That if thei wisten what it mente,   [knew]
60 Thei wolde change al here entente.   [their]
        And forto proven it is so,
I am miselven on of tho,   [one of those]
Which to this Scole am underfonge.   [received]
For it is siththe go noght longe,   [since]
As forto speke of this matiere,
I may you telle, if ye woll hiere,
A wonder hap which me befell,   [adventure]
That was to me bothe hard and fell,   [cruel]
Touchende of love and his fortune,
70 The which me liketh to comune
And pleinly forto telle it oute.
To hem that ben lovers aboute
Fro point to point I wol declare
And wryten of my woful care,
Mi wofull day, my wofull chance,
That men mowe take remembrance   [may]
Of that thei schall hierafter rede:
For in good feith this wolde I rede,   [advise]
That every man ensample take
80 Of wisdom which him is betake,   [given]
And that he wot of good aprise   [teaching]
To teche it forth, for such emprise   [enterprise]
Is forto preise; and therfor I
Woll wryte and schewe al openly
How love and I togedre mette,
Wherof the world ensample fette   [fetch (get)]
Mai after this, whan I am go,
Of thilke unsely jolif wo,   [unhappy/happy]
Whos reule stant out of the weie,

90   Nou glad and nou gladnesse aweie,
And yet it may noght be withstonde
For oght that men may understonde.

      Upon the point that is befalle[2]
Of love, in which that I am falle,
I thenke telle my matiere:
Now herkne, who that wol it hiere,
Of my fortune how that it ferde.
This enderday, as I forthferde   [other day]
To walke, as I yow telle may,—
100   And that was in the Monthe of Maii,
Whan every brid hath chose his make   [mate]
And thenkth his merthes forto make
Of love that he hath achieved;
Bot so was I nothing relieved,
For I was further fro my love
Than Erthe is fro the hevene above,
As forto speke of eny sped: [success]
So wiste I me non other red,   [knew/council]
Bot as it were a man forfare   [worn out with travel]
110   Unto the wode I gan to fare,
Noght forto singe with the briddes,
For whanne I was the wode amiddes,
I fond a swote grene pleine,   [sweet]
And ther I gan my wo compleigne
Wisshinge and wepinge al myn one,   [alone by myself]
For other merthes made I none.
So hard me was that ilke throwe,   [pain (circumstance)]
That ofte sithes overthrowe
To grounde I was withoute breth;
120   And evere I wisshide after deth,
Whanne I out of my peine awok,
And caste up many a pitous lok
Unto the hevene, and seide thus:
"O thou Cupide, O thou Venus,

Thou god of love and thou goddesse,
Wher is pite? wher is meknesse?
Now doth me pleinly live or dye,
For certes such a maladie
As I now have and longe have hadd,
130   It myhte make a wisman madd,
If that it scholde longe endure.
O Venus, queene of loves cure,
Thou lif, thou lust, thou mannes hele,
Behold my cause and my querele,
And yif me som part of thi grace,
So that I may finde in this place
If thou be gracious or non."
And with that word I sawh anon
The kyng of love and qweene bothe;
140   Bot he that kyng with yhen wrothe   [angry eyes]
His chiere aweiward fro me caste,   [countenance]
And forth he passede ate laste.
Bot natheles er he forth wente
A firy Dart me thoghte he hente   [seized]
And threw it thurgh myn herte rote:
In him fond I non other bote,   [relief (reward)]
For lenger list him noght to duelle.   [it pleased]
Bot sche that is the Source and Welle
Of wel or wo, that schal betide   [as sometimes happens]
150   To hem that loven, at that tide
Abod, bot forto tellen hiere   [wailed/speak of]
Sche cast on me no goodly chiere:
Thus natheles to me sche seide,
"What art thou, Sone?" and I abreide   [started]
Riht as a man doth out of slep,
And therof tok sche riht good kep   [notice]
And bad me nothing ben adrad:
Bot for al that I was noght glad,
For I ne sawh no cause why.
160   And eft scheo asketh, what was I:

I seide, "A Caitif that lith hiere: [captive]
What wolde ye, my Ladi diere?
Schal I ben hol or elles dye?"
Sche seide, "Tell thi maladie:
What is thi Sor of which thou pleignest?
Ne hyd it noght, for if thou feignest,
I can do the no medicine,"
"Ma dame, I am a man of thyne,
That in thi Court have longe served,
170 And aske that I have deserved,
Som wele after my longe wo."
And sche began to loure tho,
And seide, "Ther is manye of yow
Faitours, and so may be that thow   [impostors (OF *faiteor*,
                                      'contrivers')]

Art riht such on, and be feintise
Seist that thou hast me do servise."
And natheles sche wiste wel,
Mi world stod on an other whiel
Withouten eny faiterie:
180 Bot algate of my maladie   [in any case]
Sche bad me telle and seie hir trowthe.   [speak]
"Ma dame, if ye wolde have rowthe,"   [pity]
Quod I, "than wolde I telle yow."
"Sey forth," quod sche, "and tell me how;
Schew me thi seknesse everydiel."
"Ma dame, that can I do wel,
Be so my lif therto wol laste."   [providing my life]
With that hir lok on me sche caste,
And seide: "In aunter if thou live,   [in the chance that]
190 Mi will is ferst that thou be schrive;
And natheles how that it is
I wot miself, bot for al this
Unto my prest, which comth anon,
I woll thou telle it on and on,
Bothe all thi thoght and al thi werk.

O Genius myn oghne Clerk,[3]
Com forth and hier this mannes schrifte,"   [confession]
Quod Venus tho; and I uplifte
Min hefd with that, and gan beholde   [head]
200 The selve Prest, which as sche wolde   [very]
Was redy there and sette him doun
To hiere my confessioun.

    This worthi Prest, this holy man[4]
To me spekende thus began,
And seide: "Benedicite,
Mi Sone, of the felicite
Of love and ek of all the wo
Thou schalt thee schrive of bothe tuo.
What thou er this for loves sake
210 Hast felt, let nothing be forsake,
Tell pleinliche as it is befalle."
And with that word I gan doun falle
On knees, and with devocioun
And with full gret contricioun
I seide thanne: "Dominus,
Min holi fader Genius,
So as thou hast experience
Of love, for whos reverence
Thou schalt me shriven at this time,
220 I prai the let me noght mistime
Mi schrifte, for I am destourbed
In al myn herte, and so contourbed,   [perturbed]
That I ne may my wittes gete,
So schal I moche thing foryete:
Bot if thou wolt my schrifte oppose   [question me about my
                                                  confession]

Fro point to point, thanne I suppose,
Ther schal nothing be left behinde.
Bot now my wittes ben so blinde,
That I ne can miselven teche."

230 Tho he began anon to preche,
And with his wordes debonaire
He seide tome softe and faire: [to me]
"Thi schrifte to oppose and hiere,
My Sone, I am assigned hiere
Be Venus the godesse above,
Whos Prest I am touchende of love.
Bot natheles for certein skile   [moreover]
I mot algate and nedes wile
Noght only make my spekynges
240 Of love, bot of othre thinges,
That touchen to the cause of vice.
For that belongeth to thoffice
Of Prest, whos ordre that I bere,
So that I wol nothing forbere,
That I the vices on and on
Ne schal thee schewen everychon;
Wherof thou myht take evidence
To reule with thi conscience.
Bot of conclusion final
250 Conclude I wol in special
For love, whos servant I am,
And why the cause is that I cam.
So thenke I to don bothe tuo,
Ferst that myn ordre longeth to,
The vices forto telle arewe,   [in succession]
Bot next above alle othre schewe
Of love I wol the propretes,
How that thei stonde be degrees
After the disposicioun
260 Of Venus, whos condicioun
I moste folwe, as I am holde.   [bound]
For I with love am al withholde,
So that the lasse I am to wyte,   [less/blame]
Thogh I ne conne bot a lyte   [understand]

Of othre thinges that ben wise: [taught (known)]
I am noght tawht in such a wise;   [way]
For it is noght my comun us   [use]
To speke of vices and vertus,
Bot al of love and of his lore,
270 For Venus bokes of nomore
Me techen nowther text ne glose.
Bot for als moche as I suppose
It sit a prest to be wel thewed,   [mannered (disposed)]
And schame it is if he be lewed,   [ignorant]
Of my Presthode after the forme
I wol thi schrifte so enforme,
That ate leste thou schalt hiere
The vices, and to thi matiere
Of love I schal hem so remene,
280 That thou schalt knowe what thei mene.
For what a man schal axe or sein   [ask]
Touchende of schrifte, it mot be plein,   [regarding confession]
It nedeth noght to make it queinte,
For trowthe hise wordes wol noght peinte:
That I wole axe of the forthi,
My Sone, it schal be so pleinly,
That thou schalt knowe and understonde
The pointz of schrifte how that thei
     stonde."

Between the lif and deth I herde[5]
290 This Prestes tale er I answerde,
And thanne I preide him forto seie
His will, and I it wolde obeie
After the forme of his apprise.   [teaching]
Tho spak he tome in such a wise,
And bad me that I scholde schrive
As touchende of my wittes fyve,   [senses]
And schape that thei were amended   [bring about]

Of that I hadde hem misdispended.
For tho be proprely the gates, [then]
300 Thurgh whiche as to the herte algates [truly]
Comth alle thing unto the feire, [fair]
Which may the mannes Soule empeire.
And now this matiere is broght inne,
Mi Sone, I thenke ferst beginne
To wite how that thin yhe hath stonde, [know/eye]
The which is, as I understonde,
The moste principal of alle,
Thurgh whom that peril mai befalle.[6]
    And forto speke in loves kinde,
310 Ful manye suche a man mai finde,
Whiche evere caste aboute here yhe, [their]
To loke if that thei myhte aspie
Fulofte thing which hem ne toucheth,
Bot only that here herte soucheth [suspects]
In hindringe of an other wiht; [man]
And thus ful many a worthi knyht
And many a lusti lady bothe
Have be fulofte sythe wrothe. [times]
So that an yhe is as a thief
320 To love, and doth ful gret meschief;
And also for his oghne part
Fulofte thilke firy Dart [the same]
Of love, which that evere brenneth,
Thurgh him into the herte renneth:
And thus a mannes yhe ferst [eye]
Himselve grieveth alther werst, [worst of all]
And many a time that he knoweth
Unto his oghne harm it groweth.
Mi Sone, herkne now forthi
330 A tale, to be war therby
Thin yhe forto kepe and warde, [guard]
So that it passe noght his warde. [its domain]

TALE OF ACTEON

Ovide telleth in his bok[7]
Ensample touchende of mislok,
And seith hou whilom ther was on,
A worthi lord, which Acteon
Was hote, and he was cousin nyh   [called]
To him that Thebes ferst on hyh
Up sette, which king Cadme hyhte.   [was named]
340   This Acteon, as he wel myhte,
Above alle othre caste his chiere,
And used it fro yer to yere,
With Houndes and with grete Hornes
Among the wodes and the thornes
To make his hunting and his chace:
Where him best thoghte in every place
To finde gamen in his weie,
Ther rod he forto hunte and pleie.
So him befell upon a tide
350   On his hunting as he cam ride,
In a Forest al one he was: [alone]
He syh upon the grene gras
The faire freisshe floures springe,
He herde among the leves singe
The Throstle with the nyhtingale:
Thus er he wiste into a Dale
He cam, wher was a litel plein,
All round aboute wel besein
With buisshes grene and Cedres hyhe;
360   And ther withinne he caste his yhe.
Amidd the plein he syh a welle,
So fair ther myhte noman telle,
In which Diana naked stod
To bathe and pleie hire in the flod

With many a Nimphe, which hire serveth.
Bot he his yhe awey ne swerveth
Fro hire, which was naked al,
And sche was wonder wroth withal,
And him, as sche which was godesse,
370 Forschop anon, and the liknesse   [transformed]
Sche made him taken of an Hert,
Which was tofore hise houndes stert,   [before/started]
That ronne besiliche aboute   [ran]
With many an horn and many a route,   [group]
That maden mochel noise and cry:
And ate laste unhappely
This Hert his oghne houndes slowhe
And him for vengance al todrowhe.   [tore to pieces]
    Lo now, my Sone, what it is
380 A man to caste his yhe amis,
Which Acteon hath dere aboght;
Be war forthi and do it noght.
For ofte, who that hiede toke,
Betre is to winke than to loke.
And forto proven it is so,
Ovide the Poete also
A tale which to this matiere
Acordeth seith, as thou schalt hiere.

TALE OF MEDUSA

朶 In Metamor it telleth thus,[8]
390 How that a lord which Phorceüs
Was hote, hadde dowhtres thre.
Bot upon here nativite
Such was the constellacion,
That out of mannes nacion
Fro kynde thei be so miswent,
That to the liknesse of Serpent
Thei were bore, and so that on

Of hem was cleped Stellibon, [called]
That other soster Suriale,
400 The thridde, as telleth in the tale,
Medusa hihte, and natheles [was named]
Of comun name Gorgones
In every contre ther aboute,
As Monstres whiche that men doute,
Men clepen hem; and bot on yhe [one]
Among hem thre in pourpartie [share]
Thei hadde, of which thei myhte se,
Now hath it this, now hath it sche;
After that cause and nede it ladde,
410 Be throwes ech of hem it hadde. [turns]
A wonder thing yet more amis
Ther was, wherof I telle al this:
What man on hem his chiere caste
And hem behield, he was als faste
Out of a man into a Ston
Forschape, and thus ful manyon [transformed]
Deceived were, of that thei wolde
Misloke, wher that thei ne scholde.
Bot Perseüs that worthi knyht,
420 Whom Pallas of hir grete myht
Halp, and tok him a Schield therto,
And ek the god Mercurie also
Lente him a swerd, he, as it fell,
Beyende Athlans the hihe hell [Atlas]
These Monstres soghte, and there he fond
Diverse men of thilke lond
Thurgh sihte of hem mistorned were,
Stondende as Stones hiere and there.
Bot he, which wisdom and prouesse
430 Hadde of the god and the godesse,
The Schield of Pallas gan enbrace, [placed on his arm]
With which he covereth sauf his face,
Mercuries Swerd and out he drowh,

And so he bar him that he slowh
These dredful Monstres alle thre.
    Lo now, my Sone, avise the,
That thou thi sihte noght misuse:
Cast noght thin yhe upon Meduse,
That thou be torned into Ston:
440 For so wys man was nevere non,
Bot if he wel his yhe kepe
And take of fol delit no kepe,   [heed]
That he with lust nys ofte nome,   [isn't/taken]
Thurgh strengthe of love and overcome.

[Genius next warns Amans to guard his hearing, for it may
bring "tidinge of many a vanite" (450–451) to the heart. One
must turn the ear toward good so that the heart may learn virtue
and turn his ear from evil to protect the heart. Take heed of
"Aspidis" who bears the "Ston noblest of alle," the Carbuncle, in
his head (465). When men use enchantments to rob him of the
stone, he places one ear flat against the ground and stops the other
with his tail so that he might not be deceived through his ears
(480).[9] Consider also the example of Ulysses, who, by stopping the
ears of his men, escaped the Sirens, those monsters who "Lik unto
wommen of yong age/Up fro the navele/ . . . and doun benethe/
. . . bere of fishes the figure" (488–491). With their singing, sirens
make men think hell is a paradise.[10] But if one guards these two
senses (seeing and hearing) intelligently, Genius concludes, the
other three will be easy to keep.

    Genius then asks, "Hast thou thin yhen oght misthrowe?"
(549). Amans admits that he has set eyes on Medusa. His heart
has been turned to stone, and on it his love for his Lady has been
irrevocably engraved. Moreover, he has not had the wisdom of
Ulysses. The enchanting words of his Lady cause him to lose con-
trol of himself so entirely that he is left defenseless. Because the
Lover's seeing and hearing have been corrupted, Genius instructs
him in the seven deadly sins which, through "remembrance,"

must be exorcised one by one. He begins with the principal sin, Pride, who has "Ministres five ful diverse" (583), the first of which is Hypocrisy.]

 Mi Sone, an ypocrite is this,—
A man which feigneth conscience,
As thogh it were al innocence,
Withoute, and is noght so withinne;
And doth so for he wolde winne
Of his desir the vein astat.
600 And whanne he comth anon therat,
He scheweth thanne what he was,
The corn is torned into gras,
That was a Rose is thanne a thorn,
And he that was a Lomb beforn
Is thanne a Wolf, and thus malice
Under the colour of justice
Is hid; and as the poeple telleth,
These ordres witen where he duelleth,   [religious orders know]
As he that of here conseil is,   [their]
610 And thilke world which thei er this   [the same/before]
Forsoken, he drawth in ayein:
He clotheth richesse, as men sein,
Under the simplesce of poverte,
And doth to seme of gret decerte   [causes]
Thing which is litel worth withinne:
He seith in open, fy! to Sinne,
And in secre ther is no vice
Of which that he nis a Norrice: [isn't/nurse]
And evere his chiere is sobre and softe,
620 And where he goth he blesseth ofte,
Wherof the blinde world he dreccheth.   [deceives]
Bot yet al only he ne streccheth
His reule upon religioun,
Bot next to that condicioun

In suche as clepe hem holy cherche
It scheweth ek how he can werche
Among tho wyde furred hodes,
To geten hem the worldes goodes.

[Genius observes that hypocrites flourish throughout the church and secular world with "riht" on their faces but with heart "al beschrewed" (640).]

For now aday is manyon
Which spekth of Peter and of John
And thenketh Judas in his herte.
Ther schal no worldes good asterte   [escape]
His hond, and yit he yifth almesse   [alms]
660 And fasteth ofte and hiereth Messe:
With *mea culpa,* which he seith,
Upon his brest fullofte he leith
His hond, and cast upward his yhe,
As thogh he Cristes face syhe;
So that it seemeth ate syhte,
As he al one alle othre myhte
Rescoue with his holy bede.   [prayer]
Bot yet his herte in other stede   [place]
Among hise bedes most devoute
670 Goth in the worldes cause aboute,
How that he myhte his warisoun   [property]
Encresce.

[Genius compares lovers in their deceit, flattery, dress, and feigned sicknesses to hypocrites. He asks Amans if hypocrisy weighs on his conscience. Amans acknowledges that he may have been guilty in his youth, but with his present love he has not been courageous enough to say more than "ye or nay." Genius warns him against being deceitful in love and proves his "entente" (758) with the story of Mundus and Paulina.[11]]

TALE OF MUNDUS AND PAULINA

It fell be olde daies thus,
Whil themperour Tiberius
The Monarchie of Rome ladde,
Ther was a worthi Romein hadde
A wif, and sche Pauline hihte,
Which was to every mannes sihte
Of al the Cite the faireste,
And as men seiden, ek the beste.
It is and hath ben evere yit,
770 That so strong is no mannes wit,
Which thurgh beaute ne mai be drawe
To love, and stonde under the lawe
Of thilke bore frele kinde,   [born frail by nature]
Which makth the hertes yhen blinde,
Wher no reson mai be comuned:[12]
And in this wise stod fortuned   [manner]
This tale, of which I wolde mene;
This wif, which in hire lustes grene
Was fair and freissh and tendre of age,
780 Sche may noght lette the corage   [release/heart]
Of him that wole on hire assote.   [dote]
        Ther was a Duck, and he was hote   [duke/called]
Mundus, which hadde in his baillie   [charge]
To lede the chivalerie
Of Rome, and was a worthi knyht;
Bot yet he was noght of such myht
The strengthe of love to withstonde,
That he ne was so broght to honde,   [constrained]
That malgre wher he wole or no,   [despite]
790 This yonge wif he loveth so,
That he hath put al his assay   [efforts]
To wynne thing which he ne may

Gete of hire graunt in no manere,   [permission]
Be yifte of gold ne be preiere.   [gift]
And whanne he syh that be no mede   [bribery]
Toward hir love he myhte spede,   [succeed]
Be sleyhte feigned thanne he wroghte;
And therupon he him bethoghte
How that ther was in the Cite
800   A temple of such auctorite,
To which with gret Devocioun
The noble wommen of the toun
Most comunliche a pelrinage   [pilgrimage]
Gon forto preie thilke ymage
Which the godesse of childinge is,   [childbirth]
And cleped was be name Ysis:
And in hire temple thanne were,
To reule and to ministre there
After the lawe which was tho,
810   Above alle othre Prestes tuo.
This Duck, which thoghte his love gete,
Upon a day hem tuo to mete
Hath bede, and thei come at his heste;   [prayed/command]
Wher that thei hadde a riche feste,
And after mete in prive place   [secret]
This lord, which wolde his thonk
     pourchace,   [buy their gratitude]
To ech of hem yaf thanne a yifte,   [gave]
And spak so that be weie of schrifte   [confession]
He drowh hem unto his covine,   [conspiracy]
820   To helpe and schape how he Pauline
After his lust deceive myhte.
And thei here trowthes bothe plyhte,
That thei be nyhte hire scholden wynne   [entice]
Into the temple, and he therinne
Schal have of hire al his entente:
And thus acorded forth thei wente.
     Now lest thurgh which ypocrisie

Ordeigned was the tricherie,
Wherof this ladi was deceived.
830 These Prestes hadden wel conceived
That sche was of gret holinesse;
And with a contrefet simplesse,
Which hid was in a fals corage,
Feignende an hevenely message
Thei come and seide unto hir thus:
"Pauline, the god Anubus
Hath sent ous both Prestes hiere,
And seith he woll to thee appiere
Be nyhtes time himself alone,
840 For love he hath to thi persone:
And therupon he hath ous bede,
That we in Ysis temple a stede   [place]
Honestely for thee pourveie,
Wher thou be nyhte, as we thee seie,
Of him schalt take avisioun.
For upon thi condicioun,
The which is chaste and ful of feith,
Such pris, as he ous tolde, he leith,   [value]
That he wol stonde of thin acord;
850 And forto bere hierof record
He sende ous hider bothe tuo."
Glad was hire innocence tho
Of suche wordes as sche herde,
With humble chiere and thus answerde,
And seide that the goddes wille
Sche was al redy to fulfille,
That be hire housebondes leve
Sche wolde in Ysis temple at eve
Upon hire goddes grace abide,
860 To serven him the nyhtes tide.
The Prestes tho gon hom ayein,
And sche goth to hire sovereign,
Of goddes wille and as it was

Sche tolde him al the pleine cas,
Wherof he was deceived eke,
And bad that sche hire scholde meke   [submit]
Al hol unto the goddes heste.   [completely/command]
And thus sche, which as al honeste
To godward after hire entente,
870 At nyht unto the temple wente,
Wher that the false Prestes were;
And thei receiven hire there
With such a tokne of holinesse,
As thogh thei syhen a godesse,   [saw]
And al withinne in prive place
A softe bedd of large space
Thei hadde mad and encourtined,   [draped]
Wher sche was afterward engined.   [entrapped]
Bot sche, which al honour supposeth,
880 The false Prestes thanne opposeth,   [questioned]
And axeth be what observance
Sche myhte most to the plesance
Of godd that nyhtes reule kepe:
And thei hire bidden forto slepe
Liggende upon the bedd alofte,
For so, thei seide, al stille and softe
God Anubus hire wolde awake.'
The conseil in this wise take,
The Prestes fro this lady gon;
890 And sche, that wiste of guile non,
In the manere as it was seid
To slepe upon the bedd is leid,
In hope that sche scholde achieve
Thing which stod thanne upon bilieve,   [which then was thought possible]

Fulfild of alle holinesse.
Bot sche hath failed, as I gesse,
For in a closet faste by
The Duck was hid so prively   [duke/secretly]

That sche him myhte noght perceive;
900 And he, that thoghte to deceive,
Hath such arrai upon him nome,   [taken]
That whanne he wolde unto hir come,
It scholde semen at hire yhe
As thogh sche verrailiche syhe   [truly saw]
God Anubus, and in such wise
This ypocrite of his queintise   [cunning]
Awaiteth evere til sche slepte.
And thanne out of his place he crepte
So stille that sche nothing herde,
910 And to the bedd stalkende he ferde,
And sodeinly, er sche it wiste,
Beclipt in armes he hire kiste:
Wherof in wommanysshe drede
Sche wok and nyste what to rede;   [knew not what to think]
Bot he with softe wordes milde
Conforteth hire and seith, with childe
He wolde hire make in such a kynde
That al the world schal have in mynde
The worschipe of that ilke Sone;
920 For he schal with the goddes wone,   [dwell]
And ben himself a godd also.
With suche wordes and with mo,
The whiche he feigneth in his speche,
This lady wit was al to seche   [lady's wit was gone]
As sche which alle trowthe weneth: [trusts]
Bot he, that alle untrowthe meneth,   [means]
With blinde tales so hire ladde,
That all his wille of hire he hadde.
And whan him thoghte it was ynowh,
930 Ayein the day he him withdrowh
So prively that sche ne wiste
Wher he becom, bot as him liste   [it pleased him]
Out of the temple he goth his weie.
And sche began to bidde and preie

Upon the bare ground knelende,
And after that made hire offrende,
And to the Prestes yiftes grete
Sche yaf, and homward be the Strete.   [gave]
The Duck hire mette and seide thus:
940   "The myhti godd which Anubus
Is hote, he save the, Pauline,   [called]
For thou art of his discipline
So holy, that no mannes myht
Mai do that he hath do to nyht
Of thing which thou hast evere eschuied.
Bot I his grace have so poursuied,
That I was mad his lieutenant: [made]
Forthi be weie of covenant   [therefore]
Fro this day forth I am al thin,
950   And if thee like to be myn,
That stant upon thin oghne wille."
    Sche herde his tale and bar it stille,
And hom sche wente, as it befell,
Into hir chambre, and ther sche fell
Upon hire bedd to wepe and crie,
And seide: "O derke ypocrisie,
Thurgh whos dissimilacion
Of fals ymaginacion
I am thus wickedly deceived!
960   Bot that I have it aperceived   [perceived]
I thonke unto the goddes alle;
For thogh it ones be befalle,
It schal nevere eft whil that I live,
And thilke avou to godd I yive."   [vow]
And thus wepende sche compleigneth,
Hire faire face and al desteigneth   [stains]
With wofull teres of hire ÿe,
So that upon this agonie
Hire housebonde is inne come,
970   And syh how sche was overcome

With sorwe, and axeth what hire eileth. [ails]
And sche with that hirself beweileth
Welmore than sche dede afore,
And seide, "Helas, wifhode is lore [lost]
In me, which whilom was honeste, [once]
I am non other than a beste, [beast]
Now I defouled am of tuo."
And as sche myhte speke tho,
Aschamed with a pitous onde [sigh (L *anhelo*)]
980 Sche tolde unto hir housebonde
The sothe of al the hole tale,
And in hire speche ded and pale
Sche swouneth welnyh to the laste.
And he hire in hise armes faste
Uphield, and ofte swor his oth
That he with hire is nothing wroth,
For wel he wot sche may ther noght:
Bot natheles withinne his thoght
His herte stod in sori plit,
990 And seide he wolde of that despit
Be venged, how so evere it falle,
And sende unto hise frendes alle.
And whan thei weren come in fere, [together (in company)]
He tolde hem upon this matiere,
And axeth hem what was to done:
And thei avised were sone,
And seide it thoghte hem for the beste [it seemed best to them]
To sette ferst his wif in reste,
And after pleigne to the king
1000 Upon the matiere of this thing.
Tho was this wofull wif conforted
Be alle weies and desported, [cheered]
Til that sche was somdiel amended;
And thus a day or tuo despended,
The thridde day sche goth to pleigne
With many a worthi Citezeine,

And he with many a Citezein.

Whan themperour it herde sein,
And knew the falshed of the vice,
1010 He seide he wolde do justice:
And ferst he let the Prestes take,   [had the priests taken]
And for thei scholde it noght forsake,
He put hem into questioun;
Bot thei of the suggestioun
Ne couthen noght a word refuse,   [knew not how to deny]
Bot for thei wolde hemself excuse,
The blame upon the Duck thei leide.
Bot therayein the conseil seide
That thei be noght excused so,
1020 For he is on and thei ben tuo,
And tuo han more wit then on,
So thilke excusement was non.
And over that was seid hem eke,
That whan men wolden vertu seke,
Men scholde it in the Prestes finde;
Here ordre is of so hyh a kinde,
That thei be Duistres of the weie: [guides (OF *duitor*)]
Forthi, if eny man forsueie   [go astray]
Thurgh hem, thei be noght excusable.
1030 And thus be lawe resonable
Among the wise jugges there
The Prestes bothe dampned were,   [condemned]
So that the prive tricherie
Hid under fals Ipocrisie
Was thanne al openliche schewed,
That many a man hem hath beschrewed.   [cursed]
And whan the Prestes weren dede,
The temple of thilke horrible dede
Thei thoghten purge, and thilke ymage,
1040 Whos cause was the pelrinage,   [pilgrimage]
Thei drowen out and als so faste
Fer into Tibre thei it caste,

Wher the Rivere it hath defied:
And thus the temple purified
Thei have of thilke horrible Sinne,
Which was that time do therinne.
Of this point such was the juise,
Bot of the Duck was other wise:
For he with love was bestad,   [because/situated]
1050 His dom was noght so harde lad;
For Love put reson aweie
And can noght se the rihte weie.
And be this cause he was respited,
So that the deth him was acquited,
Bot for al that he was exiled,
For he his love hath so beguiled,
That he schal nevere come ayein:
For who that is to trowthe unplein,
He may noght failen of vengance.
1060   And ek to take remembrance
Of that Ypocrisie hath wroght
On other half, men scholde noght
To lihtly lieve al that thei hiere,   [believe]
Bot thanne scholde a wisman stiere
The Schip, whan suche wyndes blowe:
For ferst thogh thei beginne lowe,
At ende thei be noght menable,   [amenable (OF *amener*, 'to
                                                 lead')]

Bot al tobreken Mast and Cable,
So that the Schip with sodein blast,
1070 Whan men lest wene, is overcast;   [least expect]
As now fulofte a man mai se.

[Genius tells the story of the Trojan Horse as a second example
of hypocrisy.[13] The sleights of Calcas and Criseyde did not cause
the fall of Troy: rather it was the treacherous Brass Horse, made
by Epius and offered as a gift, which shaped the city's destruction.
The gates of Neptune which had protected the city for a thou-

sand years were torn down so that the horse, in great solemnity, might be brought in. While the city slept the Greeks crept from the horse to slay all they could find. Amans clearly should eschew hypocrisy and treachery in love (1072–1226).

The second point of Pride is Inobedience against the dictates of conscience. Amans admits to inobedience on two counts: First, his Lady commanded him to be silent about his love for her, but he has been unable to—"yit it is no pride" (1305). Secondly, she told him to leave her and choose another, but he has been unable to comply with her behest (1227–1342). So he asks for further instruction. Genius observes that "Murmur and Compleignte" are closely akin to Inobedience. Here too Amans admits that in his heavy cheer over his Lady "I grucche anon" (1385). To exemplify the rewards of Obedience over Murmur, Complaint, and Inobedience, Genius tells the Tale of Florent.[14]]

TALE OF FLORENT

🏵 Ther was whilom be daies olde	[once/in days of old]
A worthi knyht, and as men tolde	
He was Nevoeu to themperour	[nephew/th'emperor]
1410 And of his Court a Courteour:	
Wifles he was, Florent he hihte,	[wifeless/was called]
He was a man that mochel myhte,	[who might do much]
Of armes he was desirous,	
Chivalerous and amorous,	
And for the fame of worldes speche,	
Strange aventures forto seche,	[seek]
He rod the Marches al aboute.	
And fell a time, as he was oute,	
Fortune, which may every thred	
1420 Tobreke and knette of mannes sped,	[sever or tie/success]
Schop, as this knyht rod in a pas,	[contrived/traveled about]
That he be strengthe take was,	
And to a Castell thei him ladde,	
Wher that he fewe frendes hadde:	

For so it fell that ilke stounde   [in this circumstance]
That he hath with a dedly wounde
Feihtende his oghne hondes slain   [fighting/own]
Branchus, which to the Capitain
Was Sone and Heir, wherof ben wrothe
1430 The fader and the moder bothe.
That knyht Branchus was of his hond   [on his side]
The worthieste of al his lond,
And fain thei wolden do vengance
Upon Florent, bot remembrance
That thei toke of his worthinesse
Of knyhthod and of gentilesse,
And how he stod of cousinage
To themperour, made hem assuage,
And dorsten noght slen him for fere: [fear]
1440 In gret desputeisoun thei were
Among hemself, what was the beste.   [themselves]
Ther was a lady, the slyheste
Of alle that men knewe tho,   [then]
So old sche myhte unethes go,   [scarcely get about]
And was grantdame unto the dede: [dead man]
And sche with that began to rede,   [advise]
And seide how sche wol bringe him inne,   [him (Florent)]
That sche schal him to dethe winne
Al only of his oghne grant,   [even by his own agreement]
1450 Thurgh strengthe of verray covenant
Withoute blame of eny wiht.   [man]
Anon sche sende for this kniht,
And of hire Sone sche alleide   [alleged]
The deth, and thus to him sche seide:
"Florent, how so thou be to wyte   [blame]
Of Branchus deth, men schal respite
As now to take vengement,
Be so thou stonde in juggement
Upon certein condicioun,
1460 That thou unto a questioun

Which I schal axe schalt ansuere; [ask]
And over this thou schalt ek swere, [also]
That if thou of the sothe faile, [truth]
Ther schal non other thing availe,
That thou ne schalt thi deth receive.
And for men schal thee noght deceive,
That thou therof myht ben avised, [advised]
Thou schalt have day and tyme assised [allotted]
And leve saufly forto wende, [leave/go]
1470 Be so that at thi daies ende [provided that]
Thou come ayein with thin avys."
        This knyht, which worthi was and wys,
This lady preith that he may wite, [know]
And have it under Seales write,
What questioun it scholde be
For which he schal in that degree
Stonde of his lif in jeupartie.
With that sche feigneth compaignie,
And seith: "Florent, on love it hongeth
1480 Al that to myn axinge longeth:
What alle wommen most desire
This wole I axe, and in thempire
Wher as thou hast most knowlechinge
Tak conseil upon this axinge."
        Florent this thing hath undertake,
The day was set, the time take,
Under his seal he wrot his oth,
In such a wise and forth he goth
Hom to his Emes court ayein; [uncle's]
1490 To whom his aventure plein
He tolde, of that him is befalle.
And upon that thei weren alle
The wiseste of the lond asent,
Bot natheles of on assent [one]
Thei myhte noght acorde plat, [plainly]
On seide this, an othre that.

After the disposicioun
Of naturel complexioun
To som womman it is plesance,
1500 That to an other is grevance;
Bot such a thing in special,
Which to hem alle in general
Is most plesant, and most desired
Above alle othre and most conspired,   [agreed upon]
Such o thing conne thei noght finde   [one]
Be Constellacion ne kinde:
And thus Florent withoute cure
Mot stonde upon his aventure,   [must]
And is al schape unto the lere,   [prepared/loss (OE *lyre*)]
1510 As in defalte of his answere.
This knyht hath levere forto dye   [rather]
Than breke his trowthe and forto lye
In place ther as he was swore,
And schapth him gon ayein therfore.
Whan time cam he tok his leve,
That lengere wolde he noght beleve,   [remain]
And preith his Em he be noght wroth,   [uncle]
For that is a point of his oth,
He seith, that noman schal him wreke,   [avenge]
1520 Thogh afterward men hiere speke
That he par aventure deie.
And thus he wente forth his weie
Alone as knyht aventurous,
And in his thoght was curious
To wite what was best to do:
And as he rod al one so,
And cam nyh ther he wolde be,
In a forest under a tre
He syh wher sat a creature,
1530 A lothly wommannysch figure,
That forto speke of fleisch and bon
So foul yit syh he nevere non.   [saw]

This knyht behield hir redely,
And as he wolde have passed by,
Sche cleped him and bad abide;   [called]
And he his horse heved aside   [head]
Tho torneth, and to hire he rod,
And there he hoveth and abod,   [stopped/waited]
To wite what sche wolde mene.
1540 And sche began him to bemene,   [explain]
And seide: "Florent be thi name,
Thou hast on honde such a game,
That bot thou be the betre avised,   [unless]
Thi deth is schapen and devised,
That al the world ne mai the save,   [thee]
Bot if that thou my conseil have."
    Florent, whan he this tale herde,
Unto this olde wyht answerde   [creature]
And of his conseil he hir preide.
1550 And sche ayein to him thus seide:
"Florent, if I for the so schape,
That thou thurgh me thi deth ascape
And take worschipe of thi dede,
What schal I have to my mede?"   [reward]
"What thing," quod he, "that thou wolt
    axe."
"I bidde nevere a betre taxe,"   [ask for]
Quod sche, "bot ferst, er thou be sped,   [helped]
Thou schalt me leve such a wedd,   [allow]
That I wol have thi trowthe in honde
1560 Thou thou schalt be myn housebonde."
"Nay," seith Florent, "that may noght be."
"Ryd thanne forth thi wey," quod sche,
"And if thou go withoute red,   [counsel]
Thou schalt be sekerliche ded."   [certainly]
Florent behihte hire good ynowh   [promised]
Of lond, of rente, of park, of plowh,
Bot al that compteth sche at noght.   [values]

Tho fell this knyht in mochel thoght,
Now goth he forth, now comth ayein,
1570 He wot noght what is best to sein,
And thoghte, as he rod to and fro,
That chese he mot on of the tuo, [must]
Or forto take hire to his wif
Or elles forto lese his lif. [lose]
And thanne he caste his avantage,
That sche was of so gret an age,
That sche mai live bot a while,
And thoghte put hire in an Ile, [isle]
Wher that noman hire scholde knowe,
1580 Til sche with deth were overthrowe.
And thus this yonge lusti knyht
Unto this olde lothly wiht [creature]
Tho seide: "If that non other chance
Mai make my deliverance,
Bot only thilke same speche
Which, as thou seist, thou schalt me teche,
Have hier myn hond, I schal thee wedde."
And thus his trowthe he leith to wedde. [wedlock]
With that sche frounceth up the browe: [wrinkles]
1590 "This covenant I wol allowe,"
Sche seith: "if eny other thing
Bot that thou hast of my techyng
Fro deth thi body mai respite,
I woll thee of thi trowthe acquite, [promise]
And elles be non other weie.
Now herkne me what I schal seie.
Whan thou art come into the place,
Wher now thei maken gret manace
And upon thi comynge abyde,
1600 Thei wole anon the same tide [time]
Oppose thee of thin answere.
I wot thou wolt nothing forbere
Of that thou wenest be thi beste, [think]

And if thou myht so finde reste,
Wel is, for thanne is ther nomore.
And elles this schal be my lore,
That thou schalt seie, upon this Molde [earth]
That alle wommen lievest wolde [most desire]
Be soverein of mannes love:
1610 For what womman is so above, [that woman who is]
Sche hath, as who seith, al hire wille; [desire]
And elles may sche noght fulfille
What thing hir were lievest have.
With this answere thou schalt save
Thiself, and other wise noght.
And whan thou hast thin ende wroght,
Com hier ayein, thou schalt me finde,
And let nothing out of thi minde."
He goth him forth with hevy chiere,
1620 As he that not in what manere [knows not]
He mai this worldes joie atteigne:
For if he deie, he hath a peine,
And if he live, he mot him binde
To such on which of alle kinde [a one who]
Of wommen is thunsemlieste: [the most unseemly]
Thus wot he noght what is the beste:
Bot be him lief or be him loth, [glad/sad]
Unto the Castell forth he goth
His full answere forto yive,
1630 Or forto deie or forto live.
Forth with his conseil cam the lord,
The thinges stoden of record,
He sende up for the lady sone,
And forth sche cam, that olde Mone. [shrew (OE *gemaene*, 'inter-
course')]

In presence of the remenant
The strengthe of al the covenant
Tho was reherced openly,
And to Florent sche bad forthi

That he schal tellen his avis,
1640 As he that woot what is the pris.
Florent seith al that evere he couthe,
Bot such word cam ther non to mowthe,
That he for yifte or for beheste
Mihte eny wise his deth areste.
And thus he tarieth longe and late,
Til that this lady bad algate   [assuredly]
That he schal for the dom final   [judgment]
Yive his answere in special
Of that sche hadde him ferst opposed: [questioned]
1650 And thanne he hath trewly supposed
That he him may of nothing yelpe,   [boast]
Bot if so be tho wordes helpe,
Whiche as the womman hath him tawht;
Wherof he hath an hope cawht
That he schal ben excused so,
And tolde out plein his wille tho.
And whan that this Matrone herde
The manere how this knyht ansuerde,
Sche seide: "Ha treson, wo thee be,
1660 That hast thus told the privite,
Which alle wommen most desire!
I wolde that thou were afire."
Bot natheles in such a plit
Florent of his answere is quit:
And tho began his sorwe newe,
For he mot gon, or ben untrewe,
To hire which his trowthe hadde.   [pledge]
Bot he, which alle schame dradde,
Goth forth in stede of his penance,
1670 And takth the fortune of his chance,
As he that was with trowthe affaited.   [trained]
    This olde wyht him hath awaited   [creature]
In place wher as he hire lefte:
Florent his wofull heved uplefte

And syh this vecke wher sche sat,	[saw/hag]
Which was the lothlieste what	
That evere man caste on his yhe:	[cast his eye upon]
Hire Nase bass, hire browes hyhe,	[low]
Hire yhen smale and depe set,	[eyes]
1680 Hire chekes ben with teres wet,	
And rivelen as an emty skyn	[wrinkled]
Hangende doun unto the chin,	
Hire Lippes schrunken ben for age,	
Ther was no grace in the visage,	
Hir front was nargh, hir lockes hore,	[narrow]
Sche loketh forth as doth a More,	[Moor]
Hire Necke is schort, hir schuldres courbe,	
That myhte a mannes lust destroube,	
Hire body gret and nothing smal,	
1690 And schortly to descrive hire al,	
Sche hath no lith withoute a lak;	[limb]
Bot lich unto the wollesak	[woolsack]
Sche proferth hire unto this knyht,	[offers herself]
And bad him, as he hath behyht,	[promised]
So as sche hath ben his warant,	
That he hire holde covenant,	
And be the bridel sche him seseth.	
Bot godd wot how that sche him pleseth	
Of suche wordes as sche spekth:	
1700 Him thenkth welnyh his herte brekth	
For sorwe that he may noght fle,	
Bot if he wolde untrewe be.	
Loke, how a sek man for his hele	[sick/health]
Takth baldemoine with Canele,	[gentian with cinnamon]
And with the Mirre takth the Sucre,	[myrrh]
Ryht upon such a maner lucre	
Stant Florent, as in this diete:	
He drinkth the bitre with the swete,	
He medleth sorwe with likynge,	
1710 And liveth, as who seith, deyinge;	

His youthe schal be cast aweie
Upon such on which as the weie
Is old and lothly overal.
Bot nede he mot that nede schal: [must]
He wolde algate his trowthe holde, [assuredly]
As every knyht therto is holde,
What happ so evere him is befalle:
Thogh sche be the fouleste of alle,
Yet to thonour of wommanhiede [the honor]
1720 Him thoghte he scholde taken hiede;
So that for pure gentilesse,
As he hire couthe best adresce, [preparing her as best he could]

In ragges, as sche was totore, [since/tattered]
He set hire on his hors tofore
And forth he takth his weie softe;
No wonder thogh he siketh ofte. [sighs]
Bot as an oule fleth be nyhte [owl]
Out of alle othre briddes syhte,
Riht so this knyht on daies brode
1730 In clos him hield, and schop his rode
On nyhtes times, til the tyde
That he cam there he wolde abide;
And prively withoute noise
He bringth this foule grete Coise [rump (OF *cuisse*, 'thigh')]
To his Castell in such a wise
That noman myhte hire schappe avise,
Til sche into the chambre cam:
Wher he his prive conseil nam [took]
Of suche men as he most troste, [trusted]
1740 And tolde hem that he nedes moste
This beste wedde to his wif, [best woman: beast (pun)]
For elles hadde he lost his lif.
    The prive wommen were asent, [sent for]
That scholden ben of his assent:
Hire ragges thei anon of drawe, [soon took off]

And, as it was that time lawe,
She hadde bath, sche hadde reste,
And was arraied to the beste.
Bot with no craft of combes brode
1750 Thei myhte hire hore lockes schode,   [divide]
And sche ne wolde noght be schore   [shorn]
For no conseil, and thei therfore,
With such atyr as tho was used,
Ordeinen that it was excused,
And hid so crafteliche aboute,
That noman myhte sen hem oute.
Bot when sche was fulliche arraied
And hire atyr was al assaied,
Tho was sche foulere on to se: [more foul to look upon]
1760 Bot yit it may non other be,
Thei were wedded in the nyht;
So wo begon was nevere knyht
As he was thanne of mariage.
And sche began to pleie and rage,
As who seith, I am wel ynowh;
Bot he therof nothing ne lowh,   [laughed]
For sche tok thanne chiere on honde   [began to be merry]
And clepeth him hire housebonde,
And seith, "My lord, go we to bedde,
1770 For I to that entente wedde,
That thou schalt be my worldes blisse":
And profreth him with that to kisse,
As sche a lusti Lady were.
His body myhte wel be there,
Bot as of thoght and of memoire
His herte was in purgatoire.
Bot yit for strengthe of matrimoine
He myhte make non essoine,   [excuse]
That he ne mot algates plie   [comply]
1780 To gon to bedde of compaignie:
And whan thei were abedde naked,

Withoute slep he was awaked;
He torneth on that other side,
For that he wolde hise yhen hyde   [eyes]
Fro lokynge on that foule wyht.
The chambre was al full of lyht,
The courtins were of cendal thinne,   [(OF *cendal,* 'a costly
                                     fabric')]

This newe bryd which lay withinne,
Thogh it be noght with his acord,
1790 In armes sche beclipte hire lord,   [embraced]
And preide, as he was torned fro,
He wolde him torne ayeinward tho;
"For now," sche seith, "we ben bothe on."   [one]
And he lay stille as eny ston,
Bot evere in on sche spak and preide,
And bad him thenke on that he seide,
Whan that he tok hire be the hond.
      He herde and understod the bond,
How he was set to his penance,
1800 And as it were a man in trance
He torneth him al sodeinly,
And syh a lady lay him by
Of eyhtetiene wynter age,
Which was the faireste of visage
That evere in al this world he syh:
And as he wolde have take hire nyh,
Sche put hire hand and be his leve
Besoghte him that he wolde leve,   [wait]
And seith that forto wynne or lese
1810 He mot on of tuo thinges chese,
Wher he wol have hire such on nyht,
Or elles upon daies lyht,
For he schal noght have bothe tuo.
And he began to sorwe tho,
In many a wise and caste his thoght,
Bot for al that yit cowthe he noght

Devise himself which was the beste.
And sche, that wolde his hertes reste,
Preith that he scholde chese algate,
1820 Til ate laste longe and late
He seide: "O ye, my lyves hele,
Sey what you list in my querele,
I not what ansuere I schal yive: [know not/give]
Bot evere whil that I may live,
I wol that ye be my maistresse,
For I can noght miselve gesse
Which is the beste unto my chois.
Thus grante I yow myn hole vois,
Ches for ous bothen, I you preie;
1830 And what as evere that ye seie,
Riht as ye wole so wol I."
    "Mi lord," sche seide, "grant merci,
For of this word that ye now sein,
That ye have mad me soverein,
Mi destine is overpassed,
That nevere hierafter schal be lassed   [diminished]
Mi beaute, which that I now have,
Til I be take into my grave;
Bot nyht and day as I am now
1840 I schal alwey be such to yow.
The kinges dowhter of Cizile
I am, and fell bot siththe awhile,   [it befell but awhile ago]
As I was with my fader late,
That my Stepmoder for an hate,
Which toward me sche hath begonne,
Forschop me, til I hadde wonne   [transformed]
The love and sovereinete
Of what knyht that in his degre
Alle othre passeth of good name:
1850 And, as men sein, ye ben the same,
The dede proeveth it is so;
Thus am I youres evermo."

Tho was plesance and joye ynowh,
Echon with other pleide and lowh;   [laughed]
Thei live longe and wel thei ferde,
And clerkes that this chance herde
Thei writen it in evidence,
To teche how that obedience
Mai wel fortune a man to love
1860 And sette him in his lust above,
As it befell unto this knyht.

　　　Forthi, my Sone, if thou do ryht,
Thou schalt unto thi love obeie,
And folwe hir will be alle weie.

　　　Min holy fader, so I wile:
For ye have told me such a skile   [reason]
Of this ensample now tofore,
That I schal evermo therfore
Hierafterward myn observance
1870 To love and to his obeissance
The betre kepe: and over this
Of pride if ther oght elles is,
Wherof that I me schryve schal,
What thing it is in special,
Mi fader, axeth, I you preie.

[Genius now presents Surquidry (Presumption), who is the third officer in Pride's court. Surquidry deems no counsel good except his own; not once does he say "grant mercy" to God. He stands upon his own wit until he falls so far into the pit he may not arise. Only then, after his overthrow, is truth known (1876–1909).

　　　Such too is the fate of one who esteems himself too proudly in love: "Fulofte he heweth up so hihe, / That chippes fallen in his yhe" (1917–1918). Amans tells his Confessor not to worry on this point, for he finds himself so unworthy of his Lady that he can only hope for mercy. Yet, he does presume to be loved sometime, and he admits to being beguiled by his hopes: "For if a man wole in a Bot / Which is withoute botme rowe, / He moste nedes overthrowe" (1960–1962). Amans then asks penance for his presumptious hopes, and the Confessor tells him the story of the proud knight Capaneus who was struck down by lightning as he presumed to storm Thebes by himself (1977–2020).[15] To illustrate his point he tells the story of the Trump of Death.[16]]

THE TRUMP OF DEATH

    I finde upon Surquiderie,
How that whilom of Hungarie
Be olde daies was a King
Wys and honeste in alle thing:
And so befell upon a dai,
And that was in the Monthe of Maii,
As thilke time it was usance,
This kyng with noble pourveance   [provision]
Hath for himself his Charr araied,
2030 Wher inne he wolde ride amaied   [a-maying]
Out of the Cite forto pleie,
With lordes and with gret nobleie
Of lusti folk that were yonge:
Wher some pleide and some songe,
And some gon and some ryde,
And some prike here hors aside
And bridlen hem now in now oute.
The kyng his yhe caste aboute,
Til he was ate laste war
2040 And syh comende ayein his char
Two pilegrins of so gret age,
That lich unto a dreie ymage
Thei weren pale and fade hewed,
And as a bussh which is besnewed,   [covered with snow]
Here berdes weren hore and whyte;
Ther was of kinde bot a lite,
That thei ne semen fulli dede.
Thei comen to the kyng and bede   [prayed]

Som of his good par charite;
2050 And he with gret humilite
Out of his Char to grounde lepte,
And hem in bothe hise armes kepte
And keste hem bothe fot and hond
Before the lordes of his lond,
And yaf hem of his good therto:
And whanne he hath this dede do,
He goth into his char ayein.
Tho was Murmur, tho was desdeign,
Tho was compleignte on every side,
2060 Thei seiden of here oghne Pride
Eche until othre: "What is this?
Oure king hath do this thing amis,
So to abesse his realte   [abase]
That every man it myhte se,
And humbled him in such a wise
To hem that were of non emprise."   [worth]
Thus was it spoken to and fro
Of hem that were with him tho
Al prively behinde his bak;
2070 Bot to himselven noman spak.
The kinges brother in presence
Was thilke time, and gret offence
He tok therof, and was the same
Above alle othre which most blame
Upon his liege lord hath leid,
And hath unto the lordes seid,
Anon as he mai time finde,
Ther schal nothing be left behinde,
That he wol speke unto the king.
2080   Now lest what fell upon this thing.   [listen to]
The day was merie and fair ynowh,
Echon with othre pleide and lowh,
And fellen into tales newe,
How that the freisshe floures grewe,

And how the grene leves spronge,
And how that love among the yonge
Began the hertes thanne awake,
And every bridd hath chose hire make:
And thus the Maies day to thende
2090 Thei lede, and hom ayein thei wende.
The king was noght so sone come,
That whanne he hadde his chambre nome,
His brother ne was redi there,
And broghte a tale unto his Ere
Of that he dede such a schame
In hindringe of his oghne name,
Whan he himself so wolde drecche, [debase]
That to so vil a povere wrecche
Him deigneth schewe such simplesce
2100 Ayein thastat of his noblesce:
And seith he schal it nomor use,
And that he mot himself excuse
Toward hise lordes everychon.
The king stod stille as eny ston,
And to his tale an Ere he leide,
And thoghte more than he seide:
Bot natheles to that he herde
Wel cortaisly the king answerde,
And tolde it scholde be amended.
2110 And thus whan that her tale is ended,
Al redy was the bord and cloth,
The king unto his Souper goth
Among the lordes to the halle;
And whan thei hadden souped alle,
Thei token leve and forth thei go.
The king bethoghte himselve tho
How he his brother mai chastie,
That he thurgh his Surquiderie
Tok upon honde to despreise
2120 Humilite, which is to preise, [praiseworthy]

And therupon yaf such conseil
Toward his king that was noght heil;   [wholesome]
Wherof to be the betre lered,   [taught]
He thenkth to maken him afered.
    It fell so that in thilke dawe
Ther was ordeined be the lawe
A trompe with a sterne breth,
Which cleped was the Trompe of deth:
And in the Court wher the king was
2130 A certein man this Trompe of bras
Hath in kepinge, and therof serveth,
That whan a lord his deth deserveth,
He schal this dredful trompe blowe
Tofore his gate, and make it knowe
How that the jugement is yove   [given]
Of deth, which schal noght be foryove.   [forgiven]
The king, whan it was nyht, anon
This man asente and bad him gon
To trompen at his brother gate;
2140 And he, which mot so don algate,
Goth forth and doth the kynges heste.
This lord, which herde of this tempeste
That he tofore his gate blew,
Tho wiste he be the lawe and knew
That he was sikerliche ded:
And as of help he wot no red,   [counsel]
Bot sende for hise frendes alle
And tolde hem how it is befalle.
And thei him axe cause why;
2150 Bot he the sothe noght forthi   [truth]
Ne wiste, and ther was sorwe tho:
For it stod thilke tyme so,
This trompe was of such sentence,
That therayein no resistence
Thei couthe ordeine be no weie,
That he ne mot algate deie,

Bot if so that he may pourchace   [except/provide]
To gete his liege lordes grace.
Here wittes therupon thei caste,
2160 And ben apointed ate laste.   [resolved]
     This lord a worthi ladi hadde
Unto his wif, which also dradde
Hire lordes deth, and children five
Betwen hem two thei hadde alyve,
That weren yonge and tendre of age,
And of stature and of visage
Riht faire and lusty on to se.
Tho casten thei that he and sche
Forth with here children on the morwe,
2170 As thei that were full of sorwe,
Al naked bot of smok and scherte,
To tendre with the kynges herte,
His grace scholden go to seche   [seek]
And pardoun of the deth beseche.
Thus passen thei that wofull nyht,
And erly, whan thei sihe it lyht,
Thei gon hem forth in such a wise
As thou tofore hast herd devise,
Al naked bot here schortes one.
2180 Thei wepte and made mochel mone,
Here Her hangende aboute here Eres;   [hair]
With sobbinge and with sory teres
This lord goth thanne an humble pas,
That whilom proud and noble was;
Wherof the Cite sore afflyhte,   [sorely disturbed]
Of hem that sihen thilke syhte:
And natheles al openly
With such wepinge and with such cri
Forth with hise children and his wif
2190 He goth to preie for his lif.
Unto the court whan thei be come,
And men therinne have hiede nome,

Ther was no wiht, if he hem syhe,
Fro water mihte kepe his yhe
For sorwe which thei maden tho.
The king supposeth of this wo,   [anticipates]
And feigneth as he noght ne wiste;   [knew nothing at all]
Bot natheles at his upriste   [arising]
Men tolden him how that it ferde:
2200 And whan that he this wonder herde,
In haste he goth into the halle,
And alle at ones doun thei falle,
If eny pite may be founde.
The king, which seth hem go to grounde,
Hath axed hem what is the fere,   [fear]
Why thei be so despuiled there.   [despoiled (naked)]
His brother seide: "Ha lord, mercy!
I wot non other cause why,
Bot only that this nyht ful late
2210 The trompe of deth was at my gate
In tokne that I scholde deie;
Thus be we come forto preie
That ye mi worldes deth respite."
        "Ha fol, how thou art forto wyte,"   [fool/blame]
The king unto his brother seith,
"That thou art of so litel feith,
That only for a trompes soun
Hast gon despuiled thurgh the toun,
Thou and thi wif in such manere
2220 Forth with thi children that ben here,
In sihte of alle men aboute,
For that thou seist thou art in doute
Of deth, which stant under the lawe
Of man, and man it mai withdrawe,
So that it mai par chance faile.
Now schalt thou noght forthi mervaile
That I doun fro my Charr alihte,
Whanne I behield tofore my sihte

In hem that were of so gret age
2230 Min oghne deth thurgh here ymage,
Which god hath set be lawe of kynde,
Wherof I mai no bote finde: [respite]
For wel I wot, such as thei be,
Riht such am I in my degree,
Of fleissh and blod, and so schal deie.
And thus, thogh I that lawe obeie
Of which the kinges ben put under,
It oghte ben wel lasse wonder
Than thou, which art withoute nede
2240 For lawe of londe in such a drede,
Which for tacompte is bot a jape, [to account for]
As thing which thou miht overscape.
Forthi, mi brother, after this
I rede, sithen that so is [advise]
That thou canst drede a man so sore,
Dred god with al thin herte more:
For al schal deie and al schal passe,
Als wel a Leoun as an asse,
Als wel a beggere as a lord,
2250 Towardes deth in on acord
Thei schullen stonde." And in this wise
The king hath with hise wordes wise
His brother tawht and al foryive.

Forthi, mi Sone, if thou wolt live
In vertu, thou most vice eschuie,
And with low herte humblesce suie,
So that thou be noght surquidous.

Mi fader, I am amorous,
Wherof I wolde you beseche
2260 That ye me som ensample teche,
Which mihte in loves cause stonde.

Mi Sone, thou schalt understonde,
In love and othre thinges alle
If that Surquiderie falle,

It may to him noght wel betide
Which useth thilke vice of Pride,
Which torneth wisdom to wenynge   [desire (supposition)]
And Sothfastnesse into lesynge   [truth/lying]
Thurgh fol ymaginacion.
2270 And for thin enformacion,
That thou this vice as I the rede   [counsel]
Eschuie schalt, a tale I rede,   [tell]
Which fell whilom be daies olde,
So as the clerk Ovide tolde.[17]

TALE OF NARCISSUS

❦ Ther was whilom a lordes Sone,
Which of his Pride a nyce wone   [foolish (precious) habit]
Hath cawht, that worthi to his liche,   [desire]
To sechen al the worldes riche,
Ther was no womman forto love.
2280 So hihe he sette himselve above
Of stature and of beaute bothe,
That him thoghte alle wommen lothe: [loathsome]
So was ther no comparisoun
As toward his condicioun.
This yonge lord Narcizus hihte:
No strengthe of love bowe mihte
His herte, which is unaffiled;   [untrained]
Bot ate laste he was beguiled:
For of the goddes pourveance   [provision]
2290 It fell him on a dai par chance,
That he in all his proude fare   [bearing]
Unto the forest gan to fare,
Amonges othre that ther were
To hunte and to desporte him there.
And whanne he cam into the place
Wher that he wolde make his chace,
The houndes weren in a throwe   [moment]

Uncoupled and the hornes blowe:
The grete hert anon was founde,
2300 Which swifte feet sette upon grounde,
And he with spore in horse side
Him hasteth faste forto ride,
Til alle men be left behinde.
And as he rod, under a linde   [linden tree]
Beside a roche, as I thee telle,
He syh wher sprong a lusty welle:
The day was wonder hot withalle,
And such a thurst was on him falle,
That he moste owther deie or drinke;
2310 And doun he lihte and be the brinke   [alighted]
He teide his Hors unto a braunche,
And leide him lowe forto staunche
His thurst: and as he caste his lok
Into the welle and hiede tok,
He sih the like of his visage,
And wende ther were an ymage
Of such a Nimphe as tho was faie,   [magical (or fated)]
Wherof that love his herte assaie   [to try]
Began, as it was after sene,
2320 Of his sotie and made him wene   [folly/think]
It were a womman that he syh.
The more he cam the welle nyh,
The nerr cam sche to him ayein;
So wiste he nevere what to sein;
For whanne he wepte, he sih hire wepe,
And whanne he cride, he tok good kepe,
The same word sche cride also:
And thus began the newe wo,
That whilom was to him so strange;
2330 Tho made him love an hard eschange,
To sette his herte and to beginne
Thing which he mihte nevere winne.
And evere among he gan to loute,   [yield]

And preith that sche to him come oute;
And otherwhile he goth a ferr,
And otherwhile he draweth nerr,
And evere he fond hire in o place.
He wepth, he crith, he axeth grace,
There as he mihte gete non;
2340 So that ayein a Roche of Ston,
As he that knew non other red, [counsel]
He smot himself til he was ded.
Wherof the Nimphes of the welles,
And othre that ther weren elles
Unto the wodes belongende,
The body, which was ded ligende,
For pure pite that thei have
Under the grene thei begrave.
And thanne out of his sepulture
2350 Ther sprong anon par aventure
Of floures such a wonder syhte,
That men ensample take myhte
Upon the dedes whiche he dede,
As tho was sene in thilke stede; [place]
For in the wynter freysshe and faire
The floures ben, which is contraire
To kynde, and so was the folie
Which fell of his Surquiderie.
        Thus he, which love hadde in desdeign,
2360 Worste of all othre was besein,
And as he sette his pris most hyhe,
He was lest worth in loves yhe [least worthy]
And most bejaped in his wit: [mocked]
Wherof the remembrance is yit,
So that thou myht ensample take,
And ek alle othre for his sake.

[Genius introduces next the fourth aspect of Pride—Avantance,
or Boasting. The tongue of Avantance cannot be daunted, but

claps its worth abroad as does a bell; beyond measure, it is its
own herald. There are lovers of this sort too, who brag on their
rewards and triumphs. Amans claims a clear conscience here:
his Lady has never given him anything to boast about. If she
did he would not know what to do. The Confessor is well
pleased and observes that love hates no vice as much as Boasting.
He tells the story of Albinus and Rosemund to demonstrate his
point.[18]]

TALE OF ALBINUS AND ROSEMUND

⁂ Of hem that we Lombars now calle
Albinus was the ferste of alle
Which bar corone of Lombardie,
And was of gret chivalerie
In werre ayein diverse kinges.
So fell amonges othre thinges,
2465   That he that time a werre hadde
With Gurmond, which the Geptes ladde,
And was a myhti kyng also:
Bot natheles it fell him so,
Albinus slowh him in the feld,   [slew]
2470   Ther halp him nowther swerd ne scheld,
That he ne smot his hed of thanne,   [off]
Wherof he tok awey the Panne,
Of which he seide he wolde make
A Cuppe for Gurmoundes sake,
To kepe and drawe into memoire
Of his bataille the victoire.
And thus whan he the feld hath wonne,
The lond anon was overronne
And sesed in his oghne hond,   [seized]
2480   Wher he Gurmondes dowhter fond,
Which Maide Rosemounde hihte,
And was in every mannes sihte
A fair, a freissh, a lusti on.

His herte fell to hire anon,
And such a love on hire he caste,
That he hire weddeth ate laste;
And after that long time in reste
With hire he duelte, and to the beste
Thei love ech other wonder wel.
2490 Bot sche which kepth the blinde whel,
Venus, whan thei be most above,
In al the hoteste of here love,
Hire whiel sche torneth, and thei felle
In the manere as I schal telle.
　　　This king, which stod in al his welthe
Of pes, of worschipe and of helthe, [peace]
And felte him on no side grieved,
As he that hath his world achieved,
Tho thoghte he wolde a feste make;
2500 And that was for his wyves sake,
That sche the lordes ate feste,
That were obeissant to his heste,
Mai knowe: and so forth therupon
He let ordeine, and sende anon
Be lettres and be messagiers,
And warnede alle hise officiers
That every thing be wel arraied:
The grete Stiedes were assaied [steeds/readied]
For joustinge and for tornement,
2510 And many a perled garnement
Embroudred was ayein the dai.
The lordes in here beste arrai
Be comen ate time set,
On jousteth wel, an other bet, [better]
And otherwhile thei torneie,
And thus thei casten care aweie
And token lustes upon honde.
And after, thou schalt understonde,
To mete into the kinges halle [banquet]

2520 Thei come, as thei be beden alle: [bidden]
And whan thei were set and served,
Thanne after, as it was deserved,
To hem that worthi knyhtes were,
So as thei seten hiere and there,
The pris was yove and spoken oute [given]
Among the heraldz al aboute.
And thus benethe and ek above
Al was of armes and of love,
Wherof abouten ate bordes
2530 Men hadde manye sondri wordes,
That of the merthe which thei made
The king himself began to glade
Withinne his herte and tok a pride,
And sih the Cuppe stonde aside,
Which mad was of Gurmoundes hed,
As ye have herd, whan he was ded,
And was with gold and riche Stones
Beset and bounde for the nones,
And stod upon a fot on heihte
2540 Of burned gold, and with gret sleihte
Of werkmanschipe it was begrave
Of such werk as it scholde have,
And was policed ek so clene [polished]
That no signe of the Skulle is sene,
Bot as it were a Gripes Ey. [Griffin's eye]
The king bad bere his Cuppe awey,
Which stod tofore him on the bord,
And fette thilke. Upon his word [fetch the other]
This Skulle is fet and wyn therinne,
2550 Wherof he bad his wif beginne:
"Drink with thi fader, Dame," he seide.
And sche to his biddinge obeide,
And tok the Skulle, and what hire liste [pleased her]
Sche drank, as sche which nothing wiste

What Cuppe it was: and thanne al oute
The kyng in audience aboute
Hath told it was hire fader Skulle,
So that the lordes knowe schulle
Of his bataille a soth witnesse,   [true]
2560 And made avant thurgh what prouesse
He hath his wyves love wonne,
Which of the Skulle hath so begonne.
Tho was ther mochel Pride alofte,
Thei speken alle, and sche was softe,
Thenkende on thilke unkynde Pride,   [unnatural]
Of that hire lord so nyh hire side
Avanteth him that he hath slain
And piked out hire fader brain,
And of the Skulle had mad a Cuppe.
2570 Sche soffreth al til thei were uppe,
And tho sche hath seknesse feigned,
And goth to chambre and hath compleigned
Unto a Maide which sche triste,   [trusted]
So that non other wyht it wiste.
This Mayde Glodeside is hote,
To whom this lady hath behote   [promised]
Of ladischipe al that sche can,
To vengen hire upon this man,
Which dede hire drinke in such a plit   [who made her drink]
2580 Among hem alle for despit
Of hire and of hire fader bothe;
Wherof hire thoghtes ben so wrothe,
Sche seith, that sche schal noght be glad,
Til that sche se him so bestad   [situated]
That he nomore make avant.
And thus thei felle in covenant,
That thei acorden ate laste,
With suche wiles as thei caste
That thei wol gete of here acord

2590 Som orped knyht to sle this lord: [valiant]
And with this sleihte thei beginne,
How thei Helmege myhten winne,
Which was the kinges Boteler,
A proud a lusti Bacheler,
And Glodeside he loveth hote.

And sche, to make him more assote, [fond]
Hire love granteth, and be nyhte
Thei schape how thei togedre myhte
Abedde meete: and don it was
2600 This same nyht; and in this cas
The qwene hirself the nyht secounde
Wente in hire stede, and there hath
        founde
A chambre derk withoute liht,
And goth to bedde to this knyht.

And he, to kepe his observance,
To love doth his obeissance,
And weneth it be Glodeside;
And sche thanne after lay aside,
And axeth him what he hath do,
2610 And who sche was sche tolde him tho,
And seide: "Helmege, I am thi qwene,
Now schal thi love wel be sene
Of that thou hast thi wille wroght:
Or it schal sore ben aboght,
Or thou schalt worche as I thee seie.
And if thou wolt be such a weie
Do my plesance and holde it stille,
For evere I schal ben at thi wille,
Bothe I and al myn heritage."

2620 Anon the wylde loves rage,
In which noman him can governe,
Hath mad him that he can noght werne, [refuse]
Bot fell al hol to hire assent:

And thus the whiel is al miswent,
The which fortune hath upon honde;
For how that evere it after stonde,
Thei schope among hem such a wyle,
The king was ded withinne a whyle.
So slihly cam it noght aboute
2630 That thei ne ben descoevered oute,
So that it thoghte hem for the beste
To fle, for there was no reste:
And thus the tresor of the king
Thei trusse and mochel other thing, [pack]
And with a certein felaschipe
Thei fledde and wente awey be schipe,
And hielde here rihte cours fro thenne,
Til that thei come to Ravenne,
Wher thei the Dukes helpe soghte.
2640 And he, so as thei him besoghte,
A place granteth forto duelle;
Bot after, whan he herde telle
Of the manere how thei have do,
This Duk let schape for hem so,
That of a puison which thei drunke
Thei hadden that thei have beswunke. [labored for]
    And al this made avant of Pride:
Good is therfore a man to hide
His oghne pris, for if he speke, [praise]
2650 He mai lihtliche his thonk tobreke.
In armes lith non avantance [lies]
To him which thenkth his name avance
And be renomed of his dede:
And also who that thenkth to spede
Of love, he mai him noght avaunte;
For what man thilke vice haunte,
His pourpos schal fulofte faile.
In armes he that wol travaile

Or elles loves grace atteigne,
2660 His lose tunge he mot restreigne,
Which berth of his honour the keie. [bears/key]

[Amans now thanks Genius for his "gentil lore" and asks if there is anything more he should know about Pride. Genius tells him that the last form of Pride soars like a hawk, only to crumple ultimately to earth. It is Vain Glory (2662–2680). Vain Glory is like a chameleon, always changing his old guise for new. The vainglorious man forgets Purgatory and thinks his newfangled glories on earth are his heaven. More jolly than a bird in May, he wears gay colors and sings his carols (2720). Amans boldly admits to this sin. He has dressed better for love, has tried his hand at love songs, and has sung them in merry company. He never gained any favors for his efforts, however. So, despite his intentions, he has never been borne aloft or had reason to be glad. Yet fame keeps bringing to his ears reports of his Lady's beauty: "What wonder is thogh I be fain?" (2759). Genius pardons him for his vain hopes (2771) and tells him the story of Nebuchadnezzar to explain why he should eschew Vain Glory (2785 ff.).[19]]

NEBUCHADNEZZAR'S PUNISHMENT

Nebuchadnezzar was king of all the Orient. No king was so mighty. In his pride he performed many a wonder until the high King of Kings, who sees and knows all things, took vengeance on his pride (2809). He sent Nebuchadnezzar a dream of a high tree, which had large leaves and was full of fruit and birds. All kinds of beasts fed around the tree. Suddenly, a voice sounded out: "Hew doun this tree and lett it falle" (2834). Only the tree's root remained, and it had instructions to eat grass like an ox until heaven washed it seven times (2846). After awakening the king called for an explanation of the dream, but no one except Daniel knew its meaning (2882). Reluctantly Daniel explained: The tree is the king ruling over the fullness of the earth. But because of vain glory he shall be hewn down, his reign overthrown, and he shall, because of his vanity, be transformed to an ox to feed on grass for seven years, unless he change his ways (2883-2939). But vanity is blind; the king forgot the dream.]

And fell withinne a time so,
As he in Babiloine wente,
The vanite of Pride him hente; [seized]
His herte aros of veine gloire,
So that he drowh into memoire
His lordschipe and his regalie
2960 With wordes of Surquiderie.
And whan that he him most avaunteth,
That lord which veine gloire daunteth,
Al sodeinliche, as who seith treis, [quick as one, two, three]
Wher that he stod in his Paleis,
He tok him fro the mennes sihte:
Was non of hem so war that mihte
Sette yhe wher that he becom.
And thus was he from his kingdom
Into the wilde Forest drawe,
2970 Wher that the myhti goddes lawe
Thurgh his pouer dede him transforme
Fro man into a bestes forme;
And lich an Oxe under the fot
He graseth, as he nedes mot, [grazes/must]
To geten him his lives fode.
Tho thoghte him colde grases goode,
That whilom eet the hote spices, [who once ate]
Thus was he torned fro delices: [delights]
The wyn which he was wont to drinke
2980 He tok thanne of the welles brinke
Or of the pet or of the slowh, [pit/slough]
It thoghte him thanne good ynowh:
In stede of chambres wel arraied

He was thanne of a buissh wel paied,   [pleased]
The harde ground he lay upon,
For othre pilwes hath he non;
The stormes and the Reines falle,
The wyndes blowe upon him alle,
He was tormented day and nyht,
2990 Such was the hihe goddes myht,
Til sevene yer an ende toke.
Upon himself tho gan he loke;
In stede of mete gras and stres,   [meat/straw]
In stede of handes longe cles,   [claws]
In stede of man a bestes lyke   [likeness]
He syh; and thanne he gan to syke   [saw/sigh]
For cloth of gold and for perrie,   [precious stones (OF *pierre* 'stone')]

Which him was wont to magnefie.
Whan he behield his Cote of heres,
3000 He wepte and with fulwoful teres
Up to the hevene he caste his chiere   [countenance]
Wepende, and thoghte in this manere;
Thogh he no wordes myhte winne,
Thus seide his herte and spak withinne:
"O mihti godd, that al hast wroght
And al myht bringe ayein to noght,
Now knowe I wel, bot al of thee,
This world hath no prosperite:
In thin aspect ben alle liche,
3010 The povere man and ek the riche,
Withoute thee ther mai no wight,
And thou above alle othre miht.
O mihti lord, toward my vice
Thi merci medle with justice;
And I woll make a covenant,
That of my lif the remenant
I schal it be thi grace amende,
And in thi lawe so despende

That veine gloire I schal eschuie,
3020 And bowe unto thin heste and suie   [command/follow]
Humilite, and that I vowe."
And so thenkende he gan doun bowe,
And thogh him lacke vois and speche,
He gan up with his feet areche,
And wailende in his bestly stevene   [voice]
He made his pleignte unto the hevene.
He kneleth in his wise and braieth,   [manner]
To seche merci and assaieth   [tries]
His god, which made him nothing strange,
3030 Whan that he sih his pride change.
Anon as he was humble and tame,
He fond toward his god the same,
And in a twinklinge of a lok
His mannes forme ayein he tok,
And was reformed to the regne
In which that he was wont to regne;
So that the Pride of veine gloire
Evere afterward out of memoire
He let it passe. And thus is schewed
3040 What is to ben of Pride unthewed   [wrongly disposed]
Ayein the hihe goddes lawe,
To whom noman mai be felawe.

[So Genius warns Amans to take heed that he does not become like a beast. If he is humble and honest he will avoid Vain Glory and be able to stand with confidence. To conclude his diatribe against Pride, Genius tells the Tale of the Three Questions.[20]]

TALE OF THREE QUESTIONS

A king whilom was yong and wys,
The which sette of his wit gret pris.   [value]
Of depe ymaginaciouns
3070 And strange interpretaciouns,

Problemes and demandes eke,
His wisdom was to finde and seke;
Wherof he wolde in sondri wise
Opposen hem that weren wise.
Bot non of hem it myhte bere
Upon his word to yeve answere,
Outaken on, which was a knyht;   [except one]
To him was every thing so liht,   [easy]
That also sone as he hem herde,
3080 The kinges wordes he answerde;
What thing the king him axe wolde,
Therof anon the trowthe he tolde.
The king somdiel hadde an Envie,
And thoghte he wolde his wittes plie
To sette som conclusioun,
Which scholde be confusioun
Unto this knyht, so that the name
And of wisdom the hihe fame
Toward himself he wolde winne.
3090 And thus of al his wit withinne
This king began to studie and muse,
What strange matiere he myhte use
The knyhtes wittes to confounde;
And ate laste he hath it founde,
And for the knyht anon he sente,
That he schal telle what he mente.
Upon thre pointz stod the matiere
Of questions, as thou schalt hiere.
    The ferste point of alle thre
3100 Was this: "What thing in his degre
Of al this world hath nede lest,   [least need of help]
And yet men helpe it althermest?"   [most of all]
    The secounde is: "What most is worth,
And of costage is lest put forth?"   [expense/least]
    The thridde is: "Which is of most cost,
And lest is worth and goth to lost?"   [loss]

The king thes thre demandes axeth,
And to the knyht this lawe he taxeth,
That he schal gon and come ayein
3110 The thridde weke, and telle him plein
To every point, what it amonteth.
And if so be that he misconteth,
To make in his answere a faile,
Ther schal non other thing availe,
The king seith, bot he schal be ded
And lese hise goodes and his hed.
The knyht was sori of this thing
And wolde excuse him to the king,
Bot he ne wolde him noght forbere,
3120 And thus the knyht of his ansuere
Goth hom to take avisement:
Bot after his entendement   [purpose]
The more he caste his wit aboute,
The more he stant therof in doute.
Tho wiste he wel the kinges herte,
That he the deth ne scholde asterte, [escape]
And such a sorwe hath to him take,
That gladschipe he hath al forsake.
He thoghte ferst upon his lif,
3130 And after that upon his wif,
Upon his children ek also,
Of whiche he hadde dowhtres tuo;
The yongest of hem hadde of age
Fourtiene yer, and of visage
Sche was riht fair, and of stature
Lich to an hevenely figure,
And of manere and goodli speche,
Thogh men wolde alle Londes seche,
Thei scholden noght have founde hir like.
3140 Sche sih hire fader sorwe and sike,
And wiste noght the cause why;
So cam sche to him prively,

And that was where he made his mone
Withinne a Gardin al him one;   [alone by himself]
Upon hire knes sche gan doun falle
With humble herte and to him calle,
And seide: "O goode fader diere,
Why make ye thus hevy chiere,
And I wot nothing how it is?
3150 And wel ye knowen, fader, this,
What aventure that you felle
Ye myhte it saufly to me telle,
For I have ofte herd you seid,
That ye such trust have on me leid,
That to my soster ne my brother,
In al this world ne to non other,
Ye dorste telle a privite
So wel, my fader, as to me.
Forthi, my fader, I you preie,
3160 Ne casteth noght that herte aweie,
For I am sche that wolde kepe
Youre honour." And with that to wepe
Hire yhe mai noght be forbore,
Sche wissheth forto ben unbore,
Er that hire fader so mistriste
To tellen hire of that he wiste:
And evere among merci sche cride,
That he ne scholde his conseil hide
From hire that so wolde him good
3170 And was so nyh his fleissh and blod.
So that with wepinge ate laste
His chiere upon his child he caste,
And sorwfulli to that sche preide
He tolde his tale and thus he seide:
"The sorwe, dowhter, which I make
Is noght al only for my sake,
Bot for thee bothe and for you alle:
For such a chance is me befalle,

That I schal er this thridde day
3180 Lese al that evere I lese may, [lose]
Mi lif and al my good therto:
Therfore it is I sorwe so."
"What is the cause, helas!" quod sche,
"Mi fader, that ye scholden be
Ded and destruid in such a wise?"
And he began the pointz devise, [enumerate]
Whiche as the king told him be mowthe,
And seid hir pleinly that he cowthe [could]
Ansuere unto no point of this.
3190 And sche, that hiereth how it is,
Hire conseil yaf and seide tho:
"Mi fader, sithen it is so,
That ye can se non other weie,
Bot that ye moste nedes deie,
I wolde preie of you a thing:
Let me go with you to the king,
And ye schull make him understonde
How ye, my wittes forto fonde, [in order to discover]
Have leid your ansuere upon me;
3200 And telleth him, in such degre
Upon my word ye wole abide
To lif or deth, what so betide.
For yit par chaunce I may pourchace
With som good word the kinges grace,
Your lif and ek your good to save;
For ofte schal a womman have
Thing which a man mai noght areche." [reach to]
The fader herde his dowhter speche,
And thoghte ther was resoun inne,
3210 And sih his oghne lif to winne
He cowthe don himself no cure;
So betre him thoghte in aventure
To put his lif and al his good,
Than in the maner as it stod

His lif in certein forto lese. [lose]
And thus thenkende he gan to chese
To do the conseil of this Maide,
And tok the pourpos which sche saide.

    The dai was come and forth thei gon,
3220 Unto the Court thei come anon,
Wher as the king in juggement
Was set and hath this knyht assent. [sent for]
Arraied in hire beste wise
This Maiden with hire wordes wise
Hire fader ladde be the hond
Into the place, wher he fond
The king with othre whiche he wolde,
And to the king knelende he tolde
As he enformed was tofore,
3230 And preith the king that he therfore
His dowhtres wordes wolde take,
And seith that he wol undertake
Upon hire wordes forto stonde.
Tho was ther gret merveile on honde,
That he, which was so wys a knyht,
His lif upon so yong a wyht [person]
Besette wolde in jeupartie,
And manye it hielden for folie:
Bot ate laste natheles
3240 The king comandeth ben in pes,
And to this Maide he caste his chiere,
And seide he wolde hire tale hiere,
He bad hire speke, and sche began:
"Mi liege lord, so as I can,"
Quod sche, "the pointz of whiche I herde,
Thei schul of reson ben ansuerde.

    The ferste I understonde is this,
What thing of al the world it is,
Which men most helpe and hath lest nede.

3250 Mi liege lord, this wolde I rede:
The Erthe it is, which everemo
With mannes labour is bego;
Als wel in wynter as in Maii
The mannes hond doth what he mai
To helpe it forth and make it riche,
And forthi men it delve and dyche
And eren it with strengthe of plowh, [cultivate]
Wher it hath of himself ynowh,
So that his nede is ate leste.

3260 For every man and bridd and beste,
And flour and gras and rote and rinde,
And every thing be weie of kynde
Schal sterve, and Erthe it schal become; [die]
As it was out of Erthe nome, [taken]
It schal to therthe torne ayein:
And thus I mai be resoun sein
That Erthe is the most nedeles,
And most men helpe it natheles.
So that, my lord, touchende of this

3270 I have ansuerd hou that it is.
    That other point I understod, [second]
Which most is worth and most is good,
And costeth lest a man to kepe:
Mi lord, if ye woll take kepe,
I seie it is Humilite,
Thurgh which the hihe trinite
As for decerte of pure love
Unto Marie from above,
Of that he knew hire humble entente,

3280 His oghne Sone adoun he sente,
Above alle othre and hire he ches
For that vertu which bodeth pes:
So that I may be resoun calle
Humilite most worth of alle.

And lest it costeth to maintiene,
In al the world as it is sene;
For who that hath humblesce on honde,
He bringth no werres into londe,
For he desireth for the beste
3290 To setten every man in reste.
Thus with your hihe reverence
Me thenketh that this evidence
As to this point is sufficant.
     And touchende of the remenant,
Which is the thridde of youre axinges,
What leste is worth of alle thinges,
And costeth most, I telle it, Pride;
Which mai noght in the hevene abide,
For Lucifer with hem that felle
3300 Bar Pride with him into helle.   [bore]
Ther was Pride of to gret a cost,
Whan he for Pride hath hevene lost;
And after that in Paradis
Adam for Pride loste his pris: [prize]
In Midelerthe and ek also
Pride is the cause of alle wo,
That al the world ne may suffise
To stanche of Pride the reprise:
Pride is the heved of alle Sinne,
3310 Which wasteth al and mai noght winne;
Pride is of every mis the pricke,   [wrong]
Pride is the werste of alle wicke,   [wickedness]
And costneth most and lest is worth
In place where he hath his forth.
Thus have I seid that I wol seie
Of myn answere, and to you preie,
Mi liege lord, of youre office
That ye such grace and such justice
Ordeigne for mi fader hiere,

3320 That after this, whan men it hiere,
    The world therof mai speke good."
        The king, which reson understod
    And hath al herd how sche hath said,
    Was inly glad and so wel paid   [pleased]
    That al his wraththe is overgo:
    And he began to loke tho
    Upon this Maiden in the face,
    In which he fond so mochel grace,
    That al his pris on hire he leide,   [praise]
3330 In audience and thus he seide:
    "Mi faire Maide, wel thee be!
    Of thin ansuere and ek of thee
    Me liketh wel, and as thou wilt,
    Foryive be thi fader gilt.
    And if thou were of such lignage,   [lineage]
    That thou to me were of parage,   [equal rank]
    And that thi fader were a Pier,   [peer]
    As he is now a Bachilier,
    So seker as I have a lif,
3340 Thou scholdest thanne by my wif.
    Bot this I seie natheles,
    That I wol schape thin encress;
    What worldes good that thou wolt crave,
    Axe of my yifte and thou schalt have."
    And sche the king with wordes wise
    Knelende thonketh in this wise:
    "Mi liege lord, god mot you quite!   [may God requite you]
    Mi fader hier hath bot a lite
    Of warison, and that he wende   [property/thought]
3350 Hadde al be lost; bot now amende
    He mai wel thurgh your noble grace."
    With that the king riht in his place
    Anon forth in that freisshe hete   [fresh passion]
    An Erldom, which thanne of eschete   [escheat (forfeiture)]

Was late falle into his hond,
Unto this knyht with rente and lond
Hath yove and with his chartre sesed;   [given/endowed]
And thus was all the noise appesed.
    This Maiden, which sat on hire knes
3360 Tofore the king, hise charitees
Comendeth, and seide overmore:
"Mi liege lord, riht now tofore
Ye seide, as it is of record,
That if my fader were a lord
And Pier unto these othre grete,   [great men]
Ye wolden for noght elles lete,   [allow]
That I ne scholde be your wif;
And this wot every worthi lif,
A kinges word it mot ben holde.
3370 Forthi, my lord, if that ye wolde
So gret a charite fulfille,
God wot it were wel my wille:
For he which was a Bacheler,
Mi fader, is now mad a Pier;
So whenne as evere that I cam,
An Erles dowhter now I am."
    This yonge king, which peised al,   [weighed]
Hire beaute and hir wit withal,
As he that was with love hent,   [seized]
3380 Anon therto yaf his assent.
He myhte noght the maide asterte,   [escape]
That sche nis ladi of his herte;
So that he tok hire to his wif,
To holde whyl that he hath lif:
And thus the king toward his knyht
Acordeth him, as it is riht.
    And over this good is to wite,
In this Cronique as it is write,
This noble king of whom I tolde
3390 Of Spaine be tho daies olde

The kingdom hadde in governance,
And as the bok makth remembrance,
Alphonse was his propre name:
The knyht also, if I schal name,
Danz Petro hihte, and as men telle,　　　[was named Don Peter]
His dowhter wyse Peronelle
Was cleped, which was full of grace:
And that was sene in thilke place,
Wher sche hir fader out of teene　　　[trouble (OE *teona*,
　　　　　　　　　　　　　　　　　　　　　'vexation')]

3400　Hath broght and mad hirself a qweene,
Of that sche hath so wel desclosed
The pointz wherof sche was opposed.
　　　Lo now, my Sone, as thou myht hiere,
Of al this thing to my matiere
Bot on I take, and that is Pride,
To whom no grace mai betide:
In hevene he fell out of his stede,
And Paradis him was forbede,
The goode men in Erthe him hate,
3410　So that to helle he mot algate,
Where every vertu schal be weyved
And every vice be received.
Bot Humblesce is al otherwise,
Which most is worth, and no reprise
It takth ayein, bot softe and faire,
If eny thing stond in contraire,
With humble speche it is redresced:
Thus was this yonge Maiden blessed,
The which I spak of now tofore,
3420　Hire fader lif sche gat therfore,
And wan with al the kinges love.
Forthi, my Sone, if thou wolt love,
It sit thee wel to leve Pride
And take Humblesce upon thi side;
The more of grace thou schalt gete.

Mi fader, I woll noght foryete
Of this that ye have told me hiere,
And if that eny such manere
Of humble port mai love appaie,   [satisfy]
3430 Hierafterward I thenke assaie: [plan to try]
Bot now forth over I beseche
That ye more of my schrifte seche.   [confession]
    Mi goode Sone, it schal be do:
Now herkne and ley an Ere to;
For as touchende of Prides fare,
Als ferforth as I can declare
In cause of vice, in cause of love,
That hast thou pleinly herd above,
So that ther is nomor to seie
3440 Touchende of that; bot other weie
Touchende Envie I thenke telle,
Which hath the propre kinde of helle,   [very nature]
Withoute cause to misdo
Toward himself and othre also,
Hierafterward as understonde
Thou schalt the spieces, as thei stonde.

Explicit Liber Primus

INCIPIT LIBER SECUNDUS

[The vice that is second to Pride is Envy, whose fires burn end-
lessly within the man who bears this malady. Genius asks Amans
if he has had sorrow over another man's joy, for such is the
first aspect of Envy. Amans acknowledges that he has often been
guilty here. A thousand times his heart has burned, hotter than
Etna burning ceaselessly, at the sight of a rival's good cheer. His
torment is worse than a ship "forstormed and forblowe" (25).]

	Whan I the Court se of Cupide	
40	Aproche unto my ladi side	
	Of hem that lusti ben and freisshe,—	
	Thogh it availe hem noght a reisshe,	[rush]
	Bot only that thei ben in speche,—	
	My sorwe is thanne noght to seche:	[not far away]
	Bot whan thei rounen in hire Ere,	[whisper]
	Than groweth al my moste fere,	
	And namly whan thei talen longe;	
	My sorwes thanne be so stronge	
	Of that I se hem wel at ese,	
50	I can noght telle my desese.	
	Bot, Sire, as of my ladi selve,	[herself]
	Thogh sche have wowers ten or twelve,	
	For no mistrust I have of hire	
	Me grieveth noght, for certes, Sire,	
	I trowe, in al this world to seche,	[believe]
	Nis womman that in dede and speche	
	Woll betre avise hire what sche doth,	
	Ne betre, forto seie a soth,	[tell the truth]

103

Kepe hire honour ate alle tide,
60 And yit get hire a thank beside.

[Amans asks for instruction, and as an example to explain this dog-in-the-manger kind of Envy, Genius tells the story of Acis and Galatea (104 ff.).[1] The giant Polyphemous sought Galatea in love, but she loved the young knight Acis. Polyphemous lurked in the byways, trying to catch them together. After a long time he at last found them at the foot of a bank by the sea. As he spied on their lusty love play his heart was set aflame. Filled with "sorghe and gret desese" (165) at the sight of Acis in his bliss, he fled, roaring wildly like a bear, burning with the hell fires of Etna. In his rage he returned to the lovers and shoved part of the bank down onto them, burying Acis. Galatea fled into the sea where Neptune took her to a safe place. Her sorrow moved the gods, who transformed Acis into a well with ever-fresh streams. But they were angry with Polyphemous (200). Thus, Genius concludes, Amans should free himself of Envy toward his Lady.

 Amans thanks his father confessor for the excellent example and asks for further instruction, whereupon Genius tells him about the reverse of the first kind of Envy which is joy over another man's grief. Amans says he is familiar with this sin also, and has often taken pleasure in watching courtiers who climb Fortune's wheel only to be thrown down at last:]

   Thanne am I fedd of that thei faste,
245 And lawhe of that I se hem loure;   [laugh]
   And thus of that thei brewe soure
   I drinke swete, and am wel esed
   Of that I wot thei ben desesed.   [discomforted]
   Bot this which I you telle hiere
250 Is only for my lady diere;
   That for non other that I knowe
   Me reccheth noght who overthrowe,   [care]
   Ne who that stonde in love upriht.

[In response to the Lover's request for instruction, Genius tells
the story of the Travelers and the Angel.[2]]

THE TRAVELERS AND THE ANGEL

Of Jupiter this finde I write,
How whilom that he wolde wite
Upon the pleigntes whiche he herde,   [complaints]
Among the men how that it ferde,
As of here wrong condicion
To do justificacion:
And for that cause doun he sente
An Angel, which aboute wente,
That he the sothe knowe mai.
300 So it befell upon a dai
This Angel, which him scholde enforme,
Was clothed in a mannes forme,
And overtok, I understonde,
Tuo men that wenten over londe,
Thurgh whiche he thoghte to aspie
His cause, and goth in compaignie.
This Angel with hise wordes wise
Opposeth hem in sondri wise,
Now lowde wordes and now softe,
310 That mad hem to desputen ofte,
And ech of hem his reson hadde.
And thus with tales he hem ladde
With good examinacioun,
Til he knew the condicioun,
What men thei were bothe tuo;
And sih wel ate laste tho,
That on of hem was coveitous,
And his fela was envious.
And thus, whan he hath knowlechinge,

320 Anon he feigneth departinge,
And seide he mot algate wende.
Bot herkne now what fell at ende:
For thanne he made hem understonde
That he was there of goddes sonde,   [commission (sending)]
And seide hem, for the kindeschipe
That thei have don him felaschipe,
He wole hem do som grace ayein,
And bad that on of hem schal sein   [bade]
What thing him is lievest to crave,   [most dear]
330 And he it schal of yifte have;
And over that ek forth withal
He seith that other have schal
The double of that his felaw axeth;
And thus to hem his grace he taxeth.
      The coveitous was wonder glad,
And to that other man he bad
And seith that he ferst axe scholde:
For he supposeth that he wolde
Make his axinge of worldes good;
340 For thanne he knew wel how it stod,
That he himself be double weyhte
Schal after take, and thus be sleyhte,
Be cause that he wolde winne,
He bad his fela ferst beginne.
This Envious, thogh it be late,
Whan that he syh he mot algate
Make his axinge ferst, he thoghte,
If he worschipe or profit soghte,
It schal be doubled to his fiere: [companion]
350 That wolde he chese in no manere.   [choose]
Bot thanne he scheweth what he was
Toward Envie, and in this cas
Unto this Angel thus he seide
And for his yifte this he preide,
To make him blind of his on yhe,   [one eye]

So that his fela nothing syhe.
This word was noght so sone spoke,
That his on yhe anon was loke,   [locked shut]
And his felawh forthwith also
360 Was blind of bothe his yhen tuo.
Tho was that other glad ynowh,
That on wepte, and that other lowh,   [laughed]
He sette his on yhe at no cost,
Wherof that other two hath lost.
     Of thilke ensample which fell tho,
Men tellen now fulofte so,
The world empeireth comunly: [becomes worse]
And yit wot non the cause why;   [yet no one knows]
For it acordeth noght to kinde
370 Min oghne harm to seche and finde
Of that I schal my brother grieve;
It myhte nevere wel achieve.

[Amans says his Envy has not gone as far as that of the envious traveler and asks instruction on other aspects of the malady (373–382). None of Envy's brood has merit, says Genius. His next of progeny is called Detraction, who is assisted by Malebouche (Wicked Tongue). Though Detraction sometimes praises, he always finds some lack. He is like the nettle that runs up the fresh rose vine to burn it and make its roses pale. For pale is the hue of Envy. Similarly, he is like the beetle Scharnebude, who, on the hottest day of May sprouts his wings and flies high above the flowers, ignoring them in favor of the dunghill. Detraction is a backbiter who hides men's virtues by speaking the worst of them that he knows. Such men commonly haunt Love's court (383–451).

The Lover admits to some guilt here, too. He has spread tales of his rivals to his Lady. Genius warns him to guard his tongue, for his Lady will not admire him more for his detracting from others. When she knows the truth she will think the less of him for it. "For who so wole his handes lime, / Thei mosten be

the more unclene" (574–575). "For who so wol an other blame, /
He secheth ofte his oghne schame" (579–580). Genius offers the
Tale of Constance, "a tale of gret entendement" (584), as an
example of right behavior despite Envy and Detraction.[3]]

TALE OF CONSTANCE

     A worthi kniht in Cristes lawe
Of grete Rome, as is the sawe,   [saying]
The Sceptre hadde forto rihte;
590   Tiberie Constantin he hihte,
Whos wif was cleped Ytalie:
Bot thei togedre of progenie
No children hadde bot a Maide;
And sche the god so wel apaide,   [pleased]
That al the wide worldes fame
Spak worschipe of hire goode name.
Constance, as the Cronique seith,
Sché hihte, and was so ful of feith,
That the greteste of Barbarie,
600   Of hem whiche usen marchandie,   [practice merchandising]
Sche hath converted, as thei come
To hire upon a time in Rome,
To schewen such thing as thei broghte;
Whiche worthili of hem sche boghte,
And over that in such a wise   [manner]
Sche hath hem with hire wordes wise
Of Cristes feith so full enformed,
That thei therto ben all conformed,
So that baptesme thei receiven
610   And alle here false goddes weyven.   [renounce]
Whan thei ben of the feith certein,
Thei gon to Barbarie ayein,
And ther the Souldan for hem sente
And axeth hem to what entente
Thei have here ferste feith forsake.

And thei, whiche hadden undertake
The rihte feith to kepe and holde,
The matiere of here tale tolde
With al the hole circumstance.
620 And whan the Souldan of Constance
Upon the point that thei ansuerde
The beaute and the grace herde,
As he which thanne was to wedde,
In alle haste his cause spedde
To sende for the mariage.
And furthermor with good corage
He seith, be so he mai hire have,
That Crist, which cam this world to save,
He woll believe: and this recorded,
630 Thei ben on either side acorded,
And therupon to make an ende
The Souldan hise hostages sende
To Rome, of Princes Sones tuelve:
Wherof the fader in himselve
Was glad, and with the Pope avised
Tuo Cardinals he hath assissed
With othre lordes many mo,
That with his doghter scholden go,
To se the Souldan be converted.
Bot that which nevere was wel herted,
640 Envie, tho began travaile
In destourbance of this spousaile
So prively that non was war.   [no one was aware]
The Moder which this Souldan bar
Was thanne alyve, and thoghte this
Unto hirself: "If it so is
Mi Sone him wedde in this manere,
Than have I lost my joies hiere,
For myn astat schal so be lassed."   [diminished]
650 Thenkende thus sche hath compassed
Be sleihte how that sche may beguile

Hire Sone; and fell withinne a while,
Betwen hem two whan that thei were,
Sche feigneth wordes in his Ere,
And in this wise gan to seie:
"Mi Sone, I am be double weie
With al myn herte glad and blithe,
For that miself have ofte sithe   [often times]
Desired thou wolt, as men seith,   [would]

660 Receive and take a newe feith,
Which schal be forthringe of thi lif:
And ek so worschipful a wif,
The doughter of an Emperour,
To wedde it schal be gret honour.
Forthi, mi Sone, I you beseche
That I such grace mihte areche,   [attain]
Whan that my doughter come schal,
That I mai thanne in special,
So as me thenkth it is honeste,

670 Be thilke which the ferste feste   [be the one who]
Schal make unto hire welcominge."
The Souldan granteth hire axinge,   [request]
And sche therof was glad ynowh:
For under that anon she drowh
With false wordes that sche spak
Covine of deth behinde his bak.   [conspiracy]
And therupon hire ordinance
She made so, that whan Constance
Was come forth with the Romeins,

680 Of clerkes and of Citezeins,
A riche feste sche hem made:
And most whan that thei weren glade,
With fals covine which sche hadde
Hire clos Envie tho sche spradde,
And alle tho that hadden be   [those]
Or in apert or in prive   [openly or in secret]
Of conseil to the mariage,

Sche slowh hem in a sodein rage
Endlong the bord as thei be set, [along]
690 So that it myhte noght be let; [stopped]
Hire oghne Sone was noght quit, [spared]
Bot deide upon the same plit.
Bot what the hihe god wol spare
It mai for no peril misfare:
This worthi Maiden which was there
Stod thanne, as who seith, ded for feere,
To se the feste how that it stod,
Which al was torned into blod:
The Dissh forthwith the Coppe and al
700 Bebled thei weren overal; [covered with blood]
Sche sih hem deie on every side;
No wonder thogh sche wepte and cride
Makende many a wofull mone.
Whan al was slain bot sche al one,
This olde fend, this Sarazine, [fiend]
Let take anon this Constantine
With al the good sche thider broghte,
And hath ordeined, as sche thoghte,
A nakid Schip withoute stiere, [rudder]
710 In which the good and hire in fiere, [together]
Vitailed full for yeres fyve,
Wher that the wynd it wolde dryve,
Sche putte upon the wawes wilde. [waves]
     Bot he which alle thing mai schilde, [shield]
Thre yer, til that sche cam to londe,
Hire Schip to stiere hath take in honde,
And in Northumberlond aryveth;
And happeth thanne that sche dryveth
Under a Castel with the flod, [beside the tidal river]
720 Which upon Humber banke stod
And was the kynges oghne also
The which Allee was cleped tho,
A Saxon and a worthi knyht,

Bot he believeth noght ariht.
Of this Castell was Chastellein
Elda the kinges Chamberlein,
A knyhtly man after his lawe;
And whan he sih upon the wawe
The Schip drivende al one so,
730   He bad anon men scholden go
To se what it betokne mai.
This was upon a Somer dai,
The Schip was loked and sche founde;   [anchored]
Elda withinne a litel stounde
It wiste, and with his wif anon
Toward this yonge ladi gon,
Wher that thei founden gret richesse;
Bot sche hire wolde noght confesse,   [herself]
Whan thei hire axen what sche was.
740   And natheles upon the cas   [as it happened]
Out of the Schip with gret worschipe
Thei toke hire into felaschipe,
As thei that weren of hir glade:
Bot sche no maner joie made,
Bot sorweth sore of that sche fond   [because she found]
No cristendom in thilke lond;
Bot elles sche hath al hire wille,   [otherwise]
And thus with hem sche duelleth stille.
     Dame Hermyngheld, which was the wif
750   Of Elda, lich hire oghne lif
Constance loveth; and fell so,
Spekende alday betwen hem two,
Thurgh grace of goddes pourveance
This maiden tawhte the creance   [faith]
Unto this wif so parfitly,
Upon a dai that faste by
In presence of hire housebonde,
Wher thei go walkende on the Stronde,
A blind man, which cam there lad,   [led]

760 Unto this wif criende he bad,
With bothe hise hondes up and preide
To hire, and in this wise he seide:
"O Hermyngeld, which Cristes feith,
Enformed as Constance seith,
Received hast, yif me my sihte."
　　　Upon his word hire herte afflihte　　　[trembled]
Thenkende what was best to done,
Bot natheles sche herde his bone　　　[prayer]
And seide, "In trust of Cristes lawe,
770 Which don was on the crois and slawe,　　　[who was put on the cross/ slain]

Thou bysne man, behold and se."　　　[blind (OE *bisene*, 'near-sighted')]

With that to god upon his kne
Thonkende he tok his sihte anon,
Wherof thei merveile everychon,
Bot Elda wondreth most of alle:
This open thing which is befalle
Concludeth him be such a weie,
That he the feith mot nede obeie.
　　　Now lest what fell upon this thing.　　　[listen]
780 This Elda forth unto the king
A morwe tok his weie and rod,
And Hermyngeld at home abod
Forth with Constance wel at ese.
Elda, which thoghte his king to plese,
As he that thanne unwedded was,
Of Constance al the pleine cas
Als goodliche as he cowthe tolde.
The king was glad and seide he wolde
Come thider upon such a wise
790 That he him mihte of hire avise,
The time apointed forth withal.
This Elda triste in special　　　[trusted]
Upon a knyht, whom fro childhode

He hadde updrawe into manhode:
To him he tolde al that he thoghte,
Wherof that after him forthoghte;   [repented]
And natheles at thilke tide   [time]
Unto his wif he bad him ride
To make redi alle thing
800   Ayein the cominge of the king,
And seith that he himself tofore
Thenkth forto come, and bad therfore
That he him kepe, and told him whanne.   [await]
This knyht rod forth his weie thanne;
And soth was that of time passed
He hadde in al his wit compassed
How he Constance myhte winne;
Bot he sih tho no sped therinne,   [luck]
Wherof his lust began tabate,   [to abate]
810   And that was love is thanne hate;
Of hire honour he hadde Envie,
So that upon his tricherie
A lesinge in his herte he caste.   [deceit]
Til he cam home he hieth faste,   [hurries]
And doth his ladi tunderstonde
The Message of hire housebonde:
And therupon the longe dai
Thei setten thinges in arrai,
That al was as it scholde be
820   Of every thing in his degree;   [its]
And whan it cam into the nyht,
This wif hire hath to bedde dyht,   [retired]
Wher that this Maiden with hire lay.
This false knyht upon delay
Hath taried til thei were aslepe,
As he that wolde his time kepe
His dedly werkes to fulfille;
And to the bed he stalketh stille,
Wher that he wiste was the wif,

830 And in his hond a rasour knif
    He bar, with which hire throte he cutte,
    And prively the knif he putte
    Under that other beddes side,
    Wher that Constance lai beside.
    Elda cam hom the same nyht,
    And stille with a prive lyht,
    As he that wolde noght awake
    His wif, he hath his weie take
    Into the chambre, and ther liggende
840 He fond his dede wif bledende,
    Wher that Constance faste by
    Was falle aslepe; and sodeinly
    He cride alowd, and sche awok,
    And forth withal sche caste a lok
    And sih this ladi blede there,
    Wherof swounende ded for fere
    Sche was, and stille as eny Ston
    She lay, and Elda therupon
    Into the Castell clepeth oute,
850 And up sterte every man aboute,
    Into the chambre and forth thei wente.
    Bot he, which alle untrouthe mente,
    This false knyht, among hem alle
    Upon this thing which is befalle
    Seith that Constance hath don this dede;
    And to the bed with that he yede   [went]
    After the falshed of his speche,
    And made him there forto seche,
    And fond the knif, wher he if leide,
860 And thanne he cride and thanne he seide,
    "Lo, seth the knif al blody hiere!
    What nedeth more in this matiere
    To axe?" And thus hire innocence
    He sclaundreth there in audience
    With false wordes whiche he feigneth.

Bot yit for al that evere he pleigneth,
Elda no full credence tok:
And happeth that ther lay a bok,
Upon the which, when he it sih,
870　This knyht hath swore and seid on hih,
That alle men it mihte wite,
"Now be this bok, which hier is write,
Constance is gultif, wel I wot."
With that the hond of hevene him smot
In tokne of that he was forswore,　　　　　[guilty of perjury]
That he hath bothe hise yhen lore,　　　　　[lost]
Out of his hed the same stounde　　　　　　[instant]
Thei sterte, and so thei weren founde.
A vois was herd, whan that they felle,
880　Which seide, "O dampned man to helle,
Lo, thus hath god the sclaundre wroke　　　[avenged]
That thou ayein Constance hast spoke:
Beknow the sothe er that thou dye."　　　[make known the truth]
And he told out his felonie,
And starf forth with his tale anon.　　　　[died]
Into the ground, wher alle gon,
This dede lady was begrave:
Elda, which thoghte his honour save,
Al that he mai restreigneth sorwe.
890　　　For the seconde day a morwe
The king cam, as thei were acorded;
And whan it was to him recorded
What god hath wroght upon this chaunce,
He tok it into remembrance
And thoghte more than he seide.
For al his hole herte he leide
Upon Constance, and seide he scholde
For love of hire, if that sche wolde,
Baptesme take and Cristes feith
900　Believe, and over that he seith
He wol hire wedde, and upon this

Asseured ech til other is. [betrothed]
And forto make schorte tales,
Ther cam a Bisschop out of Wales
Fro Bangor, and Lucie he hihte,
Which thurgh the grace of god almihte
The king with many an other mo
Hath cristned, and betwen hem tuo
He hath fulfild the mariage.
910 Bot for no lust ne for no rage
Sche tolde hem nevere what sche was;
And natheles upon the cas
The king was glad, how so it stod,
For wel he wiste and understod
Sche was a noble creature.
The hihe makere of nature
Hire hath visited in a throwe, [in a moment]
That it was openliche knowe
Sche was with childe be the king,
920 Wherof above al other thing
He thonketh god and was riht glad.
And fell that time he was bestad [engaged]
Upon a werre and moste ride;
And whil he scholde there abide,
He lefte at hom to kepe his wif
Suche as he knew of holi lif,
Elda forth with the Bisschop eke;
And he with pouer goth to seke [troops]
Ayein the Scottes forto fonde [wage]
930 The werre which he tok on honde.
      The time set of kinde is come,
This lady hath hire chambre nome,
And of a Sone bore full,
Wherof that sche was joiefull,
Sche was delivered sauf and sone.
The bisshop, as it was to done,
Yaf him baptesme and Moris calleth;

And therupon, as it befalleth,
With lettres writen of record
940 Thei sende unto here liege lord,
That kepers weren of the qweene:
And he that scholde go betwene,
The Messager, to Knaresburgh,
Which toun he scholde passe thurgh,
Ridende cam the ferste day.
The kinges Moder there lay,
Whos rihte name was Domilde,
Which after al the cause spilde: [afterward/upset]
For he, which thonk deserve wolde,
950 Unto this ladi goth and tolde
Of his Message al how it ferde.
And sche with feigned joie it herde
And yaf him yiftes largely,
Bot in the nyht al prively
Sche tok the lettres whiche he hadde,
Fro point to point and overradde,   [read them over point by
                                                point]

As sche that was thurghout untrewe,
And let do wryten othre newe   [had other new ones
                                                written]

In stede of hem, and thus thei spieke:
960   "Oure liege lord, we thee beseke
That thou with ous ne be noght wroth,
Though we such thing as is thee loth
Upon oure trowthe certefie.
Thi wif, which is of faierie,
Of such a child delivered is
Fro kinde which stant al amis:
Bot for it scholde noght be seie,
We have it kept out of the weie
For drede of pure worldes schame,
970 A povere child and in the name

Of thilke which is so misbore
We toke, and therto we be swore,
That non bot only thou and we
Schal knowen of this privete:
Moris it hatte, and thus men wene   [is named/think]
That it was boren of the qweene
And of thin oghne bodi gete.
Bot this thing mai noght be foryete,
That thou ne sende ous word anon
980   What is thi wille therupon."
    This lettre, as thou has herd devise,
Was contrefet in such a wise
That noman scholde it aperceive:
And sche, which thoghte to deceive,
It leith wher sche that other tok.
This Messager, whan he awok,
And wiste nothing how it was,
Aros and rod the grete pas
And tok this lettre to the king.
990   And whan he sih this wonder thing,
He makth the Messager no chiere,
Bot natheles in wys manere
He wrot ayein, and yaf hem charge
That thei ne soffre noght at large
His wif to go, bot kepe hire stille,
Til thei have herd mor of his wille.
This Messager was yifteles,   [giftless]
Bot with this lettre natheles,
Or be him lief or be him loth,   [happy or sad]
1000   In alle haste ayein he goth
Be Knaresburgh, and as he wente,
Unto the Moder his entente
Of that he fond toward the king
He tolde; and sche upon this thing
Seith that he scholde abide al nyht

And made him feste and chiere ariht,
Feignende as thogh sche cowthe him
    thonk.
Bot he with strong wyn which he dronk
Forth with the travail of the day
1010 Was drunke, aslepe and while he lay,
Sche hath hise lettres overseie
And formed in an other weie.
    Ther was a newe lettre write,
Which seith: "I do you forto wite,   [I command you to know]
That thurgh the conseil of you tuo
I stonde in point to ben undo,
As he which is a king deposed.
For every man it hath supposed,
How that my wif Constance is faie;   [fairy]
1020 And if that I, thei sein, delaie
To put hire out of compaignie,
The worschipe of my Regalie
Is lore; and over this thei telle,   [lost]
Hire child schal noght among hem duelle,
To cleymen eny heritage.
So can I se non avantage,
Bot al is lost, if sche abide:
Forthi to loke on every side
Toward the meschief as it is,
1030 I charge you and bidde this,
That ye the same Schip vitaile,
In which that sche tok arivaile,
Therinne and putteth bothe tuo,
Hireself forthwith hire child also,
And so forth broght unto the depe
Betaketh hire the See to kepe.
Of foure daies time I sette,
That ye this thing no longer lette,   [allow]
So that your lif be noght forsfet."   [forfeited]
1040 And thus this lettre contrefet

The Messager, which was unwar,
Upon the kingeshalve bar,   [bore on the king's behalf]
And where he scholde it hath betake.
Bot whan that thei have hiede take,
And rad that writen is withinne,
So gret a sorwe thei beginne,
As thei here oghne Moder sihen
Brent in a fyr before here yhen:
Ther was wepinge and ther was wo,
1050 Bot finaly the thing is do.
    Upon the See thei have hire broght,
Bot sche the cause wiste noght,
And thus upon the flod thei wone,   [dwelt]
This ladi with hire yonge Sone:
And thanne hire handes to the hevene
Sche strawhte, and with a milde stevene   [voice]
Knelende upon hire bare kne
Sche seide, "O hihe mageste,
Which sest the point of every trowthe,   [sees]
1060 Tak of thi wofull womman rowthe   [compassion]
And of this child that I schal kepe."
And with that word sche gan to wepe,
Swounende as ded, and ther sche lay;
Bot he which alle thinges may
Conforteth hire, and ate laste
Sche loketh and hire yhen caste
Upon hire child and seide this:
"Of me no maner charge it is
What sorwe I soffre, bot of thee
1070 Me thenkth it is a gret pite,
For if I sterve thou schalt deie: [die]
So mot I nedes be that weie
For Moderhed and for tendresse
With al myn hole besinesse
Ordeigne me for thilke office,
As sche which schal be thi Norrice."

Thus was sche strengthed forto stonde;
And tho sche tok hire child in honde
And yaf it sowke, and evere among
1080 Sche wepte, and otherwhile song
To rocke with hire child aslepe:
And thus hire oghne child to kepe
Sche hath under the goddes cure.   [care (L *cura*)]
  And so fell upon aventure,   [by chance]
Whan thilke yer hath mad his ende,
Hire Schip, so as it moste wende
Thurgh strengthe of wynd which god
      hath yive,
Estward was into Spaigne drive
Riht faste under a Castell wall,
1090 Wher that an hethen Amirall   [admiral]
Was lord, and he a Stieward hadde,
Oon Theloüs, which al was badde,
A fals knyht and a renegat.
He goth to loke in what astat
The Schip was come, and there he fond
Forth with a child upon hire hond
This lady, wher sche was al one.
He tok good hiede of the persone,
And sih sche was a worthi wiht,   [creature]
1100 And thoghte he wolde upon the nyht
Demene hire at his oghne wille,   [command (OF *demener*,
                                       'drive')

And let hire be therinne stille,
That mo men sih sche noght that dai.
At goddes wille and thus sche lai,
Unknowe what hire schal betide;
And fell so that be nyhtes tide
This knyht withoute felaschipe
Hath tak a bot and cam to Schipe,
And thoghte of hire his lust to take,
1110 And swor, if sche him daunger make,   [resists his desire]

That certeinly sche scholde deie.
Sche sih ther was non other weie,
And seide he scholde hire wel comforte,
That he ferst loke out ate porte,   [but first he should]
That noman were nyh the stede,   [near the place]
Which myhte knowe what thei dede,
And thanne he mai do what he wolde.
He was riht glad that sche so tolde,
And to the porte anon he ferde:
1120 Sche preide god, and he hire herde,
And sodeinliche he was out throwe
And dreynt, and tho began to blowe
A wynd menable fro the lond   [leading]
And thus the myhti goddes hond
Hire hath conveied and defended.
        And whan thre yer be full despended,
Hire Schip was drive upon a dai,
Wher that a gret Navye lay
Of Schipes, al the world at ones:
1130 And as god wolde for the nones,   [this time]
Hire Schip goth in among hem alle,
And stinte noght, er it be falle   [stopped/until it befell]
And hath the vessell undergete,   [come under]
Which Maister was of al the Flete,
Bot there it resteth and abod.
This grete Schip on Anker rod;
The Lord cam forth, and whan he sih
That other ligge abord so nyh,
He wondreth what it myhte be,
1140 And bad men to gon in and se.
This ladi tho was crope aside,   [had crept]
As sche that wolde hireselven hide,
For sche ne wiste what thei were:
Thei soghte aboute and founde hir there
And broghten up hire child and hire;
And therupon this lord to spire   [probe]

Began, fro whenne that sche cam,
And what sche was. Quod sche, "I am
A womman wofully bestad. [situated]
1150 I hadde a lord, and thus he bad,
That I forth with my litel Sone
Upon the wawes scholden wone, [dwell]
Bot why the cause was, I not:
Bot he which alle thinges wot
Yit hath, I thonke him, of his miht
Mi child and me so kept upriht,
That we be save bothe tuo."
This lord hire axeth overmo
How sche believeth, and sche seith,
1160 "I lieve and triste in Cristes feith,
Which deide upon the Rode tree."
"What is thi name?" tho quod he.
"Mi name is Couste," sche him seide:
Bot forthermor for noght he preide
Of hire astat to knowe plein,
Sche wolde him nothing elles sein
Bot of hir name, which sche feigneth;
Alle othre thinges sche restreigneth,
That a word more sche ne tolde.
1170 This lord thanne axeth if sche wolde
With him abide in compaignie,
And seide he cam fro Barbarie
To Romeward, and hom he wente.
Tho sche supposeth what it mente,
And seith sche wolde with him wende
And duelle unto hire lyves ende,
Be so it be to his plesance. [providing he agreed]
And thus upon here aqueintance
He tolde hire pleinly as it stod,
1180 Of Rome how that the gentil blod
In Barbarie was betraied,
And therupon he hath assaied [undertaken]

Be werre, and taken such vengance,
That non of al thilke alliance,
Be whom the tresoun was compassed,
Is from the swerd alyve passed;
Bot of Constance hou it was,
That cowthe he knowe be no cas,
Wher sche becam, so as he seide.　　　　　[what became of her]
1190　　Hire Ere unto his word sche leide,
Bot forther made sche no chiere.　　　　[no open acknowledgment]
And natheles in this matiere
It happeth thilke time so:
This Lord, with whom sche scholde go,
Of Rome was the Senatour,
And of hir fader themperour
His brother doughter hath to wyve,
Which hath hir fader ek alyve,
And was Salustes cleped tho;
1200　This wif Heleine hihte also,
To whom Constance was Cousine.
Thus to the sike a medicine
Hath god ordeined of his grace,
That forthwith in the same place
This Senatour his trowthe plihte,　　　　[pledged]
For evere, whil he live mihte,
To kepe in worschipe and in welthe,
Be so that god wol yive hire helthe,
This ladi, which fortune him sende.
1210　And thus be Schipe forth sailende
Hire and hir child to Rome he broghte,
And to his wif tho he besoghte
To take hire into compaignie:
And sche, which cowthe of courtesie
Al that a good wif scholde konne,
Was inly glad that sche hath wonne
The felaschip of so good on.
Til tuelve yeres were agon,

This Emperoures dowhter Custe
1220 Forth with the dowhter of Saluste
Was kept, bot noman redily
Knew what sche was, and noght forthi
Thei thoghten wel sche hadde be
In hire astat of hih degre,
And every lif hire loveth wel.
      Now herke how thilke unstable whel,
Which evere torneth, wente aboute.
The king Allee, whil he was oute,
As thou tofore hast herd this cas,
1230 Deceived thurgh his Moder was:
Bot whan that he cam hom ayein,
He axeth of his Chamberlein
And of the Bisschop ek also,
Wher thei the qweene hadden do.
And thei answerde, there he bad,
And have him thilke lettre rad,
Which he hem sende for warant,
And tolde him pleinli as it stant,
And sein, it thoghte hem gret pite
1240 To se so worthi on as sche,
With such a child as ther was bore,
So sodeinly to be forlore.   [lost]
He axeth hem what child that were;
And thei him seiden, that naghere,   [nowhere]
In al the world thogh men it soghte,
Was nevere womman that forth broghte
A fairer child than it was on.
And thanne he axede hem anon,
Whi thei ne hadden write so:
1250 Thei tolden, so thei hadden do.
He seide, "Nay." Thei seiden, "Yis."
The lettre schewed rad it is,
Which thei forsoken everidel.
Tho was it understonde wel

That ther is tresoun in the thing:
The Messager tofore the king
Was broght and sodeinliche opposed;
And he, which nothing hath supposed
Bot alle wel, began to seie
1260 That he nagher upon the weie
Abod, bot only in a stede;
And cause why that he so dede
Was, as he wente to and fro,
At Knaresburgh be nyhtes tuo
The kinges Moder made him duelle.
And whan the king it herde telle,
Withinne his herte he wiste als faste
The treson which his Moder caste;
And thoghte he wolde noght abide,
1270 Bot forth riht in the same tide
He tok his hors and rod anon.
With him ther riden manion,
To Knaresburgh and forth thei wente,
And lich the fyr which tunder hente,   [tinder seizes]
In such a rage, as seith the bok,
His Moder sodeinliche he tok
And seide unto hir in this wise:
"O beste of helle, in what juise   [justice (right)]
Hast thou deserved forto deie,
1280 That hast so falsly put aweie
With tresoun of thi bacbitinge
The treweste at my knowlechinge
Of wyves and the most honeste?
Bot I wol make this beheste,   [vow]
I schal be venged er I go."
And let a fyr do make tho,
And bad men forto caste hire inne:
Bot ferst sche tolde out al the sinne,
And dede hem alle forto wite
1290 How sche the lettres hadde write,

Fro point to point as it was wroght. [done]
And tho sche was to dethe broght
And brent tofore hire Sones yhe:
Wherof these othre, whiche it sihe
And herden how the cause stod,
Sein that the juggement is good,
Of that hir Sone hire hath so served;
For sche it hadde wel deserved
Thurgh tresoun of hire false tunge,
1300 Which thurgh the lond was after sunge,
Constance and every wiht compleigneth. [everybody mourns for Constance]

Bot he, whom alle wo distreigneth, [torments]
This sorghfull king, was so bestad, [upset]
That he schal nevermor be glad,
He seith, eftsone forto wedde,
Til that he wiste how that sche spedde,
Which hadde ben his ferste wif:
And thus his yonge unlusti lif
He dryveth forth so as he mai.
1310   Til it befell upon a dai,
Whan he hise werres hadde achieved,
And thoghte he wolde be relieved [restored]
Of Soule hele upon the feith [health/by way of]
Which he hath take, thanne he seith
That he to Rome in pelrinage
Wol go, wher Pope was Pelage,
To take his absolucioun.
And upon this condicioun
He made Edwyn his lieutenant,
1320 Which heir to him was apparant,
That he the lond in his absence
Schal reule: and thus be providence
Of alle thinges wel begon
He tok his leve and forth is gon.
Elda, which tho was with him there,

Er thei fulliche at Rome were,
Was sent tofore to pourveie;
And he his guide upon the weie,
In help to ben his herbergour,
1330 Hath axed who was Senatour,
That he his name myhte kenne.
Of Capadoce, he seide, Arcenne
He hihte, and was a worthi kniht.
To him goth Elda tho forth riht
And tolde him of his lord tidinge,
And preide that for his comynge
He wolde assigne him herbergage;   [lodging]
And he so dede of good corage.
      Whan al is do that was to done,
1340 The king himself cam after sone.
This Senatour, whan that he com,
To Couste and to his wif at hom
Hath told how such a king Allee
Of gret array to the Citee
Was come, and Couste upon his tale,
With herte clos and colour pale
Aswoune fell, and he merveileth
So sodeinly what thing hire eyleth,
And cawhte hire up, and whan sche wok,
1350 Sche syketh with a pitous lok
And feigneth seknesse of the See;
Bot it was for the king Allee,
For joie which fell in hire thoght
That god him hath to toune broght.
This king hath spoke with the Pope
And told al that he cowthe agrope,   [discover]
What grieveth in his conscience;
And thanne he thoghte in reverence
Of his astat, er that he wente,
1360 To make a feste, and thus he sente
Unto the Senatour to come

Upon the morwe and othre some,
To sitte with him at the mete.
This tale hath Couste noght foryete,
Bot to Moris hire Sone tolde
That he upon the morwe scholde
In al that evere he cowthe and mihte
Be present in the kinges sihte,
So that the king him ofte sihe.   [might see]
1370 Moris tofore the kinges yhe
Upon the morwe, wher he sat,
Fulofte stod, and upon that
The king his chiere upon him caste,
And in his face him thoghte als faste
He sih his oghne wif Constance;
For nature as in resemblance
Of face hem liketh so to clothe,
That thei were of a suite bothe.
The king was moeved in his thoght
1380 Of that he seth, and knoweth it noght;
This child he loveth kindely,
And yit he wot no cause why.
Bot wel he sih and understod
That he toward Arcenne stod,
And axeth him anon riht there,
If that this child his Sone were.
He seide, "Yee, so I him calle,
And wolde it were so befalle,
Bot it is al in other wise."
1390   And tho began he to devise
How he the childes Moder fond
Upon the See from every lond
Withinne a Schip was stiereles,
And how this ladi helpeles
Forth with hir child he hath forthdrawe.
The king hath understonde his sawe,
The childes name and axeth tho,

And what the Moder hihte also
That he him wolde telle he preide.
1400 "Moris this child is hote,' he seide,
"His Moder hatte Couste, and this
I not what maner name it is."
But Allee wiste wel ynowh,
Wherof somdiel smylende he lowh;   [laughed]
For Couste in Saxoun is to sein
Constance upon the word Romein.
Bot who that cowthe specefie
What tho fell in his fantasie,
And how his wit aboute renneth
1410 Upon the love in which he brenneth,
It were a wonder forto hiere:
For he was nouther ther ne hiere,
Bot clene out of himself aweie,
That he not what to thenke or seie,
So fain he wolde it were sche.   [eagerly he wished]
Wherof his hertes privete
Began the werre of yee and nay,
The which in such balance lay,
That contenance for a throwe
1420 He loste, til he mihte knowe
The sothe: bot in his memoire
The man which lith in purgatoire
Desireth noght the hevene more,
That he ne longeth al so sore
To wite what him schal betide.
And whan the bordes were aside
And every man was rise aboute,
The king hath weyved al the route,   [dismissed the company]
And with the Senatour al one
1430 He spak and preide him of a bone,   [boon]
To se this Couste, wher sche duelleth
At hom with him, so as he telleth.
The Senatour was wel appaied,

This thing no lengere is delaied,
To se this Couste goth the king;
And sche was warned of the thing,
And with Heleine forth sche cam
Ayein the king, and he tho nam
Good hiede, and whan he sih his wif,
1440 Anon with al his hertes lif
He cawhte hire in his arm and kiste.
Was nevere wiht that sih ne wiste
A man that more joie made,
Wherof thei weren alle glade
Whiche herde tellen of this chance.
    This king tho with his wif Constance,
Which hadde a gret part of his wille,
In Rome for a time stille
Abod and made him wel at ese:
1450 Bot so yit cowthe he nevere plese
His wif, that sche him wolde sein
Of hire astat the trowthe plein,
Of what contre that sche was bore,
Ne what sche was, and yit therfore
With al his wit he hath don sieke.
Thus as they lihe abedde and spieke
Sche preide him and conseileth bothe,
That for the worschipe of hem bothe,
So as hire thoghte it were honeste,
1460 He wolde an honourable feste
Make, er he wente, in the Cite,
Wher themperour himself schal be:
He graunteth al that sche him preide.
Bot as men in that time seide,
This Emperour fro thilke day
That ferst his dowhter wente away
He was thanne after nevere glad;
Bot what that eny man him bad
Of grace for his dowhter sake,

1470 That grace wolde he noght forsake;
And thus ful gret almesse he dede,
Wherof sche hadde many a bede.   [prayer]
      This Emperour out of the toun
Withinne a ten mile enviroun,
Where as it thoghte him for the beste,
Hath sondry places forto reste;
And as fortune wolde tho,
He was duellende at on of tho.
The king Allee forth with thassent
1480 Of Couste his wif hath thider sent
Moris his Sone, as he was taght,
To themperour and he goth straght,
And in his fader half besoghte,
As he which his lordschipe soghte,
That of his hihe worthinesse
He wolde do so gret meknesse,
His oghne toun to come and se,
And yive a time in the cite,
So that his fader mihte him gete
1490 That he wolde ones with him ete.
This lord hath granted his requeste;
And whan the dai was of the feste,
In worschipe of here Emperour
The king and ek the Senatour
Forth with here wyves bothe tuo,
With many a lord and lady mo,
On horse riden him ayein;
Til it befell, upon a plein
Thei sihen wher he was comende.
1500 With that Constance anon preiende
Spak to hir lord that he abyde,
So that sche mai tofore ryde,
To ben upon his bienvenue   [welcoming feast]
The ferste which schal him salue;
And thus after hire lordes graunt

Upon a Mule whyt amblaunt
Forth with a fewe rod this qweene.
Thei wondren what sche wolde mene,
And riden after softe pas;
1510 Bot whan this ladi come was
To themperour, in his presence
Sche seide alowd in audience,
"Mi lord, mi fader, wel you be!
And of this time that I se
Youre honour and your goode hele,
Which is the helpe of my querele,   [complaint]
I thonke unto the goddes myht."
For joie his herte was affliht   [aflutter]
Of that sche tolde in remembrance;
1520 And whanne he wiste it was Constance,
Was nevere fader half so blithe.
Wepende he keste hire ofte sithe,
So was his herte al overcome;
For thogh his Moder were come
Fro deth to lyve out of the grave,
He mihte nomor wonder have
Than he hath whan that he hire sih.
With that hire oghne lord cam nyh
And is to themperour obeied;   [received in obedience]
1530 Bot whan the fortune is bewreied,   [revealed]
How that Constance is come aboute,
So hard an herte was non oute,
That he for pite tho ne wepte.
       Arcennus, which hire fond and kepte,
Was thanne glad of that is falle,
So that with joie among hem alle
Thei riden in at Rome gate.
This Emperour thoghte al to late,
Til that the Pope were come,
1540 And of the lordes sende some
To preie him that he wolde haste:

And he cam forth in alle haste,
And whan that he the tale herde,
How wonderly this chance ferde,
He thonketh god of his miracle,
To whos miht mai be non obstacle:
The king a noble feste hem made,
And thus thei weren alle glade.
A parlement, er that thei wente,
1550 Thei setten unto this entente,
To puten Rome in full espeir   [hope (OF *esperer*)]
That Moris was apparant heir
And scholde abide with hem stille,
For such was al the londes wille.
   Whan every thing was fulli spoke,
Of sorwe and queint was al the smoke,   [stopped]
Tho tok his leve Allee the king,
And with full many a riche thing,
Which themperour him hadde yive,
1560 He goth a glad lif forto live;
For he Constance hath in his hond,
Which was the confort of his lond.
For whan that he cam hom ayein,
Ther is no tunge it mihte sein
What joie was that ilke stounde   [time]
Of that he hath his qweene founde,
Which ferst was sent of goddes sonde,
Whan sche was drive upon the Stronde,
Be whom the misbelieve of Sinne
1570 Was left, and Cristes feith cam inne
To hem that whilom were blinde.
   Bot he which hindreth every kinde
And for no gold mai be forboght,
The deth comende er he be soght,
Tok with this king such aqueintance,
That he with al his retenance
Ne mihte noght defende his lif;

And thus he parteth from his wif,
Which thanne made sorwe ynowh.
1580 And therupon hire herte drowh
To leven Engelond for evere
And go wher that sche hadde levere,   [rather]
To Rome, whenne that sche cam:
And thus of al the lond sche nam
Hir leve, and goth to Rome ayein.
And after that the bokes sein,
She was noght there bot a throwe,   [little while]
Whan deth of kinde hath overthrowe
Hir worthi fader, which men seide
1590 That he betwen hire armes deide.
And afterward the yer suiende   [following]
The god hath mad of hire an ende,
And fro this worldes faierie   [deceits]
Hath take hire into compaignie.
Moris hir Sone was corouned,
Which so ferforth was abandouned
To Cristes feith, that men him calle
Moris the cristeneste of alle.

And thus the wel meninge of love
1600 Was ate laste set above;
And so as thou hast herd tofore,
The false tunges weren lore,   [lost]
Whiche upon love wolden lie.

[As a second example of the mischief which comes from Envy and Backbiting, Genius tells the story of Demetrius and Perseus,[4] two sons of Philip of Macedonia (1604–1861). Demetrius was the elder brother and was deemed the better knight. But Envy burned in the heart of his brother who accused him behind his back of selling out to Rome. King Philip believed Perseus and brought Demetrius to trial. But Perseus bribed the judge so that the guiltless man was condemned and slain. Then Perseus waxed proud and vain and rebelled against his father, whom he declared was incompetent. The king then saw the treachery to which he had been victim, but too late. Now he could do nothing: "The lond was torned up so doun" (1745). He died of sorrow. Then false-tongued Perseus set out to destroy Rome.]

Bot ther mai nothing stonde longe
Which is noght upon trowthe grounded;
For god, which alle thing hath bounded
1755 And sih the falshod of his guile,
Hath set him bot a litel while,
That he schal regne upon depos;
For sodeinliche as he aros
So sodeinliche doun he fell.

[His march was anticipated in Rome, and the Counsel Paul Emilius prepared to defend the city. As Paul was setting out for battle he saw his young daughter weeping. Upon inquiry she said she wept over the death of Perseus, "hir litel hound." The Counsel thought this a good omen, prognosticating success, for he thought that the backbiting Perseus was much like a hound. And, indeed, the daughter proved a prophetess. While Perseus was trying to cross the frozen Danube the ice broke and a great number of his men were drowned. Paul attacked the disordered Macedonians and won the victory. Perseus ended his days in exile disguised as a leather and brass worker in Rome.]

1862 Lo, what profit a man mai finde,
Which hindre wole an other wiht.
Forthi with al thin hole miht,
Mi Sone, eschuie thilke vice.

[Genius next speaks of False-Semblant, Envy's fourth officer. False-Semblant is the well of Deceit. He is always in council with Hypocrisy; they are of one household.]

Of Falssemblant it nedeth noght
To telle of olde ensamples oght;
For al dai in experience
1900 A man mai se thilke evidence
Of faire wordes whiche he hiereth;
Bot yit the barge Envie stiereth
And halt it evere fro the londe,
Wher Falssemblant with Ore on honde
It roweth, and wol noght arive,
Bot let it on the wawes dryve
In gret tempeste and gret debat,
Wherof that love and his astat
Empeireth.

[When his countenance is most clear, False-Semblant's intent is most dark. Flee this vice and let your semblance be clear. Amans is uncertain whether he is guilty here or not. He asks to be questioned further to find out. Genius inquires whether he has ever gained the confidence of a friend to find out secrets which he then might use against the friend in Love's game; or has he thought to advance himself through the disturbance of another? Amans says that he has not done so for the most part although he is not entirely without stain. He has feigned good cheer with his fellows until he knows their intentions, and he has been deceitful, if what he learns touches on his Lady.]

And if so be myn herte soucheth   [suspicious]
1970 That oght unto my ladi toucheth   [whatever/pertains]
Of love that he wol me telle,
Anon I renne unto the welle
And caste water in the fyr,
So that his carte amidd the Myr,
Be that I have his conseil knowe,
Fulofte sithe I overthrowe,
Whan that he weneth best to stonde.
Bot this I do you understonde,

If that a man love elles where,
1980 So that my ladi be noght there,
And he me telle, I wole it hide,
Ther schal no word ascape aside,
For with deceipte of no semblant
To him breke I no covenant.

[He behaves in this way for two reasons. First, to excuse his
Lady if they speak ill of her, and second, to know who her
lovers are. But he is never deceitful if their confidence has noth-
ing to do with his Lady. What is his punishment to be? Genius
says it is best to avoid all disguises. False-Semblant is most com-
mon among those whom we call Lombards, who dwell among
us using their cunning to cheat us of the profits of our own land.
They know a craft called *Fa crere* (make believe), so subtle that
no door can protect one against them. Thereby they get the best
goods of the land. Having been forewarned of them we must be
all the more wary. Thus hear the story of Deianira and Nessus.[5]]

TALE OF DEIANIRA AND NESSUS

☘ Of Falssemblant which is believed
Ful many a worthi wiht is grieved,
And was long time er we wer bore.
To thee, my Sone, I wol therfore
A tale telle of Falssemblant,
2150 Which falseth many a covenant,
And many a fraude of fals conseil
Ther ben hangende upon his Seil:
And that aboghten gulteles
Bothe Deianire and Hercules,
The whiche in gret desese felle
Thurgh Falssemblant, as I schal telle.
Whan Hercules withinne a throwe   [short time]
Al only hath his herte throwe   [cast]
Upon this faire Deianire,

2160 It fell him on a dai desire,
Upon a Rivere as he stod,
That passe he wolde over the flod
Withoute bot, and with him lede
His love, bot he was in drede
For tendresce of that swete wiht,
For he knew noght the forde ariht.
Ther was a Geant thanne nyh,
Which Nessus hihte, and whanne he sih
This Hercules and Deianyre,
2170 Withinne his herte he gan conspire,
As he which thurgh his tricherie
Hath Hercules in gret envie,
Which he bar in his herte loke,
And thanne he thoghte it schal be wroke.   [satisfied]
Bot he ne dorste natheles
Ayein this worthi Hercules
Falle in debat as forto feihte;
Bot feigneth Semblant al be sleihte
Of frendschipe and of alle goode,
2180 And comth where as thei bothe stode,
And makth hem al the chiere he can,
And seith that as here oghne man
He is al redy forto do
What thing he mai; and it fell so
That thei upon his Semblant triste,   [trusted]
And axen him if that he wiste
What thing hem were best to done,
So that thei mihten sauf and sone
The water passe, he and sche.
2190 And whan Nessus the privete   [secret]
Knew of here herte what it mente,
As he that was of double entente,
He made hem riht a glad visage;
And whanne he herde of the passage
Of him and hire, he thoghte guile,

And feigneth Semblant for a while
To don hem plesance and servise,
Bot he thoghte al an other wise.
This Nessus with hise wordes slyhe
2200 Yaf such conseil tofore here yhe
Which semeth outward profitable
And was withinne deceivable.
He bad hem of the Stremes depe
That thei be war and take kepe,
So as thei knowe noght the pas;
Bot forto helpe in such a cas,
He seith himself that for here ese
He wolde, if that it mihte hem plese,
The passage of the water take,
2210 And for this ladi undertake
To bere unto that other stronde
And sauf to sette hire up alonde,
And Hercules may thanne also
The weie knowe how he schal go:
And herto thei acorden alle.
Bot what as after schal befalle,
Wel payd was Hercules of this,   [pleased]
And this Geant also glad is,
And tok this ladi up alofte
2220 And set hire on his schuldre softe,
And in the flod began to wade,
As he which no grucchinge made,   [complaining]
And bar hire over sauf and sound.
Bot whanne he stod on dreie ground
And Hercules was fer behinde,
He sette his trowthe al out of mynde,
Who so therof be lief or loth,   [happy/sad]
With Deianyre and forth he goth,
As he that thoghte to dissevere
2230 The compaignie of hem for evere.
Whan Hercules therof tok hiede,

Als faste as evere he mihte him spiede
He hyeth after in a throwe;
And hapneth that he hadde a bowe,
The which in alle haste he bende,
As he that wolde an Arwe sende,
Which he tofore hadde envenimed.
He hath so wel his schote timed,
That he him thurgh the bodi smette,
2240 And thus the false wiht he lette.   [halted]
    Bot lest now such a felonie:
Whan Nessus wiste he scholde die,
He tok to Deianyre his scherte,   [gave]
Which with the blod was of his herte
Thurghout desteigned overal,
And tolde how sche it kepe schal
Al prively to this entente,
That if hire lord his herte wente
To love in eny other place,
2250 The scherte, he seith, hath such a grace,
That if sche mai so mochel make
That he the scherte upon him take,
He schal alle othre lete in vein   [leave]
And torne unto hire love ayein.
Who was tho glad bot Deianyre?
Hire thoghte hire herte was afyre
Til it was in hire cofre loke,
So that no word therof was spoke.
    The daies gon, the yeres passe,
2260 The hertes waxen lasse and lasse
Of hem that ben to love untrewe:
This Hercules with herte newe
His love hath set on Eolen,
And therof spieken alle men.
This Eolen, this faire maide,
Was, as men thilke time saide,
The kinges dowhter of Eurice;

And sche made Hercules so nyce [foolish]
Upon hire Love and so assote, [befuddled]
2270 That he him clotheth in hire cote,
And sche in his was clothed ofte;
And thus fieblesce is set alofte,
And strengthe was put under fote,
Ther can noman therof do bote. [remedy]
Whan Deianyre hath herd this speche,
Ther was no sorwe forto seche:
Of other helpe wot sche non,
Bot goth unto hire cofre anon;
With wepende yhe and woful herte
2280 Sche tok out thilke unhappi scherte,
As sche that wende wel to do,
And broghte hire werk aboute so
That Hercules this scherte on dede, [put on]
To such entente as she was bede
Of Nessus, so as I seide er.
Bot therof was sche noght the ner,
As no fortune may be weyved; [avoided]
With Falssemblant sche was deceived,
That whan sche wende best have wonne,
2290 Sche lost al that sche hath begonne.
For thilke scherte unto the bon
His body sette afyre anon,
And cleveth so, it mai noght twinne, [taken off]
For the venym that was therinne.
And he thanne as a wilde man
Unto the hihe wode he ran,
And as the Clerk Ovide telleth,
The grete tres to grounde he felleth
With strengthe al of his oghne myght,
2300 And made an huge fyr upriht,
And lepte himself therinne at ones
And brende him bothe fleissh and bones.
Which thing cam al thurgh Falssemblant,

That false Nessus the Geant
Made unto him and to his wif;
Wherof that he hath lost his lif,
And sche sori for everemo.
    Forthi, my Sone, er thee be wo,
I rede, be wel war therfore;
2310 For whan so gret a man was lore,
It oghte yive a gret conceipte
To warne alle othre of such deceipte.
    Grant mercy, fader, I am war
So fer that I nomore dar
Of Falssemblant take aqueintance;
Bot rathere I wol do penance
That I have feigned chiere er this.

[Genius next tells Amans of the fifth kind of Envy, this called
Supplantation. Most of all the supplanter's heart is set upon
great offices or benefices. Often he exchanges chalk for cheese,
whereby others lose while he gains profit. He follows Fortune's
wheel to trade his woe for another man's weal. He takes the
bird to market while others beat the bushes (2318–2356). There
are supplanters in love, too, who claim other men's rights. Have
you, my son, been of such profession? Amans does not think so,
though that hardly clears his conscience. Only lack of might, not
intent, has kept him from such Supplantation. Yet even if he
had the strength of Alexander he would be fearful of slander.
He would rather die than risk his reputation. He would use
Supplantation to secure his love only if he found a foolproof
way. If this is sin, he concludes, what should his redress be?
(2357–2428).

Genius advises that he would be more fearful of this sin if
he realized that God sees man's thoughts. And if he knew what
it is to be a supplanter he would be doubly wary. Remember the
fate of Agamemnon who supplanted Achilles's love, Breseida; or
Criseyde, who supplanted Troilus with Diomedes (2429–2458).
Consider, moreover, the story of Geta and Amphitrion.[6] Almena

loved Geta, but Amphitrion disguised his voice as Geta's and made his way to her bedroom. She let him in and welcomed him to her warm bed. Thus he supplanted Geta's love, leaving him like a ship without rudder (2459–2495). Consider also the Tale of the False Bachelor.[7] Before the time that Rome was a Christian city, there lived an emperor who ruled his realm in peace. His chivalrous son grew restless, however, and desiring to be a warrior beseeched his father to let him ride into strange lands in search of adventure. The emperor refused him permission. So the venturesome prince took as his squire a knight whom he trusted, and under disguise they slipped away by sea to join the Sultan of Persia in his war against the Caliphe of Egypt. The emperor's son won great glory in the war and thus the admiration of the sultan. The sultan had a beautiful daughter who was his heir and ripe for marriage. For love of her the prince fought like a lion. As Fortune would have it, the sultan and the caliphe agreed to end the war with one great battle to the death. Prior to the battle the sultan took a gold ring from his daughter and told her that if he should be killed she should marry the man to whom he gave the ring. In battle the Roman prince above all deserved the prize. All Egypt fled in his presence. Persia followed in pursuit, until, by chance, an arrow struck the sultan, who was borne to his tent. Before he died he gave his daughter's ring to the prince and told him what it meant. After the sultan's burial a parliament was called to determine the new emperor. In anticipation the prince confided his good news about the ring to the squire. But that night the squire stole the ring and went to court where the sultan's daughter had announced her father's promise. The false bachelor presented the ring and, despite protest, soon was married and crowned lord of the land. The deceived prince was stricken with deadly sorrow. On his deathbed, he called the worthiest of the land to him and revealed his true identity. He sent a letter of reconciliation to his father, the Emperor of Rome; then, after a farewell to his lady sweet, he died. The false steward was arrested. But because he was the crowned king they could not execute him by Persian law. Instead, they returned him to the Romans who soon dispatched justice (2496–2781).

Genius warns the Lover to heed the evils of Supplantation so that he might never be found guilty. For when Pride and Envy join, no man profits. Consider further an example of Supplantation within the Holy Church.[8] When Pope Nicholas died, the conclave of cardinals assembled to elect Celestin, a virtuous recluse, to be his successor. But one cardinal's envy burned like Etna in his heart, engendering treachery. He bribed a clerk to visit Celestin at night while he slept. From behind a wall the clerk spoke through a brass trumpet, advising Celestin thrice over to give up the papacy. The new pope, full of innocence, conceived in his conscience that it was God's will that he should resign. So the next day he went to the consistory to find out if the pope could quit, but no one knew. Then the treacherous cardinal spoke up to point out that the pope ordained what laws he chose and that he could declare his own right to resign. The resignation took place and soon the insidious cardinal was named pope in Celestin's place. He was called Pope Boniface. Unable to hide his treachery, Boniface now openly boasted about how he won the papacy. In his pride he quarreled with King Louis of France from whom he demanded personal homage. Louis refused and the pope sentenced him with cursing and interdict. In response the King sent William of Langharet who captured the pope near Avignon:]

> Lo, thus the Supplantour was served;
> For thei him ladden into France
> And setten him to his penance
> Withinne a tour in harde bondes,
> Wher he for hunger bothe hise hondes
> Eet of and deide, god wot how:
> 3030 Of whom the wrytinge is yit now
> Registred, as a man mai hiere,
> Which spekth and seith in this manere:
> Thin entre lich the fox was slyh,
> Thi regne also with pride on hih

Was lich the Leon in his rage;
Bot ate laste of thi passage
Thi deth was to the houndes like.

[Such was the letter that was proclaimed in Rome. Take heed;
keep Simon from the fold. Joachim the Abbot forwarned us that
mercenary chapmen would buy and sell many with their fraud
and supplantation. To prefer envy, men defer their consciences.
Envy moved Joab to slay Abner treacherously and caused
Achitophel to hang himself when his counsel was not prefered
at court.[9]]

    Senec witnesseth openly
How that Envie proprely
Is of the Court the comun wenche,
And halt taverne forto schenche   [pour out]
That drink which makth the herte
    brenne,
3100 And doth the wit aboute renne,
Be every weie to compasse
How that he mihte alle othre passe,
As he which thurgh unkindeschipe
Envieth every felaschipe.

[There is no vice as abominable toward God or unprofitable for
man as Envy. It is of no value in love. Amans agrees that
Envy is a vice to be eschewed, but wonders how he can avoid it.
Genius informs him that Charity, the Mother of Pity, is the best
remedy against Envy and tells him the Tale of Constantine and
Sylvester.[10]]

TALE OF CONSTANTINE
AND SYLVESTER

Among the bokes of latin
I finde write of Constantin

The worthi Emperour of Rome,
3190 Suche infortunes to him come,
Whan he was in his lusti age,
The lepre cawhte in his visage [leprosy]
And so forth overal aboute,
That he ne mihte ryden oute:
So lefte he bothe Schield and spere,
As he that mihte him noght bestere, [go out]
And hield him in his chambre clos.
Thurgh al the world the fame aros,
The grete clerkes ben asent
3200 And come at his comandement
To trete upon this lordes hele. [health]
So longe thei togedre dele, [consult]
That thei upon this medicine
Apointen hem, and determine
That in the maner as it stod
Thei wolde him bathe in childes blod
Withinne sevene wynter age:
For, as thei sein, that scholde assuage
The lepre and al the violence,
3210 Which that thei knewe of Accidence
And noght be weie of kinde is falle.
And therto thei acorden alle
As for final conclusioun,
And tolden here opinioun
To themperour: and he anon
His conseil tok, and therupon
With lettres and with seales oute
Thei sende in every lond aboute
The yonge children forto seche,
3220 Whos blod, thei seiden, schal be leche [remedy]
For themperoures maladie.
Ther was ynowh to wepe and crie
Among the Modres, whan thei herde
Hou wofully this cause ferde,

Bot natheles thei moten bowe;
And thus wommen ther come ynowhe
With children soukende on the Tete.
Tho was ther manye teres lete,
Bot were hem lieve or were hem lothe,
3230 The wommen and the children bothe
Into the Paleis forth be broght
With many a sory hertes thoght
Of hem whiche of here bodi bore
The children hadde, and so forlore
Withinne a while scholden se.
The Modres wepe in here degre,
And manye of hem aswoune falle,
The yonge babes criden alle:
This noyse aros, the lord it herde,
3240 And loked out, and how it ferde
He sih, and as who seith abreide   [started]
Out of his slep, and thus he seide:
    "O thou divine pourveance,
Which every man in the balance
Of kinde hast formed to be liche,
The povere is bore as is the riche
And deieth in the same wise,
Upon the fol, upon the wise
Siknesse and hele entrecomune;
3250 Mai non eschuie that fortune
Which kinde hath in hire lawe set;
Hire strengthe and beaute ben beset
To every man aliche fre,
That sche preferreth no degre
As in the disposicioun
Of bodili complexioun:
And ek of Soule resonable
The povere child is bore als able
To vertu as the kinges Sone;
3260 For every man his oghne wone   [in his own manner]

After the lust of his assay
The vice or vertu chese may.
Thus stonden alle men franchised,
Bot in astat thei ben divised;
To some worschipe and richesse,
To some poverte and distresse,
On lordeth and an other serveth;
Bot yit as every man deserveth
The world yifth noght his yiftes hiere.
3270 Bot certes he hath gret matiere
To ben of good condicioun,
Which hath in his subjeccioun
The men that ben of his semblance."
And ek he tok a remembrance
How he that made lawe of kinde
Wolde every man to lawe binde,
And bad a man, such as he wolde
Toward himself, riht such he scholde
Toward an other don also.
3280 And thus this worthi lord as tho
Sette in balance his oghne astat
And with himself stod in debat,
And thoghte hou that it was noght good
To se so mochel mannes blod
Be spilt for cause of him alone.
He sih also the grete mone,
Of that the Modres were unglade,
And of the wo the children made,
Wherof that al his herte tendreth,
3290 And such pite withinne engendreth,
That him was levere forto chese   [rather/choose]
His oghne bodi forto lese,
Than se so gret a moerdre wroght
Upon the blod which gulteth noght.   [was not guilty]
Thus for the pite which he tok
Alle othre leches he forsok,   [doctors]

And put him out of aventure
Al only into goddes cure;
And seith, "Who that woll maister be,
3300 He mot be servant to pite."
So ferforth he was overcome
With charite, that he hath nome   [taken]
His conseil and hise officers,
And bad unto hise tresorers
That thei his tresour al aboute
Departe among that povere route
Of wommen and of children bothe,
Wherof thei mihte hem fede and clothe
And saufli tornen hom ayein
3310 Withoute lost of eny grein.
Thurgh charite thus he despendeth
His good, wherof that he amendeth
The povere poeple, and contrevaileth
The harm, that he hem so travaileth:
And thus the woful nyhtes sorwe
To joie is torned on the morwe;
Al was thonkinge, al was blessinge,
Which erst was wepinge and cursinge;
Thes wommen gon hom glade ynowh,
3320 Echon for joie on other lowh,   [laughed]
And preiden for this lordes hele,
Which hath relessed the querele,
And hath his oghne will forsake
In charite for goddes sake.

    Bot now hierafter thou schalt hiere
What god hath wroght in this matiere,
As he which doth al equite.
To him that wroghte charite
He was ayeinward charitous,
3330 And to pite he was pitous:
For it was nevere knowe yit
That charite goth unaquit.

The nyht, whan he was leid to slepe,
The hihe god, which wolde him kepe,
Seint Peter and seint Poul him sende,
Be whom he wolde his lepre amende.
Thei tuo to him slepende appiere
Fro god, and seide in this manere:
"O Constantin, for thou hast served
3340 Pite, thou hast pite deserved:
Forthi thou schalt such pite have
That god thurgh pite woll thee save.
So schalt thou double hele finde,
Ferst for this bodiliche kinde,
And for this wofull Soule also,
Thou schalt ben hol of bothe tuo.
And for thou schalt thee noght despeire,
Thi lepre schal nomore empeire
Til thou wolt sende therupon
3350 Unto the Mont of Celion,
Wher that Silvestre and his clergie
Togedre duelle in compaignie
For drede of thee, which many day
Hast ben a fo to Cristes lay,
And hast destruid to mochel schame
The prechours of his holy name.
Bot now thou hast somdiel appesed
Thi god, and with good dede plesed,
That thou thi pite hast bewared   [employed]
3360 Upon the blod which thou hast spared.
Forthi to thi salvacion
Thou schalt have enformacioun,
Such as Silvestre schal the teche:
The nedeth of non other leche."
    This Emperour, which al this herde,
"Grant merci lordes," he ansuerde,
"I wol do so as ye me seie.
Bot of o thing I wolde preie:

What schal I telle unto Silvestre
3370 Or of youre name or of youre estre?"   [abode]
And thei him tolden what thei hihte,
And forth withal out of his sihte
Thei passen up into the hevene.
And he awok out of his swevene,
And clepeth, and men come anon:
He tolde his drem, and therupon
In such a wise as he hem telleth
The Mont wher that Silvestre duelleth
Thei have in alle haste soght,
3380 And founde he was and with hem broght
To themperour, which to him tolde
His swevene and elles what he wolde.
And whan Silvestre hath herd the king,
He was riht joiful of this thing,
And him began with al his wit
To techen upon holi writ
Ferst how mankinde was forlore,   [lost]
And how the hihe god therfore
His Sone sende from above,
3390 Which bore was for mannes love,
And after of his oghne chois
He tok his deth upon the crois;
And how in grave he was beloke,   [shut up]
And how that he hath helle broke
And tok hem out that were him lieve;   [who believed in him]
And forto make ous full believe
That he was verrai goddes Sone,
Ayein the kinde of mannes wone   [custom]
Fro dethe he ros the thridde day,
3400 And whanne he wolde, as he wel may,
He styh up to his fader evene   [ascended]
With fleissh and blod into the hevene;
And riht so in the same forme
In fleissh and blod he schal reforme,

Whan time comth, the qwike and dede
At thilke woful dai of drede,
Where every man schal take his dom, [judgment]
Als wel the Maister as the grom.
The mihti kinges retenue
3410 That dai may stonde of no value
With worldes strengthe to defende;
For every man mot thanne entende
To stonde upon his oghne dedes
And leve alle othre mennes nedes.
That dai mai no consail availe,
The pledour and the plee schal faile,
The sentence of that ilke day
Mai non appell sette in delay;
Ther mai no gold the Jugge plie,
3420 That he ne schal the sothe trie
And setten every man upriht,
Als wel the plowman as the kniht:
The lewed man, the grete clerk
Schal stonde upon his oghne werk,
And such as he is founde tho,
Such schal he be for everemo.
Ther mai no peine be relessed,
Ther mai no joie ben encressed,
Bot endeles, as thei have do,
3430 He schal receive on of the tuo.
And thus Silvestre with his sawe [saying]
The ground of al the newe lawe
With gret devocion he precheth,
Fro point to point and pleinly techeth
Unto this hethen Emperour;
And seith, the hihe creatour
Hath underfonge his charite, [undertaken]
Of that he wroghte such pite,
Whan he the children hadde on honde.
3440 Thus whan this lord hath understonde

Of al this thing how that it ferde,
Unto Silvestre he thanne ansuerde,
With al his hole herte and seith
That he is redi to the feith.
And so the vessel which for blod
Was mad, Silvestre, ther it stod,
With clene water of the welle
In alle haste he let do felle, [caused to be filled]
And sette Constantin therinne
3450 Al naked up unto the chinne.
And in the while it was begunne,
A liht, as thogh it were a Sunne,
Fro hevene into the place com
Wher that he tok his cristendom;
And evere among the holi tales [reckoning]
Lich as thei weren fisshes skales
Ther fellen from him now and eft,
Til that ther was nothing beleft
Of al his grete maladie.
3460 For he that wolde him purefie,
The hihe god hath mad him clene,
So that ther lefte nothing sene;
He hath him clensed bothe tuo,
The bodi and the Soule also.
      Tho knew this Emperour in dede
That Cristes feith was forto drede,
And sende anon hise lettres oute
And let do crien al aboute,
Up peine of deth noman weyve [refuse]
3470 That he baptesme ne receive:
After his Moder qweene Heleine
He sende, and so betwen hem tweine
Thei treten, that the Cite all
Was cristned, and sche forth withall.
This Emperour, which hele hath founde,
Withinne Rome anon let founde

Tuo cherches, whiche he dede make
For Peter and for Poules sake,
Of whom he hadde avisioun;
3480 And yaf therto possessioun
Of lordschipe and worldes good.
Bot how so that his will was good   [but even though]
Toward the Pope and his Franchise,
Yit hath it proved other wise,
To se the worchinge of the dede:
For in Cronique this I rede;
Anon as he hath mad the yifte,
A vois was herd on hih the lifte,   [in the air on high]
Of which al Rome was adrad,
3490 And seith: "To day is venym schad
In holi cherche of temporal,
Which medleth with the spirital."
And hou it stant of that degree
Yit mai a man the sothe se:
God mai amende it, whan he wile,
I can ther to non other skile.

    Bot forto go ther I began,
How charite mai helpe a man
To bothe worldes, I have seid:
3500 And if thou have an Ere leid,
Mi Sone, thou miht understonde,
If charite be take on honde,
Ther folweth after mochel grace.
Forthi, if that thou wolt pourchace
How that thou miht Envie flee,
Aqueinte thee with charite,
Which is the vertu sovereine.

    Mi fader, I schal do my peine:
For this ensample which ye tolde
3510 With al myn herte I have withholde,
So that I schal for everemore
Eschuie Envie wel the more:

And that I have er this misdo,
Yif me my penance er I go.
And over that to mi matiere
Of schrifte, why we sitten hiere
In privete betwen ous tweie,
Now axeth what ther is, I preie.
  Mi goode Sone, and for thi lore   [education]
3520 I woll thee telle what is more,
So that thou schalt the vices knowe:
For whan thei be to thee full knowe,
Thou miht hem wel the betre eschuie.
And for this cause I thenke suie
The forme bothe and the matiere,
As now suiende thou schalt hiere
Which vice stant next after this:
And whan thou wost how that it is,
As thou schalt hiere me devise,
3530 Thow miht thiself the betre avise.

Explicit Liber Secundus

INCIPIT LIBER TERCIUS

[Wrath is the next sin, a particular enemy to Patience. Wrath has five servants to help him strive:]

The ferst of hem Malencolie
Is cleped, which in compaignie
An hundred times in an houre
30   Wol as an angri beste loure,   [scowl]
And noman wot the cause why.

[Amans admits to guilt here. Often he is inwardly angry at the successes of other men and at his own lost opportunities. He spends his waking hours dreaming of meeting his Lady and praying for some good answer to his suit. But also he dreams of her refusal. Then, as her "nay" sounds a thousand times in his ears, his wrath grows, and he loses his wits. He reckons the years he has wasted on her. Yet, when she refuses to see him, he falls into such a fit of melancholy that all his servants suffer until it passes. But, when he sees her again and she speaks sweetly to him, he could not be angry for all the gold in Rome. Nevertheless, when she afterward ignores or scorns him, his rage returns as before.]

And thus myn hand ayein the pricke
I hurte and have do many day,
And go so forth as I go may,
Fulofte bitinge on my lippe,
120   And make unto miself a whippe,
With which in many a chele and hete   [chill]
Mi wofull herte is so tobete,
That all my wittes ben unsofte

And I am wroth, I not how ofte;
125 And al it is Malencolie,
Which groweth of the fantasie
Of love, that me wol noght loute: [will not yield to me]
So bere I forth an angri snoute
Ful manye times in a yer.

[Genius offers the story of Canace and Machaire as an example which may help him to understand in sober moments the folly of such behavior.[1]]

TALE OF CANACE AND MACHAIRE

   ❧ Ther was a king which Eolus
Was hote, and it befell him thus,
That he tuo children hadde faire,
The Sone cleped was Machaire,
The dowhter ek Canace hihte.
Be daie bothe and ek be nyhte,
Whil thei be yonge, of comun wone   [custom]
150 In chambre thei togedre wone,   [dwell]
And as thei scholden pleide hem ofte,
Til thei be growen up alofte
Into the youthe of lusti age,
Whan kinde assaileth the corage
With love and doth him forto bowe,
That he no reson can allowe,
Bot halt the lawes of nature:
For whom that love hath under cure,
As he is blind himself, riht so
160 He makth his client blind also.
In such manere as I you telle
As thei al day togedre duelle,
This brother mihte it noght asterte   [escape]
That he with al his hole herte
His love upon his Soster caste:

And so it fell hem ate laste,
That this Machaire with Canace
Whan thei were in a prive place,
Cupide bad hem ferst to kesse,
170 And after sche which is Maistresse
In kinde and techeth every lif
Withoute lawe positif,[2]
Of which sche takth nomaner charge,
Bot kepth hire lawes al at large,
Nature, tok hem into lore   [learning]
And tawht hem so, that overmore
Sche hath hem in such wise daunted,
That thei were, as who seith, enchaunted.
And as the blinde an other ledeth
180 And til thei falle nothing dredeth,
Riht so thei hadde non insihte;
Bot as the bridd which wole alihte
And seth the mete and noght the net,
Which in deceipte of him is set,
This yonge folk no peril sihe,
Bot that was likinge in here yhe,
So that thei felle upon the chance
Where witt hath lore his remembrance.   [lost]
So longe thei togedre assemble,
190 The wombe aros, and sche gan tremble,
And hield hire in hire chambre clos
For drede it scholde be disclos
And come to hire fader Ere:
Wherof the Sone hadde also fere,
And feigneth cause forto ryde;
For longe dorste he noght abyde,
In aunter if men wolde sein   [on the chance that]
That he his Soster hath forlein:
For yit sche hadde it noght beknowe
200 Whos was the child at thilke throwe.
Machaire goth, Canace abit,   [stays]

The which was noght delivered yit,
Bot riht sone after that sche was.
      Now lest and herkne a woful cas.
The sothe, which mai noght ben hid,
Was ate laste knowe and kid   [known and conveyed]
Unto the king, how that it stod.
And whan that he it understod,
Anon into Malencolie,
210 As thogh it were a frenesie,
He fell, as he which nothing cowthe
How maistrefull love is in yowthe:
And for he was to love strange,
He wolde noght his herte change
To be benigne and favorable
To love, bot unmerciable
Betwen the wawe of wod and wroth   [wave/madness/anger]
Into his dowhtres chambre he goth,
And sih the child was late bore,
220 Wherof he hath hise othes swore
That sche it schal ful sore abye.
And sche began merci to crie,
Upon hire bare knes and preide,
And to hire fader thus sche seide:
"Ha mercy! fader, thenk I am
Thi child, and of thi blod I cam.
That I misdede yowthe it made,
And in the flodes bad me wade,
Wher that I sih no peril tho:
230 Bot now it is befalle so,
Merci, my fader, do no wreche!"   [vengeance]
And with that word sche loste speche
And fell doun swounende at his fot,
As sche for sorwe nedes mot.   [must]
Bot his horrible crualte
Ther mihte attempre no pite:
Out of hire chambre forth he wente

Al full of wraththe in his entente,
And tok the conseil in his herte
240 That sche schal noght the deth asterte,
As he which Malencolien
Of pacience hath no lien, [bond]
Wherof his wraththe he mai restreigne.
And in this wilde wode peine,
Whanne al his resoun was untame,
A kniht he clepeth be his name,
And tok him as be weie of sonde [messenger]
A naked swerd to bere on honde,
And seide him that he scholde go
250 And telle unto his dowhter so
In the manere as he him bad,
How sche that scharpe swerdes blad
Receive scholde and do withal
So as sche wot wherto it schal.
Forth in message goth this kniht
Unto this wofull yonge wiht,
This scharpe swerd to hire he tok:
Wherof that al hire bodi qwok,
For wel sche wiste what it mente,
260 And that it was to thilke entente
That sche hireselven scholde slee.
And to the kniht sche seide: "Yee,
Now that I wot my fadres wille,
That I schal in this wise spille, [perish]
I wole obeie me therto,
And as he wole it schal be do.
Bot now this thing mai be non other,
I wole a lettre unto mi brother,
So as my fieble hand may wryte,
270 With al my wofull herte endite."
Sche tok a Penne on honde tho,
Fro point to point and al the wo,
Als ferforth as hireself it wot,

Unto hire dedly frend sche wrot,
And tolde how that hire fader grace
Sche mihte for nothing pourchace;
And overthat, as thou schalt hiere,
Sche wrot and seide in this manere:
"O thou my sorwe and my gladnesse,
280 O thou myn hele and my siknesse,
O my wanhope and al my trust,   [despair]
O my desese and al my lust,
O thou my wele, o thou my wo,
O thou my frend, o thou my fo,
O thou my love, o thou myn hate,
For thee mot I be ded algate.
Thilke ende may I noght asterte,
And yit with al myn hole herte,
Whil that me lasteth eny breth,
290 I wol the love into my deth,
Bot of o thing I schal thee preie,
If that my litel Sone deie,
Let him be beried in my grave
Beside me, so schalt thou have
Upon ous bothe remembrance.
For thus it stant of my grevance;
Now at this time, as thou schalt wite,
With teres and with enke write
This lettre I have in cares colde:
300 In my riht hond my Penne I holde,
And in my left the swerd I kepe,
And in my barm ther lith to wepe   [lap]
Thi child and myn, which sobbeth faste.
Now am I come unto my laste:
Fare wel, for I schal sone deie,
And thenk how I thi love abeie."
The pomel of the swerd to grounde
Sche sette, and with the point a wounde
Thurghout hire herte anon sche made,

310   And forth with that al pale and fade
      Sche fell doun ded fro ther sche stod.
      The child lay bathende in hire blod
      Out rolled fro the moder barm,
      And for the blod was hot and warm,
      He basketh him aboute thrinne.   [therein]
      Ther was no bote forto winne,   [reward]
      For he, which can no pite knowe,
      The king cam in the same throwe,   [instant]
      And sih how that his dowhter dieth
320   And how this Babe al blody crieth;
      Bot al that mihte him noght suffise,
      That he ne bad to do juise   [justice]
      Upon the child, and bere him oute,
      And seche in the Forest aboute
      Som wilde place, what it were,
      To caste him out of honde there,
      So that som beste him mai devoure,
      Where as noman him schal socoure.
      Al that he bad was don in dede:
330   Ha, who herde evere singe or rede
      Of such a thing as that was do?
      Bot he which ladde his wraththe so
      Hath knowe of love bot a lite
      Bot for al that he was to wyte,   [to be blamed]
      Thurgh his sodein Malencolie
      To do so gret a felonie.
          Forthi, my Sone, how so it stonde,
      Be this cas thou miht understonde
      That if thou evere in cause of love
340   Schalt deme, and thou be so above   [judge]
      That thou miht lede it at thi wille,
      Let nevere thurgh thi Wraththe spille   [destroy]
      Which every kinde scholde save.
      For it sit every man to have
      Reward to love and to his miht,

Ayein whos strengthe mai no wiht:
And siththe an herte is so constreigned,
The reddour oghte be restreigned   [harshness]
To him that mai no bet aweie,
350 Whan he mot to nature obeie.
For it is seid thus overal,
That nedes mot that nede schal
Of that a lif doth after kinde,
Wherof he mai no bote finde.
What nature hath set in hir lawe
Ther mai no mannes miht withdrawe,
And who that worcheth therayein,
Fulofte time it hath be sein,
Ther hath befalle gret vengance,
360 Wherof I finde a remembrance.

TIRESIAS AND THE SNAKES

杩 Ovide after the time tho
Tolde an ensample and seide so,
How that whilom Tiresias,[3]
As he walkende goth per cas,
Upon an hih Montaine he sih
Tuo Serpentz in his weie nyh,   [nearby]
And thei, so as nature hem tawhte,
Assembled were, and he tho cawhte
A yerde which he bar on honde,   [stick]
370 And thoghte that he wolde fonde   [try]
To letten hem, and smot hem bothe: [separate]
Wherof the goddes weren wrothe;
And for he hath destourbed kinde
And was so to nature unkinde,
Unkindeliche he was transformed,
That he which erst a man was formed
Into a womman was forschape.
That was to him an angri jape;

Bot for that he with Angre wroghte,
380 Hise Angres angreliche he boghte.

[Thus Ovid writes so that we might know by reason that man is
more than a beast, that he must appreciate nature and let every
creature love as it should. Amans agrees to let every man love as
he chooses, providing it be not his Lady, for then, regardless, he
would be angry (381–416).

Upon request Genius tells Amans about Cheste (chiding),
the second servant to Wrath. Cheste is the most unbecoming
creature who ever broke up love (417–423).]

For he berth evere his mowth unpinned,
So that his lippes ben unloke
And his corage is al tobroke,
That every thing which he can telle,
It springeth up as doth a welle,
Which mai non of his stremes hyde,
430 Bot renneth out on every syde.
So buillen up the foule sawes   [boil/sayings]
That Cheste wot of his felawes:
For as a Sive kepeth Ale,
Riht so can Cheste kepe a tale;
Al that he wot he wol desclose,
And speke er eny man oppose.   [inquire]
As a Cite withoute wal,
Wher men mai gon out overal
Withouten eny resistence,
440 So with his croked eloquence
He spekth al that he wot withinne:
Wherof men lese mor than winne,
For ofte time of his chidinge
He bringth to house such tidinge,
That makth werre ate beddeshed.   [bed's head]
He is the levein of the bred,
Which soureth al the past aboute: [dough]

Men oghte wel such on to doute,   [such a person]
For evere his bowe is redi bent,
450 And whom he hit I telle him schent,   [call/ruined]
If he mai perce him with his tunge.
And ek so lowde his belle is runge,
That of the noise and of the soun
Men feeren hem in al the toun
Welmore than thei don of thonder.
For that is cause of more wonder;
For with the wyndes whiche he bloweth
Fulofte sythe he overthroweth
The Cites and the policie,
460 That I have herd the poeple crie,
And echon seide in his degre,
"Ha wicke tunge, wo thee be!"
For men sein that the harde bon,   [bone]
Althogh himselven have non,
A tunge brekth it al to pieces.

[Genius asks Amans if he has been guilty of chiding. He says he is not guilty, though he often has complained to his Lady. If, however, self-accusation is chiding, then he is guilty, for often he chides his heart for a word misspoken or unspoken. He would take vengeance on himself, but to no avail.]

Bot Oule on Stock and Stock on Oule;   [owl/perch]
The more that a man defoule,   [befoul]
Men witen wel which hath the werse;
And so to me nys worth a kerse,   [sprig of cress]
Bot torneth on myn oghne hed,
590 Thogh I, til that I were ded,
Wolde evere chyde in such a wise
Of love as I to you devise.

[Genius urges Amans to be debonair. He must learn to hold his tongue and get to know Patience, the cure for all offenses; to be like patient Socrates, and learn to suffer as he did.[4]]

THE PATIENCE OF SOCRATES

    Althogh it be now litel sene
Among the men thilke evidence,
Yit he was upon pacience   [he (Socrates)]
So sett, that he himself assaie   [to try]
In thing which mihte him most mispaie   [displease]
Desireth, and a wickid wif
650   He weddeth, which in sorwe and strif
Ayein his ese was contraire.
Bot he spak evere softe and faire,
Til it befell, as it is told,
In wynter, whan the dai is cold,
This wif was fro the welle come,
Wher that a pot with water nome
Sche hath, and broghte it into house,
And sih how that hire seli spouse   [simple]
Was sett and loked on a bok
660   Nyh to the fyr, as he which tok
His ese for a man of age.
And sche began the wode rage,   [mad rage]
And axeth him what devel he thoghte,
And bar on hond that him ne roghte   [upbraided him for not
                                    troubling himself over]

What labour that sche toke on honde,
And seith that such an Housebonde
Was to a wif noght worth a Stre.
He seide nowther nay ne ye,
Bot hield him stille and let hire chyde;
670   And sche, which mai hirself noght hyde,
Began withinne forto swelle,
And that sche broghte in fro the welle,
The waterpot sche hente alofte   [heaved aloft]
And bad him speke, and he al softe
Sat stille and noght a word ansuerde;

And sche was wroth that he so ferde,   [over his behavior]
And axeth him if he be ded;
And al the water on his hed
Sche pourede oute and bad awake.
680 Bot he, which wolde noght forsake
His Pacience, thanne spak,
And seide how that he fond no lak
In nothing which sche hadde do:
For it was wynter time tho,
And wynter, as be weie of kinde
Which stormy is, as men it finde,
Ferst makth the wyndes forto blowe,
And after that withinne a throwe
He reyneth and the watergates
690 Undoth; "and thus my wif algates,
Which is with reson wel besein,   [in accord]
Hath mad me bothe wynd and rein
After the Sesoun of the yer."
And thanne he sette him nerr the fer,
And as he miht hise clothes dreide,
That he nomore o word ne seide;
Wherof he gat him somdel reste,
For that him thoghte was the beste.

[Genius admits that he is uncertain whether it suits a man to
suffer as Socrates did, but he should at least be patient in Love's
court. He tells another tale to illustrate the need of restraining
one's words:[5] Tiresias, who had lived as both man and woman,
was called by the debating Jupiter and Juno to declare which
sex is the more amorous. He heedlessly gave judgment against
Juno who in her anger blinded both his eyes. As recompense
Jupiter made him a soothsayer; yet he would rather have had his
eyesight. Therefore, you should hold your tongue still close, and
if you know other men's secrets, keep your own counsel—reveal
it to no one. Keep in mind the old example of Phebus and
Cornide:[6]]

TALE OF PHEBUS AND CORNIDE

    Phebus, which makth the daies lihte,
A love he hadde, which tho hihte
Cornide, whom aboven alle
He pleseth: bot what schal befalle
Of love ther is noman knoweth,
Bot as fortune hire happes throweth.　　　　　　　[circumstances]
So it befell upon a chaunce,
790   A yong kniht tok hire aqueintance
And hadde of hire al that he wolde:
Bot a fals bridd, which sche hath holde　　　　　　[bird]
And kept in chambre of pure yowthe,
Discoevereth all that evere he cowthe.
This briddes name was as tho
Corvus, the which was thanne also
Welmore whyt than eny Swan,
And he that schrewe al that he can
Of his ladi to Phebus seide;
800   And he for wraththe his swerd outbreide,　　　[drew out]
With which Cornide anon he slowh.
Bot after he was wo ynowh,　　　　　　　　　　[unhappy]
And tok a full gret repentance,
Wherof in tokne and remembrance
Of hem whiche usen wicke speche,
Upon this bridd he tok this wreche,　　　　　　　[vengeance]
That ther he was snow whyt tofore,
Evere afterward colblak therfore
He was transformed, as it scheweth,
810   And many a man yit him beschreweth,
And clepen him into this day
A Raven, be whom yit men mai
Take evidence, whan he crieth,
That som mishapp it signefieth.
Be war therfore and sei the beste,

If thou wolt be thiself in reste,
Mi goode Sone, as I the rede.

[As a final example of Cheste, Genius tells the story of the nymph Laar[7] who spied on Jupiter and Jutorne as they lay together, then told all she saw. Jupiter cut her tongue out and cast her into hell. So do not jangle or tell tales (818–842).

The third servant to Wrath is Hate, who is Cheste's own brother. Hate is slow showing, but long gathering. It dwells in the heart until the time it can be satisfied. Then, suddenly it shows more rage than a wild beast and knows no mercy (843–864). Amans says he knows something of what Genius speaks, though he never behaved that way with his Lady. Still, he is not entirely guiltless, for when he cries mercy from day to day and gets only short words from her, he hates her words: "The word I hate and hire I love" (883). Also he has hated janglers who in their envy lie about him to his Lady; he hopes Love, the mighty Cupid, will smite them with the same rod with which he has been smitten, so that they might know how evil their attempts to hinder him are (884–932). Genius is not pleased with Amans for his hate. He should hate no man, only man's condition. Genius says he will tell the story of King Namplus and the Greeks to teach him to beware the hatred of others (933–972):[8] After the destruction of Troy the Greeks set out for home. But Juno sent a great tempest against them, and they sought haven as best they might. It befell that King Namplus, whose son Palamades the Greeks had treacherously slain, knew of their plight at sea and sought vengeance. Seeing how the wind blew he set up beacon fires which drew the Greeks blithfully not to good haven but onto the rocks, so that ten or twelve died. The others who followed the first heard their death cries and set back to sea. The next day they realized the treachery and stayed on the high sea where they were safe (973–1066). Beware, then, how Fraud beguiles men. There is no scribe who can write with ink half the manners of Fraud (1067–1088).

The two remaining deadly varieties of Wrath are Contek

(Strife), who has Foolhaste as his chamberlain, and Homicide; both despise Patience, and the one often leads to the other (1089–1120). The Lover says he has been guilty of Contek only in his heart, where debate ever stands, much to the disease of his estate. When Fortune casts him down in love, he broods on her injustices, and his heart is in jeopardy (1192). Genius warns him against the evils of Contek and tells him the "Tale of Diogenes and Alexander" to teach him how to govern his will with reason.[9]]

TALE OF DIOGENES

A Philosophre of which men tolde
Ther was whilom be daies olde,
And Diogenes thanne he hihte.
So old he was that he ne mihte
The world travaile, and for the beste
He schop him forto take his reste,
And duelte at hom in such a wise,
That nyh his hous he let devise
Endlong upon an Axeltre   [axletree]
1210 To sette a tonne in such degre,   [barrel]
That he it mihte torne aboute;
Wherof on hed was taken oute,   [head]
For he therinne sitte scholde
And torne himself so as he wolde,
To take their and se the hevene   [the air]
And deme of the planetes sevene,   [consider]
As he which cowthe mochel what.
And thus fulofte there he sat
To muse in his philosophie
1220 Solein withoute compaignie: [alone]
So that upon a morwetyde,
As thing which scholde so betyde,
Whan he was set ther as him liste
To loke upon the Sonne ariste,
Wherof the propretes he sih,

It fell ther cam ridende nyh
King Alisandre with a route;   [retinue]
And as he caste his yhe aboute,
He sih this Tonne, and what it mente
1230 He wolde wite, and thider sente
A knyht, be whom he mihte it knowe,
And he himself that ilke throwe
Abod, and hoveth there stille.   [waited/stays]
This kniht after the kinges wille
With spore made his hors to gon
And to the tonne he cam anon,
Wher that he fond a man of Age,
And he him tolde the message,
Such as the king him hadde bede,   [commanded]
1240 And axeth why in thilke stede
The Tonne stod, and what it was.
And he, which understod the cas,
Sat stille and spak no word ayein.
The kniht bad speke and seith, "Vilein,
Thou schalt me telle, er that I go;
It is thi king which axeth so."
"Mi king," quod he, "that were unriht."   [not true]
"What is he thanne?" seith the kniht,
"Is he thi man?" "That seie I noght,"
1250 Quod he, "bot this I am bethoght,
Mi mannes man hou that he is."
"Thou lyest, false cherl, ywiss,"   [truly]
The kniht him seith, and was riht wroth,
And to the king ayein he goth
And tolde him how this man ansuerde.
The king, whan he this tale herde,
Bad that thei scholden alle abyde,
For he himself wol thider ryde.
And whan he cam tofore the tonne,
1260 He hath his tale thus begonne:

"Alheil," he seith, "what man art thou?"
Quod he, "Such on as thou sest now."
The king, which hadde wordes wise,
His age wolde noght despise,
Bot seith, "Mi fader, I thee preie
That thou me wolt the cause seie,
How that I am thi mannes man."
"Sire king," quod he, "and that I can,
If that thou wolt." "Yis," seith the king.
1270 Quod he, "This is the sothe thing:
Sith I ferst resoun understod,
And knew that thing was evel and good,
The will which of my bodi moeveth,
Whos werkes that the god reproeveth,
I have restreigned everemore,
As him which stant under the lore
Of reson, whos soubgit he is,
So that he mai noght don amis:
And thus be weie of covenant
1280 Will is my man and my servant,
And evere hath ben and evere schal.
And thi will is thi principal,
And hath the lordschipe of thi witt,
So that thou cowthest nevere yit
Take o dai reste of thi labour;
Bot forto ben a conquerour
Of worldes good, which mai noght laste,
Thou hiest evere aliche faste,   [hasten]
Wher thou no reson hast to winne:
1290 And thus thi will is cause of Sinne,
And is thi lord, to whom thou servest,
Wherof thou litel thonk deservest."
The king of that he thus answerde
Was nothing wroth, bot whanne he herde
The hihe wisdom which he seide,

With goodly wordes this he preide,
That he him wolde telle his name.
"I am," quod he, "that ilke same,
The which men Diogenes calle."
1300 Tho was the king riht glad withalle,
For he hadde often herd tofore
What man he was, so that therfore
He seide, "O wise Diogene,
Now schal thi grete witt be sene;
For thou schalt of my yifte have
What worldes thing that thou wolt crave."
Quod he, "Thanne hove out of my Sonne,   [stay]
And let it schyne into mi Tonne;
For thou benymst me thilke yifte   [take from me]
1310 Which lith noght in thi miht to schifte: [to dispose]
Non other good of thee me nedeth."
      This king, whom every contre dredeth,
Lo, thus he was enformed there:
Wherof, my Sone, thou miht lere
How that thi will schal noght be lieved,   [trusted]
Where it is noght of wit relieved.   [assisted]
And thou hast seid thiself er this
How that thi will thi maister is;
Thurgh which thin hertes thoght withinne
1320 Is evere of Contek to beginne,
So that it is gretli to drede
That it non homicide brede.
For love is of a wonder kinde,
And hath hise wittes ofte blinde,
That thei fro mannes reson falle;
Bot whan that it is so befalle
That will schal the corage lede,   [heart]
In loves cause it is to drede:
Wherof I finde ensample write,
1330 Which is behovely forto wite.   [helpful]

TALE OF PYRAMUS
AND THISBE

I rede a tale, and telleth this:[10]
The Cite which Semiramis
Enclosed hath with wall aboute,
Of worthi folk with many a route
Was enhabited here and there;
Among the whiche tuo ther were
Above alle othre noble and grete,
Dwellende tho withinne a Strete
So nyh togedre, as it was sene,
1340 That ther was nothing hem betwene,
Bot wow to wow and wall to wall.   [wall (wow)]
This o lord hadde in special
A Sone, a lusti Bacheler,
In al the toun was non his pier:
That other hadde a dowhter eke,
In al the lond that forto seke
Men wisten non so faire as sche.
And fell so, as it scholde be,
This faire dowhter nyh this Sone
1350 As thei togedre thanne wone,
Cupide hath so the thinges schape,
That thei ne mihte his hand ascape,
That he his fyr on hem ne caste:
Wherof her herte he overcaste
To folwe thilke lore and suie   [obey]
Which nevere man yit miht eschuie;
And that was love, as it is happed,
Which hath here hertes so betrapped,
That thei be alle weies seche
1360 How that thei mihten winne a speche,
Here wofull peine forto lisse.

     Who loveth wel, it mai noght misse,

And namely whan ther be tuo
Of on acord, how so it go,
Bot if that thei som weie finde;
For love is evere of such a kinde
And hath his folk so well affaited,   [trained]
That howso that it be awaited,
Ther mai noman the pourpos lette:
1370 And thus betwen hem tuo thei sette
An hole upon a wall to make,
Thurgh which thei have her conseil take
At alle times, whan thei myhte.
This faire Maiden Tisbee hihte,
And he whom that sche loveth hote
Was Piramus be name hote.
So longe here lecoun thei recorden,
Til ate laste thei acorden
Be nihtes time forto wende
1380 Al one out fro the tounes ende,
Wher was a welle under a Tree;
And who cam ferst, or sche or he,
He scholde stille there abide.
So it befell the nyhtes tide
This maiden, which desguised was,
Al prively the softe pas
Goth thurgh the large toun unknowe,
Til that sche cam withinne a throwe
Wher that sche liketh forto duelle,
1390 At thilke unhappi freisshe welle,
Which was also the Forest nyh.
Wher sche comende a Leoun syh
Into the feld to take his preie,
In haste and sche tho fledde aweie,
So as fortune scholde falle,
For feere and let hire wympel falle
Nyh to the welle upon therbage.   [the grass]
This Leoun in his wilde rage

A beste, which that he fond oute,
1400 Hath slain, and with his blodi snoute,
Whan he hath eten what he wolde,
To drynke of thilke stremes colde
Cam to the welle, where he fond
The wympel, which out of hire hond
Was falle, and he it hath todrawe,
Bebled aboute and al forgnawe;   [bloodied]
And thenne he strawhte him forto drinke
Upon the freisshe welles brinke,
And after that out of the plein
1410 He torneth to the wode ayein.
And Tisbee dorste noght remue,   [move]
Bot as a bridd which were in Mue
Withinne a buissh sche kepte hire clos
So stille that sche noght aros
Unto hirself and pleigneth ay.   [ever complains to herself]
        And fell, whil that sche there lay,
This Piramus cam after sone
Unto the welle, and be the Mone   [moon]
He fond hire wimpel blodi there.
1420 Cam nevere yit to mannes Ere
Tidinge, ne to mannes sihte
Merveile, which so sore aflihte   [afflicted]
A mannes herte, as it tho dede
To him, which in the same stede
With many a wofull compleignynge
Began his handes forto wringe,
As he which demeth sikerly   [judged certainly]
That sche be ded: and sodeinly
His swerd al nakid out he breide   [took]
1430 In his folhaste, and thus he seide:
"I am cause of this felonie,
So it is resoun that I die,
As sche is ded be cause of me."
And with that word upon his kne

He fell, and to the goddes alle
Up to the hevene he gan to calle,
And preide, sithen it was so
That he may noght his love as tho
Have in this world, that of her grace
1440 He miht hire have in other place,
For hiere wolde he noght abide,
He seith: bot as it schal betide,
The Pomel of his swerd to grounde
He sette, and thurgh his herte a wounde
He made up to the bare hilte:
And in this wise himself he spilte
With his folhaste and deth he nam;
For sche withinne a while cam,
Wher he lai ded upon his knif.
1450 So wofull yit was nevere lif
As Tisbee was, whan sche him sih:
Sche mihte noght o word on hih
Speke oute, for hire herte schette,   [shut]
That of hir lif no pris sche sette,   [value]
Bot ded swounende doun sche fell.
Til after, whanne it so befell
That sche out of hire traunce awok,
With many a wofull pitous lok
Hire yhe alwei among sche caste
1460 Upon hir love, and ate laste
Sche cawhte breth and seide thus:
"O thou which cleped art Venus,
Goddesse of love, and thou, Cupide,
Which loves cause hast forto guide,
I wot now wel that ye be blinde,
Of thilke unhapp which I now finde
Only betwen my love and me.
This Piramus, which hiere I se
Bledende, what hath he deserved?
1470 For he youre heste hath kept and served,

And was yong and I bothe also:
Helas, why do ye with ous so?
Ye sette oure herte bothe afyre,   [both our hearts]
And maden ous such thing desire
Wherof that we no skile cowthe;   [reason]
Bot thus oure freisshe lusti yowthe
Withoute joie is al despended,
Which thing mai nevere ben amended:
For as of me this wol I seie,
1480 That me is levere forto deie
Than live after this sorghful day."
And with this word, where as he lay,
Hire love in armes sche embraseth,
Hire oghne deth and so pourchaseth
That now sche wepte and nou sche kiste,
Til ate laste, er sche it wiste,
So gret a sorwe is to hire falle,
Which overgoth hire wittes alle.
As sche which mihte it noght asterte,
1490 The swerdes point ayein hire herte
Sche sette, and fell doun therupon,
Wherof that sche was ded anon:
And thus bothe on o swerd bledende
Thei weren founde ded liggende.

[Beware of your sadness which may cause you to act in Fool-
haste; waste not your life, Genius exhorts. Amans admits that
because of love he has wished to die a thousand times in a single
day. He is culpable because of his will. Yet his Lady is never
the more merciful for it. He knows who the hinderer of his
grace is, and gold from the land of nine kings would not save
the scoundrel if he could get his hands on him. It is Daunger, his
Lady's counsellor, who thwarts him. Regardless of where or
when he approaches his Lady, Daunger is always ready. Daunger
is so glued to her and so secret in his counsel that Amans stands
no chance of obtaining her grace. He would gladly kill Daunger

ere Daunger kills him. But if Daunger did kill him, would that make his Lady guilty of homicide? Would she even feel bad? "Mi goode fader, if ye rewe / Upon mi tale, tell me now," he pleads (1610–1611).

Genius advises Amans to temper his heart from Wrath. A man who is foolhasty often falls, and seldom is he ready when love calls. Better it is to suffer than to be wild and overthrown. What may a mouse do against a cat? Who may make war against love without faring the worse? Love demands peace. Whoever fights most conquers least. Remember Pyramus and do not be overhasty (1612–1684). Consider also the Tale of Phebus and Daphne.[11] Phebus, enamored of Daphne's beauty, was smitten with Cupid's hot, golden dart. So he pursued her in foolhaste. But Daphne was struck with a leaden dart and remained cold and aloof. Thus ever she fled and ever he pursued. To make him understand fully that nothing in love might be accomplished in Foolhaste, she was turned into a laurel tree which, like her maidenhood, is ever green (1685–1728).

Amans thanks Genius for this story, but allows that as long as his Lady is no tree but still true to her own form he will serve her, regardless of Fortune. Genius says no more on the subject, except to warn Amans to beware of Phebus's plight and then to urge him to heed good counsel (1729–1756). To illustrate his point he tells the Tale of Athemas and Demephon.[12] After the Trojan War was over the Greek kings found in many places that during their absence their people had fallen into disobedience. Such was true with Demephon and Athemas. But before these returning kings brought their power against their own people, wise old Nestor advised them to patch up their troubles: To what purpose is a king's throne if his people have been slain; better it is to win by fair speech than by vengeance. When the country heard Nestor's wise words and saw the power of the kings, none were so bold to go to war against them. So the kings were appeased. The strife was forgotten and not recorded. Follow this example, my son, and temper your heart (1757–1862).

Consider next Homicide which sometimes brings great woe to

man when his reason is away and his will becomes malicious. Then the peril is great and piteous, as you will understand from the Tale of Orestes.[13]]

TALE OF ORESTES

  Of Troie at thilke noble toun
Whos fame stant yit of renoun
And evere schal to mannes Ere,
The Siege laste longe there,
Er that the Greks it mihten winne,
1890 Whil Priamus was king therinne;
Bot of the Greks that lyhe aboute
Agamenon ladde al the route.
This thing is knowen overal,
Bot yit I thenke in special
To my matiere therupon
Telle in what wise Agamenon,
Thurgh chance which mai noght be
    weived,
Of love untrewe was deceived.
An old sawe is, "Who that is slyh
1900 In place where he mai be nyh,
He makth the ferre Lieve loth":   [distant loved one
                             loathsome]

Of love and thus fulofte it goth.
Ther while Agamenon batailleth
To winne Troie, and it assailleth,
Fro home and was long time ferr,
Egistus drowh his qweene nerr,
And with the leiser which he hadde
This ladi at his wille he ladde:
Climestre was hire rihte name,
1910 Sche was therof gretli to blame,
To love there it mai noght laste.
Bot fell to meschief ate laste;

Fro whan this noble worthi kniht
Fro Troie cam, the ferste nyht
That he at home abedde lay,
Egistus, longe er it was day,
As this Climestre him hadde asent,
And weren bothe of on assent,
Be treson slowh him in his bedd.
1920 Bot moerdre, which mai noght ben hedd,   [hidden]
Sprong out to every mannes Ere,
Wherof the lond was full of fere.
    Agamenon hath be this qweene
A Sone, and that was after sene;
Bot yit as thanne he was of yowthe,
A babe, which no reson cowthe,
And as godd wolde, it fell him thus.
A worthi kniht Taltabius
This yonge child hath in kepinge,
1930 And whan he herde of this tidinge,
Of this treson, of this misdede,
He gan withinne himself to drede,
In aunter if this false Egiste   [if by chance]
Upon him come, er he it wiste,
To take and moerdre of his malice
This child, which he hath to norrice:
And for that cause in alle haste
Out of the lond he gan him haste
And to the king of Crete he strawhte
1940 And him this yonge lord betawhte,   [delivered]
And preide him for his fader sake
That he this child wolde undertake
And kepe him til he be of Age,
So as he was of his lignage;
And tolde him over al the cas,
How that his fadre moerdred was,
And hou Egistus, as men seide,
Was king, to whom the lond obeide.

And whanne Ydomeneux the king
1950   Hath understondinge of this thing,
Which that this kniht him hadde told,
He made sorwe manyfold,
And tok this child into his warde,
And seide he wolde him kepe and warde,
Til that he were of such a myht
To handle a swerd and ben a knyht,
To venge him at his oghne wille.
And thus Horestes duelleth stille,
Such was the childes rihte name,
1960   Which after wroghte mochel schame
In vengance of his fader deth.

The time of yeres overgeth,
That he was man of brede and lengthe,
Of wit, of manhod and of strengthe,
A fair persone amonges alle.
And he began to clepe and calle,
As he which come was to manne,
Unto the King of Crete thanne,
Preiende that he wolde him make
1970   A kniht and pouer with him take,
For lengere wolde he noght beleve,   [remain]
He seith, bot preith the king of leve
To gon and cleyme his heritage
And vengen him of thilke oultrage
Which was unto his fader do.
The king assenteth wel therto,
With gret honour and knyht him makth,
And gret pouer to him betakth,
And gan his journe forto caste: [plan]
1980   So that Horestes ate laste
His leve tok and forth he goth.
As he that was in herte wroth,
His ferste pleinte to bemene,
Unto the Cite of Athene

He goth him forth and was received,
So there was he noght deceived.
The Duc and tho that weren wise
Thei profren·hem to his servise;
And he hem thonketh of here profre
1990 And seith himself he wol gon offre
Unto the goddes for his sped,
As alle men him yeven red.
So goth he to the temple forth:
Of yiftes that be mochel worth
His sacrifice and his offringe
He made; and after his axinge
He was ansuerd, if that he wolde
His stat recovere, thanne he scholde
Upon his Moder do vengance
2000 So cruel, that the remembrance
Therof mihte everemore abide,
As sche that was an homicide
And of hire oghne lord Moerdrice.
Horestes, which of thilke office
Was nothing glad, as thanne he preide
Unto the goddes there and seide
That thei the juggement devise,
How sche schal take the juise.   [be given justice]
And therupon he hadde ansuere,
2010 That he hire Pappes scholde of tere   [tear off]
Out of hire brest his oghne hondes,   [with his own hands]
And for ensample of alle londes
With hors sche scholde be todrawe,
Til houndes hadde hire bones gnawe
Withouten eny sepulture:
This was a wofull aventure.
And whan Horestes hath al herd,
How that the goddes have ansuerd,
Forth with the strengthe which he ladde
2020 The Duc and his pouer he hadde,

And to a Cite forth thei gon,
The which was cleped Cropheon,
Where as Phoieus was lord and Sire,
Which profreth him withouten hyre
His help and al that he mai do,
As he that was riht glad therto,
To grieve his mortiel enemy:
And tolde hem certein cause why,
How that Egiste in Mariage
2030 His dowhter whilom of full Age
Forlai, and afterward forsok,
Whan he Horestes Moder tok.
    Men sein, "Old Senne newe schame":
Thus more and more aros the blame
Ayein Egiste on every side.
Horestes with his host to ride
Began, and Phoieus with hem wente;
I trowe Egiste him schal repente.
Thei riden forth unto Micene,
2040 Wher lay Climestre thilke qweene,
The which Horestes moder is:
And whan sche herde telle of this,
The gates weren faste schet,
And thei were of here entre let.   [delayed]
Anon this Cite was withoute
Belein and sieged al aboute,
And evere among thei it assaile,
Fro day to nyht and so travaile,
Til ate laste thei it wonne;
2050 Tho was ther sorwe ynowh begonne.
    Horestes dede his moder calle
Anon tofore the lordes alle
And ek tofor the poeple also,
To hire and tolde his tale tho,
And seide, "O cruel beste unkinde,
How mihtest thou thin herte finde,

For eny lust of loves drawhte, [draught]
That thou acordest to the slawhte [slaughter]
Of him which was thin oghne lord?
2060 Thi treson stant of such record,
Thou miht thi werkes noght forsake;
So mot I for mi fader sake
Vengance upon thi bodi do,
As I comanded am therto.
Unkindely for thou hast wroght,
Unkindeliche it schal be boght,
The Sone schal the Moder sle,
For that whilom thou seidest yee
To that thou scholdest nay have seid."
2070 And he with that his hond hath leid
Upon his Moder brest anon,
And rente out fro the bare bon
Hire Pappes bothe and caste aweie
Amiddes in the carte weie,
And after tok the dede cors
And let it drawe awey with hors
Unto the hound and to the raven;
Sche was non other wise graven. [buried]
Egistus, which was elles where,
2080 Tidinges comen to his Ere
How that Micenes was belein, [besieged]
Bot what was more herd he noght sein;
With gret manace and mochel bost
He drowh pouer and made an host
And cam in rescousse of the toun.
Bot al the sleyhte of his tresoun
Horestes wiste it be aspie, [by spies]
And of his men a gret partie
He made in buisshement abide, [ambush]
2090 To waite on him in such a tide
That he ne mihte here hond ascape:
And in this wise as he hath schape

The thing befell, so that Egiste
Was take, er he himself it wiste,
And was forth broght hise hondes bounde,
As whan men han a tretour founde.
And tho that weren with him take,
Whiche of tresoun were overtake,
Togedre in o sentence falle;
2100 Bot false Egiste above hem alle
Was demed to diverse peine, [condemned to]
The worste that men cowthe ordeigne,
And so forth after be the lawe
He was unto the gibet drawe,
Where he above alle othre hongeth,
As to a tretour it belongeth.
　　　Tho fame with hire swifte wynges
Aboute flyh and bar tidinges,
And made it cowth in alle londes
2110 How that Horestes with hise hondes
Climestre his oghne Moder slowh.
Some sein he dede wel ynowh,
And som men sein he dede amis,
Diverse opinion ther is:
That sche is ded thei speken alle,
Bot pleinli hou it is befalle,
The matiere in so litel throwe
In soth ther mihte noman knowe
Bot thei that weren ate dede: [who were involved]
2120 And comunliche in every nede
The worste speche is rathest herd [heard first]
And lieved, til it be ansuerd. [believed]
The kinges and the lordes grete
Begonne Horestes forto threte
To puten him out of his regne:
"He is noght worthi forto regne,
The child which slowh his moder so,"

Thei saide; and therupon also
The lordes of comun assent
2130 A time sette of parlement,
And to Athenes king and lord
Togedre come of on acord,
To knowe hou that the sothe was:
So that Horestes in this cas
Thei senden after, and he com.
King Menelay the wordes nom
And axeth him of this matiere:
And he, that alle it mihten hiere,
Ansuerde and tolde his tale alarge,
2140 And hou the goddes in his charge
Comanded him in such a wise
His oghne hond to do juise.
And with this tale a Duc aros,
Which was a worthi kniht of los,   [fame (OF *los*, 'praise')]
His name was Menesteüs,
And seide unto the lordes thus:
"The wreeche of which Horestes dede,   [vengeance]
It was thing of goddes bede,   [command]
And nothing of his crualte;
2150 And if ther were of mi degree
In al this place such a kniht
That wolde sein it was no riht,
I wole it with my bodi prove."
And therupon he caste his glove,
And ek this noble Duc alleide
Ful many an other skile, and seide   [reason]
Sche hadde wel deserved wreche,
Ferst for the cause of Spousebreche,
And after wroghte in such a wise
2160 That al the world it oghte agrise,   [terrify]
Whan that sche for so foul a vice
Was of hire oghne lord moerdrice.

Thei seten alle stille and herde,
Bot therto was noman ansuerde,
It thoughte hem alle he seide skile,
Ther is noman withseie it wile;
Whan thei upon the reson musen,
Horestes alle thei excusen:
So that with gret solempnete
2170 He was unto his dignete
Received, and coroned king.
And tho befell a wonder thing:
Egiona, whan sche this wiste,
Which was the dowhter of Egiste
And Soster on the moder side
To this Horeste, at thilke tide,
Whan sche herde how hir brother spedde,   [fared]
For pure sorwe, which hire ledde,
That he ne hadde ben exiled,
2180 Sche hath hire oghne lif beguiled
Anon and hyng hireselve tho.
It hath and schal ben everemo,
To moerdre who that wole assente,
He mai noght faille to repente:
This false Egiona was on,
Which forto moerdre Agamenon
Yaf hire acord and hire assent,
So that be goddes juggement,
Thogh that non other man it wolde,
2190 Sche tok hire juise as sche scholde;
And as sche to an other wroghte,
Vengance upon hirself sche soghte,
And hath of hire unhappi wit
A moerdre with a moerdre quit.
Such is of moerdre the vengance.
    Forthi, mi Sone, in remembrance
Of this ensample tak good hiede:
For who that thenkth his love spiede   [to advance]

With moerdre, he schal with worldes
    schame
2200 Himself and ek is love schame.

[Amans asks if there is any lawful way to slay without com-
mitting sin.]

2210 Mi Sone, in sondri wise ye.
    What man that is of traiterie,   [treason]
    Of moerdre of elles robberie
    Atteint, the jugge schal noght lette,   [convicted/release]
    Bot he schal slen of pure dette,
    And doth gret Senne, if that he wonde.   [turn aside (from justice)]
    For who that lawe hath upon honde,
    And spareth forto do justice
    For merci, doth noght his office,
    That he his mercy so bewareth,   [employs]
2220 Whan for o schrewe which he spareth
    A thousand goode men he grieveth:
    With such merci who that believeth
    To plese god, he is deceived,
    Or elles resoun mot be weyved.
    The lawe stod er we were bore,
    How that a kinges swerd is bore
    In signe that he schal defende
    His trewe poeple and make an ende
    Of suche as wolden hem devoure.
2230 Lo thus, my Sone, to socoure
    The lawe and comun riht to winne,
    A man mai sle withoute Sinne,
    And do therof a gret almesse,   [good deed]
    So forto kepe rihtwisnesse.
    And over this for his contre
    In time of werre a man is fre
    Himself, his hous and ek his lond
    Defende with his oghne hond,

And slen, if that he mai no bet,
2240 After the lawe which is set.

[Amans then asks if wars are justified. Genius attempts to explain: God told Moses that homicide was forbidden; moreover, He sent His angels to sing of peace to the shepherds. Thus, according to the law of charity, there should be no war. War conspires with pestilence and famine, poverty and woe. It brings all to nothing. The church is burned, the priest slain, the wife and maiden raped. No man really gains by war. Christ commanded love and peace; whoever works the reverse must expect no reward in heaven. Sin is the cause of war and the reward of sin is death. Better to be at peace than doubly lost. The first wars grew out of covetousness. So it was in Greece and Persia. Only Arcadia, because it was barren and poor, was free from war. It is a wonder that a rich king will claim property to which he has no right simply because he is powerful. Every man knows that such behavior is against both law and nature. But covetousness causes man to put aside reason to find a way to war. Always he feigns some cause and convinces himself that he will gain by war. Such men have no time for conscience (2241–2360).

Consider the example of Alexander and the Pirate, which shows how men excuse their tyranny and how rich and poor alike make war and pillage for lucre.[14] Once, after Alexander had conquered all the world, it happened by chance that a famous pirate who had slain and stolen from many men was captured and brought before the king. In response to the king's accusations the pirate maintained that his heart was one with Alexander's, his will being to rifle and get wealth throughout the world. For such behavior he is labeled "pirate," while Alexander, because of his greater number of followers, is named "emperor," though their deeds are essentially the same. Upon hearing the pirate's defense and upon observing his hardy countenance, the king placed the pirate in his own service and after a time made him a knight and gave him land.

Such men are of one accord, but consider their end. When

men become falcons, their rapine is never satisfied. After conquering the world, Alexander was poisoned and died miserably. He who slew was slain. Lo, what profit war, where covetous, proud men behave as beasts (2361–2480).

Amans next questions the legality of war against the Saracens. Genius says he has often heard that men should preach and suffer for the faith; but he has heard nothing said in favor of slaughter. Christ, with His death, bought all men and, as a sign of perfect charity, made them free. He instructed the Apostles to spread the faith, fearless of death. In their suffering Christianity arose. Whether the faith would have grown by war is not known. It is known, however, that since the Church has received the sword, a great part of what once was Christian has been lost. May God amend as He knows best. If you wish to rest well with your conscience, consider well before you slay. For man is ordained the principal of God's earthly creations; his soul bears the likeness of God. Yet homicide has become so general now that it exists even within Holy Church. We preach charity, but do nothing as we teach. Thus blind conscience has lost evidence of the peace that Christ taught on earth (2481–2546).

In Greece, before the time of Christ, Peleus slew his brother Phocus but was given dispensation by paying gold. So also Medea, after slaying her two sons, and also the son of Amphioras, who slew his mother, got penance by paying gold. And thus for reward of the world's goods, homicide is still bought off. But in the next life one's sins may not be bought off. Man should follow natural law, not make himself worse than a beast (2547–2598).

Solinus gives the wonderous account of a bird that has a face of blood and bone like a man's. If by chance the bird finds a man in his way he slays him and eats his fill beside a well. When he drinks he sees the likeness of the slain man in the well and becomes so distraught with his misdeed that he dies before morning. This example shows that men should eschew homicide. For men, especially knights whose might is greatest, are beholden to mercy by every law of nature, as the Tale of Telaphus and Teucer exemplifies (2638):[15] He who has mercy may not fail of his reward. When Achilles with his son Telaphus went to Troy it happened that they attacked Teucer, King of Mese, along the way. Achilles himself smote Teucer from his saddle and was about to kill him when Telaphus interceded for the fallen king. The reason for Telaphus's intercession was that Teucer had shown Telaphus mercy in a battle of another time. So Achilles did not slay the king. The rest of Teucer's company, upon seeing their king fall, fled, but many were captured. The Greeks that day won great possessions. Later, Teucer, in memory of Telaphus's mercy, made him his heir (2639-2717).

Thus, Genius concludes, you should have pity and compassion on the passions of other men. In order to stand against Wrath, you should take counsel of Patience and let mercy govern your conscience. Then you will feel no rancor and will put away Cheste and Melancholy, Foolhaste and Contek. Amans says he will try. They agree to speak next of Sloth (2718-2774).]

Explicit Liber Tercius

INCIPIT LIBER QUARTUS

[Sloth is the next vice, of which Lachesce (procrastination) is the first kind. Lachesce tarries, always putting things off until to-morrow. The Lover confesses he is guilty of Lachesce. Often he has avoided speaking to his Lady because Lachesce says, "Another time is better; write a letter rather than speak now." Yet although his tongue is slow, his heart busily asks grace (1–72). To instruct Amans on the evil of Lachesce, Genius tells the story of Aeneas and Dido.[1]]

TALE OF AENEAS AND DIDO

    Ayein Lachesce in loves cas
I finde how whilom Eneas,
Whom Anchises to Sone hadde,
80   With gret navie, which he ladde
Fro Troie, aryveth at Cartage,
Wher for a while his herbergage   [lodging]
He tok; and it betidde so,
With hire which was qweene tho
Of the Cite his aqueintance
He wan, whos name in remembrance
Is yit, and Dido sche was hote;
Which loveth Eneas so hote
Upon the wordes which he seide,
90   That al hire herte on him sche leide
And dede al holi what he wolde.
      Bot after that, as it be scholde,
Fro thenne he goth toward Ytaile
Be Schipe, and there his arivaile

Hath take, and schop him forto ryde.
Bot sche, which mai noght longe abide
The hote peine of loves throwe,
Anon withinne a litel throwe
A lettre unto hir kniht hath write,
100 And dede him pleinly forto wite,
If he made eny tariinge,
To drecche of his ayeincomynge,   [put off]
That sche ne mihte him fiele and se,
Sche scholde stonde in such degre
As whilom stod a Swan tofore,
Of that sche hadde hire make lore;   [lost her mate]
For sorwe a fethere into hire brain
She schof and hath hireselve slain;
As king Menander in a lay   [song]
110 The sothe hath founde, wher sche lay
Sprantlende with hire wynges tweie,   [sprawling]
As sche which scholde thanne deie
For love of him which was hire make.
    "And so schal I do for thi sake,"
This qweene seide, "wel I wot."
Lo, to Enee thus sche wrot
With many an other word of pleinte:
Bot he, which hadde hise thoghtes feinte
Towardes love and full of Slowthe,
120 His time lette, and that was rowthe: [delayed]
For sche, which loveth him tofore,
Desireth evere more and more,
And whan sche sih him tarie so,
Hire herte was so full of wo,
That compleignende manyfold
Sche hath hire oghne tale told,
Unto hirself and thus sche spak:
"Ha, who fond evere such a lak   [such a fault]
Of Slowthe in eny worthi kniht?
130 Now wot I wel my deth is diht

Thurgh him which scholde have be mi
    lif."
Bot forto stinten al this strif,
Thus whan sche sih non other bote,
Riht evene unto hire herte rote   [heart's root]
A naked swerd anon sche threste,
And thus sche gat hireselve reste
In remembrance of alle slowe.
     Wherof, my Sone, thou miht knowe
How tariinge upon the nede
140 In loves cause is forto drede;
And that hath Dido sore aboght,
Whos deth schal evere be bethoght.

[As a second illustration of Lachesce Genius tells how Ulysses
stayed so long at Troy that Penelope finally wrote him to com-
plain of his sloth.[2] The letter was delivered, and Ulysses set out
for home as soon as the war was won. So desirous he was of
the "visage of Penelope" that each day of his return journey
seemed to him a thousand years. Finally he got home and thus
the debate of love ceased. Sloth was excused (143-233). Recall
also the fate of the great clerk Grosseteste who worked seven years
forging a head of brass which would be able to speak, only to
lose his reward when he dozed for half a minute (234-249).[3]
Similarly the story of the Foolish Virgins who lost their grooms
for lack of oil in their lamps demonstrates that no profit comes
from Sloth (250-260).[4] Love must be waited on; love eschews
Sloth.

    Amans observes that he has never broken any appointment
with his Lady since she has never graced him with one; he would
unjoint every limb before he failed to keep his promise. As is, she
lights on none of his lures. The more he cries out, the less atten-
tion she pays. He seeks what he may not find; always he is be-
hind in love. Genius advises as shrift for Lachesce that Amans
become busy, thus avoiding the vices hanging in Sloth's lap
(261-312).

Hear what else pertains to Sloth. Consider Pusillanimity, that is, the fear to speak or begin an action. For the pusillanimous always makes excuses; the wolf is always in his way. He has illnesses that no man may cure. Thus he wins nothing (313–354). The Lover admits guilt here too. Genius tells him the story of Pygmalion to demonstrate the rewards that follow perseverance.[5]]

TALE OF PYGMALION

❦ I finde hou whilom ther was on,
Whos name was Pymaleon,
Which was a lusti man of yowthe:
The werkes of entaile he cowthe   [sculpture (OF *taillier*, "to cut')]

Above alle othre men as tho;
And thurgh fortune it fell him so,
As he whom love schal travaile,
He made an ymage of entaile
Lich to a womman in semblance
380 Of feture and of contienance,
So fair yit nevere was figure.
Riht as a lyves creature
Sche semeth, for of yvor whyt
He hath hire wroght of such delit,
That sche was rody on the cheke
And red on bothe hire lippes eke;
Wherof that he himself beguileth.
For with a goodly lok sche smyleth,
So that thurgh pure impression
390 Of his ymaginacion
With al the herte of his corage
His love upon this faire ymage
He sette, and hire of love preide;
Bot sche no word ayeinward seide.
The longe day, what thing he dede,
This ymage in the same stede

Was evere bi, that ate mete   [at dinner]
He wolde hire serve and preide hire ete,
And putte unto hire mowth the cuppe;
400 And whan the bord was taken uppe,
He hath hire into chambre nome,
And after, whan the nyht was come,
He leide hire in his bed al nakid.
He was forwept, he was forwakid,
He keste hire colde lippes ofte,
And wissheth that thei weren softe,
And ofte he rouneth in hire Ere,   [whispers]
And ofte his arm now hier now there
He leide, as he hir wolde embrace,
410 And evere among he axeth grace,
As thogh sche wiste what he mente:
And thus himself he gan tormente
With such desese of loves peine,
That noman mihte him more peine.
Bot how it were, of his penance
He made such continuance
Fro dai to nyht, and preith so longe,
That his preiere is underfonge,   [accepted]
Which Venus of hire grace herde;
420 Be nyhte and whan that he worst ferde,
And it lay in his nakede arm,
The colde ymage he fieleth warm
Of fleissh and bon and full of lif.
    Lo, thus he wan a lusti wif,
Which obeissant was at his wille;
And if he wolde have holde him stille
And nothing spoke, he scholde have
    failed:
Bot for he hath his word travailed
And dorste speke, his love he spedde,
430 And hadde al that he wolde abedde.
For er thei wente thanne atwo,

A knave child betwen hem two
Thei gete, which as after hote
Paphus, of whom yit hath the note
A certein yle, which Paphos
Men clepe, and of his name it ros.
    Be this ensample thou miht finde
That word mai worche above kinde.
Forthi, my Sone, if that thou spare
440 To speke, lost is al thi fare,
For Slowthe bringth in alle wo.
And over this to loke also,
The god of love is favorable
To hem that ben of love stable,
And many a wonder hath befalle.

[As a further example of wonders wrought by love, Genius tells the Tale of Iphis.[6] In anger King Ligdus said to his pregnant wife Thelecuse that if she gave birth to a daughter it would be slain. When the queen was delivered of a daughter, however, Isis, goddess of childbirth, told Thelecuse to keep her child and say it was a boy. Thus the child was named Iphis and was raised as the king's son. When Iphis was ten years old he was given in marriage to Iante, a duke's daughter. Often the couple lay abed together, fresh in play, she and she, until Cupid took pity on their love and transformed Iphis into a man. Then they led a merry life without offense to nature. Thus it seems that love is well disposed towards those who pursue with busy heart that which is their due, for see what riches love without sloth can bring (446–515).

Amans says that he has been diligent night and day as a lover, yet he is no nearer Love's miracle. What is to be done? Genius tells Amans that he has lost his memory. He has no wit to maintain what he should and thus often grieves. For there is a servant of Sloth called Forgetfulness. Forgetfulness makes lovers forget two thirds of what they meant to say of love. Amans says he knows this problem; in the presence of his Lady he is more frightened than of a ghost and stands deaf and dumb, not worth an ivy leaf. Afterward he debates with himself, chides his foolish heart, complaining of his forgetfulness. Yet he never in his heart forgets his Lady, nor could he ever, even with the enchanted Ring of Oblivion which Moses had made for Tharbis. Yet he clean forgets his speech when next he sees her. How may Forgetfulness and Pusillanimity be redressed? (516–709) Genius notes that Love will not send his grace to a man who asks for none; God knows man's thought, yet still it is His will that we pray. Pull up a busy heart and let nothing hinder your business. Many are the examples against Forgetfulness (710–730).]

TALE OF DEMEPHON AND PHYLLIS

King Demephon, whan he be Schipe
To Troieward with felaschipe
Sailende goth, upon his weie
It hapneth him at Rodopeie,
As Eolus him hadde blowe,
To londe, and rested for a throwe.[7]
And fell that ilke time thus,
The dowhter of Ligurgius,
Which qweene was of the contre,
740 Was sojournende in that Cite
Withinne a Castell nyh the stronde,
Wher Demephon cam up to londe.
Phillis sche hihte, and of yong age
And of stature and of visage
Sche hadde al that hire best besemeth.
Of Demephon riht wel hire qwemeth,   [is pleasing to her]
Whan he was come, and made him chiere;
And he, that was of his manere
A lusti knyht, ne myhte asterte
750 That he ne sette on hire his herte;
So that withinne a day or tuo
He thoghte, how evere that it go,

He wolde assaie the fortune,
And gan his herte to commune
With goodly wordes in hire Ere;
And forto put hire out of fere,
He swor and hath his trowthe pliht   [pledged]
To be for evere hire oghne knyht.
And thus with hire he stille abod,
760   Ther while his Schip on Anker rod,
And hadde ynowh of time and space
To speke of love and seche grace.
      This ladi herde al that he seide,
And hou he swor and hou he preide,
Which was as an enchantement
To hire, that was innocent:
As thogh it were trowthe and feith,
Sche lieveth al that evere he seith,
And as hire infortune scholde,
770   Sche granteth him al that he wolde.
Thus was he for the time in joie,
Til that he scholde go to Troie;
Bot tho sche made mochel sorwe,
And he his trowthe leith to borwe   [places in pledge]
To come, if that he live may,
Ayein withinne a Monthe day,
And therupon thei kisten bothe:
Bot were hem lieve or were hem lothe,
To Schipe he goth and forth he wente
780   To Troie, as was his ferste entente.
      The daies gon, the Monthe passeth,
Hire love encresceth and his lasseth,
For him sche lefte slep and mete,   [food]
And he his time hath al foryete;
So that this wofull yonge qweene,
Which wot noght what it mihte meene,
A lettre sende and preide him come,
And seith how sche is overcome

With strengthe of love in such a wise,
790 That sche noght longe mai suffise
To liven out of his presence
And putte upon his conscience
The trowthe which he hath behote, [promised]
Wherof sche loveth him so hote,
Sche seith, that if he lengere lette
Of such a day as sche him sette,
Sche scholde sterven in his Slowthe,
Which were a schame unto his trowthe.
This lettre is forth upon hire sonde,
800 Wherof somdiel confort on honde
Sche tok, as sche that wolde abide
And waite upon that ilke tyde
Which sche hath in hire lettre write.
    Bot now is pite forto wite,
As he dede erst, so he foryat
His time eftsone and oversat.
Bot sche, which mihte noght do so,
The tyde awayteth everemo,
And caste hire yhe upon the See:
810 Somtime nay, somtime yee,
Somtime he cam, somtime noght,
Thus sche desputeth in hire thoght
And wot noght what sche thenke mai;
Bot fastende al the longe day
Sche was into the derke nyht,
And tho sche hath do set up lyht
In a lanterne on hih alofte
Upon a Tour, wher sche goth ofte,
In hope that in his cominge
820 He scholde se the liht brenninge,
Wherof he mihte his weies rihte [amend]
To come wher sche was by nyhte.
Bot al for noght, sche was deceived,
For Venus hath hire hope weyved,

And schewede hire upon the Sky
How that the day was faste by,
So that withinne a litel throwe
The daies lyht sche mihte knowe.
Tho sche behield the See at large;
830 And whan sche sih ther was no barge
Ne Schip, als ferr as sche may kenne,
Doun fro the Tour sche gan to renne
Into an Herber all hire one, [arbor]
Wher many a wonder woful mone
Sche made, that no lif it wiste,
As sche which all hire joie miste,
That now sche swouneth, now sche
    pleigneth,
And al hire face sche desteigneth
With teres, whiche, as of a welle
840 The stremes, from hire yhen felle;
So as sche mihte and evere in on
Sche clepede upon Demephon,
And seide, "Helas, thou slowe wiht,
Wher was ther evere such a knyht,
That so thurgh his ungentilesce
Of Slowthe and of foryetelnesse
Ayein his trowthe brak his stevene?" [word]
And tho hire yhe up to the hevene
Sche caste, and seide, "O thou unkinde,
850 Hier schalt thou thurgh thi Slowthe finde,
If that thee liste to come and se,
A ladi ded for love of thee,
So as I schal myselve spille;
Whom, if it hadde be thi wille,
Thou mihtest save wel ynowh."
With that upon a grene bowh
A Ceinte of Selk, which sche ther hadde, [girdle]
Sche knette, and so hireself sche ladde, [tied up]
That sche aboute hire whyte swere [neck (OE *sweora*)]

860 It dede, and hyng hirselven there.
    Wherof the goddes were amoeved,
    And Demephon was so reproeved,
    That of the goddes providence
    Was schape such an evidence
    Evere afterward ayein the slowe,
    That Phillis in the same throwe
    Was schape into a Notetre,   [nut tree]
    That alle men it mihte se,
    And after Phillis Philliberd
870 This tre was cleped in the yerd,
    And yit for Demephon to schame
    Into this dai it berth the name.
    This wofull chance how that it ferde
    Anon as Demephon it herde,
    And every man it hadde in speche,
    His sorwe was noght tho to seche;
    He gan his Slowthe forto banne,
    Bot it was al to late thanne.
        Lo thus, my Sone, miht thou wite
880 Ayein this vice how it is write;
    For noman mai the harmes gesse,
    That fallen thurgh foryetelnesse,
    Wherof that I thi schrifte have herd.
    Bot yit of Slowthe hou it hath ferd
    In other wise I thenke oppose,
    If thou have gult, as I suppose.

[Sloth's secretary is Negligence, who stands ever behind, saying afterward, "Ha, wolde god I hadde knowe!" (899). After the steed is stolen he locks up the stable. He never learns by example, for he prizes not virtue (887–915). Amans says he has a clean conscience here: Though he may not be wise, he is truly so amorous that he diligently searches ways to fathom love's craft. Though he has been unsuccessful so far, his pursuit is unwavering. Genius is pleased with the Lover's ambition, though he tells the

Tale of Phaeton[8] as warning, nonetheless: For never yet was there science or virtue which was not destroyed and lost once Negligence occurred (978). Phebus, who heats the earth and gives health to all living things, had a son who was named Phaeton. The son conspired with his mother Clemenee to get Phebus to let him drive the sun cart. The father agreed and gave the boy useful instruction: do not drive the horses too hard, nor reign them back too much; keep the right gait; drive them neither too high nor too low. But in his negligence Phaeton paid no heed. When his chance came he drove the cart wantonly, flying high as it pleased him, and too low, scorching the earth. Men cried out to god for help. When Phebus saw his son's negligence he ordained that the cart fall into the ocean where Phaeton was drowned. See how the negligent fares, where from the high firmament, because he would be low, he is soon overthrown (979–1034). Similarly, consider the Tale of Icarus.[9] Dedalus and his son Icarus were both imprisoned with the Minotaur. Dedalus, a man who was crafty from his youth, devised wings from feathers and other things so that he and his son might fly high out of the prison. He charged his son to beware of the sun which might melt the wax which held the feathers; then, out from their prison they both flew. Icarus mounted higher and higher and paid no heed to his father's advice. The sun melted the wax, and he fell to his destruction. So do men who lack governance often fall (1035–1071).

But the worst kind of "Slowthe," "of slowe the sloweste," is Idleness. Idleness is the nurse of every vice in man's nature. In winter he does nothing because of the cold; in summer, nothing because of the heat. So whether he freeze or sweat, be in or out, he is idle, playing games. He is like a cat who would eat a fish without getting his claws wet. Amans says he has not been idle in Love. Genius replies by asking how he has kept busy.]

Mi fader, evere yit er this
In every place, in every stede,
What so mi lady hath me bede,   [bidden me]
With al myn herte obedient

I have therto be diligent.
And if so is sche bidde noght,
What thing that thanne into my thoght
Comth ferst of that I mai suffise,
1130 I bowe and profre my servise,
Somtime in chambre, somtime in halle,
Riht as I se the times falle.
And whan sche goth to hiere masse,
That time schal noght overpasse,
That I naproche hir ladihede,
In aunter if I mai hire lede   [in order that I]
Unto the chapelle and ayein.
Thanne is noght al mi weie in vein,
Somdiel I mai the betre fare,
1140 Whan I, that mai noght fiele hir bare,
Mai lede hire clothed in myn arm:
Bot afterward it doth me harm
Of pure ymaginacioun;
For thanne this collacioun   [(OF *collacion*, 'discourse')]
I make unto miselven ofte,
And seie, "Ha lord, hou sche is softe,
How sche is round, hou sche is smal!
Now wolde god I hadde hire al
Withoute danger at mi wille!"
1150 And thanne I sike and sitte stille,   [sigh]
Of that I se mi besi thoght
Is torned ydel into noght.
Bot for al that lete I ne mai,   [bother]
Whanne I se time an other dai,
That I ne do my besinesse
Unto mi ladi worthinesse.
For I therto mi wit afaite   [prepare]
To se the times and awaite
What is to done and what to leve:
1160 And so, whan time is, be hir leve,
What thing sche bit me don, I do,   [bids]

And wher sche bidt me gon, I go,
And whanne hir list to clepe, I come.
Thus hath sche fulliche overcome
Min ydelnesse til I sterve,   [die]
So that I mot hire nedes serve,
For as men sein, nede hath no lawe.
Thus mot I nedly to hire drawe,
I serve, I bowe, I loke, I loute,   [bend]
1170 Min yhe folweth hire aboute,
What so sche wole so wol I,
Whan sche wol sitte, I knele by,
And whan sche stant, than wol I stonde:
Bot whan sche takth hir werk on honde
Of wevinge or enbrouderie,
Than can I noght bot muse and prie   [peer]
Upon hir fingres longe and smale,
And now I thenke, and now I tale,   [speak]
And now I singe, and now I sike,
1180 And thus mi contienance I pike.   [countenance/choose]
And if it falle, as for a time
Hir liketh noght abide bime,
Bot besien hire on other thinges,
Than make I othre tariinges
To dreche forth the longe dai,   [while away]
For me is loth departe away.
And thanne I am so simple of port,
That forto feigne som desport
I pleie with hire litel hound
1190 Now on the bedd, now on the ground,
Now with hir briddes in the cage;
For ther is non so litel page,
Ne yit so simple a chamberere,
That I ne make hem alle chere,
Al for thei scholde speke wel:
Thus mow ye sen mi besi whiel,
That goth noght ydeliche aboute.

And if hir list to riden oute
On pelrinage or other stede,
1200 I come, thogh I be noght bede,   [invited]
And take hire in min arm alofte
And sette hire in hire sadel softe,
And so forth lede hire be the bridel,
For that I wolde noght ben ydel.
And if hire list to ride in Char,
And thanne I mai therof be war,
Anon I schape me to ryde
Riht evene be the Chares side;
And as I mai, I speke among,
1210 And otherwhile I singe a song,
Which Ovide in his bokes made,
And seide, "O whiche sorwes glade,
O which wofull prosperite
Belongeth to the proprete
Of love, who so wole him serve!
And yit therfro mai noman swerve,
That he ne mot his lawe obeie."
And thus I ryde forth mi weie,
And am riht besi overal
1220 With herte and with mi body al,
As I have said you hier tofore.
My goode fader, tell therfor,
Of Ydelnesse if I have gilt.

[Genius excuses him, but notes that not all men are so diligent
in love. Hear the story of a king's daughter who refused to love.]

TALE OF ROSIPHELEE

🙰 Of Armenye, I rede thus,[10]
Ther was a king, which Herupus
Was hote, and he a lusti Maide
To dowhter hadde, and as men saide

Hire name was Rosiphelee;
1250 Which tho was of gret renomee,
For sche was bothe wys and fair
And scholde ben hire fader hair.　　　　　　[heir]
Bot sche hadde o defalte of Slowthe
Towardes love, and that was rowthe;
For so wel cowde noman seie,
Which mihte sette hire in the weie
Of loves occupacion
Thurgh non ymaginacion;
That scole wolde sche noght knowe.
1260 And thus sche was on of the slowe
As of such hertes besiness,
Til whanne Venus the goddesse,
Which loves court hath forto reule,
Hath broght hire into betre reule,
Forth with Cupide and with his miht:
For thei merveille how such a wiht,
Which tho was in hir lusti age,
Desireth nother Mariage
Ne yit the love of paramours,
1270 Which evere hath be the comun cours
Amonges hem that lusti were.
So was it schewed after there:
For he that hihe hertes loweth　　　　　　[makes low]
With fyri Dartes whiche he throweth,
Cupide, which of love is godd,
In chastisinge hath mad a rodd
To dryve awei hir wantounesse;
So that withinne a while, I gesse,
Sche hadde on such a chance sporned,
1280 That al hire mod was overtorned,
Which ferst sche hadde of slow manere:
For thus it fell, as thou schalt hiere.
Whan come was the Monthe of Maii,
Sche wolde walke upon a dai,

And that was er the Sonne Ariste;
Of wommen bot a fewe it wiste,
And forth sche wente prively
Unto the Park was faste by,
Al softe walkende on the gras,
1290 Til sche cam ther the Launde was,
Thurgh which ther ran a gret rivere.
It thoghte hir fair, and seide, "Here
I wole abide under the schawe":   [wood (grove)]
And bad hire wommen to withdrawe,
And ther sche stod al one stille,
To thenke what was in hir wille.
Sche sih the swote floures springe,
Sche herde glade foules singe,
Sche sih the bestes in her kinde,   [their natural behavior]
1300 The buck, the do, the hert, the hinde,
The madle go with the femele;   [male]
And so began ther a querele
Betwen love and hir oghne herte,
Fro which sche couthe noght asterte.   [escape]
And as sche caste hire yhe aboute,
Sche syh clad in o suite a route
Of ladis, wher thei comen ryde
Along under the wodes syde:
On faire amblende hors thei sete,
1310 That were al whyte, fatte and grete,
And everichon thei ride on side.   [sidesaddle]
The Sadles were of such a Pride,
With Perle and gold so wel begon,
So riche syh sche nevere non;
In kertles and in Copes riche
Thei weren clothed, alle liche,
Departed evene of whyt and blew;
With alle lustes that sche knew   [joys]
Thei were enbrouded overal.   [adorned]
1320 Here bodies weren long and smal,

The beaute faye upon her face
Non erthly thing it may desface;
Corones on here hed thei beere,
As ech of hem a qweene weere,
That al the gold of Cresus halle
The leste coronal of alle
Ne mihte have boght after the worth:
Thus come thei ridende forth.
    The kinges dowhter, which this syh,
1330 For pure abaissht drowh hire adryh   [abashment/aside]
And hield hire clos under the bowh,
And let hem passen stille ynowh;
For as hire thoghte in hire avis,
To hem that were of such a pris
Sche was noght worthi axen there,
Fro when they come or what thei were:
Bot levere than this worldes good
Sche wolde have wist hou that it stod,
And putte hire hed alitel oute;
1340 And as sche lokede hire aboute,
Sche syh comende under the linde   [along the trees]
A womman up an hors behinde.
The hors on which sche rod was blak,
Al lene and galled on the back,
And haltede, as he were encluyed,   [hurt with a nail (OF *en-*
                                           cloer, 'to nail')]

Wherof the womman was annuied;
Thus was the hors in sori plit,
Bot for al that a sterre whit
Amiddes in the front he hadde.
1350 Hir Sadel ek was wonder badde,
In which the wofull womman sat,
And natheles ther was with that
A riche bridel for the nones
Of gold and preciouse Stones.
Hire cote was somdiel totore;

Aboute hir middel twenty score
Of horse haltres and wel mo
Ther hyngen ate time tho.
  Thus whan sche cam the ladi, nyh,
1360 Than tok sche betre hiede and syh
This womman fair was of visage,
Freyssh, lusti, yong and of tendre age;
And so this ladi, ther sche stod,
Bethoghte hire wel and understod
That this, which com ridende tho,
Tidinges couthe telle of tho,
Which as sche sih tofore ryde,
And putte hir forth and preide abide,
And seide "Ha, Suster, let me hiere,
1370 What ben thei, that now riden hiere,
And ben so richeliche arraied?"
  This womman, which com so esmaied, [troubled]
Ansuerde with ful softe speche,
And seith, "Ma Dame, I schal you teche.
These ar of tho that whilom were
Servantz to love, and trowthe beere,
Ther as thei hadde here herte set.
Fare wel, for I mai noght be let: [delay]
Ma Dame, I go to mi servise,
1380 So moste I haste in alle wise;
Forthi, ma Dame, yif me leve,
I mai noght longe with you leve,"
  "Ha, goode Soster, yit I preie,
Tell me whi ye ben so beseie
And with these haltres thus begon."
  "Ma Dame, whilom I was on
That to mi fader hadde a king;
Bot I was slow, and for no thing
Me liste noght to love abeie,
1390 And that I now ful sore abeie. [sorely pay for]
For I whilom no love hadde, [because]

Min hors is now so fièble and badde,
And al totore is myn arai,
And every yeer this freisshe Maii
These lusti ladis ryde aboute,
And I mot nedes suie here route   [follow]
In this manere as ye now se,
And trusse here haltres forth with me,   [pack their halters]
And am bot as here horse knave.
1400 Non other office I ne have,
Hem thenkth I am worthi nomore,
For I was slow in loves lore,
Whan I was able forto lere,   [learn]
And wolde noght the tales hiere
Of hem that couthen love teche."
    "Now tell me thanne, I you beseche,
Wherof that riche bridel serveth."
    With that hire chere awei sche swerveth, [face/turns]
And gan to wepe, and thus sche tolde:
1410 "This bridel, which ye nou beholde
So riche upon myn horse hed,—
Ma Dame, afore, er I was ded,
Whan I was in mi lusti lif,
Ther fel into myn herte a strif
Of love, which me overcom,
So that therafter hiede I nom
And thoghte I wolde love a kniht:
That laste wel a fourtenyht,
For it no lengere mihte laste,
1420 So nyh my lif was ate laste.
Bot now, allas, to late war
That I ne hadde him loved ar:
For deth cam so in haste bime,
Er I therto hadde eny time,
That it ne mihte ben achieved.
Bot for al that I am relieved,
Of that mi will was good therto,

That love soffreth it be so
That I schal swiche a bridel were.
1430 Now have ye herd al myn ansuere:
To godd, ma Dame, I you betake,
And warneth alle for mi sake,
Of love that thei ben noght ydel,
And bidd hem thenke upon my brydel."
And with that word al sodeinly
Sche passeth, as it were a Sky,
Al clene out of this ladi sihte:
And tho for fere hire herte afflihte,   [was afflicted]
And seide to hirself, "Helas!
1440 I am riht in the same cas.
Bot if I live after this day,
I schal amende it, if I may."
And thus homward this lady wente,
And changede al hire ferste entente,
Withinne hire herte and gan to swere
That sche none haltres wolde bere.

    Lo, Sone, hier miht thou taken hiede,
How ydelnesse is forto drede,
Namliche of love, as I have write.
1450 For thou miht understonde and wite,
Among the gentil nacion
Love is an occupacion,
Which forto kepe hise lustes save
Scholde every gentil herte have:
For as the ladi was chastised,
Riht so the knyht mai ben avised,
Which ydel is and wol noght serve
To love, he mai per cas deserve
A grettere peine than sche hadde,
1460 Whan sche aboute with hire ladde
The horse haltres; and forthi
Good is to be wel war therbi.   [careful]
Bot forto loke aboven alle,

These Maidens, hou so that it falle,
Thei scholden take ensample of this
Which I have told, for soth it is.

    Mi ladi Venus, whom I serve,
What womman wole hire thonk deserve,
Sche mai noght thilke love eschuie
1470 Of paramours, bot sche mot suie
Cupides lawe; and natheles
Men sen such love sielde in pes,
That it nys evere upon aspie
Of janglinge and of fals Envie,
Fulofte medlid with disese:
Bot thilke love is wel at ese,
Which set is upon mariage;
For that dar schewen the visage
In alle places openly.
1480 A gret mervaile it is forthi,
How that a Maiden wolde lette,
That sche hir time ne besette
To haste unto that ilke feste,
Wherof the love is al honeste.
Men mai recovere lost of good,
Bot so wys man yit nevere stod,
Which mai recovere time lore:
So mai a Maiden wel therfore
Ensample take, of that sche strangeth
1490 Hir love, and longe er that sche changeth
Hir herte upon hir lustes greene
To mariage, as it is seene.
For thus a yer or tuo or thre
Sche lest, er that sche wedded be,   [loses]
Whyl sche the charge myhte bere
Of children, whiche the world forbere
Ne mai, bot if it scholde faile.
Bot what Maiden hire esposaile
Wol tarie, whan sche take mai,

1500   Sche schal per chance an other dai
        Be let, whan that hire lievest were.   [put off/most desirous]

[To illustrate his point Genius tells the story of Jephthah's daughter.[11] Among the Jews there once lived a duke named Jephthah who vowed that if God would give him the victory he would sacrifice the first man or woman he saw upon returning home from war. His prayer was answered, the victory his. As he returned home his lovely daughter came out to meet him, dancing and caroling in celebration of her father's fame. She it was whom he saw first. Tearing his clothes and weeping he moaned the lack of true felicity in this life. His daughter comforted him but bade him keep his covenant. Yet she too mourned her fate. She got forty days respite to bewail her maidenhood, for since she had not yet married she had borne no children for the increase of her people. With other maidens she traveled over down and dale bewailing her lost youth which was to be wasted without fruit. Thus she died a woeful maiden (1505–1595).

The Lover thanks Genius for this story and says the point is clear for women, though he does not understand how it applies to men. A man's worthiness in love is manifested, says Genius, through feats of arms. Lovers should travel even across the sea seeking worship, sometimes in Prussia, now in Rhodes, now Tartary, until heralds cry out, "Valiant, valiant, lo, wher he goth!" (1633). Then his fame will come home to his Lady's ear.

Amans acknowledges that many men are more successful in arms than he, though he wonders if it is right to shed blood at all. Christ bid that no man should slay another. Besides, what good would winning across the sea be if he lost his Lady at home? Books say we should convert men to Christ's faith, not kill them. To kill a Saracen is to kill a soul, and killing was never Christ's teaching. Amans says he would rather serve in Cupid's arms and go where love bids him. Did not Achilles himself leave his arms and the Greek cause because of his love of Polexenen? There is no gain in winning chaff and losing wheat. Nevertheless, if his Lady bid him to fly through the sky or go through the deep sea, he would. Yet all his labor seems fruitless. Cupid always sets things in discord. The busier he is and the more he kneels and prays with soft words, the more he is refused. All his efforts come to idleness in the end (1698–1770).

Genius tells Amans that he cares too much and is too hasty. Better to wait for tide than to row against the stream. Perchance the revolutions of the heavens are not yet in accord with his condition. Genius says he will vouch to Venus, whose priest he is, that Amans has tried hard (1771–1810). But to demonstrate the Lover's sloth in refusing to bear arms and to counter his example of Achilles' refusal to bear arms, Genius tells the story of Nauplus and Ulysses.[12] When King Nauplus, father of Palamades, asked Ulysses to join the other Greeks in the seige of Troy, Ulysses, because of his love for Penelope with whom he would dwell in love at home, tried to beguile the king by feigning madness. He arose early and yoked foxes instead of oxen to his plow and sowed the land with salt. Nauplus saw through the ruse and played a trick in return. He placed Ulysses' son in the furrow before the plow and when Ulysses turned aside, he chastised him for feigning madness and thus forsaking honor because of love. Ulysses answered not one word, but turned and went home in shame to prepare himself for war (1811–1895).

Thus, a knight who refuses his responsibilities will find no ease. He must put aside fear as did the worthy King Protesilaus when he ignored the warnings of his wife that he not go to Troy.[13] He was the first to land, choosing rather to die in battle than be reproved for cowardice (1934). Similarly, Saul, when the spirit of Samuel told him that he and his son Jonathan would be slain in battle, did not hold back from the enemy but met them on Mount Gelboe, and although he was slain, his knighthood is known throughout the world (1962).[14]

Prowess in knighthood is grounded in hardiness. He who would become a knight should take example of Achilles who was trained by Chiro, called Centaurus.[15] Chiro taught Achilles when he was twelve years old to enter into a wilderness filled with lions and lionesses, leopards and tigers, there to pursue no beast which fled before him such as hart and hind, but to take his game from that which withstood him. Everyday, without fail, he kept his covenant with Chiro and slew or at least wounded fierce beasts to bring blood tokens to Chiro as he was taught. He no more feared a lion than an ass, and thus came to surpass all other knights in prowess (1963–2013).

Genius notes that books are full of examples of bravery, such as Lancelot's, which bring the knight success in love, but one story especially comes to mind, that of Hercules and Achelons.[16] King Oënes of Chalcedon had a daughter named Deianire with whom Hercules, the son of Mercury, fell in love. The fame of Hercules, who had set the two brass pillars in the desert of India, was endless, and when he asked Oënes for Deianire's hand in marriage the king was filled with fear. He said that Deianire was already betrothed to Achelons, a giant and a sorcerer, but that the matter might be settled through a combat between the contestants in love. Achelons readily accepted the contest. The day was set, the field chosen, and the two knights fought. Soon Hercules caught the giant in his powerful arms and lifted him into the air. But the sorcerer turned himself into an adder and slipped away. Next he changed into a bull which spurned the earth and charged Hercules. But Hercules seized the bull's great horns and cast him to the ground, there to hold him fast. Thus Hercules won what he otherwise would not have had (2014–2134).

Another example of love and war's acquaintance is seen in Pantasilee, Queen of Feminee, who, for love of Hector, led her maidens against the Greeks in hope of rescuing Troy. After Pirrus slew her, Philemenis brought her body back to the land of the Amazons and was granted three lusty maidens a year as a reward. Thus his labor brought him ease. Aeneas also won his bride Lavinia by defeating Turnus. These examples show how love is won by manhood and gentilesse (2135–2199).[17]

Amans asks Genius the meaning of Gentilesse. Some say that Gentilesse comes with riches which are passed down from past time, but Genius says they are wrong.[18] Riches do not last and have no merit in themselves. Nor are men born gentle, for all are descended alike from Adam and Eve. All are born naked into the world and are subject to death whether they be rich or poor. No worldly goods accompany man beyond the grave; nor is there virtue in such possessions.]

Bot of the bodi, which schal deie,
Althogh ther be diverse weie
To deth, yit is ther bot on ende,
To which that every man schal wende,
Als wel the beggere as the lord,
2250 Of o nature, of on acord:
Sche which oure Eldemoder is,   [ancient mother]
The Erthe, bothe that and this
Receiveth and alich devoureth,
That sche to nouther part favoureth.
So wot I nothing after kinde
Where I mai gentilesse finde.

[Virtue alone which is set in the heart and which may not be taken away offers the certainty of Gentilesse.]

For after the condicion
2270 Of resonable entencion,
The which out of the Soule groweth
And the vertu fro vice knoweth,
Wherof a man the vice eschuieth,
Withoute Slowthe and vertu suieth,   [follows]
That is a verrai gentil man,   [truly]
And nothing elles which he can,
Ne which he hath, ne which he mai.
Bot for al that yit nou aday,
In loves court to taken hiede,
2280 The povere vertu schal noght spiede,   [succeed]
Wher that the riche vice woweth;
For sielde it is that love alloweth   [seldom]
The gentil man withoute good,

Thogh his condicion be good.
Bot if a man of bothe tuo
Be riche and vertuous also,
Thanne is he wel the more worth:
Bot yit to putte himselve forth
He mostc don his besinesse,
2290 For nowther good ne gentilesse
Mai helpen hem whiche ydel be.

[If one works hard according to his degree, it often happens that
he achieves both worship and ease. Honest love has many ways of
profit: It makes the villain courteous and the coward hardy; it
rules men and women alike.]

For love hath evere hise lustes grene
2310 In gentil folk, as it is sene,
Which thing ther mai no kinde areste:
I trowe that ther is no beste,   [no man of highest gen-
                                                    tilesse]

If he with love scholde aqueinte,
That he ne wolde make it queinte   [consummate the love]
As for the while that it laste.
And thus I conclude ate laste,
That thei ben ydel, as me semeth,
Whiche unto thing that love demeth
Forslowthen that thei scholden do.   [neglect through sloth]
2320   And overthis, mi Sone, also
After the vertu moral eke
To speke of love if I schal seke,
Among the holi bokes wise
I finde write in such a wise,
"Who loveth noght is hier as ded";[19]
For love above alle othre is hed,
Which hath the vertus forto lede,
Of al that unto mannes dede   [behavior (deed)]
Belongeth: for of ydelschipe

2330 He hateth all the felaschipe.
    For Slowthe is evere to despise,
    Which in desdeign hath al apprise,   [teaching (OF *apprendre*,
                                              'to teach, inform')]

    And that acordeth noght to man:
    For he that wit and reson kan,
    It sit him wel that he travaile
    Upon som thing which mihte availe,
    For ydelschipe is noght comended,
    Bot every lawe it hath defended.   [forbidden (OF *defendre*,
                                              'to ward off')

[Solomon says, "Just as birds are made for flight, so man is born to labor." [20] We who now live may take from antiquity examples of man's wit and strength. In order that we might draw to memory the names and history of man's labors, Genius reviews the uses of labor as found in many books.[21] The high God gave to men the perfect form and matter of wisdom which men must repeatedly labor to learn anew. Men labor over books as well as plows. The names of great inventors have come down to us through the chronicles. Cham invented the Hebrew alphabet and was the first man to be learned in natural philosophy. Cadmus made the first Greek letters. Theges was the first augur, and Philemon the first to describe the countenance of the heart. The first authors (enditours) were Cladyns, Esdras, Sulpices, Termegis, Pandulf, Frigidilles, Menander, Ephiloquorus, Solins, Pandas, and Josephus. Heredot was the first man notable in the science of meter, rime, and cadence. Jubal was the first musician, and Poulins invented the harp. Zenzis was the first painter, Prometheus the first sculptor. Tubal first worked with iron and steel, while Jadahel was the first fisherman and hunter. Veronius made first the delicacies of cooking, and Minerve was first to weave wool. Delbora first made linen. It was Saturn who taught men to work in the fields and vineyards for meat and drink; he also introduced merchants and the coining of money (2450). But how the precious metals came to be, men do not know, though philosophers have sought many ways through alchemy. Each planet has its appropriate metal (the Sun gold, the Moon silver, Mars iron, Saturn lead, Jupiter brass, Venus copper, and Mercury quicksilver), and there are four spirits (quicksilver, sal amoniac, sulphur, and arsenic). Men have learned how to refine them with hot, well-blown fires. In order to work with the body and spirit of metals, men, in hope of finding the philosopher's stone, use seven established forms (distillation, congelation, solution, descension, sublimation, calcination, fixation). These wise old philosophers made three stones: *lapis vegetabilis,* whose virtue it is to heal men and keep them from sickness until natural death befalls them; *lapis animalis,* which protects the five senses and keeps them keen; and a third called *Mineral,* which can restore metals to their original purity, that is, return them to gold and silver (the red and the white of the sun and moon), the two extremes to which all metals desire to return. This last stone not only multiplies gold, but also it is an elixir for men and is much sought after by alchemists.]

Thei speken faste of thilke Ston,
Bot hou to make it, nou wot non
After the sothe experience.
And natheles gret diligence
Thei setten upon thilke dede,
And spille more than thei spede;
For allewey thei finde a lette,   [hindrance]
Which bringeth in poverte and dette
To hem that riche were afore:
2590   The lost is had, the lucre is lore,
To gete a pound thei spenden fyve;
I not hou such a craft schal thryve
In the manere as it is used:
It were betre be refused
Than forto worchen upon weene   [expectation]
In thing which stant noght as thei weene.   [think]

[Hermes was the very first alchemist to whom most still apply. Geber, Ortolan, Morien, and Avicen also wrote about the practice of alchemy, though few understand their books. Those who found the way wrote in Greek, Arabic, and Chaldean (2632).

Among the Latin speaking kingdoms Carmente invented the use of letters, and Aristarchus, Donat, and Dindimus were the first grammarians. "Tullius with cithero" wrote about rhetoric.[22] Jerome translated the Bible from Hebrew to Latin, while other writers translated into Latin books from the Chaldean, Greek, and Arabic. Ovid wrote Latin poetry and if you want council in love you should read him (2671).

Amans says he would read Ovid if it would help speed his love; it would be pointless to read him if he counseled restraint. To learn a thing which may not be is like trying to keep green a tree whose roots have been cut off. Genius admits that one must venture in love if he hopes to win and warns Amans of other kinds of sloth which obstruct love (2700). Somnolence is chamberlain to Sloth and many a hundred has he laid to sleep when they should be awake. Often he retires unkissed, saying that he will not leave his sluggardy for any drury. When knights and women revel, he skulks off like a hare and goes to bed, there to dream that he is stuck in the mire, or that he is sitting by the fire clawing his bare shanks, or that he is climbing up banks and falling into deep slades. All the while he snores louder than a ship running against the current; he sputters like a monk's pancake just thrown into the pan. At other times (though seldom) he dreams he is in Lover's Heaven and that all the world is his and has to listen to whatever exposition suits his disposition. Be careful not to be like the somnolent, Genius advises (2701–2745).

Amans says he would rather lose both eyes before he would be such a sluggard. Better to have died in his mother's womb. He would never sleep when he had the opportunity to dance or play near his love. No one skips as light as he if he should get to kiss her hand. He readily consents to play dice or talk of love, or read about Troilus if she does not want to dance. And if the occasion to speak his desire arises he speaks, and if she says it is

time to go home because of darkness he says it is still light. But
if she insists, how piteously he looks on her when he takes his
leave, hoping she may slacken her Daunger. Even so he tarries,
finally kneeling to kiss her good night; then, just before he
reaches the door he feigns losing his ring, or something else, and
returns for a last kiss, though seldom does he get one. And when
he finally does leave, he curses that ever sleep was made for eyes,
and wishes night were passed so that he might see her again.
When at last he goes to bed his mind wanders beyond locks and
walls and enters her bed and softly takes her in his arms and
feels the warmth of her body and wishes his body were there.
Thus he torments himself at night until sleep finally takes him.
Then a thousand score greater is his torment as he dreams. If, in
his dream, Daunger leaves, then he wishes never to wake, but
would dream that dream forever (2746–2916). Genius observes
that dreams have sometimes been prophetic and tells the story of
Ceïx and Alceone[23] as proof.]

TALE OF CEÏX AND ALCEONE

    This finde I write in Poesie:
Ceïx the king of Trocinie
Hadde Alceone to his wif,
2930 Which as hire oghne hertes lif
Him loveth; and he hadde also
A brother, which was cleped tho
Dedalion, and he per cas
Fro kinde of man forschape was
Into a Goshauk of liknesse;
Wherof the king gret hevynesse
Hath take, and thoghte in his corage
To gon upon a pelrinage
Into a strange regioun,
2940 Wher he hath his devocioun
To don his sacrifice and preie,

If that he mihte in eny weie
Toward the goddes finde grace
His brother hele to pourchace,
So that he mihte be reformed
Of that he hadde be transformed.
To this pourpos and to this ende
This king is redy forto wende,
As he which wolde go be Schipe;
2950 And forto don him felaschipe
His wif unto the See him broghte,
With al hire herte and him besoghte,
That he the time hire wolde sein,
Whan that he thoghte come ayein:
"Withinne," he seith, "tuo Monthe day."
And thus in al the haste he may
He tok his leve, and forth he seileth
Wepende, and sche hirself beweileth,
And torneth hom, ther sche cam fro.
2960 Bot whan the Monthes were ago,
The whiche he sette of his comynge,
And that sche herde no tydinge,
Ther was no care forto seche:
Wherof the goddes to beseche
Tho sche began in many wise,
And to Juno hire sacrifise
Above alle othre most sche dede,
And for hir lord sche hath no bede
To wite and knowe hou that he ferde,
2970 That Juno the goddesse hire herde,
Anon and upon this matiere
Sche bad Yris hir Messagere
To Slepes hous that sche schal wende,
And bidde him that he make an ende
Be swevene and schewen al the cas   [dream]
Unto this ladi, hou it was.

    This Yris, fro the hihe stage

Which undertake hath the Message,
Hire reyny Cope dede upon,   [cloak]
2980 The which was wonderli begon
With colours of diverse hewe,
An hundred mo than men it knewe;
The hevene lich unto a bowe
Sche bende, and so she cam doun lowe,
The god of Slep wher that sche fond.
And that was in a strange lond,
Which marcheth upon Chymerie: [borders on]
For ther, as seith the Poesie,
The god of Slep hath mad his hous,
2990 Which of entaille is merveilous.   [construction]
Under an hell ther is a Cave,   [hill]
Which of the Sonne mai noght have,
So that noman mai knowe ariht
The point betwen the dai and nyht:
Ther is no fyr, ther is no sparke,
Ther is no dore, which mai charke,   [creak]
Wherof an yhe scholde unschette,
So that inward ther is no lette.   [disturbance]
And forto speke of that withoute,
3000 Ther stant no gret Tree nyh aboute
Wher on ther myhte crowe or pie
Alihte, forto clepe or crie:
Ther is no cok to crowe day,
Ne beste non which noise may
The hell, bot al aboute round
Ther is growende upon the ground
Popi, which berth the sed of slep,
With othre herbes suche an hep.   [great quality (heap)]
A stille water for the nones   [quiet stream]
3010 Rennende upon the smale stones,
Which hihte of Lethes the rivere,
Under that hell in such manere
Ther is, which yifth gret appetit

To slepe. And thus full of delit
Slep hath his hous; and of his couche
Withinne his chambre if I schal touche,
Of hebenus that slepi Tree   [ebony]
The bordes al aboute be,
And for he scholde slepe softe,
3020   Upon a fethrebed alofte
He lith with many a pilwe of doun:
The chambre is strowed up and doun
With swevenes many thousendfold.   [dreams]
Thus cam Yris into this hold,
And to the bedd, which is al blak,
Sche goth, and ther with Slep sche spak,
And in the wise as sche was bede   [ordered]
The Message of Juno sche dede.
Fulofte hir wordes sche reherceth,
3030   Er sche his slepi Eres perceth;
With mochel wo bot ate laste
His slombrende yhen he upcaste
And seide hir that it schal be do
Wherof among a thousend tho,
Withinne his hous that slepi were,
In special he ches out there
Thre, whiche scholden do this dede:
The ferste of hem, so as I rede,
Was Morpheüs, the whos nature   [the one whose]
3040   Is forto take the figure
Of what persone that him liketh,
Wherof that he fulofte entriketh   [ensnares]
The lif which slepe schal be nyhte;
And Ithecus that other hihte,
Which hath the vois of every soun,
The chiere and the condicioun   [countenance]
Of every lif, what so it is:
The thridde suiende after this
Is Panthasas, which may transforme

3050 Of every thing the rihte forme,
　　　And change it in an other kinde.
　　　Upon hem thre, so as I finde,
　　　Of swevenes stant al thapparence,
　　　Which otherwhile is evidence
　　　And otherwhile bot a jape.　　　　　　　[jest]
　　　Bot natheles it is so schape,
　　　That Morpheüs be nyht al one
　　　Appiereth until Alceone
　　　In liknesse of hir housebonde
3060 Al naked ded upon the stronde,
　　　And hou he dreynte in special
　　　These othre tuo it schewen al.
　　　The tempeste of the blake cloude,
　　　The wode See, the wyndes loude,　　　　[raging sea]
　　　Al this sche mette, and sih him dyen;　　[dreamed]
　　　Wherof that sche began to crien,
　　　Slepende abedde ther sche lay,
　　　And with that noise of hire affray　　　　[fright]
　　　Hir wommen sterten up aboute,
3070 Whiche of here ladi were in doute,
　　　And axen hire hou that sche ferde;
　　　And sche, riht as sche syh and herde,
　　　Hir swevene hath told hem everydel.
　　　And thei it halsen alle wel　　　　　　　[explain]
　　　And sein it is a tokne of goode;
　　　Bot til sche wiste hou that it stode,
　　　Sche hath no confort in hire herte,
　　　Upon the morwe and up sche sterte,
　　　And to the See, wher that sche mette　　[dreamed]
3080 The bodi lay, withoute lette　　　　　　　[delay]
　　　Sche drowh, and whan that sche cam nyh,
　　　Stark ded, hise armes sprad, sche syh
　　　Hire lord flietende upon the wawe.　　　[wave]
　　　Wherof hire wittes ben withdrawe,
　　　And sche, which tok of deth no kepe,

Anon forth lepte into the depe
And wolde have cawht him in hire arm.
    This infortune of double harm
The goddes fro the hevene above
3090 Behielde, and for the trowthe of love,
Which in this worthi ladi stod,
Thei have upon the salte flod
Hire dreinte lord and hire also
Fro deth to lyve torned so,
That thei ben schapen into briddes   [birds]
Swimmende upon the wawe amiddes.
And whan sche sih hire lord livende
In liknesse of a bridd swimmende,
And sche was of the same sort,
3100 So as sche mihte do desport,
Upon the joie which sche hadde
Hire wynges bothe abrod sche spradde,
And him, so as sche mai suffise,
Beclipte and keste in such a wise,
As sche was whilom wont to do:
Hire wynges for hire armes tuo
Sche tok, and for hire lippes softe
Hire harde bile, and so fulofte
Sche fondeth in hire briddes forme,
3110 If that sche mihte hirself conforme
To do the plesance of a wif,
As sche dede in that other lif:
For thogh sche hadde hir pouer lore,
Hir will stod as it was tofore,
And serveth him so as sche mai.
Wherof into this ilke day
Togedre upon the See thei wone,
Wher many a dowhter and a Sone
Thei bringen forth of briddes kinde;
3120 And for men scholden take in mynde
This Alceoun the trewe queene,

Hire briddes yit, as it is seene,
Of Alceoun the name bere.

[Thus it is that men's dreams often prove true. Amans observes that he is watchful when he is near his Lady, but when he is far away he spends his time abed, trying to sleep, sighing to make time pass, hating all the while his waking hours. Is this Somnolence? Genius says the Lover has been so dedicated that he is forgiven (3124–3186). To reassure him and to show how incompatible love and sleep are, he recounts the "Prayer of Cephalus."[24] Cephalus lay all night with Aurora in his arms, but as day drew near he prayed: "O Phebus, governor of the day's light, though you make glad all creatures according to nature's law, nevertheless, love likes secrecy and desires to be shaded. I pray with all my heart that you withdraw your light from which nothing may be hidden. Remain unborn in the sign of Capricorn in the house of Saturn that I may love longer. Drive your fiery chariot the long way around. And Diana also, goddess of the moon, be gracious. Stand all the while opposite Phebus in your house in Cancer so that we might beget children." Thus he prayed that he might love and enjoy the feast of night without the sleep of sluggardy. Sloth knows neither night from day, but sleeps and snores till noon. Cephalus did otherwise (3187–3275).

Amans says he knows of no man who would sleep if he had his love by him. He has not had the good fortune of such circumstances, so as far as he is concerned the sun can keep on moving. In sleep he at least dreams sometimes. Genius agrees but warns him not to sleep too much (3276–3316). There is a time to sleep and a time not to, as the story of Argus and Mercury exemplifies.[25] Ovid tells how Jupiter lay with Io, whereupon Juno, in her wrath, turned Io into a cow and set Argus with his hundred eyes to keep track of her. But Mercury devised a pipe which played so sweetly that Argus, for all his eyes, fell asleep, and Mercury cut off his head and stole the cow away. Much woe may thus befall a man who sleeps when he should not. Amans reminds Genius that he himself has already made the same point and wonders if there is any other aspect of Sloth which they might next consider (3317–3379). Genius says there is, and that is Tristesse, that is to say, wanhope or despondency. After Sloth has done all it can, at last the slothful one sees how his time has been lost and conceives Tristesse in his heart. He then despairs. In one breath he wishes a thousand times for death. He laments, "Alas that I was born," yet he makes no effort to help himself; his sorrow merely confirms the desperate world he is in. He thinks himself beyond mercy and inconsolable. He obstinately refuses to listen to reason. Thus he dwindles till he dies, hindering his own welfare. So it is too with lovers. "Are you such a one?" Genius asks (3380–3457).

Amans says he is, except in one point. He is bound to sorrow and has no real hope; nevertheless, he still prays. He asks for penance. Genius says he knows of no cure for such a condition. Lovers are always sorrowful and only love can give them grace. But do not despair, for when the heart fails there is no cure and the gods are vengeful (3458–3514). Witness the Tale of Iphis and Araxarathen.[26]]

TALE OF IPHIS
AND ARAXARATHEN

Whilom be olde daies fer
Of Mese was the king Theucer,
Which hadde a kniht to Sone, Iphis:
Of love and he so maistred is,
That he hath set al his corage,
3520   As to reguard of his lignage,
Upon a Maide of lou astat.
Bot thogh he were a potestat
Of worldes good, he was soubgit
To love, and put in such a plit,
That he excedeth the mesure
Of reson, that himself assure

He can noght; for the more he preide,
The lasse love on him sche leide.
He was with love unwys constreigned,
3530 And sche with resoun was restreigned:
The lustes of his herte he suieth,
And sche for drede schame eschuieth,
And as sche scholde, tok good hiede
To save and kepe hir wommanhiede.
And thus the thing stod in debat
Betwen his lust and hire astat:
He yaf, he sende, he spak be mouthe,
Bot yit for oght that evere he couthe
Unto his sped he fond no weie,   [success]
3540 So that he caste his hope aweie,
Withinne his herte and gan despeire
Fro dai to dai, and so empeire,   [becomes worse]
That he hath lost al his delit
Of lust, of Slep, of Appetit,
That he thurgh strengthe of love lasseth   [diminishes]
His wit, and resoun overpasseth.
As he which of his lif ne rowhte,   [cared not]
His deth upon himself he sowhte,
So that be nyhte his weie he nam,
3550 Ther wiste non wher he becam;
The nyht was derk, ther schon no Mone,
Tofore the gates he cam sone,
Wher that this yonge Maiden was,
And with this wofull word, "Helas!"
Hise dedli pleintes be began
So stille that ther was noman
It herde, and thanne he seide thus:
"O thou Cupide, o thou Venus,
Fortuned be whos ordinaunce
3560 Of love is every mannes chaunce,
Ye knowen al min hole herte,
That I ne mai your hond asterte;   [escape]

On you is evere that I crie,
And yit you deigneth noght to plie,   [yield]
Ne toward me youre Ere encline.
Thus for I se no medicine
To make an ende of mi querele,
My deth schal be in stede of hele.
    Ha, thou mi wofull ladi diere
3570 Which duellest with thi fader hiere
And slepest in thi bedd at ese,
Thou wost nothing of my desese,
Hou thou and I be now unmete.   [far apart]
Ha lord, what swevene schalt thou mete,
What dremes hast thou nou on honde?
Thou slepest there, and I hier stonde.
Thogh I no deth to the deserve,
Hier schal I for thi love sterve,
Hier schal a kinges Sone dye
3580 For love and for no felonie;
Wher thou therof have joie or sorwe,
Hier schalt thou se me ded tomorwe.
O herte hard aboven alle,
This deth, which schal to me befalle
For that thou wolt noght do me grace,
Yit schal be told in many a place,
Hou I am ded for love and trouthe
In thi defalte and in thi slouthe:
Thi Daunger schal to manye mo
3590 Ensample be for everemo,
Whan thei my wofull deth recorde."
And with that word he tok a Corde,
With which upon the gate tre
He hyng himself, that was pite.
    The morwe cam, the nyht is gon,
Men comen out and syhe anon
Wher that this yonge lord was ded:
Ther was an hous withoute red,   [counsel]

For noman knew the cause why;
3600 Ther was wepinge and ther was cry.
This Maiden, whan that sche it herde,
And sih this thing hou it misferde,
Anon sche wiste what it mente,
And al the cause hou it wente
To al the world sche tolde it oute,
And preith to hem that were aboute,
To take of hire the vengance,
For sche was cause of thilke chaunce,
Why that this kinges Sone is split.
3610 Sche takth upon hirself the gilt,
And is al redi to the peine
Which eny man hir wole ordeigne:
And bot if eny other wolde,
Sche seith that sche hirselve scholde
Do wreche with hire oghne hond,
Thurghout the world in every lond
That every lif therof schal speke,
Hou sche hirself it scholde wreke.
Sche wepth, sche crith, sche swouneth ofte,
3620 Sche caste hire yhen up alofte
And seide among ful pitously:
"A godd, thou wost wel it am I,
For whom Iphis is thus besein:
Ordeine so, that men mai sein
A thousend wynter after this,
Hou such a Maiden dede amis,
And as I dede, do to me:
For I ne dede no pite
To him, which for mi love is lore,
3630 Do no pite to me therfore."
And with this word sche fell to grounde
Aswoune, and ther sche lay a stounde.
The goddes, whiche hir pleigntes herde
And syhe hou wofully sche ferde,

Hire lif thei toke awey anon,
And schopen hire into a Ston
After the forme of hire ymage
Of bodi bothe and of visage.
And for the merveile of this thing
3640 Unto the place cam the king
And ek the queene and manye mo;
And whan thei wisten it was so,
As I have told it hier above,
Hou that Iphis was ded for love,
Of that he hadde be refused,
Thei hielden alle men excused
And wondren upon the vengance.
And forto kepe in remembrance,
This faire ymage mayden liche
3650 With compaignie noble and riche
With torche and gret sollempnite
To Salamyne the Cite
Thei lede, and carie forth withal
The dede corps, and sein it schal
Beside thilke ymage have
His sepulture and be begrave: [buried]
This corps and this ymage thus
Into the Cite to Venus,
Wher that goddesse hire temple hadde,
3660 Togedre bothe tuo thei ladde.
This ilke ymage as for miracle
Was set upon an hyh pinacle,
That alle men it mihte knowe,
And under that thei maden lowe
A tumbe riche for the nones
Of marbre and ek of jaspre stones,
Wherin this Iphis was beloken,
That evermor it schal be spoken.
And for men schal the sothe wite,
3670 Thei have here epitaphe write,

As thing which scholde abide stable:
The lettres graven in a table
Of marbre were and seiden this:
"Hier lith, which slowh himself, Iphis,
For love of Araxarathen:
And in ensample of tho wommen,
That soffren men to deie so,
Hire forme a man mai sen also,
Hou it is torned fleissh and bon
3680 Into the figure of a Ston:
He was to neysshe and sche to hard.   [soft (OE *hnesce*)]
Be war forthi hierafterward;
Ye men and wommen bothe tuo,
Ensampleth you of that was tho."
      Lo thus, mi Sone, as I thee seie,
It grieveth be diverse weie
In desespeir a man to falle,
Which is the laste branche of alle
Of Slouthe, as thou hast herd devise.
3690 Whereof that thou thiself avise
Good is, er that thou be deceived,
Wher that the grace of hope is weyved.

[Amans says he now understands the meaning of Sloth and its
court and asks if there are other sins in which he should be in-
structed, for he would be "clene schryve." Genius says he will
next speak of one of the seven sins that has set the world at odds
with itself and has caused much wrong (3693–3712).]

Explicit Liber Quartus

INCIPIT LIBER QUINTUS

[At first, after God created the world, men held property in common. They spoke not of winning or losing, for there was little to be had. But as men, horses, oxen, and sheep increased, and as men began to use money, Avarice sprang up. Then war replaced peace; instead of the spade and shovel men took in hand the sharp sword. They hoarded their gold behind walls and ditches, and the more they got the more they sought, thinking ever that the world lasts. Thus their state became a hell, filled with worry, their only pleasure being in looking at gold. But their profit was worth no more than the plow to the ox or the sheared wool to the sheep. They became slaves to their own wealth (1–59).

Amans says he has not been avaricious in love, since he has never been in full possession of his woman. Yet he should not be excused, for if once he got her he would hold on to her till death parted them. He would be more strongly welded to her than to his own wife, if he had one, and would not fast even on Friday. Fie on bags in a chest. He would have enough if he but kissed her. She would be worth more to him than a whole mine full of gold. Yet he is like the avaricious man in his concern over his treasure, and, like the ox which Genius mentioned, he gets no real profit for his labor (60–116).

Genius does not wonder about the Lover's thraldom in love, but warns him that thraldom to gold goes against nature, as the story of Midas demonstrates.[1] Bacchus, god of wine, had a priest named Cillenus, who got drunk and wandered into Frigia, there to be seized, bound in chains, and taken to King Midas. Midas, who saw what the trouble was, had him unbound and placed in a chamber on a soft couch, where he might sleep at leisure. When

238

Cillenus awoke to discover Midas's courtesy, he prayed to Bacchus to reward Midas. So Bacchus did by granting him one wish. Three choices Midas debated. The first, delight, he rejected, since he would not be able to appreciate delights in old age. The second, worship, he rejected because of the responsibilities which accompany it. So he decided to wish for wealth; he asked that all that he touched might be turned to gold. The god granted his wish. Midas was glad: he touched this and that, and stone, tree, leaf, grass, flour, fruit—all became gold. But soon he became hungry. His board was set, but all that came near his mouth turned to gold. Then he saw his folly. He cried to Bacchus to be forgiven of his avarice. The god took pity on him and bade him go bathe in the river Paceole. He did and recovered his first estate, but as he did so the bed of the stream turned to gold. On his return home he put aside Avarice forever, and saw that food and clothes sufficed. He advised his people to till their lands and to live according to nature's law (117–332).

So it was that before gold was smelted into coins there were scarcely any untrue men. Towns needed no walls; there were no property contracts (*brocage*). The florin was the mother of malignity and war. Avarice is its own wondrous hell, for it is never satisfied. Avoid Avarice; hold to Largess. Give to the poor, for he who is niggardly here suffers elsewhere. Remember the suffering of Tantalus.[2] The flood was at his lower lip and fruit hung against his upper lip. But neither could he reach to quench his thirst or satisfy his hunger. If he bowed to drink, the water bowed too; and if he reached to eat, the fruit withdrew. Such is the torment of the avaricious. If you wish to be beloved, you must be gracious and eschew the sickness of Avarice (333–428).

A jealous lover is like an avaricious man.[3] Both see a potential thief in every man. Jealousy is a feverous malady which afflicts the eyes so that the jealous man may never take them off his woman. He watches her every smile or frown. If she dresses well, he thinks she is luring men on; if she dresses poorly, he thinks she does not love him. He gives her no rest. His spies watch her while he is away. If she shows the least favor to another man he turns the occasion into a quarrel. Like a blind man he finds fault where there is none. Woe to the woman who is married to such a man. If it is the woman who is jealous, her pain is double, for she must keep it to herself. Jealousy grows from foolish love and distrust. Just as a sick man hates his food, so the jealous man, in his fever, loses his appetite for love. Love hates nothing more than Avarice, as the Tale of Vulcan and Venus shows.[4]]

TALE OF VULCAN AND VENUS

Ovide wrot of manye thinges,
Among the whiche in his wrytinges
He tolde a tale in Poesie,
Which toucheth unto Jelousie,
Upon a certein cas of love.
640 Among the goddes alle above
It fell at thilke time thus:
The god of fyr, which Vulcanus
Is hote, and hath a craft forthwith
Assigned, forto be the Smith
Of Jupiter, and his figure
Bothe of visage and of stature
Is lothly and malgracious,
Bot yit he hath withinne his hous
As for the likynge of his lif
650 The faire Venus to his wif.
Bot Mars, which of batailles is
The god, an yhe hadde unto this:
As he which was chivalerous,
It fell him to ben amerous,
And thoghte it was a gret pite
To se so lusti on as sche
Be coupled with so lourde a wiht: [clumsy]
So that his peine day and nyht
He dede, if he hire winne myhte;

660 And sche, which hadde a good insihte
Toward so noble a knyhtli lord
In love fell of his acord.
Ther lacketh noght bot time and place,
That he nys siker of hire grace: [certain]
Bot whan tuo hertes falle in on,
So wys await was nevere non,
That at som time thei ne mete;
And thus this faire lusti swete
With Mars hath ofte compaignie.
670 Bot thilke unkynde Jelousie,
Which everemor the herte opposeth,
Makth Vulcanus that he supposeth
That it is noght wel overal,
And to himself he seide, he schal
Aspie betre, if that he may;
And so it fell upon a day,
That he this thing so slyhli ledde,
He fond hem bothe tuo abedde
Al warm, echon with other naked.
680 And he with craft al redy maked
Of stronge chenes hath hem bounde,
As he togedre hem hadde founde,
And lefte hem bothe ligge so,
And gan to clepe and crie tho
Unto the goddes al aboute;
And thei assembled in a route
Come alle at ones forto se.
Bot none amendes hadde he,
Bot was rebuked hiere and there
690 Of hem that loves frendes were;
And seiden that he was to blame,
For if ther fell him eny schame,
It was thurgh his misgovernance:
And thus he loste contienance,
This god, and let his cause falle;

And thei to skorne him lowhen alle,   [laugh]
And losen Mars out of hise bondes.
Wherof these erthli housebondes
For evere myhte ensample take,
700   If such a chaunce hem overtake:
For Vulcanus his wif bewreide,   [exposed]
The blame upon himself he leide,
Wherof his schame was the more;
Which oghte forto ben a lore
For every man that liveth hiere,
To reulen him in this matiere.
Thogh such an happ of love asterte,
Yit scholde he noght apointe his herte
With Jelousie of that is wroght,
710   Bot feigne, as thogh he wiste it noght:
For if he lete it overpasse,
The sclaundre schal be wel the lasse,
And he the more in ese stonde.
For this thou myht wel understonde,
That where a man schal nedes lese,   [lose]
The leste harm is forto chese.
Bot Jelousie of his untrist
Makth that full many an harm arist,
Which elles scholde noght arise;
720   And if a man him wolde avise
Of that befell to Vulcanus,
Him oghte of reson thenke thus,
That sithe a god therof was schamed,
Wel scholde an erthli man be blamed
To take upon him such a vice.
     Forthi, my Sone, in thin office
Be war that thou be noght jelous,
Which ofte time hath schent the hous.   [ruined]

[Amans says this example is hard to understand. How may such things befall gods when there is only one God who is Lord over both heaven and hell?[5] How did the notion of such gods come about? Genius explains that among the ignorant much is taken for true which is mistaken. Before Christ was born among us there were four forms of religion. The religion of the Chaldeans was based on the twelve signs of the Zodiac and the seven planets. They depicted in their imaginations gods in the various constellations. They also worshipped the elements. These beliefs were unreasonable, for the elements are mutable and clearly not gods, and the sun and moon suffer eclipses. He who worships the stars detracts from the Creator by placing the creation above him. Nevertheless, that is what the Chaldeans did, and consequently they do penance in hell (729–786).

The second form of religion was that of the Egyptians, and their false faith was the worst of all. They honored as gods various beasts and also three brothers (Orus, Typhon, and Isirus) and their sister (Isis). Isirus slept with Isis and for that Typhon slew him. But Isirus's son Orayn later slew Typhon in return. The Chronicle says that Isis came to Egypt from Greece and taught the Egyptians how to till the soil. She is their goddess of birth. So they believed in their ignorance (787–834).

The third form of religion before Christ's time was that of the Greeks. The Greeks sacrificed to gods and goddesses who were many and full of vice. Saturn, King of Crete, was their high god. In a frenzy he ate his own children. In vengeance his son Jupiter bound him, cut off his genitals, and cast them into the sea, from whence Venus sprang up. Saturn then was exiled to an island where he lived full of malice. What a god to have as chief! Jupiter was the next chief of gods. Juno was his wife, yet he was a lecher and committed adultery so much and played so many tricks that he was called the god of delight. Mars was the god of war. He came from Dace to Italy where he seduced the prioress of Vesta's Temple, a woman named Ilia, who was the daughter of King Numitor. She gave birth to Romulus and Remus who became great knights in their father's name and founded Rome. Mars, like Jupiter and Saturn, has a star named for him. Apollo was brother to Venus. He was a huntsman and also played the harp, whereby he often got sustenance by deceiving the ignorant. He was called the god of wit and is still so called by fools. Mercury was a thief who knew sorcery. He could transform himself into a woman and was a crafty orator. He was god of merchants and thieves; he too has his star among the seven planets. Vulcan was a hunchback. He was Jupiter's smith. King Hippotas of Sicily had a son named Aeolus whom the Greeks called their god of wind. How blind their religion is! Jupiter's brother Neptune was lord of the sea and wrought tyranny over islands and sailors. He was the first founder of Troy. The teacher of shepherds and goatherds was Pan. He taught men how to domesticate animals and how to play the pipes. Practical experience gave him a ready wit. Another god was Bacchus, begat upon Semele by Jupiter. To hide his lechery, Jupiter kept him in a mountain in India which was named Dion. He grew up a waster and spent all his income on wine and women. Yet despite his gluttony the Greeks made him their god of wine. Esculapius, son of Apollo, was also a Greek god. His craft was surgery. But he loved Darius's daughter and Jupiter slew him for it, thus depriving him of godhood. The Romans thought he was a god too. He destroyed a plague for them once, but he died among the Greeks. Still, he is called the god of medicine. Hercules was another god. No man was as strong as he. He performed twelve marvels against giants and loathsome monsters. Yet he was a man full of sin and in the end burned himself up in a rage. Pluto, another brother of Jupiter, was god of hell. Whenever he was angry he would swear by Lethe, Phlegethon, Cocytus, or Acheron, which were his rivers. He also swore by "Segne and Stige," which were the two deepest pits of hell. He got out of his pits by sacrificing to Jupiter (835–1126).

These and many more are the Greek gods. Yet they had many goddesses too. Just as Saturn was chief of the false gods, so Cybele was the mother of goddesses. She bore three children by Saturn—Juno, Neptune, and Pluto. Saturn heard that he was fated to be overthrown by his own son so he began to hate Cybele. In his anger he begat Jupiter in adultery with Philerem. Jupiter married Juno, his own sister. The water nymphs were her handmaidens and the rainbow her messenger. What foolishness! Minerva is another goddess whom the Greeks served. She founded cloth making and is called the goddess of sapience. Much is said about the goddess Pallas. Her father was Pallant, a cruel giant. She was the cause of his death. Some say she was Mars's wife. Thus she is called goddess of battle. After his exile Saturn came to Italy and introduced farming. His wife came with him. Her name was Ceres and she became goddess of corn and crops. In his lechery Jupiter begat his daughter Diana on Latona. He kept Latona on the island of Delos where she bore and raised her child. Diana took no liking to men but preferred hunting in forests and wilderness. She is worshipped by gentility and is goddess of high hills, green trees, and fresh wells.]

    Proserpina, which dowhter was
Of Cereres, befell this cas:
Whil sche was duellinge in Cizile,
1280 Hire moder in that ilke while
Upon hire blessinge and hire heste
Bad that sche scholde ben honeste,
And lerne forto weve and spinne,
And duelle at hom and kepe hire inne.
Bot sche caste al that lore aweie,
And as sche wente hir out to pleie,
To gadre floures in a pleine,
And that was under the monteine
Of Ethna, fell the same tyde
1290 That Pluto cam that weie ryde,
And sodeinly, er sche was war,
He tok hire up into his char.
And as thei riden in the field,
Hire grete beaute he behield,
Which was so plesant in his ÿe,
That forto holde in compainie
He weddeth hire and hield hire so
To ben his wif for everemo.

And as thou hast tofore herd telle
1300 Hou he was cleped god of helle,
So is sche cleped the goddesse
Be cause of him, ne mor ne lesse.

[These were the gods of the Greeks, whom the Romans honored too with temples for each. In their fantasy they also honored satyrs and nymphs in the hills, oreads in the mountains, dryads in the woods, naiads in fresh wells and, in the sea, nymphs who are said to come from the wife of King Dorus who, with all her daughters, drowned in the sea. Nymphs, wherever they dwell, are obedient attendants and serve the goddesses. The Greeks even had gods for the dead, of whom Manes was chief. But it would take too long to rime all their gods, they had so many (1303-1373).

Amans asks Genius if he would speak about the gods and goddesses of love. Genius says he has been ashamed to mention them because he is their own priest. But since Amans is a lover he will continue. Venus, who puts "daunger" away and finds a way for love, was Saturn's daughter. She had many children: Harmonia was her child by Mars; Mercury fathered Androgynus on her; Anchises begat Aeneas by her; and Butes begat Eryx. She lay with Jupiter her own brother to conceive Cupid, and that child, when he came of age, fell lecherously in love with his mother. When they were together he kissed his mother as if he had no eyes to see reason with, and she too, who knew nothing but lust, took him as lover. Thus he was blind and she unwise. So Cupid became the god of love, for he dared love his mother. Venus had many other lovers. Her law of deportment was that every woman should take any man she wanted. She also was the first to advise women to sell their bodies. Semiramis followed her advice, and so did Neabole. She is goddess of love and gentilesse, and also of lust for the world and pleasance (1374-1443).

See the foul misbelief of the Greeks who made up a god or goddess for every occasion. Dindimus, King of the Brahmins, wrote to Alexander to blame Greek religion for having separate gods for all parts of the body: Minerva for the head, Mercury for the tongue, Bacchus for the throat, Hercules for arms and shoulders, Mars for the breast, Juno for gall, Cupid for the stomach, Ceres for the womb, and lecherous Venus for the rest that pertains "to thilke office appourtenant" (1496). Their religion involves many images made by themselves before which they kneel. How dark such belief; how far from reasonable wit! What was today a ragged tree stands tomorrow majestically in a temple. Prometheus first devised the craft of idolatry, and Cirophanes made the first idol in commemoration of his deceased son. Ninus, King of Assyria, was the second idolater; he made an image of gold and stone of his father, Belus, and demanded by law that every man sacrifice to the image. In time the name became Bel, then Beelzebub. The third image to be made honored King Apis of Greece, later called Serapis. When Alexander rode from Candace's kingdom he thought he talked to Serapis in a cave in the wilderness. Thus the fiend blinds idolaters in their fantasy (1444–1590).

The fourth form of religion prior to Christianity was that of the Jews. Genesis tells us that the Jews were a chosen people. After the flood Noah was assured that the world would not be destroyed again. But the Jews broke their covenant and turned to false gods. Faith and obedience were renewed by Abraham who became father of a great progeny, which extended even into Egypt. There Pharaoh oppressed them until Moses delivered them, taking great vengeance on the Egyptians. The Pharaoh was slain and the land flooded, but God divided the sea for the Jews who passed on dry foot into the desert. There they were guided by a pillar of fire and were fed manna from heaven; they got water from a hard rock, and later Moses gave them the law. Then they were led to the Promised Land where Caleb and Joshua were their leaders. Thus this belief long endured under the guidance of prophets. But at their greatest moment, when Christ was born, they failed.

But this matter is generally known to those of the Christian faith: how Lucifer debated with God and lost heaven, and how Adam even in Paradise broke away from God and fell out of his place; just so the Jews in their best moment, when they most perfect might have stood, fell in greatest folly. The Son of God took flesh from a maid and was born and fed among them, but they with one voice slew Him on the cross. Therefore the keeping of God's law was taken from them, and they live dispersed in alien lands, outside God's grace (1591–1736).

Almighty God, in justice and pity, sent Christ to answer for Adam's sin and to buy man again. Gregory says that it would help man none to be born if it were not for Christ.[6] Yet through Christ, man's soul is reconciled and, despite the original sin, may attain heaven. But faith alone without good works is not enough. Therefore we must be careful not to be oppressed "with Anticristes lollardie" (1807) which threatens us all. Our priests are like the Priest Thoas who left the temple of Minerva unguarded while Antenor stole the Palladion. The theft led to the overthrow of Troy. The priests bear the keys to heaven, yet in these times of adversity they fail to steer men's spiritual eyes. Christ died for the faith, yet our prelates now say, "Life is sweet," so that faith, unaided, sleeps. The world stands in a mist where no man sees the right way, while the keepers of the Church's key misobey. Peter's ship is nearly drowning. False prelates sow "cokkel with the corn" (1881) so that the crop that Christ first sowed with His own hand is nearly lost. In the cause of ignorance the people are estranged from the love of truth. Take example of Gregory, who stood against slothful prelates warning that they would stand at Judgment with empty hands. Be not like the man who hid his lord's bezant and got no increase from it. Our spiritual labor is dull and slow, yet we are swift enough towards Avarice. Avarice is a form of idolatry which changes virtues into vice (1737–1959).

Amans asks what other kinds of Avarice there are and how they pertain to love, whereupon Genius explains Covetousness to him. Covetousness is captain of Avarice's court and has many servants abroad in the world winning profit for Avarice. As a hungry magpie awaits the death of beasts, so Coveitise greedily waits to take his fill of the world. Never satisfied, he forgets conscience and takes all he can. Thus men often destroy themselves, as the Tale of Virgil's Mirror exemplifies (1960–2030):[7] Once when Rome was threatened by invaders the magician Virgil built a mirror that he set on marble pillars in the heart of town. In the mirror one could behold any enemy within thirty miles, whether it be day or night. It happened that Carthage went to war against Rome, but as long as the mirror stood they could get nowhere. So Hannibal sought counsel with the King of Puile and together they made their plan. Crassus, the Roman emperor, was known for his covetousness, so they secretly sent into the city three philosophers laden with gold. The philosophers divided the gold into two treasures which they hid in the ground, and then went to Crassus to tell him of their marvelous abilities to know in dreams where treasures were hidden. They told him they had dreamed of treasure hidden beneath Rome. The covetous emperor set his miners to digging the very next day, whereupon they found one of the treasures. The emperor was ecstatic. The next day the second philosopher dreamed; the men dug and found the second treasure. Now the emperor honored the three philosophers as if they were gods. Then the third told the emperor right in his ear that he knew where the greatest treasure of all was hidden —more jewels and precious stones than all the emperor's horses could carry. It was hidden under the mirror, but might be mined if the foundation were propped up with pillars. So the emperor set his miners to work, digging and propping until the mirror stood on nothing but pillars. That night the philosophers slipped into the mine, covered the pillars with pitch, sulphur, and resin, and while the city slept set the timberwork afire. They slipped out of town to watch the mirror fall. They laughed together and said, "Lo, what coveitise /Mai do with hem that be noght wise!" (2187–2188). With the mirror gone, subjects all aròund rose up in rebellion. Hannibal led the way. In a single day he gathered three bushels full of gold rings taken from the hands of gentlemen whom he slew. He felled so many Romans that their corpses made a bridge clear across the Tiber. But justice came to the covetous emperor. The Romans put him in a chair and said that since he wanted gold he would have it; they melted gold in a pan, and when it was boiling hot they poured it down his throat. Thus his thirst for gold was quenched (2031–2224).

Covetousness in kings is a terrible thing. They watch the harvests more eagerly than the farmers. But Fortune stands against kings as well as poor men, as the Tale of the Two Coffers[8] will demonstrate (2272). A certain king had about him many knights and squires. Some of his older servants who had failed to gain advancement complained when they saw younger men preferred before them. Their complaints became known to the king who devised a means of showing them that the fault lay with Fortune, not himself. He placed two identical coffers in his chamber and secretly put gold in one and straw and rubbish in the other. Then he called the grumblers to him. "You have all done well," he said to them, "and all deserve advancement. But to prove that I have not held you back and to stop your complaints, I have prepared two boxes, one with gold and the other with rubbish in it. Choose whichever you wish." The courtiers thanked him for his kindness and debated which coffer to choose. At last they sent their representative to single out their choice. When the coffer was opened it contained straw and rubbish. The king then opened the other to prove his good faith and said, "You see, the fault lies not with me. You have been refused by Fortune." And thus the king was excused, and his courtiers stopped their grumbling and sought his mercy (2273–2390).

A comparable story is told of the Emperor Frederick who met two beggars along the way.[9] One said, "Well may a man whom the king favors be rich." The other said contrary: "That man is rich to whom God sends good fortune." Their dispute came to the attention of the king who invited them to his palace and offered them two pasties. A capon was baked in one and florins in the other, though both looked the same from the outside. The beggar who had put faith in the generosity of kings chose first but unfortunately got meat instead of money. In his chagrin he said, "How easily deceived is he who trusts in man's help. But well off is the man whom God helps. My fellow is rich, but I am still poor." Fortune left him nothing (2391–2441).

Fortune treats covetous lovers in a similar way. They are never satisfied, but they get no more than Fortune allows. Some set their hearts on all women, here to be attracted by this one's white skin, there by that one's noble kin, elsewhere by a meek expression, or a gray eye, a rosy cheek, a playful laugh, a flat nose, or soft speech. It takes little to whet the love of covetous men, for they are color blind and make no effort at discriminating (2498). Amans says he is no such lover. He has been most discriminating. Though he were as poor as Job he would consider none but his lady (2513). Genius observes that other men are less virtuous than Amans. Some in fact marry women purely for their money (2533). Amans is shocked: Though his lady were poor as the exiled Medea he would not love her less; she is more to him than the rich queen Candace whom Alexander chose, or Pantasilee who was Queen of Feminie and gave her fortune to Hector. He doubts that any man could be so covetous as to prefer gold to his lady. She is better than a woman with millions. In actual fact she is not poor, but that makes no difference either way. He is drawn to her for pure love (2625). Genius admits that that is the best way to love, but he tells the Tale of the King and His Steward's Wife to show how powerfully covetousness may interfere in love (2642).[10]]

TALE OF THE KING AND
HIS STEWARD'S WIFE

Of Puile whilom was a king,
A man of hih complexioun
And yong, bot his affeccioun
After the nature of his age
2650 Was yit noght falle in his corage
The lust of wommen forto knowe.
So it betidde upon a throwe

This lord fell into gret seknesse:
Phisique hath don the besinesse
Of sondri cures manyon
To make him hol; and therupon
A worthi maister which ther was
Yaf him conseil upon this cas,
That if he wolde have parfit hele,   [health]
2660   He scholde with a womman dele,
A freissh, a yong, a lusti wiht,
To don him compaignie a nyht;
For thanne he seide him redily,
That he schal be al hol therby,
And otherwise he kneu no cure.
     This king, which stod in aventure
Of lif and deth, for medicine
Assented was, and of covine   [confidence]
His Steward, whom he tristeth wel,
2670   He tok, and tolde him everydel,
Hou that this maister hadde seid:
And therupon he hath him preid
And charged upon his ligance,   [allegiance]
That he do make porveance   [provision]
Of such on as be convenable
For his plesance and delitable;
And bad him, hou that evere it stod,
That he schal spare for no good,
For his will is riht wel to paie.
2680   The Steward seide he wolde assaie: [try]
Bot nou hierafter thou schalt wite,
As I finde in the bokes write,
What coveitise in love doth.
This Steward, forto telle soth,
Amonges al the men alyve
A lusti ladi hath to wyve,
Which natheles for gold he tok
And noght for love, as seith the bok.

A riche Marchant of the lond
2690 Hir fader was, and hire fond
So worthily, and such richesse
Of worldes good and such largesse
With hire he yaf in mariage,
That only for thilke avantage
Of good this Steward hath hire take,
For lucre and noght for loves sake,
And that was afterward wel seene;
Nou herkne what it wolde meene.

This Steward in his oghne herte
2700 Sih that his lord mai noght asterte   [escape]
His maladie, bot he have   [unless]
A lusti womman him to save,
And thoghte he wolde yive ynowh
Of his tresor; wherof he drowh
Gret coveitise into his mynde,
And sette his honour fer behynde.
Thus he, whom gold hath overset,
Was trapped in his oghne net;
The gold hath mad hise wittes lame,
2710 So that sechende his oghne schame
He rouneth in the kinges Ere,   [whispers]
And seide him that he wiste where
A gentile and a lusti on
Tho was, and thider wolde he gon:
Bot he mot yive yiftes grete;
For bot it be thurgh gret beyete   [enticements (gain)]
Of gold, he seith, he schal noght spede.
The king him bad upon the nede
That take an hundred pound he scholde,
2720 And yive it where that he wolde,
Be so it were in worthi place:
And thus to stonde in loves grace
This king his gold hath abandouned.
And whan this tale was full rouned,   [told]

The Steward tok the gold and wente,
Withinne his herte and many a wente   [turn]
Of coveitise thanne he caste,
Wherof a pourpos ate laste
Ayein love and ayein his riht
2730 He tok, and seide hou thilke nyht
His wif schal ligge be the king;
And goth thenkende upon this thing
Toward his In, til he cam hom
Into the chambre, and thanne he nom   [took]
His wif, and tolde hire al the cas.
And sche, which red for schame was,
With bothe hire handes hath him preid
Knelende and in this wise seid,
That sche to reson and to skile   [common sense]
2740 In what thing that he bidde wile
Is redy forto don his heste,
Bot this thing were noght honeste,
That he for gold hire scholde selle.
And he tho with hise wordes felle   [cruel]
Forth with his gastly contienance
Seith that sche schal don obeissance
And folwe his will in every place;
And thus thurgh strengthe of his manace
Hir innocence is overlad,
2750 Wherof sche was so sore adrad
That sche his will mot nede obeie.
And therupon was schape a weie,
That he his oghne wif be nyhte
Hath out of alle mennes sihte
So prively that non it wiste
Broght to the king, which as him liste
Mai do with hire what he wolde.
For whan sche was ther as sche scholde,
With him abedde under the cloth,
2760 The Steward tok his leve and goth

Into a chambre faste by;
Bot hou he slep, that wot noght I,
For he sih cause of jelousie.
    Bot he, which hath the compainie
Of such a lusti on as sche,
Him thoghte that of his degre
Ther was noman so wel at ese:
Sche doth al that sche mai to plese,
So that his herte al hol sche hadde;
2770 And thus this king his joie ladde,
Til it was nyh upon the day.
The Steward thanne wher sche lay
Cam to the bedd, and in his wise
Hath bede that sche scholde arise.
The king seith, "Nay, sche schal noght
    go."
His Steward seide ayein, "Noght so;
For sche mot gon er it be knowe,
And so I swor at thilke throwe,
Whan I hire fette to you hiere."   [fetched]
2780 The king his tale wol noght hiere,
And seith hou that he hath hire boght,
Forthi sche schal departe noght,
Til he the brighte dai beholde.
And cawhte hire in hise armes folde,
As he which liste forto pleie,
And bad his Steward gon his weie,
And so he dede ayein his wille.
And thus his wif abedde stille
Lay with the king the longe nyht,
2790 Til that it was hih Sonne lyht;
Bot who sche was he knew nothing.
    Tho cam the Steward to the king
And preide him that withoute schame
In savinge of hire goode name
He myhte leden hom ayein

This lady, and hath told him plein
Hou that it was his oghne wif.
The king his Ere unto this strif
Hath leid, and whan that he it herde,
2800 Welnyh out of his wit he ferde,
And seide, "Ha, caitif most of alle,   [vagabond]
Wher was it evere er this befalle,
That eny cokard in this wise   [fool]
Betok his wif for coveitise?   [delivered]
Thou hast both hire and me beguiled
And ek thin oghne astat reviled,
Wherof that buxom unto thee   [obedient]
Hierafter schal sche nevere be.
For this avou to god I make,
2810 After this day if I thee take,
Thou schalt ben honged and todrawe.
Nou loke anon thou be withdrawe,
So that I se thee neveremore."
This Steward thanne dradde him sore,
With al the haste that he mai
And fledde awei that same dai,
And was exiled out of londe.
   Lo, there a nyce housebonde,   [foolish]
Which thus hath lost his wif for evere!
2820 Bot natheles sche hadde a levere;   [better fate]
The king hire weddeth and honoureth,
Wherof hire name sche socoureth,
Which erst was lost thurgh coveitise
Of him, that ladde hire other wise,
And hath himself also forlore.

[Covetousness is a great disease in love which poisons the sugar.
Amans observes that some wealth is convenient in love, but that
he would never marry for riches. He asks for neither park nor
plow; to have her love would be enough. Genius next points out
that Covetousness has two counsellors, False-witness and Perjury,

who act as procurers and make false bargains. Lovers are guilty
of these sins when they beguile women with oaths of fidelity,
then break their trust. Amans says he is not guilty here. He loves
his Lady most faithfully. Even if a thousand men knew it and
spoke of it they would only be spreading truth. Still, says Genius,
False-witness is always speeding his cause; we must be wary, as
the Tale of Achilles and Deidamia shows us.[11]]

TALE OF ACHILLES
AND DEIDAMIA

The Goddesse of the See Thetis,
Sche hadde a Sone, and his name is
Achilles, whom to kepe and warde,
Whil he was yong, as into warde
Sche thoghte him salfly to betake,   [safely to deliver]
As sche which dradde for his sake
Of that was seid in prophecie,
That he at Troie scholde die,
Whan that the Cite was belein.   [besieged]
2970 Forthi, so as the bokes sein,
Sche caste hire wit in sondri wise,
Hou sche him mihte so desguise
That noman scholde his bodi knowe:
And so befell that ilke throwe,
Whil that sche thoghte upon this dede,
Ther was a king, which Lichomede
Was hote, and he was wel begon
With faire dowhtres manyon,
And duelte fer out in an yle.
2980   Nou schalt thou hiere a wonder wyle: [wonder of cunning]
This queene, which the moder was
Of Achilles, upon this cas
Hire Sone, as he a Maiden were,
Let clothen in the same gere
Which longeth unto wommanhiede:

And he was yong and tok non hiede,
Bot soffreth al that sche him dede.
Wherof sche hath hire wommen bede
And charged be here othes alle,
2990 Hou so it afterward befalle,
That thei discovere noght this thing,
Bot feigne and make a knowleching,
Upon the conseil which was nome,
In every place wher thei come
To telle and to witnesse this,
Hou he here ladi dowhter is.   [their lady's daughter]
And riht in such a maner wise
Sche bad thei scholde hire don servise,
So that Achilles underfongeth   [receives]
3000 As to a yong ladi belongeth
Honour, servise and reverence.
For Thetis with gret diligence
Him hath so tawht and so afaited,   [prepared]
That, hou so that it were awaited,
With sobre and goodli contenance
He scholde his wommanhiede avance,
That non the sothe knowe myhte,
Bot that in every mannes syhte
He scholde seme a pure Maide.
3010 And in such wise as sche him saide,
Achilles, which that ilke while
Was yong, upon himself to smyle
Began, whan he was so besein.

And thus, after the bokes sein,
With frette of Perle upon his hed,   [ornamental diadem]
Al freissh betwen the whyt and red,
As he which tho was tendre of Age,
Stod the colour in his visage,
That forto loke upon his cheke
3020 And sen his childly manere eke,
He was a womman to beholde.

And thanne his moder to him tolde,
That sche him hadde so begon
Be cause that sche thoghte gon
To Lichomede at thilke tyde,
Wher that sche seide he scholde abyde
Among hise dowhtres forto duelle.
    Achilles herde his moder telle,
And wiste noght the cause why;
3030 And natheles ful buxomly   [obediently]
He was redy to that sche bad,
Wherof his moder was riht glad,
To Lichomede and forth thei wente.
And whan the king knew hire entente,
And sih this yonge dowhter there,
And that it cam unto his Ere
Of such record, of such witnesse,
He hadde riht a gret gladnesse   [truly]
Of that he bothe syh and herde,
3040 As he that wot noght hou it ferde
Upon the conseil of the nede.
Bot for al that king Lichomede
Hath toward him this dowhter take,
And for Thetis his moder sake
He put hire into compainie
To duelle with Deïdamie,
His oghne dowhter, the eldeste,
The faireste and the comelieste
Of alle hise doghtres whiche he hadde.
3050   Lo, thus Thetis the cause ladde,
And lefte there Achilles feigned,
As he which hath himself restreigned
In al that evere he mai and can
Out of the manere of a man,
And tok his wommannysshe chiere,
Wherof unto his beddefere   [bedfellow]
Deïdamie he hath be nyhte.

Wher kinde wole himselve rihte,
After the Philosophres sein,
3060 Ther mai no wiht be therayein:
And that was thilke time seene.
The longe nyhtes hem betuene
Nature, which mai noght forbere,
Hath mad hem bothe forto stere: [stir]
Thei kessen ferst, and overmore
The hihe weie of loves lore
Thei gon, and al was don in dede,
Wherof lost is the maydenhede;
And that was afterward wel knowe.
3070   For it befell that ilke throwe
At Troie, wher the Siege lay
Upon the cause of Menelay
And of his queene dame Heleine,
The Gregois hadden mochel peine
Alday to fihte and to assaile.
Bot for thei mihten noght availe
So noble a Cite forto winne,
A prive conseil thei beginne,
In sondri wise wher thei trete;
3080 And ate laste among the grete
Thei fellen unto this acord,
That Protheüs, of his record
Which was an Astronomien
And ek a gret Magicien,
Scholde of his calculacion
Seche after constellacion,
Hou thei the Cite mihten gete:
And he, which hadde noght foryete
Of that belongeth to a clerk,
3090 His studie sette upon this werk.
So longe his wit aboute he caste,
Til that he fond out ate laste,
Bot if they hadden Achilles

Here werre schal ben endeles.
And over that he tolde hem plein
In what manere he was besein,
And in what place he schal be founde;
So that withinne a litel stounde
Ulixes forth with Diomede
3100 Upon this point to Lichomede
Agamenon togedre sente.
Bot Ulixes, er he forth wente,
Which was on of the moste wise,
Ordeigned hath in such a wise,
That he the moste riche aray,
Wherof a womman mai be gay,
With him hath take manyfold,
And overmore, as it is told,
An harneis for a lusti kniht,
3110 Which burned was as Selver bryht,
Of swerd, of plate and ek of maile,
As thogh he scholde to bataille,
He tok also with him be Schipe.
And thus togedre in felaschipe
Forth gon this Diomede and he
In hope til thei mihten se
The place where Achilles is.
        The wynd stod thanne noght amis,
Bot evene topseilcole it blew,
3120 Til Ulixes the Marche knew,   [country]
Wher Lichomede his Regne hadde.
The Stieresman so wel hem ladde,
That thei ben comen sauf to londe,
Wher thei gon out upon the stronde
Into the Burgh, wher that thei founde
The king, and he which hath facounde,   [eloquence]
Ulixes, dede the message.
Bot the conseil of his corage,
Why that he cam, he tolde noght,

3130 Bot undernethe he was bethoght
In what manere he mihte aspie
Achilles fro Deïdamie
And fro these othre that ther were,
Full many a lusti ladi there.
 Thei pleide hem there a day or tuo,
And as it was fortuned so,
It fell that time in such a wise,
To Bachus that a sacrifise
Thes yonge ladys scholden make;
3140 And for the strange mennes sake,
That comen fro the Siege of Troie,
Thei maden wel the more joie.
Ther was Revel, ther was daunsinge,
And every lif which coude singe
Of lusti wommen in the route   [company]
A freissh carole hath sunge aboute;
Bot for al this yit natheles
The Greks unknowe of Achilles
So weren, that in no degre
3150 Thei couden wite which was he,
Ne be his vois, ne be his pas.   [pace]
Ulixes thanne upon this cas
A thing of hih Prudence hath wroght:
For thilke aray, which he hath broght
To yive among the wommen there,
He let do fetten al the gere   [caused to be fetched]
Forth with a knihtes harneis eke,—
In al a contre forto seke
Men scholden noght a fairer se,—
3160 And every thing in his degre
Endlong upon a bord he leide.
To Lichomede and thanne he preide
That every ladi chese scholde
What thing of alle that sche wolde,
And take it as be weie of yifte;

For thei hemself it scholde schifte,   [should dispose of it]
He seide, after here oghne wille.
    Achilles thanne stod noght stille:
Whan he the bryhte helm behield,
3170 The swerd, the hauberk and the Schield,
His herte fell therto anon;
Of all that othre wolde he non,
The knihtes gere he underfongeth,   [takes]
And thilke aray which that belongeth
Unto the wommen he forsok.
And in this wise, as seith the bok,
Thei knowen thanne which he was:
For he goth forth the grete pas
Into the chambre where he lay;
3180 Anon, and made no delay,
He armeth him in knyhtli wise,
That bettre can noman devise,
And as fortune scholde falle,
He cam so forth tofore hem alle,
As he which tho was glad ynowh.
But Lichomede nothing lowh,   [laughed]
Whan that he syh hou that it ferde,
For thanne he wiste wel and herde,
His dowhter hadde be forlein;
3190 Bot that he was so oversein,   [imprudent]
The wonder overgoth his wit.
For in Cronique is write yit
Thing which schal nevere be foryete,
Hou that Achilles hath begete
Pirrus upon Deïdamie,
Wherof cam out the tricherie
Of Falswitnesse, whan thei saide
Hou that Achilles was a Maide.
Bot that was nothing sene tho,
3200 For he is to the Siege go
Forth with Ulixe and Diomede.

[How, Genius concludes, may women find security against men who bear false witness when they betray each other as Thetis did Deidamia? Then, to illustrate the evils of Perjury, he tells the story of Jason and Medea.[12]]

TALE OF JASON AND MEDEA

     In Grece whilom was a king,
Of whom the fame and knowleching
Beleveth yit, and Peleüs
3250 He hihte; bot it fell him thus,
That his fortune hir whiel so ladde
That he no child his oghne hadde
To regnen after his decess.
He hadde a brother natheles,
Whos rihte name was Eson,
And he the worthi kniht Jason
Begat, the which in every lond
Alle othre passede of his hond
In Armes, so that he the beste
3260 Was named and the worthieste,
He soghte worschipe overal.
Nou herkne, and I thee telle schal
An aventure that he soghte,
Which afterward ful dere he boghte.
    Ther was an yle, which Colchos
Was cleped, and therof aros
Gret speche in every lond aboute,
That such merveile was non oute
In al the wyde world nawhere,
3270 As tho was in that yle there.
Ther was a Schiep, as it was told,
The which his flees bar al of gold,
And so the goddes hadde it set,
That it ne mihte awei be fet
Be pouer of no worldes wiht:

And yit ful many a worthi kniht
It hadde assaied, as thei dorste,
And evere it fell hem to the worste.
Bot he, that wolde it noght forsake,
3280 Bot of his knyhthod undertake
To do what thing therto belongeth,
This worthi Jason, sore alongeth
To se the strange regiouns
And knowe the condiciouns
Of othre Marches, where he wente;
And for that cause his hole entente
He sette Colchos forto seche,
And therupon he made a speche
To Peleüs his Em the king.   [uncle]
3290 And he wel paid was of that thing;   [pleased]
And schop anon for his passage,   [arranged]
And suche as were of his lignage,
With othre knihtes whiche he ches,
With him he tok, and Hercules,
Which full was of chivalerie,
With Jason wente in compaignie;
And that was in the Monthe of Maii,
Whan colde stormes were away.
The wynd was good, the Schip was yare,
3300 Thei tok here leve, and forth thei fare
Toward Colchos: bot on the weie
What hem befell is long to seie;
Hou Lamedon the king of Troie,
Which oghte wel have mad hem joie,
Whan thei to reste a while him preide,
Out of his lond he hem congeide;   [dismissed]
And so fell the dissencion,
Which after was destruccion
Of that Cite, as men mai hiere:
3310 Bot that is noght to mi matiere.
Bot thus this worthi folk Gregeis

Fro that king, which was noght curteis,
And fro his lond with Sail updrawe
Thei wente hem forth, and many a sawe
Thei made and many a gret manace,
Til ate laste into that place
Which as thei soghte thei aryve,
And striken Sail, and forth as blyve   [quickly]
Thei sente unto the king and tolden
3320 Who weren ther and what thei wolden.
Oëtes, which was thanne king,
Whan that he herde this tyding
Of Jason, which was comen there,
And of these othre, what thei were,
He thoghte don hem gret worschipe:
For thei anon come out of Schipe,
And strawht unto the king thei wente,
And be the hond Jason he hente,
And that was ate paleis gate,
3330 So fer the king cam on his gate
Toward Jason to don him chiere;
And he, whom lacketh no manere,
Whan he the king sih in presence,
Yaf him ayein such reverence
As to a kinges stat belongeth.
And thus the king him underfongeth,   [receives]
And Jason in his arm he cawhte,
And forth into the halle he strawhte,   [went directly]
And ther they siete and spieke of thinges,
3340 And Jason tolde him tho tidinges,
Why he was come, and faire him preide
To haste his time, and the kyng seide,
"Jason, thou art a worthi kniht,
Bot it lith in no mannes myht
To don that thou art come fore:
Ther hath be many a kniht forlore
Of that thei wolden it assaie."

Bot Jason wolde him noght esmaie,   [be frightened by]
And seide, "Of every worldes cure
3350 Fortune stant in aventure,
Per aunter wel, per aunter wo:
Bot hou as evere that it go,
It schal be with myn hond assaied."
The king tho hield him noght wel paied,   [pleased]
For he the Grekes sore dredde,
In aunter, if Jason ne spedde,   [indeed/fared not well]
He mihte therof bere a blame;
For tho was al the worldes fame
In Grece, as forto speke of Armes.
3360 Forthi he dredde him of his harmes,
And gan to preche him and to preie;
Bot Jason wolde noght obeie,
Bot seide he wolde his porpos holde
For ought that eny man him tolde.
The king, whan he thes wordes herde,
And sih hou that this kniht ansuerde,
Yit for he wolde make him glad,
After Medea gon he bad,
Which was his dowhter, and sche cam.
3370 And Jason, which good hiede nam,
Whan he hire sih, ayein hire goth;   [goes toward her]
And sche, which was him nothing loth,
Welcomede him into that lond,
And softe tok him be the hond,
And doun thei seten bothe same.   [together]
Sche hadde herd spoke of his name
And of his grete worthinesse;
Forthi sche gan hir yhe impresse
Upon his face and his stature,
3380 And thoghte hou nevere creature
Was so wel farende as was he.
And Jason riht in such degre
Ne mihte noght withholde his lok,

Bot so good hiede on hire he tok,
That him ne thoghte under the hevene
Of beaute sawh he nevere hir evene,
With al that fell to wommanhiede.
Thus ech of other token hiede,
Thogh ther no word was of record;
3390 Here hertes bothe of on acord
Ben set to love, bot as tho
Ther mihten be no wordes mo.
The king made him gret joie and feste,
To alle his men he yaf an heste,
So as thei wolde his thonk deserve,
That thei scholde alle Jason serve,
Whil that he wolde there duelle.
And thus the dai, schortly to telle,
With manye merthes thei despente,
3400 Til nyht was come, and tho thei wente,
Echon of other tok his leve,
Whan thei no lengere myhten leve.   [remain]
I not hou Jason that nyht slep,
Bot wel I wot that of the Schep,
For which he cam into that yle,
He thoghte bot a litel whyle;
Al was Medea that he thoghte,
So that in many a wise he soghte
His witt wakende er it was day,
3410 Som time yee, som time nay,
Som time thus, som time so,
As he was stered to and fro   [stirred]
Of love, and ek of his conqueste
As he was holde of his beheste.
And thus he ros up be the morwe
And tok himself seint John to borwe,   [committed himself to St. John's care]

And seide he wolde ferst beginne
At love, and after forto winne

The flees of gold, for which he com,
3420 And thus to him good herte he nom.
    Medea riht the same wise,
Til dai cam that sche moste arise,
Lay and bethoughte hire al the nyht,
Hou sche that noble worthi kniht
Be eny weie mihte wedde:
And wel sche wiste, if he ne spedde
Of thing which he hadde undertake,
Sche mihte hirself no porpos take;
For if he deide of his bataile,
3430 Sche most thanne algate faile
To geten him, whan he were ded.
Thus sche began to sette red   [make plans]
And torne aboute hir wittes alle,
To loke hou that it mihte falle
That sche with him hadde a leisir
To speke and telle of hir desir.
And so it fell that same day
That Jason with that suete may   [sweet maiden]
Togedre sete and hadden space
3440 To speke, and he besoughte hir grace.
And sche his tale goodli herde,
And afterward sche him ansuerde
And seide, "Jason, as thou wilt,
Thou miht be sauf, thou miht be spilt;   [safe/killed]
For wite wel that nevere man,
Bot if he couthe that I can,   [knows what I know]
Ne mihte that fortune achieve
For which thou comst: bot as I lieve,   [trust]
If thou wolt holde covenant
3450 To love, of al the remenant
I schal thi lif and honour save,
That thou the flees of gold schalt have."
He seide, "Al at youre oghne wille,
Ma dame, I schal treuly fulfille

Youre heste, whil mi lif mai laste."
Thus longe he preide, and ate laste
Sche granteth, and behihte him this,
That whan nyht comth and it time is,
Sche wolde him sende certeinly
3460 Such on that scholde him prively
Al one into hire chambre bringe.
He thonketh hire of that tidinge,
For of that grace him is begonne
Him thenkth alle othre thinges wonne.

  The dai made ende and lost his lyht,
And comen was the derke nyht,
Which al the daies yhe blente.
Jason tok leve and forth he wente,
And whan he cam out of the pres,   [crowd]
3470 He tok to conseil Hercules,
And tolde him hou it was betid,
And preide it scholde wel ben hid,
And that he wolde loke aboute,
Therwhiles that he schal ben oute.
Thus as he stod and hiede nam,
A Mayden fro Medea cam
And to hir chambre Jason ledde,
Wher that he fond redi to bedde
The faireste and the wiseste eke;
3480 And sche with simple chiere and meke,
Whan sche him sih, wax al aschamed.
Tho was here tale newe entamed;   [renewed (OF *entamer*, 'to
                    wound or lay open')]

For sikernesse of Mariage   [security]
Sche fette forth a riche ymage,
Which was figure of Jupiter,
And Jason swor and seide ther,
That also wiss god scholde him helpe,
That if Medea dede him helpe,
That he his pourpos myhte winne,

3490 Thei scholde nevere parte atwinne,
     Bot evere whil him lasteth lif,
     He wolde hire holde for his wif.
     And with that word thei kisten bothe;
     And for thei scholden hem unclothe,
     Ther cam a Maide, and in hir wise
     Sche dede hem bothe full servise,
     Til that thei were in bedde naked:
     I wot that nyht was wel bewaked,
     Thei hadden both what thei wolde.
3500 And thanne of leisir sche him tolde,
     And gan fro point to point enforme
     Of his bataile and al the forme,
     Which as he scholde finde there,
     Whan he to thyle come were.   [the island]
           Sche seide, at entre of the pas   [passage (adventure)]
     Hou Mars, which god of Armes was,
     Hath set tuo Oxen sterne and stoute,
     That caste fyr and flamme aboute
     Bothe at the mouth and ate nase,   [nose]
3510 So that thei setten al on blase
     What thing that passeth hem betwene:
     And forthermore upon the grene
     Ther goth the flees of gold to kepe
     A Serpent, which mai nevere slepe.
     Thus who that evere scholde it winne,
     The fyr to stoppe he mot beginne,
     Which that the fierce bestes caste,
     And daunte he mot hem ate laste,   [control]
     So that he mai hem yoke and dryve;
3520 And therupon he mot as blyve
     The Serpent with such strengthe assaile,
     That he mai slen him be bataile;
     Of which he mot the teth outdrawe,   [extract]
     As it belongeth to that lawe,
     And thanne he mot the Oxen yoke,

Til thei have with a plowh tobroke
A furgh of lond, in which arowe   [furrow]
The teth of thaddre he moste sowe,   [the serpent (adder)]
And therof schule arise knihtes
3530 Wel armed up at alle rihtes.
Of hem is noght to taken hiede,
For ech of hem in hastihiede
Schal other slen with dethes wounde:
And thus whan thei ben leid to grounde,
Than mot he to the goddes preie,
And go so forth and take his preie.   [prey]
Bot if he faile in eny wise
Of that ye hiere me devise,
Ther mai be set non other weie,
3540 That he ne moste algates deie.
"Nou have I told the peril al:
I woll you tellen forth withal,"
Quod Medea to Jason tho,
"That ye schul knowen er ye go,
Ayein the venym and the fyr
What schal ben the recoverir.
Bot, Sire, for it is nyh day,
Ariseth up, so that I may
Delivere you what thing I have,
3550 That mai youre lif and honour save."
Thei weren bothe loth to rise,
Bot for thei weren bothe wise,
Up thei arisen ate laste:
Jason his clothes on him caste
And made him redi riht anon,
And sche hir scherte dede upon
And caste on hire a mantel clos,
Withoute more and thanne aros.
Tho tok sche forth a riche Tye   [casket]
3560 Mad al of gold and of Perrie,   [jewels]
Out of the which sche nam a Ring,

The Ston was worth al other thing.
Sche seide, whil he wolde it were,
Ther myhte no peril him dere, [injure (OE *daru*)]
In water mai it noght be dreynt,
Wher as it comth the fyr is queynt,
It daunteth ek the cruel beste,
Ther may no qued that man areste, [evil thing]
Wher so he be on See or lond,
3570 Which hath that ring upon his hond:
And over that sche gan to sein,
That if a man wol ben unsein,
Withinne his hond hold clos the Ston, [let him hold]
And he mai invisible gon.
The Ring to Jason sche betauhte, [entrusted]
And so forth after sche him tauhte
What sacrifise he scholde make;
And gan out of hire cofre take
Him thoughte an hevenely figure,
3580 Which ai be charme and be conjure
Was wroght, and ek it was thurgh write
With names, which he scholde wite,
As sche him tauhte tho to rede;
And bad him, as he wolde spede,
Withoute reste of eny while,
Whan he were londed in that yle,
He scholde make his sacrifise
And rede his carecte in the wise [charm]
As sche him tauhte, on knes doun bent,
3590 Thre sithes toward orient;
For so scholde he the goddes plese
And winne himselven mochel ese.
And whanne he hadde it thries rad,
To opne a buiste sche him bad, [box]
Which sche ther tok him in present,
And was full of such oignement,
That ther was fyr ne venym non

That scholde fastnen him upon,
Whan that he were enoynt withal.
3600 Forthi sche tauhte him hou he schal
Enoignte his armes al aboute,
And for he scholde nothing doute,
Sche tok him thanne a maner glu,   [gave him]
The which was of so gret vertu,
That where a man it wolde caste,
It scholde binde anon so faste
That noman mihte it don aweie.
And that sche bad be alle weie
He scholde into the mouthes throwen
3610 Of tho tweie Oxen that fyr blowen,
Therof to stoppen the malice;
The glu schal serve of that office.
And over that hir oignement,
Hir Ring and hir enchantement
Ayein the Serpent scholde him were,   [defend (OE *warian*)]
Til he him sle with swerd or spere:
And thanne he may saufliche ynowh
His Oxen yoke into the plowh
And the teth sowe in such a wise,
3620 Til he the knyhtes se arise,
And ech of other doun be leid
In such manere as I have seid.
        Lo, thus Medea for Jason
Ordeigneth, and preith therupon
That he nothing foryete scholde,
And ek sche preith him that he wolde,
Whan he hath alle his Armes don,   [finished]
To grounde knele and thonke anon
The goddes, and so forth be ese
3630 The flees of gold he scholde sese.
And whanne he hadde it sesed so,
That thanne he were sone ago

Withouten eny tariynge.
    Whan this was seid, into wepinge
Sche fell, as sche that was thurgh nome
With love, and so fer overcome,
That al hir world on him sche sette.
Bot whan sche sih ther was no lette,
That he mot nedes parte hire fro,
3640 Sche tok him in hire armes tuo,
An hundred time and gan him kisse,
And seide, "O, al mi worldes blisse,
Mi trust, mi lust, mi lif, min hele,
To be thin helpe in this querele
I preie unto the goddes alle."
And with that word sche gan doun falle
On swoune, and he hire uppe nam,
And forth with that the Maiden cam,
And thei to bedde anon hir broghte,
3650 And thanne Jason hire besoghte,
And to hire seide in this manere:
"Mi worthi lusti ladi dere,
Conforteth you, for be my trouthe
It schal noght fallen in mi slouthe
That I ne wol thurghout fulfille
Youre hestes at youre oghne wille.
And yit I hope to you bringe
Withinne a while such tidinge,
The which schal make ous bothe game."
3660   Bot for he wolde kepe hir name,
Whan that he wiste it was nyh dai,
He seide, "A dieu, mi swete mai."
And forth with him he nam his gere,
Which as sche hadde take him there,
And strauht unto his chambre he wente,
And goth to bedde and slep him hente,
And lay, that noman him awok,

For Hercules hiede of him tok,
Til it was undren hih and more. [9:00 A.M. (*tierce* in Benoît)]

3670 And thanne he gan to sighe sore
And sodeinliche abreide of slep; [started]
And thei that token of him kep,
His chamberleins, be sone there,
And maden redi al his gere,
And he aros and to the king
He wente, and seide hou to that thing
For which he cam he wolde go.
The king therof was wonder wo,
And for he wolde him fain withdrawe,
3680 He tolde him many a dredful sawe,
Bot Jason wolde it noght recorde, [take note]
And ate laste thei acorde.
Whan that he wolde noght abide,
A Bot was redy ate tyde,
In which this worthi kniht of Grece
Ful armed up at every piece,
To his bataile which belongeth,
Tok ore on honde and sore him longeth,
Til he the water passed were.
3690 Whan he cam to that yle there,
He set him on his knes doun strauht,
And his carecte, as he was tawht, [charm]
He radde, and made his sacrifise,
And siththe enoignte him in that wise, [next]
As Medea him hadde bede
And thanne aros up fro that stede,
And with the glu the fyr he queynte,
And anon after he atteinte
The grete Serpent and him slowh.
3700 Bot erst he hadde sorwe ynowh,
For that Serpent made him travaile
So harde and sore of his bataile,

That nou he stod and nou he fell:
For longe time it so befell,
That with his swerd ne with his spere
He mihte noght that Serpent dere.　　　　　[injure]
He was so scherded al aboute,　　　　　　　[scaled]
It hield all eggetol withoute,　　　　　　　[edge tools]
He was so ruide and hard of skin,
3710　Ther mihte nothing go therin;
Venym and fyr togedre he caste,
That he Jason so sore ablaste,
That if ne were his oignement,
His Ring and his enchantement,
Which Medea tok him tofore,
He hadde with that worm be lore;　　　　　[dragon/lost]
Bot of vertu which therof cam
Jason the Dragon overcam.
And he anon the teth outdrouh,
3720　And sette his Oxen in a plouh,
With which he brak a piece of lond
And sieu hem with his oghne hond.　　　　[sowed]
Tho mihte he gret merveile se:
Of every toth in his degre
Sprong up a kniht with spere and schield,
Of whiche anon riht in the field
Echon slow other; and with that
Jason Medea noght foryat,
On bothe his knes he gan doun falle,
3730　And yaf thonk to the goddes alle.
The Flees he tok and goth to Bote,
The Sonne schyneth bryhte and hote,
The Flees of gold schon forth withal,
The water glistreth overal.
　　　Medea wepte and sigheth ofte,
And stod upon a Tour alofte:
Al prively withinne hirselve,
Ther herde it nouther ten ne tuelve,

Sche preide, and seide, "O, god him spede,
3740 The kniht which hath mi maidenhiede!"
And ay sche loketh toward thyle.
Bot whan sche sih withinne a while
The Flees glistrende ayein the Sonne,
Sche saide, "Ha lord, now al is wonne,
Mi kniht the field hath overcome:
Nou wolde god he were come;
Ha lord, that he ne were alonde!"
Bot I dar take this on honde,
If that sche hadde wynges tuo,
3750 Sche wolde have flowe unto him tho
Strawht ther he was into the Bot.
    The dai was clier, the Sonne hot,
The Gregeis weren in gret doute,
The whyle that here lord was oute:
Thei wisten noght what scholde tyde,
Bot waiten evere upon the tyde,
To se what ende scholde falle.
Ther stoden ek the nobles alle
Forth with the comun of the toun;
3760 And as thei loken up and doun,
Thei weren war withinne a throwe,
Wher cam the bot, which thei wel knowe,
And sihe hou Jason broghte his preie.
And tho thei gonnen alle seie,
And criden alle with o stevene,   [voice]
"Ha, wher was evere under the hevene
So noble a knyht as Jason is?"
And welnyh alle seiden this,
That Jason was a faie kniht,   [fairy (enchanted)]
3770 For it was nevere of mannes miht
The Flees of gold so forto winne;
And thus to talen thei beginne.
With that the king com forth anon,
And sih the Flees, hou that it schon;

And whan Jason cam to the lond,
The king himselve tok his hond
And kist him, and gret joie him made.
The Gregeis weren wonder glade,
And of that thing riht merie hem thoghte,
3780 And forth with hem the Flees thei broghte,
And ech on other gan to leyhe;   [laugh]
Bot wel was him that mihte neyhe,   [draw near]
To se therof the proprete.
And thus thei passen the cite
And gon unto the Paleis straght.
　　Medea, which foryat him naght,
Was redy there, and seide anon,
"Welcome, O worthi kniht Jason."
Sche wolde have kist him wonder fayn,
3790 Bot schame tornede hire agayn;
It was noght the manere as tho,
Forthi sche dorste noght do so.
Sche tok hire leve, and Jason wente
Into his chambre, and sche him sente
Hire Maide to sen hou he ferde;
The which whan that sche sih and herde,
Hou that he hadde faren oute
And that it stod wel al aboute,
Sche tolde hire ladi what sche wiste,
3800 And sche for joie hire Maide kiste.
The bathes weren thanne araied,
With herbes tempred and assaied,
And Jason was unarmed sone
And dede as it befell to done:
Into his bath he wente anon
And wyssh him clene as eny bon;
He tok a sopp, and oute he cam,
And on his beste aray he nam,
And kempde his hed, whan he was clad,
3810 And goth him forth al merie and glad

Riht strawht into the kinges halle.
The king cam with his knihtes alle
And maden him glad welcominge;
And he hem tolde the tidinge
Of this and that, hou it befell,
Whan that he wan the schepes fell.   [skin]
    Medea, whan sche was asent,   [sent for]
Com sone to that parlement,
And whan sche mihte Jason se,
3820 Was non so glad of alle as sche.
Ther was no joie forto seche,
Of him mad every man a speche,
Som man seide on, som man seide other;
Bot thogh he were goddes brother
And mihte make fyr and thonder,
Ther mihte be nomore wonder
Than was of him in that cite.
Echon tauhte other, "This is he,
Which hath in his pouer withinne
3830 That al the world ne mihte winne:
Lo, hier the beste of alle goode."
Thus saiden thei that there stode,
And ek that walkede up and doun,
Bothe of the Court and of the toun.
    The time of Souper cam anon,
Thei wisshen and therto thei gon,
Medea was with Jason set:
Tho was ther many a deynte fet
And set tofore hem on the bord,
3840 Bot non so likinge as the word
Which was ther spoke among hem tuo,
So as thei dorste speke tho.
Bot thogh thei hadden litel space,
Yit thei acorden in that place
Hou Jason scholde come at nyht,
Whan every torche and every liht

Were oute, and thanne of other thinges
Thei spieke aloud for supposinges
Of hem that stoden there aboute:
3850 For love is everemore in doute,
If that it be wisly governed
Of hem that ben of love lerned.
    Whan al was don, that dissh and cuppe
And cloth and bord and al was uppe,
Thei waken whil hem lest to wake,
And after that thei leve take
And gon to bedde forto reste.
And whan him thoghte for the beste,
That every man was faste aslepe,
3860 Jason, that wolde his time kepe,
Goth forth stalkende al prively
Unto the chambre, and redely
Ther was a Maide, which him kepte.
Medea wok and nothing slepte,
Bot natheles sche was abedde,
And he with alle haste him spedde
And made him naked and al warm.
Anon he tok hire in his arm:
What nede is forto speke of ese?
3870 Hem list ech other forto plese,
So that thei hadden joie ynow:
And tho thei setten whanne and how
That sche with him awey schal stele.
With wordes suche and othre fele   [many]
Whan al was treted to an ende,
Jason tok leve and gan forth wende
Unto his oughne chambre in pes;
Ther wiste it non bot Hercules.
    He slepte and ros whan it was time,
3880 And whanne it fell towardes prime,
He tok to him suche as he triste   [trusted]
In secre, that non other wiste,

And told hem of his conseil there,
And seide that his wille were
That thei to Schipe hadde alle thinge
So priveliche in thevenynge,   [secretly]
That noman mihte here dede aspie
Bot tho that were of compaignie:
For he woll go withoute leve,
3890   And lengere woll he noght beleve;   [remain]
Bot he ne wolde at thilke throwe
The king or queene scholde it knowe.
Thei saide, "Al this schal we be do":
And Jason truste wel therto.
     Medea in the mene while,
Which thoghte hir fader to beguile,
The Tresor which hir fader hadde
With hire al priveli sche ladde,
And with Jason at time set
3900   Awey sche stal and fond no let,   [delay]
And straght sche goth hire unto schipe
Of Grece with that felaschipe,
And thei anon drowe up the Seil.
And al that nyht this was conseil,   [a secret]
Bot erly, whan the Sonne schon,
Men syhe hou that thei were agon,
And come unto the king and tolde:
And he the sothe knowe wolde,
And axeth where his dowhter was.
3910   Ther was no word bot Out, Allas!
Sche was ago. The moder wepte,
The fader as a wod man lepte,
And gan the time forto warie,   [curse]
And swor his oth he wol noght tarie,
That with Caliphe and with galeie   [caliph (a kind of ship)]
The same cours, the same weie,
Which Jason tok, he wolde take,
If that he mihte him overtake.

To this thei seiden alle yee:
3920 Anon thei weren ate See,
And alle, as who seith, at a word
Thei gon withinne schipes bord,
The Sail goth up, and forth thei strauhte.
Bot non espleit therof thei cauhte,   [success (OF *esploit*)]
And so thei tornen hom ayein,
For al that labour was in vein.
    Jason to Grece with his preie
Goth thurgh the See the rihte weie:
Whan he ther com and men it tolde,
3930 Thei maden joie yonge and olde.
Eson, whan that he wiste of this,
Hou that his Sone comen is,
And hath achieved that he soughte
And hom with him Medea broughte,
In al the wyde world was non
So glad a man as he was on.
Togedre ben these lovers tho,
Til that thei hadden sones tuo,
Wherof thei weren bothe glade,
3940 And olde Eson gret joie made
To sen thencress of his lignage;
For he was of so gret an Age,
That men awaiten every day,
Whan that he scholde gon away.
Jason, which sih his fader old,
Upon Medea made him bold,
Of art magique, which sche couthe,
And preith hire that his fader youthe
Sche wolde make ayeinward newe:
3950 And sche, that was toward him trewe,
Behihte him that sche wolde it do,
Whan that sche time sawh therto.
Bot what sche dede in that matiere
It is a wonder thing to hiere,

Bot yit for the novellerie
I thenke tellen a partie.
Thus it befell upon a nyht,
Whan ther was noght bot sterreliht,
Sche was vanyssht riht as hir liste,
3960 That no wyht bot hirself it wiste,
And that was ate mydnyht tyde.
The world was stille on every side;
With open hed and fot al bare,
Hir her tosprad sche gan to fare,   [hair]
Upon hir clothes gert sche was,
Al specheles and on the gras
Sche glod forth as an Addre doth:
Non otherwise sche no goth,
Til sche cam to the freisshe flod,
3970 And there a while sche withstod.
Thries sche torned hire aboute,
And thries ek sche gan doun loute   [bow]
And in the flod sche wette hir her,
And thries on the water ther
Sche gaspeth with a drecchinge onde,   [troubled breath]
And tho sche tok hir speche on honde.
Ferst sche began to clepe and calle
Upward unto the sterres alle,
To Wynd, to Air, to See, to lond
3980 Sche preide, and ek hield up hir hond
To Echates, and gan to crie,
Which is goddesse of Sorcerie.
Sche seide, "Helpeth at this nede,
And as ye maden me to spede,
Whan Jason cam the Flees to seche,
So help me nou, I you beseche."
With that sche loketh and was war,
Doun fro the Sky ther cam a char,
The which Dragouns aboute drowe:
3990 And tho sche gan hir hed doun bowe,

And up sche styh, and faire and wel   [ascended (OE *stigan*)]
Sche drof forth bothe char and whel
Above in thair among the Skyes.
The lond of Crete and tho parties
Sche soughte, and faste gan hire hye,
And there upon the hulles hyhe
Of Othrin and Olimpe also,
And ek of othre hullés mo,
Sche fond and gadreth herbes suote,   [sweet]
4000 Sche pulleth up som be the rote,
And manye with a knyf sche scherth,   [shears]
And alle into hir char sche berth.
Thus whan sche hath the hulles sought,
The flodes ther foryat sche nought,
Eridian and Amphrisos,
Peneie and ek Spercheïdos,
To hem sche wente and ther sche nom
Bothe of the water and the fom,
The sond and ek the smale stones,
4010 Whiche as sche ches out for the nones,
And of the rede See a part,
That was behovelich to hire art,
Sche tok, and after that aboute
Sche soughte sondri sedes oute
In feldes and in many greves,
And ek a part sche tok of leves:
Bot thing which mihte hire most availe
Sche fond in Crete and in Thessaile.
    In daies and in nyhtes Nyne,
4020 With gret travaile and with gret pyne,   [pain]
Sche was pourveid of every piece,   [provided]
And torneth homward into Grece.
Before the gates of Eson
Hir char sche let awai to gon,
And tok out ferst that was therinne;
For tho sche thoghte to beginne

Such thing as semeth impossible,
And madé hirselven invisible,
As sche that was with Air enclosed
4030 Añd mihte of noman be desclosed.
Sche tok up turves of the lond
Withoute helpe of mannes hond,
Al heled with the grene gras, [covered]
Of which an Alter mad ther was
Unto Echates the goddesse
Of art magique and the maistresse,
And eft an other to Juvente,
As sche which dede hir hole entente.
Tho tok sche fieldwode and verveyne, [gentian/vervain]
4040 Of herbes ben noght betre tueine,
Of which anon withoute let
These alters ben aboute set:
Tuo sondri puttes faste by [pits]
Sche made, and with that hastely
A wether which was blak sche slouh,
And out therof the blod sche drouh
And dede into the pettes tuo;
Warm melk sche putte also therto
With hony meynd: and in such wise [mingled]
4050 Sche gan to make hir sacrifice,
And cride and preide forth withal
To Pluto the god infernal,
And to the queene Proserpine.
And so sche soghte out al the line
Of hem that longen to that craft,
Behinde was no name laft,
And preide hem alle, as sche wel couthe,
To grante Eson his ferste youthe.
This olde Eson broght forth was tho,
4060 Awei sche bad alle othre go
Upon peril that mihte falle;
And with that word thei wenten alle,

And leften there hem tuo al one.
And tho sche gan to gaspe and gone,
And made signes manyon,
And seide hir wordes therupon;
So that with spellinge of hir charmes
Sche tok Eson in bothe hire armes,
And made him forto slepe faste,
4070 And him upon hire herbes caste.
The blake wether tho sche tok,
And hiewh the fleissh, as doth a cok;   [hewed]
On either alter part sche leide,
And with the charmes that sche seide
A fyr down fro the Sky alyhte
And made it forto brenne lyhte.
Bot whan Medea sawh it brenne,
Anon sche gan to sterte and renne
The fyri aulters al aboute:
4080 Ther was no beste which goth oute
More wylde than sche semeth ther:
Aboute hir schuldres hyng hir her,
As thogh sche were oute of hir mynde
And torned in an other kynde.
Tho lay ther certein wode cleft,
Of which the pieces nou and eft
Sche made hem in the pettes wete,
And put hem in the fyri hete,
And tok the brond with al the blase,
4090 And thries sche began to rase
Aboute Eson, ther as he slepte;
And eft with water, which sche kepte,
Sche made a cercle aboute him thries,
And eft with fyr of sulphre twyes:
Ful many an other thing sche dede,
Which is noght writen in this stede.
Bot tho sche ran so up and doun,
Sche made many a wonder soun,

Somtime lich unto the cock,
4100 Somtime unto the Laverock,
Somtime kacleth as a Hen,
Somtime spekth as don the men:
And riht so as hir jargoun strangeth,
In sondri wise hir forme changeth,
Sche semeth faie and no womman;   [fairy]
For with the craftes that sche can
Sche was, as who seith, a goddesse,
And what hir liste, more or lesse,
Sche dede, in bokes as we finde,
4110 That passeth over manneskinde.   [beyond man's nature]
Bot who that wole of wondres hiere,
What thing sche wroghte in this matiere,
To make an ende of that sche gan,
Such merveile herde nevere man.

    Apointed in the newe Mone,
Whan it was time forto done,
Sche sette a caldron on the fyr,
In which was al the hole atir,
Wheron the medicine stod,
4120 Of jus, of water and of blod,
And let it buile in such a plit,
Til that sche sawh the spume whyt;
And tho sche caste in rynde and rote,
And sed and flour that was for bote,
With many an herbe and many a ston,
Wherof sche hath ther many on:
And ek Cimpheius the Serpent
To hire hath alle his scales lent,
Chelidre hire yaf his addres skin,
4130 And sche to builen caste hem in;   [boil]
A part ek of the horned Oule,
The which men hiere on nyhtes houle;
And of a Raven, which was told
Of nyne hundred wynter old,

Sche tok the hed with al the bile;
And as the medicine it wile,
Sche tok therafter the bouele   [bowel]
Of the Seewolf, and for the hele   [shark]
Of Eson, with a thousand mo
4140 Of thinges that sche hadde tho,
In that Caldroun togedre as blyve
Sche putte, and tok thanne of Olyve
A drie branche hem with to stere,   [stir]
The which anon gan floure and bere
And waxe al freissh and grene ayein.
Whan sche this vertu hadde sein,
Sche let the leste drope of alle
Upon the bare flor doun falle;
Anon ther sprong up flour and gras,
4150 Where as the drope falle was,
And wox anon al medwe grene,   [meadow]
So that it mihte wel be sene.
Medea thanne knew and wiste
Hir medicine is forto triste,   [to be trusted]
And goth to Eson ther he lay,
And tok a swerd was of assay,
With which a wounde upon his side
Sche made, that therout mai slyde
The blod withinne, which was old
4160 And sek and trouble and fieble and cold.
And tho sche tok unto his us
Of herbes al the beste jus,
And poured it into his wounde;
That made his veynes fulle and sounde:
And tho sche made his wounde clos,
And tok his hand, and up he ros;
And tho sche yaf him drinke a drauhte,
Of which his youthe ayein he cauhte,
His hed, his herte and his visage
4170 Lich unto twenty wynter Age;

Hise hore heres were away,
And lich unto the freisshe Maii,
Whan passed ben the colde schoures,
Riht so recovereth he his floures.

    Lo, what mihte eny man devise,
A womman schewe in eny wise
Mor hertly love in every stede,
Than Medea to Jason dede?
Ferst sche made him the flees to winne,
4180 And after that fro kiththe and kinne   [acquaintances]
With gret tresor with him sche stal,
And to his fader forth withal
His Elde hath torned into youthe,
Which thing non other womman couthe:
Bot hou it was to hire aquit,
The remembrance duelleth yit.

    King Peleüs his Em was ded,   [uncle]
Jason bar corone on his hed,
Medea hath fulfild his wille:
4190 Bot whanne he scholde of riht fulfille
The trouthe, which to hire afore
He hadde in thyle of Colchos swore,   [the island]
Tho was Medea most deceived.
For he an other hath received,
Which dowhter was to king Creon,
Creusa sche hihte, and thus Jason,
As he that was to love untrewe,
Medea lefte and tok a newe.
Bot that was after sone aboght:
4200 Medea with hire art hath wroght
Of cloth of gold a mantel riche,
Which semeth worth a kingesriche,   [kingdom]
And that was unto Creusa sent
In name of yifte and of present,
For Sosterhode hem was betuene;
And whan that yonge freisshe queene

That mantel lappeth hire aboute,
Anon therof the fyr sprong oute
And brente hir bothe fleissh and bon.
4210 Tho cam Medea to Jason
With bothe his Sones on hire hond,
And seide, "O thou of every lond
The moste untrewe creature,
Lo, this schal be thi forfeture."
With that sche bothe his Sones slouh
Before his yhe, and he outdrouh
His swerd and wold have slayn hir tho,
Bot farewel, sche was ago
Unto Pallas the Court above,
4220 Wher as sche pleigneth upon love,
As sche that was with that goddesse,
And he was left in gret destresse.
  Thus miht thou se what sorwe it doth
To swere an oth which is noght soth,
In loves cause namely.
Mi Sone, be wel war forthi,
And kep that thou be noght forswore:
For this, which I have told tofore,
Ovide telleth everydel.

[Amans wonders how the Golden Fleece got to Colchos in the first place, so Genius tells the Tale of Phrixus and Helen.[13] King Athemas and his wife Philen had two children, a son named Phrixus and a daughter named Helen. But before the children became of age their mother died. So King Athemas remarried, his bride being a maiden named Yno, daughter of Cadmus. After the marriage Yno, in her disdain, schemed to make the children loathsome to the king. For a year or two she had the land sown with sodden wheat that would not germinate. As famine grew throughout the land the king went to the Temple of Ceres to make sacrifices. But Yno plotted with the priests who told the king that Phrixus and Helen must be cast out of the land before wheat might grow again. So the children were thrown into the sea. But Juno took pity on them and sent a sheep with golden fleece that picked up the children to carry them to safety. So strange a creature it was, however, that Helen, in her fear, fainted and was drowned. The sheep carried Phrixus safely to Colchos, and what happened afterward you already have heard (4243–4361).

Amans notes that he who breaks his troth is not worthy of love at all; he then asks if there is further instruction pertaining to Avarice. There is, says Genius, a conscienceless brood called Usurers who run about like hounds, tracking down money to drive into their net. Always the Usurer is out for himself, seeking double measure. He lends a pea and demands a bean in return. There are many lovers of this sort too, whose love is worth no more than a mite but who want a pound repayment. Always they take advantage of love. With the help of their brokers they make false seem true. They buy love for little, then with their false weights gain much (4434). Amans says he is not guilty of Usury. He gives much more in love than ever he gets in return. He would gladly give double weight to get half in return. But if she does not reward him he fears he will never recover from the cost. No broker has brought him gain. Indeed, it is remarkable that his Lady has ignored him so successfully. Amans wonders (thought being free) if his Lady may not be a little bit guilty of usury herself. She certainly leads him on with her looks, yet gives him no real gain. How can her conscience excuse her when she sees him so spent, yet so loveless? He prays to God that she, for her own sake, will mend her ways (4532).

Genius admonishes Amans not to be too quick to accuse his Lady, for he has admitted that she has moved his heart by looking on him. It may be that her one look is worth many hearts like his, in which case he has sold his heart well. Common notions of justice do not apply to love. Love hinders and advances as he chooses. But the one part Genius admires in Amans's confession is his reluctance to use guile. For the vengeance upon beguilers is great, as the Tale of Echo makes clear (4572):[14]

Juno once had in her company a treacherous maiden named Echo who played lovebroker for Jupiter. But Juno found out and reproved her in this manner: "O traitress, who has misused your lady so, you deserve great pain. You used sly words to hide my husband's infidelities from me. As punishment you shall henceforth clap out as loud as a bell whatever you hear men say." And with that she was cast from her chamber into the hills and woods where no word spoken by man may escape her mouth (4652). In conclusion Genius advises Amans that if he should marry, he should be true to his wife. One love is sufficient: do not ask for more. Amans says his conscience is free; he has not been guilty of "brocage" (4664).

Genius next speaks of Parsimony (Skarsnesse) who is counsel and housekeeper for blind Avarice and who lets nothing escape. God himself goes wanting. It would be easier to flay flint than to get a reed's worth of goods from Skarsnesse, even if the man in need were his brother. Parsimony is love's enemy (4728). Amans says that if he had the treasure of Cresus, the gold of Octavian, and the wealth of India he would give it all to his sweet maid. But in fact he gives her nothing since she will not take anything he offers. She takes gifts from others, but that is because they are friends. Yet whoever is master of one's heart is master of one's goods; she commands all that Amans has whether she will or not (4775). Genius commends the Lover's attitude, for he who is parsimonious over small things in love will lose everything. Witness the Tale of Babio and Croceus.[15] Babio had a lover in his keeping whose name was Viola. None was fairer for her age than she. She was free and generous, full of youth and game. But he was the biggest "chinche" (miser) in all the land. Viola was woebegone until she met a fresh, free, and friendly man named Croceus. He knew no Avarice. He gave her gifts, and soon the medicine of Cupid and Venus cured her sadness. She forsook the begrudging Babio, bejaped for his scarcity, to enjoy Croceus. For the niggardly may not dwell in Love's court (4869).

Avarice's next fellow, a fiendish vice who was never man's

friend, is Ingratitude (Unkindeschipe). Ingratitude thinks he is not beholden to anyone, even his mother who bore him. He takes what any man will give him, but grumbles if he has to return a single grain, even though his barn is full. Nature damns so unkind a man. Even animals are grateful for kindness, for that is Nature's law. An authority in this matter is the Tale of Adrian and Bardus.[16]]

TALE OF ADRIAN AND BARDUS

To speke of an unkinde man,
I finde hou whilom Adrian,
Of Rome which a gret lord was,
4940 Upon a day as he per cas   [by chance]
To wode in his huntinge wente,
It hapneth at a soudein wente,   [turn]
After his chace as he poursuieth,
Thurgh happ, the which noman eschuieth,   [chance]
He fell unwar into a pet,   [pit]
Wher that it mihte noght be let.
The pet was dep and he fell lowe,
That of his men non myhte knowe
Wher he becam, for non was nyh,
4950 Which of his fall the meschief syh.
And thus al one ther he lay
Clepende and criende al the day
For socour and deliverance,
Til ayein Eve it fell per chance,
A while er it began to nyhte,
A povere man, which Bardus hihte,
Cam forth walkende with his asse,
And hadde gadred him a tasse   [heap]
Of grene stickes and of dreie
4960 To selle, who that wolde hem beie,
As he which hadde no liflode,
Bot whanne he myhte such a lode

To toune with his Asse carie.
And as it fell him forto tarie
That ilke time nyh the pet,
And hath the trusse faste knet,
He herde a vois, which cride dimme,
And he his Ere to the brimme
Hath leid, and herde it was a man,
4970 Which seide, "Ha, help hier Adrian,
And I wol yiven half mi good."
    The povere man this understod,
As he that wolde gladly winne,
And to this lord which was withinne
He spak and seide, "If I thee save,
What sikernesse schal I have   [security]
Of covenant, that afterward
Thou wolt me yive such reward
As thou behihtest nou tofore?"   [promised]
4980   That other hath his othes swore
Be hevene and be the goddes alle,
If that it myhte so befalle
That he out of the pet him broghte,
Of all the goodes whiche he oghte
He schal have evene halvendel.
    This Bardus seide he wolde wel;
And with this word his Asse anon
He let untrusse, and therupon
Doun goth the corde into the pet,
4990 To which he hath at ende knet
A staf, wherby, he seide, he wolde
That Adrian him scholde holde.
Bot it was tho per chance falle,
Into that pet was also falle
An Ape, which at thilke throwe,   [moment]
Whan that the corde cam doun lowe,
Al sodeinli therto he skipte
And it in bothe hise armes clipte.

And Bardus with his Asse anon
5000 Him hath updrawe, and he is gon.
But what he sih it was an Ape,
He wende al hadde ben a jape
Of faierie, and sore him dradde:
And Adrian eftsone gradde   [cried aloud (OE *graedan*)]
For help, and cride and preide faste,
And he eftsone his corde caste;
Bot whan it cam unto the grounde,
A gret Serpent it hath bewounde,
The which Bardus anon up drouh.
5010 And thanne him thoghte wel ynouh,
It was fantosme, bot yit he herde
The vois, and he therto ansuerde,
"What wiht art thou in goddes name?"
      "I am," quod Adrian, "the same,
Whos good thou schalt have evene half."
Quod Bardus, "Thanne a goddes half
The thridde time assaie I schal":
And caste his corde forth withal
Into the pet, and whan it cam
5020 To him, this lord of Rome it nam,
And therupon him hath adresced,
And with his hand fulofte blessed,
And thanne he bad to Bardus hale.   [haul]
And he, which understod his tale,
Betwen him and his Asse al softe
Hath drawe and set him up alofte
Withouten harm al esely.
He seith noght ones "grant merci,"
Bot strauhte him forth to the cite,
5030 And let this povere Bardus be.
And natheles this simple man
His covenant, so as he can,
Hath axed; and that other seide,
If so be that he him umbreide   [reproached]

Of oght that hath be speke or do,
It schal ben venged on him so,
That him were betre to be ded.
And he can tho non other red,
But on his asse ayein he caste
5040 His trusse, and hieth homward faste:
And whan that he cam hom to bedde,
He tolde his wif hou that he spedde.
Bot finaly to speke oght more
Unto this lord he dradde him sore,
So that a word ne dorste he sein:
And thus upon the morwe ayein,
In the manere as I recorde,
Forth with his Asse and with his corde
To gadre wode, as he dede er,
5050 He goth; and whan that he cam ner
Unto the place where he wolde,
He hath his Ape anon beholde,
Which hadde gadred al aboute
Of stickes hiere and there a route,
And leide hem redy to his hond,
Wherof he made his trosse and bond;
Fro dai to dai and in this wise
This Ape profreth his servise,
So that he hadde of wode ynouh.
5060 Upon a time and as he drouh
Toward the wode, he sih besyde
The grete gastli Serpent glyde,
Til that sche cam in his presence,
And in hir kinde a reverence
Sche hath him do, and forth withal
A Ston mor briht than a cristall
Out of hir mouth tofore his weie
Sche let doun falle, and wente aweie,
For that he schal noght ben adrad.
5070 Tho was this povere Bardus glad,

Thonkende god, and to the Ston
He goth and takth it up anon,
And hath gret wonder in his wit
Hou that the beste him hath aquit,
Wher that the mannes Sone hath failed,
For whom he hadde most travailed.
Bot al he putte in goddes hond,
And torneth hom, and what he fond
Unto his wif he hath it schewed;
5080 And thei, that weren bothe lewed, [ignorant]
Acorden that he scholde it selle.
And he no lengere wolde duelle,
Bot forth anon upon the tale
The Ston he profreth to the sale;
And riht as he himself it sette,
The jueler anon forth fette
The gold and made his paiement,
Therof was no delaiement.
    Thus whan this Ston was boght and sold,
5090 Homward with joie manyfold
This Bardus goth; and whan he cam
Hom to his hous and that he nam
His gold out of his Purs, withinne
He fond his Ston also therinne,
Wherof for joie his herte pleide,
Unto his wif and thus he seide,
"Lo, hier my gold, lo, hier mi Ston!"
His wif hath wonder therupon,
And axeth him hou that mai be.
5100 "Nou be mi trouthe I not," quod he,
"Bot I dar swere upon a bok,
That to my Marchant I it tok,
And he it hadde whan I wente:
So knowe I noght to what entente
It is nou hier, bot it be grace.
Forthi tomorwe in other place

I wole it fonde forto selle,   [attempt]
And if it wol noght with him duelle,
Bot crepe into mi purs ayein,
5110 Than dar I saufly swere and sein,
It is the vertu of the Ston."
        The morwe cam, and he is gon
To seche aboute in other stede
His Ston to selle, and he so dede,
And lefte it with his chapman there.
Bot whan that he cam elleswhere,
In presence of his wif at hom,
Out of his Purs and that he nom
His gold, he fond his Ston withal:
5120 And thus it fell him overal,   [again and again]
Where he it solde in sondri place,
Such was the fortune and the grace.
Bot so wel may nothing ben hidd,
That it nys ate laste kidd: [known]
This fame goth aboute Rome
So ferforth, that the wordes come
To themperour Justinian;
And he let sende for the man,
And axede him hou that it was.
5130 And Bardus tolde him al the cas,
Hou that the worm and ek the beste,
Althogh thei maden no beheste,
His travail hadden wel aquit;
Bot he which hadde a mannes wit,
And made his covenant be mouthe
And swor therto al that he couthe
To parte and yiven half his good,
Hath nou foryete hou that it stod,
As he which wol no trouthe holde.
5140   This Emperour al that he tolde
Hath herd, and thilke unkindenesse
He seide he wolde himself redresse.

And thus in court of juggement
This Adrian was thanne assent,
And the querele in audience
Declared was in the presence
Of themperour and many mo;
Wherof was mochel speche tho
And gret wondringe among thet press.
5150 Bot ate laste natheles
For the partie which hath pleigned
The lawe hath diemed and ordeigned
Be hem that were avised wel,
That he schal have the havendel
Thurghout of Adrianes good.
And thus of thilke unkinde blod
Stant the memoire into this day,
Wherof that every wysman may
Ensamplen him, and take in mynde
5160 What schame it is to ben unkinde;
Ayein the which reson debateth,
And every creature it hateth.

[There are many lovers who are guilty of Ingratitude, too, Genius says, but Amans insists that he is not one of them. He has not been successful enough to have anything to be ungrateful about. He will not accuse his Lady of unkindness, but he cannot say she has been kind either. Genius responds that Amans is to blame for complaining of his Lady. It may be that she cannot honor his desires for some good reason. Still it is commendable that Amans is free from Ingratitude and to prove that he has chosen the right path Genius tells the Tale of Theseus and Ariadne.[17]]

TALE OF THESEUS AND ARIADNE

Mynos, as telleth the Poete,
The which whilom was king of Crete,
A Sone hadde and Androchee

He hihte: and so befell that he
Unto Athenes forto lere   [study]
Was send, and so he bar him there,
For that he was of hih lignage,
Such pride he tok in his corage,
That he foryeten hath the Scoles,
5240 And in riote among the foles
He dede manye thinges wronge;
And useth thilke lif so longe
Til ate laste of that he wroghte
He fond the meschief which he soghte,
Wherof it fell that he was slain.
His fader, which it herde sain,
Was wroth, and al that evere he mihte,
Of men of Armes he him dighte   [prepared]
A strong pouer, and forth he wente
5250 Unto Athenys, where he brente
The pleine contre al aboute:
The Cites stode of him in doute,
As thei that no defence hadde
Ayein the pouer which he ladde.
　　Egeüs, which was there king,
His conseil tok upon this thing,
For he was thanne in the Cite:
So that of pes into tretee
Betwen Mynos and Egeüs
5260 Thei felle, and ben acorded thus;
That king Mynos fro yer to yeere
Receive schal, as thou schalt here,
Out of Athenys for truage   [tribute]
Of men that were of myhti Age
Persones nyne, of whiche he schal
His wille don in special
For vengance of his Sones deth.
Non other grace ther ne geth,
Bot forto take the juise;

5270 And that was don in such a wise
      Which stod upon a wonder cas.
      For thilke time so it was,
      Wherof that men yit rede and singe,
      King Mynos hadde in his kepinge
      A cruel Monstre, as seith the geste: [tale]
      For he was half man and half beste,
      And Minotaurus he was hote,
      Which was begete in a riote
      Upon Pasiphe, his oghne wif,
5280 Whil he was oute upon the strif
      Of thilke grete Siege at Troie.
      Bot sche, which lost hath alle joie,
      Whan that sche syh this Monstre bore,
      Bad men ordeigne anon therfore:
      And fell that ilke time thus,
      Ther was a Clerk, on Dedalus,
      Which hadde ben of hire assent   [sent for by her]
      Of that hir world was so miswent;
      And he made of his oghne wit,
5290 Wherof the remembrance is yit,
      For Minotaure such an hous,
      Which was so strange and merveilous,
      That what man that withinne wente,
      Ther was so many a sondri wente,   [turn]
      That he ne scholde noght come oute,
      But gon amased al aboute.
      And in this hous to loke and warde
      Was Minotaurus put in warde,
      That what lif that therinne cam,
5300 Of man or beste, he overcam
      And slow, and fedde him therupon;
      And in this wise many on
      Out of Athenys for truage
      Devoured weren in that rage.
      For every yeer thei schope hem so,

Thei of Athenys, er thei go
Toward that ilke wofull chance,
As it was set in ordinance,
Upon fortune here lot thei caste;
5310 Til that Theseüs ate laste,
Which was the kinges Sone there,
Amonges othre that ther were
In thilke yeer, as it befell,
The lot upon his chance fell.
He was a worthi kniht withalle;
And whan he sih this chance falle,
He ferde as thogh he tok non hiede,   [behaved]
Bot al that evere he mihte spiede,
With him and with his felaschipe
5320 Forth into Crete he goth be Schipe;
Wher that the king Mynos he soghte,
And profreth all that he him oghte
Upon the point of here acord.
   This sterne king, this cruel lord
Tok every day on of the Nyne,
And put him to the discipline
Of Minotaure, to be devoured;
Bot Theseüs was so favoured,
That he was kept til ate laste.
5330 And in the meene while he caste
What thing him were best to do:
And fell that Adriagne tho,
Which was the dowhter of Mynos,
And hadde herd the worthi los   [fame]
Of Theseüs and of his myht,
And syh he was a lusti kniht,
Hire hole herte on him sche leide,
And he also of love hir preide,
So ferforth that thei were al on.
5340 And sche ordeigneth thanne anon
In what manere he scholde him save,

And schop so that sche dede him have
A clue of thred, of which withinne
Ferst ate dore he schal beginne
With him to take that on ende,
That whan he wolde ayeinward wende,
He mihte go the same weie.
And over this, so as I seie,
Of pich sche tok him a pelote,   [pitch/ball]
5350 The which he scholde into the throte
Of Minotaure caste rihte:
Such wepne also for him sche dighte,
That he be reson mai noght faile
To make an ende of his bataile;
For sche him tawhte in sondri wise,
Til he was knowe of thilke emprise,
Hou he this beste schulde quelle.
And thus, schort tale forto telle,
So as this Maide him hadde tawht,
5360 Theseüs with this Monstre fawht,
Smot of his hed, the which he nam,
And be the thred, so as he cam,
He goth ayein, til he were oute.
Tho was gret wonder al aboute:
Mynos the tribut hath relessed,
And so was al the werre cessed
Betwen Athene and hem of Crete.

        Bot now to speke of thilke suete,   [sweetheart]
Whos beaute was withoute wane,   [was undiminished]
5370 This faire Maiden Adriane,
Whan that sche sih Theseüs sound,
Was nevere yit upon the ground
A gladder wyht than sche was tho.
Theseüs duelte a dai or tuo
Wher that Mynos gret chiere him dede:
Theseüs in a prive stede
Hath with this Maiden spoke and rouned,   [whispered]

That sche to him was abandouned
In al that evere that sche couthe,
5380 So that of thilke lusty youthe
Al prively between hem tweie
The ferste flour he tok aweie.
For he so faire tho behihte   [promised]
That evere, whil he live mihte,
He scholde hire take for his wif,
And as his oghne hertes lif
He scholde hire love and trouthe bere;
And sche, which mihte noght forbere,
So sore loveth him ayein,
5390 That what as evere he wolde sein
With al hire herte sche believeth.
And thus his pourpos he achieveth,
So that assured of his trouthe
With him sche wente, and that was
    routhe.
    Fedra hire yonger Soster eke,
A lusti Maide, a sobre, a meke,
Fulfild of alle curtesie,
For Sosterhode and compainie
Of love, which was hem betuene,
5400 To sen hire Soster mad a queene,
Hire fader lefte and forth sche wente
With him, which al his ferste entente
Foryat withinne a litel throwe,
So that it was al overthrowe,
Whan sche best wende it scholde stonde.
The Schip was blowe fro the londe,
Wherin that thei seilende were;
This Adriagne hath mochel fere
Of that the wynd so loude bleu,
5410 As sche which of the See ne kneu,
And preide forto reste a whyle.
And so fell that upon an yle,

Which Chyo hihte, thei ben drive,
Where he to hire his leve hath yive
That sche schal londe and take hire reste.
Bot that was nothing for the beste:
For whan sche was to londe broght,
Sche, which that time thoghte noght
Bot alle trouthe, and tok no kepe,
5420 Hath leid hire softe forto slepe,
As sche which longe hath ben forwacched;   [worn out with watching]
Bot certes sche was evele macched
And fer from alle loves kinde;
For more than the beste unkinde   [beast]
Theseüs, which no trouthe kepte,
Whil that this yonge ladi slepte,
Fulfild of his unkindeschipe
Hath al foryete the goodschipe
Which Adriane him hadde do,
5430 And bad unto the Schipmen tho
Hale up the seil and noght abyde,
And forth he goth the same tyde
Toward Athene, and hire alonde
He lefte, which lay nyh the stronde
Slepende, til that sche awok.
Bot whan that sche cast up hire lok
Toward the stronde and sih no wyht,
Hire herte was so sore aflyht,
That sche ne wiste what to thinke,
5440 Bot drouh hire to the water brinke,
Wher sche behield the See at large.
Sche sih no Schip, sche sih no barge
Als ferforth as sche mihte kenne: [see]
"Ha lord," sche seide, "which a Senne,
As al the world schal after hiere,
Upon this woful womman hiere
This worthi kniht hath don and wroght!
I wende I hadde his love boght,   [thought]

And so deserved ate nede,
5450 Whan that he stod upon his drede,
And ek the love he me behihte.
It is gret wonder hou he mihte
Towardes me nou ben unkinde,
And so to lete out of his mynde
Thing which he seide his oghne mouth.
Bot after this whan it is couth
And drawe into the worldes fame,
It schal ben hindringe of his name:
For wel he wot and so wot I,
5460 He yaf his trouthe bodily,
That he myn honour scholde kepe."
And with that word sche gan to wepe,
And sorweth more than ynouh:
Hire faire tresces sche todrouh,
And with hirself tok such a strif,
That sche betwen the deth and lif
Swounende lay fulofte among.
And al was this on him along,
Which was to love unkinde so,
5470 Wherof the wrong schal everemo
Stonde in Cronique of remembrance.
And ek it asketh a vengance
To ben unkinde in loves cas,
So as Theseüs thanne was,
Al thogh he were a noble kniht;
For he the lawe of loves riht
Forfeted hath in alle weie,
That Adriagne he putte aweie,
Which was a gret unkinde dede:
5480 And after this, so as I rede,
Fedra, the which hir Soster is,
He tok in stede of hire, and this
Fel afterward to mochel teene.   [trouble (OE *teona*)]
For thilke vice of which I meene,

Unkindeschipe, where it falleth,
The trouthe of mannes herte it palleth,
That he can no good dede aquite:
So mai he stonde of no merite
Towardes god, and ek also
5490 Men clepen him the worldes fo;
For he nomore than the fend
Unto non other man is frend,
Bot al toward himself al one.
Forthi, mi Sone, in thi persone
This vice above alle othre fle.

[The next in the lineage of Avarice is Ravine. He thrives on
extortion, filling his larder at the expense of others. He gets people
in his debt, and then when they cannot pay, he takes by force
what he chooses. There are lovers who behave in this way, too,
taking by force what they want. Amans says he is no raviner in
love. Were he as strong as Pompeii or Alexander, whom all the
world obeyed, he would do nothing that might bring slander on
his Lady. But he requests, nonetheless, an example of such be-
havior. So Genius tells the Tale of Tereüs.[18]]

TALE OF TEREÜS

🔖 Ther was a real noble king,   [royal]
And riche of alle worldes thing,
Which of his propre enheritance
Athenes hadde in governance,
And who so thenke therupon,
His name was king Pandion.
Tuo douhtres hadde he be his wif,
The whiche he lovede as his lif;
The ferste douhter Progne hihte,
5560 And the secounde, as sche wel mihte,
Was cleped faire Philomene,
To whom fell after mochel tene.   [vexation]

The fader of his pourveance
His doughter Progne wolde avance,
And yaf hire unto mariage
A worthi king of hih lignage,
A noble kniht eke of his hond,
So was he kid in every lond, [known]
Of Trace he hihte Tereüs;
5570 The clerk Ovide telleth thus.
This Tereüs his wif hom ladde,
A lusti lif with hire he hadde;
Til it befell upon a tyde,
This Progne, as sche lay him besyde,
Bethoughte hir hou it mihte be
That sche hir Soster myhte se,
And to hir lord hir will sche seide,
With goodly wordes and him preide
That sche to hire mihte go:
5580 And if it liked him noght so,
That thanne he wolde himselve wende,
Or elles be som other sende,
Which mihte hire diere Soster griete, [greet]
And schape hou that thei mihten miete. [plan]
Hir lord anon to that he herde
Yaf his acord, and thus ansuerde:
"I wole," he seide, "for thi sake
The weie after thi Soster take
Miself, and bringe hire, if I may."
5590 And sche with that, there as he lay,
Began him in hire armes clippe,
And kist him with hir softe lippe,
And seide, "Sire, grant mercy."
And he sone after was redy,
And tok his leve forto go;
In sori time dede he so.
This Tereüs goth forth to Schipe
With him and with his felaschipe;

Be See the rihte cours he nam,
5600 Into the contre til he cam,
Wher Philomene was duellinge,
And of hir Soster the tidinge
He tolde, and tho thei weren glade,
And mochel joie of him thei made.
The fader and the moder bothe
To leve here douhter weren lothe,
Bot if thei weren in presence;
And natheles at reverence
Of him, that wolde himself travaile,
5610 Thei wolden noght he scholde faile
Of that he preide, and yive hire leve:
And sche, that wolde noght beleve,   [stay behind]
In alle haste made hire yare   [ready]
Toward hir Soster forto fare,
With Tereüs and forth sche wente.
And he with al his hole entente,
Whan sche was fro hir frendes go,
Assoteth of hire love so,   [dotes]
His yhe myhte he noght withholde,
5620 That he ne moste on hir beholde;
And with the sihte he gan desire,
And sette his oghne herte on fyre;
And fyr, whan it to tow aprocheth,   [straw (OE *tow*)]
To him anon the stengthe acrocheth,   [increases]
Til with his hete it be devoured,
The tow ne mai noght be socoured.
And so that tirant raviner,
Whan that sche was in his pouer,
And he therto sawh time and place,
5630 As he that lost hath alle grace,
Foryat he was a wedded man,
And in a rage on hire he ran,
Riht as a wolf which takth his preie.
And sche began to crie and preie,

"O fader, o mi moder diere,
Nou help!" Bot thei ne mihte it hiere,
And sche was of to litel myht
Defense ayein so ruide a knyht
To make, whanne he was so wod
5640 That he no reson understod,
Bot hield hire under in such wise,
That sche ne myhte noght arise,
Bot lay oppressed and desesed,
As if a goshauk hadde sesed
A brid, which dorste noght for fere
Remue: and thus this tirant there
Beraft hire such thing as men sein
Mai neveremor be yolde ayein,   [given]
And that was the virginite:
5650 Of such Ravine it was pite.
        Bot whan sche to hirselven com,
And of hir meschief hiede nom,
And knew hou that sche was no maide,
With wofull herte thus sche saide:
"O thou of alle men the worste,
Wher was ther evere man that dorste
Do such a dede as thou hast do?
That dai schal falle, I hope so,
That I schal telle out al mi fille,
5660 And with my speche I schal fulfille
The wyde world in brede and lengthe.
That thou hast do to me be strengthe,
If I among the poeple duelle,
Unto the poeple I schal it telle;
And if I be withinne wall
Of Stones closed, thanne I schal
Unto the Stones clepe and crie,
And tellen hem thi felonie;
And if I to the wodes wende,
5670 Ther schal I tellen tale and ende,

And crie it to the briddes oute,
That thei schul hiere it al aboute.
For I so loude it schal reherce,
That my vois schal the hevene perce,
That it schal soune in goddes Ere.
Ha, false man, where is thi fere?
O mor cruel than eny beste,
Hou hast thou holden thi beheste
Which thou unto my Soster madest?
5680 O thou, which alle love ungladest,
And art ensample of alle untrewe,
Nou wolde god mi Soster knewe,
Of thin untrouthe, hou that it stod!"
And he than as a Lyon wod   [raging]
With hise unhappi handes stronge
Hire cauhte be the tresses longe,
With whiche he bond ther bothe hire
    armes,
That was fieble dede of armes,
And to the grounde anon hire caste,
5690 And out he clippeth also faste
Hire tunge with a peire scheres.
So what with blod and what with teres
Out of hire yhe and of hir mouth,
He made hire faire face uncouth:
Sche lay swounende unto the deth,
Ther was unethes eny breth;   [scarcely]
Bot yit whan he hire tunge refte,
A litel part therof belefte,
Bot sche with al no word mai soune,
5700 Bot chitre and as a brid jargoune.
And natheles that wode hound   [mad]
Hir bodi hent up fro the ground,
And sente hir there as be his wille
Sche scholde abyde in prison stille
For everemo: bot nou tak hiede

What after fell of this misdede.
    Whanne al this meschief was befalle,
This Tereüs, that foule him falle,
Unto his contre hom he tyh;   [came (OE *teon,* 'to draw')]
5710 And vhan he com his paleis nyh,
His wif al redi there him kepte.
Whan he hir sih, anon he wepte,
And that he dede for deceite,
For sche began to axe him streite,
"Wher is mi Soster?" And he seide
That sche was ded; and Progne abreide,   [started]
As sche that was a wofull wif,
And stod betuen hire deth and lif,
Of that sche herde such tidinge:
5720 Bot for sche sih hire lord wepinge,
She wende noght bot alle trouthe,
And hadde wel the more routhe.
The Perles weren tho forsake   [adornments]
To hire, and blake clothes take;
As sche that was gentil and kinde,
In worschipe of hir Sostres mynde   [her sister's memory]
Sche made a riche enterement,
For sche fond non amendement
To syghen or to sobbe more:
5730 So was ther guile under the gore.   [cloak]
    Nou leve we this king and queene,
And torne ayein to Philomene,
As I began to tellen erst.
Whan sche cam into prison ferst,
It thoghte a kinges douhter strange
To maken so soudein a change
Fro welthe unto so grete a wo;
And sche began to thenke tho,
Thogh sche be mouthe nothing preide,
5740 Withinne hir herte thus sche seide:
"O thou, almyhty Jupiter,

That hihe sist and lokest fer,
Thou soffrest many a wrong doinge,
And yit it is noght thi willinge.
To thee ther mai nothing ben hid,
Thou wost hou it is me betid:
I wolde I hadde noght be bore,   [been born]
For thanne I hadde noght forlore
Mi speche and mi virginite.
5750 Bot, goode lord, al is in thee,
Whan thou therof wolt do vengance
And schape mi deliverance."
And evere among this ladi wepte,
And thoghte that sche nevere kepte
To ben a worldes womman more,
And that sche wissheth everemore.
Bot ofte unto hir Soster diere
Hire herte spekth in this manere,
And seide, "Ha, Soster, if ye knewe
5760 Of myn astate, ye wolde rewe,
I trowe, and my deliverance
Ye wolde schape, and do vengance
On him that is so fals a man:
And natheles, so as I can,
I wol you sende som tokninge,
Wherof ye schul have knowlechinge
Of thing I wot, that schal you lothe,
The which you toucheth and me bothe."
And tho withinne a whyle als tyt   [promptly]
5770 Sche waf a cloth of Selk al whyt   [wove]
With lettres and ymagerie,
In which was al the felonie,
Which Tereüs to hire hath do;
And lappede it togedre tho
And sette hir signet therupon
And sende it unto Progne anon.
The messager which forth it bar,

What it amonteth is noght war;
And natheles to Progne he goth
5780 And prively takth hire the cloth,
And wente ayein riht as he cam,
The court of him non hiede nam.
    Whan Progne of Philomene herde,
Sche wolde knowe hou that it ferde,
And opneth that the man hath broght,
And wot therby what hath be wroght
And what meschief ther is befalle.
In swoune tho sche gan doun falle,
And efte aros and gan to stonde,
5790 And eft sche takth the cloth on honde,
Behield the lettres and thymages;
Bot ate laste, "Of suche oultrages,"
Sche seith, "wepinge is noght the bote":   [remedy]
And swerth, if that sche live mote,
It schal be venged otherwise.
And with that sche gan hire avise
Hou ferst sche mihte unto hire winne
Hir Soster, that noman withinne,
Bot only thei that were suore,   [sworn]
5800 It scholde knowe, and schop therfore   [arranged (shaped)]
That Tereüs nothing it wiste;
And yit riht as hirselven liste,   [desired]
Hir Soster was delivered sone
Out of prison, and be the mone
To Progne sche was broght be nyhte.
    Whan ech of other hadde a sihte,
In chambre, ther thei were al one,
Thei maden many a pitous mone;
Bot Progne most of sorwe made,
5810 Which sihe hir Soster pale and fade
And specheles and deshonoured,
Of that sche hadde be defloured;
And ek upon hir lord sche thoghte,

Of that he so untreuly wroghte
And hadde his espousaile broke. [wedding vows]
Sche makth a vou it schal be wroke, [avenged]
And with that word sche kneleth doun
Wepinge in gret devocioun:
Unto Cupide and to Venus
5820 Sche preide, and seide thanne thus:
"O ye, to whom nothing asterte
Of love mai, for every herte
Ye knowe, as ye that ben above
The god and the goddesse of love;
Ye witen wel that evere yit
With al mi will and al my wit,
Sith ferst ye schopen me to wedde,
That I lay with mi lord abedde,
I have be trewe in mi degre,
5830 And evere thoghte forto be,
And nevere love in other place,
Bot al only the king of Trace,
Which is mi lord and I his wif.
Bot nou allas this wofull strif!
That I him thus ayeinward finde
The most untrewe and most unkinde
That evere in ladi armes lay.
And wel I wot that he ne may
Amende his wrong, it is so gret;
5840 For he to lytel of me let,
Whan he myn oughne Soster tok,
And me that am his wif forsok."
    Lo, thus to Venus and Cupide
Sche preide, and furthermor sche cride
Unto Appollo the hiheste,
And seide, "O myghti god of reste,
Thou do vengance of this debat.
Mi Soster and al hire astat
Thou wost, and hou sche hath forlore

5850 Hir maidenhod, and I therfore
In al the world schal bere a blame
Of that mi Soster hath a schame,
That Tereüs to hire I sente:
And wel thou wost that myn entente
Was al for worschipe and for goode.
O lord, that yifst the lives fode
To every wyht, I prei thee hiere
Thes wofull Sostres that ben hiere,
And let ous noght to the ben lothe;
5860 We ben thin oghne wommen bothe."
    Thus pleigneth Progne and axeth
    wreche,   [vengeance]
And thogh hire Soster lacke speche,
To him that alle thinges wot
Hire sorwe is noght the lasse hot:
Bot he that thanne had herd hem tuo,
Him oughte have sorwed everemo
For sorwe which was hem betuene.
With signes pleigneth Philomene,
And Progne seith, "It schal be wreke,
5870 That al the world therof schal speke."
And Progne tho seknesse feigneth,
Wherof unto hir lord sche pleigneth,
And preith sche moste hire chambres kepe,
And as hir liketh wake and slepe.
And he hire granteth to be so;
And thus togedre ben thei tuo,
That wolde him bot a litel good.
Nou herk hierafter hou it stod
Of wofull auntres that befelle:
5880 Thes Sostres, that ben bothe felle,—
And that was noght on hem along,
Bot onliche on the grete wrong
Which Tereüs hem hadde do,—
Thei schopen forto venge hem tho.

This Tereüs be Progne his wif
A Sone hath, which as his lif
He loveth, and Ithis he hihte:
His moder wiste wel sche mihte
Do Tereüs no more grief
5890 Than sle this child, which was so lief.
Thus sche, that was, as who seith, mad
Of wo, which hath hir overlad,
Withoute insihte of moderhede
Foryat pite and loste drede
And in hir chambre prively
This child withouten noise or cry
Sche slou, and hieu him al to pieces: [cut]
And after with diverse spieces
The fleissh, whan it was so toheewe,
5900 Sche takth, and makth therof a sewe,   [stew]
With which the fader at his mete
Was served, til he hadde him ete;
That he ne wiste hou that it stod,
Bot thus his oughne fleissh and blod
Himself devoureth ayein kinde,
As he that was tofore unkinde.
And thanne, er that he were arise,
For that he scholde ben agrise,   [aggrieved]
To schewen him the child was ded,
5910 This Philomene tok the hed
Betwen tuo disshes, and al wrothe
Tho comen forth the Sostres bothe,
And setten it upon the bord.
And Progne tho began the word,
And seide, "O werste of alle wicke,
Of conscience whom no pricke
Mai stere, lo, what thou hast do!
Lo, hier ben nou we Sostres tuo;
O Raviner, lo hier thi preie,
5920 With whom so falsliche on the weie

Thou hast thi tirannye wroght.
Lo, nou it is somdel aboght,
And bet it schal, for of thi dede
The world schal evere singe and rede
In remembrance of thi defame:
For thou to love hast do such schame,
That it schal nevere be foryete."
With that he sterte up fro the mete,
And schof the bord unto the flor,
5930 And cauhte a swerd anon and suor
That thei scholde of his handes dye.
And thei unto the goddes crie
Begunne with so loude a stevene,   [voice]
That thei were herd unto the hevene;
And in a twinclinge of an yhe
The goddes, that the meschief syhe,
Here formes changen alle thre.
Echon of hem in his degre
Was torned into briddes kinde;
5940 Diverseliche, as men mai finde,
After thastat that thei were inne,
Here formes were set atwinne.
And as it telleth in the tale,
The ferst into a nyhtingale
Was schape, and that was Philomene,
Which in the wynter is noght sene,
For thanne ben the leves falle
And naked ben the buisshes alle.
For after that sche was a brid,
5950 Hir will was evere to ben hid,
And forto duelle in prive place,
That noman scholde sen hir face
For schame, which mai noght be lassed,
Of thing that was tofore passed,
Whan that sche loste hir maidenhiede:
For evere upon hir wommanhiede,

Thogh that the goddes wolde hire change,
Sche thenkth, and is the more strange,
And halt hir clos the wyntres day.
5960 Bot whan the wynter goth away,
And that Nature the goddesse
Wole of hir oughne fre largesse
With herbes and with floures bothe
The feldes and the medwes clothe, [meadows]
And ek the wodes and the greves [groves]
Ben heled al with grene leves, [covered]
So that a brid hire hyde mai,
Betwen Averil and March and Maii,
Sche that the wynter hield hir clos,
5970 For pure schame and noght aros,
Whan that sche seth the bowes thikke,
And that ther is no bare sticke,
Bot al is hid with leves grene,
To wode comth this Philomene
And makth hir ferste yeres flyht;
Wher as sche singeth day and nyht,
And in hir song al openly
Sche makth hir pleignte and seith, "O
            why,
O why ne were I yit a maide?"
5980 For so these olde wise saide,
Which understoden what sche mente,
Hire notes ben of such entente.
And ek thei seide hou in hir song
Sche makth gret joie and merthe among,
And seith, "Ha, nou I am a brid,
Ha, nou mi face mai ben hid:
Thogh I have lost mi Maidenhede,
Schal noman se my chekes rede."
Thus medleth sche with joie wo
5990 And with hir sorwe merthe also,
So that of loves maladie

Sche makth diverse melodie,
And seith love is a wofull blisse,
A wisdom which can noman wisse,
A lusti fievere, a wounde softe:
This note sche reherceth ofte
To hem whiche understonde hir tale.
Nou have I of this nyhtingale,
Which erst was cleped Philomene,
6000 Told al that evere I wolde mene,
Bothe of hir forme and of hir note,
Wherof men mai the storie note.
      And of hir Soster Progne I finde,
Hou sche was torned out of kinde
Into a Swalwe swift of winge,
Which ek in wynter lith swounynge,
Ther as sche mai nothing be sene:
Bot whan the world is woxe grene
And comen is the Somertide,
6010 Than fleth sche forth and ginth to chide,
And chitreth out in her langage
What falshod is in mariage,
And telleth in a maner speche
Of Tereüs the Spousebreche.   [adulterer]
Sche wol noght in the wodes duelle,
For sche wolde openliche telle;
And ek for that sche was a spouse,
Among the folk sche comth to house,
To do thes wyves understonde
6020 The falshod of hire housebonde,
That thei of hem be war also,
For ther ben manye untrewe of tho.
Thus ben the Sostres briddes bothe,
And ben toward the men so lothe,
That thei ne wole of pure schame
Unto no mannes hand be tame;
For evere it duelleth in here mynde

Of that thei founde a man unkinde,
And that was false Tereüs.
6030 If such on be amonges ous
I not, bot his condicion
Men sein in every region
Withinne toune and ek withoute
Nou regneth comunliche aboute.
And natheles in remembrance
I wol declare what vengance
The goddes hadden him ordeined,
Of that the Sostres hadden pleigned:
For anon after he was changed
6040 And from his oghne kinde stranged,
A lappewincke mad he was,
And thus he hoppeth on the gras,
And on his hed ther stant upriht
A creste in tokne he was a kniht;
And yit unto this dai men seith,
A lappewincke hath lore his feith
And is the brid falseste of alle.

    Bewar, mi Sone, er thee so falle;
For if thou be of such covine,   [conspiracy]
6050 To gete of love be Ravine
Thi lust, it mai the falle thus,
As it befell of Tereüs.

    Mi fader, goddes forebode!
Me were levere be fortrode
With wilde hors and be todrawe,
Er I ayein love and his lawe
Dede eny thing or loude or stille,
Which were noght mi ladi wille.

[Genius speaks next of Robbery, a henchman of Avarice who
gets his sustenance by ransacking whomever he can, whether by
land or water. So too there are thieves of love who, if they find
an able woman in a convenient place, take part of her wares,

regardless of who she is. Meanwhile the wife of such a villain, who loves her lord as her own life, sits home wishing for his return; later she learns how well his hounds ran, how bright the sun shone, and how well his hawks flew, but not how he robbed in the woods and was untrue in love (6134). There can be no justification for such behavior, as Ovid's story of Neptune and Cornix shows.[19] Cornix was a maiden servant of Pallas, the wife of Mars, who helps all who fight under his banner. Once as Cornix was walking upon the strand, Neptune saw her and was so struck by her beauty that he plotted how he might rob her, not of rings, brooches, or other things small, but to seize her in his arms and put his hand into the coffer containing the greatest of all treasures called maidenhead. But Cornix was a proud woman, dreadful of shame, and when she saw that she might not oppose the thief she prayed to Pallas to save her honor, whereupon suddenly she was transformed into a crow, delighted more to keep her maidenhead white beneath black feathers than to lose it and be adorned in white pearls. Thus the maiden escaped, and Neptune was forever japed and scorned for his loss (6217).

As a further warning against robbing women of their maidenhead Genius tells the Tale of Calistona.[20] King Lichaon had a daughter named Calistona who swore in her heart forever to be a maiden. She kept company with nymphs and woodmaidens who one spring took her to the Wood of Tegea where she was received by Diana into the company of Virgins. But one day Jupiter came suddenly upon her and robbed her of her treasure. Later, as she bathed with the Virgins in the presence of Diana her guilt was made known by her swelling womb. Full of shame she was cast out to give birth in the woods to a boy, named Archas. But Juno learned of the robbery and in her wrath transformed Calistona into a hideous bear. Some years later Archas happened to be hunting in the woods and came upon the bear. His mother recognized him and rushed to him, both arms spread, to embrace her son. Quickly he seized an arrow and bent his bow, but Jupiter intervened and saved them both (6337).

Robbing of maidenhead is a dreadful thing. Hear a tale of

old days when Virginity was esteemed. Valerius says that the Emperor of Rome should honor virgins, and when he meets one along the way he should pay homage.[21] In those days not only women but men also were virgins. One man named Phyryns put out his eyes so that his virginity might not be threatened by the looks of appealing women. Indeed, the Apocalypse records that virgins are esteemed above all others in heaven. When the Emperor Valentinian was a hundred winters old and still a virgin, he rejoiced more in his victory over the flesh than in all his conquests of kingdoms (6417).

Amans acknowledges that such achievements are remarkable, but he wonders how the world could keep going if everybody turned virgin. The world of men would soon be gone. What of God's command to multiply? (6428) Genius says that he is speaking of theft of maidenhood outside the laws of ordinance— that is what is bad. Evil always follows when Virginity is taken in a lawless manner. Witness the fate of Agamemmon when he took from the city of Lesbon the virgin Criseide, daughter of Crisis, who was priestess for Phebus.[22] Phebus was so enraged when she was taken that he sent a plague as vengeance until Agamemnon acknowledged his folly and repented by returning the girl with prayers and sacrifices (6475).

Covetousness has two other companions, Stealth and Michery, who stalk as a peacock, taking their prey in secret where none may see. The stealthy thief works by night, trying doors, creeping in at windows while the lord sleeps. In daylight he picks pockets and cuts purse strings. Like a hound he slips into the fold, takes what he wants, then, after wiping his mouth on the grass, feigns cheer the next day as he sleeps (6542). There are lovers, too, who practice stealth, seeking ways to steal a kiss or two. Amans says he is no thief. Never has he dared in secrecy to take his Lady by the knee or steal this or that from her. Men say that where the heart fails there shall no castle be assailed. Even if he had ten hearts of the strongest men it would be no use, for they would all be hers. Besides, his Lady has a guardian named Daunger who is more wakeful than the serpent who guarded the golden fleece in Colchos. Whether she is clothed or naked, Daunger is right there. All her treasure he keeps under lock and key. Even the least glance may not be stolen if he sees it. One could stalk and creep and wait all night, but, with Daunger on guard, get nothing. With him around no one can really be guilty of Stealth. Nevertheless, Amans admits that at night, when others are asleep, he slips to his window to look at the houses all about, trying to imagine what it must be like in the chamber where his Lady lies soft asleep in bed. Then he wishes he were the magician Nectanabus or Protheus, that he might transform himself and fly into the chamber to pick and steal something of love. But at last, when he comes to his senses and realizes how long he has been standing there, he stalks back to bed. That is all he ever wins by Stealth at night, a thought of embrace, no more (6700). Genius reassures Amans by telling him that little good ever comes of Stealth, as the Tale of Leucothoe demonstrates:[23] Venus, whom none can restrain, caused Phebus to fall in love with Leucothoe, a maiden who was kept under close guard by her mother. But Phebus was so smitten with love that in broad daylight he slipped past her chamber wall and all of a sudden took what he was after. But Venus, who hates Michery, discovered the deed to Clymene, Phebus's concubine, who told the maiden's father. In a rage he buried his daughter alive in a pit. But Phebus, out of reverence for Leucothoe, changed her into a flower named "golde," which ever follows the sun (6783).

Amans says he is not surprised that Phebus was caught, since he tried his game in broad daylight, and asks for a story of Stealth by night. So Genius tells the story of Hercules and Faunus.[24]]

TALE OF HERCULES AND FAUNUS

    The myhtieste of alle men
Whan Hercules with Eolen,
Which was the love of his corage,
6810 Togedre upon a Pelrinage

Towardes Rome scholden go,
It fell hem be the weie so,
That thei upon a dai a Cave
Withinne a roche founden have,
Which was real and glorious   [royal]
And of Entaile curious,   [design]
Be name and Thophis it was hote.
The Sonne schon tho wonder hote,
As it was in the Somer tyde;
6820 This Hercules, which be his syde
Hath Eolen his love there,
Whan thei at thilke cave were,
He seide it thoghte him for the beste
That sche hire for the hete reste
Al thilke day and thilke nyht;
And sche, that was a lusti wyht,
It liketh hire al that he seide:
And thus thei duelle there and pleide
The longe dai. And so befell,
6830 This Cave was under the hell   [hill]
Of Tymolus, which was begrowe
With vines, and at thilke throwe
Faunus with Saba the goddesse,
Be whom the large wildernesse
In thilke time stod governed,
Weere in a place, as I am lerned,
Nyh by, which Bachus wode hihte.
This Faunus tok a gret insihte
Of Eolen, that was so nyh;
6840 For whan that he hire beaute syh,
Out of his wit he was assoted,   [befuddled]
And in his herte it hath so noted,
That he forsok the Nimphes alle,
And seide he wolde, hou so it falle,
Assaie an other forto winne;
So that his hertes thoght withinne

He sette and caste hou that he myhte
Of love pyke awey be nyhte
That he be daie in other wise
6850 To stele mihte noght suffise:
And therupon his time he waiteth.
    Nou tak good hiede hou love afaiteth   [tames]
Him which withal is overcome.
Faire Eolen, whan sche was come
With Hercules into the Cave,
Sche seide him that sche wolde have
Hise clothes of and hires bothe,
That ech of hem scholde other clothe.
And al was do riht as sche bad,
6860 He hath hire in hise clothes clad
And caste on hire his gulion,   [tunic]
Which of the Skyn of a Leoun
Was mad, as he upon the weie
It slouh, and overthis to pleie   [slew]
Sche tok his grete Mace also
And knet it at hir gerdil tho.
So was sche lich the man arraied,
And Hercules thanne hath assaied
To clothen him in hire array:
6870 And thus thei jape forth the dai,
Til that her Souper redy were.
And whan thei hadden souped there,
Thei schopen hem to gon to reste;   [prepared themselves]
And as it thoghte hem for the beste,
Thei bede, as for that ilke nyht,   [ordered]
Tuo sondri beddes to be dyht,
For thei togedre ligge nolde,
Be cause that thei offre wolde
Upon the morwe here sacrifice.
6880 The servantz deden here office
And sondri beddes made anon,
Wherin that thei to reste gon

Ech be himself in sondri place.
Faire Eole hath set the Mace
Beside hire beddes hed above,
And with the clothes of hire love
Sche helede al hire bed aboute;   [covered (heeled)]
And he, which hadde of nothing doute,
6890 Hire wympel wond aboute his cheke,
Hire kertell and hire mantel eke
Abrod upon his bed he spredde.
And thus thei slepen bothe abedde;
And what of travail, what of wyn,
The servantz lich to drunke Swyn
Begunne forto route faste.   [snore]
        This Faunus, which his Stelthe caste,
Was thanne come to the Cave,
And fond thei weren alle save
Withoute noise, and in he wente.
6900 The derke nyht his sihte blente,   [blinded]
And yit it happeth him to go
Where Eolen abedde tho
Was leid al one for to slepe;
Bot for he wolde take kepe
Whos bed it was, he made assai,
And of the Leoun, where it lay,
The Cote he fond, and ek he fieleth
The Mace, and thanne his herte kieleth,   [grows cool]
That there dorste he noght abyde,
6910 Bot stalketh upon every side
And soghte aboute with his hond,
That other bedd til that he fond,
Wher lai bewympled a visage.
Tho was he glad in his corage,
For he hir kertell fond also
And ek hir mantell bothe tuo
Bespred upon the bed alofte.
He made him naked thanne, and softe

Into the bedd unwar he crepte,
6920 Wher Hercules that time slepte,
And wende wel it were sche;
And thus in stede of Eole
Anon he profreth him to love.
But he, which felte a man above,
This Hercules, him threw to grounde
So sore, that thei have him founde
Liggende there upon the morwe;
And tho was noght a litel sorwe,
That Faunus of himselve made,
6930 Bot elles thei were alle glade   [but the rest were]
And lowhen him to scorne aboute: [laughed]
Saba with Nimphis al a route
Cam doun to loke hou that he ferde,
And whan that thei the sothe herde,
He was bejaped overal.

[Genius warns Amans that unless he has better sense than Faunus he had better avoid Michery. Amans says that his conscience is not worried, for his heart is too faint to try (6953).

The last division of Covetousness is Sacrilege. God bade Adam labor and gave Moses the Law, but nowadays men use Stealth to avoid work and overrun the Law, even in the Church itself.[25] Such offenses are Sacrilege, whose heritage is in Hell. Three princes of old were culpable of Sacrilege—Antiochus, Nabuzardan, and Nabugodonosor. Balthazar paid for their Sacrilege in Jerusalem when the writing appeared on the wall. Lovers are sometimes guilty of Sacrilege at Mass when they ignore the priest and the bells in order to spend their time whispering in their girlfriend's ear, asking for a ring or glove. Such lovers dress up gayly and hover around the most attractive women in the congregation. To appear fresh they comb their croquet curls and set therein a brooch or chaplet, or some green leaves which of late grew in the grove. Thus they look fresh as a hawk about to capture fowl. In hope of making women's hearts fiit, they appear in holy places to enhance the magic of their charm. They keep track of the number of glances they get, but none of them offer love. They come only to steal a heart or two (7095).

Amans denies that he goes to church to look over the women, but admits that he does go there when his Lady goes, and that he looks at her all he can, and prays that she might have a change of heart towards him. Eagerly he hopes to steal a favorable glance from her, and when she goes to offering he accompanies her if he possibly can and slips his arm about her waist until she says, "Grant mercy." Thus he at least gets a lusty touch and a good word, though her purpose is far from his. If this is Sacrilege it seems a grace, but no other kind of Sacrilege does he know (7182). Genius warns Amans that the church is no place for love games but rather a place for prayer and confession. As a warning he tells the Tale of Paris and Helen.[26] All men know how the Trojan King Lamedon denied Hercules and Jason a resting place as they sailed to Colchos. After their return to Greece they sailed against Troy and destroyed the king and his city, leaving only a burned wall behind. Among the prisoners they took was Esiona, Lamedon's daughter, whom Hercules gave to King Thelamon. Thus Greece got vengeance on Troy. But Lamedon had a son named Priam who was away during the slaughter. When Priam heard how the city had fallen he returned, restored the wall, and built a new city of stone. None was so fair in all the world. On one side of the town he built Ylioun, a high tower so strong that no engine could menace it. Moreover, it was built on rock so that no tunnel might undermine it. The town was laid out in perfect proportion with six gates, and it was surrounded with broad and deep ditches so that a few men might protect the city from the whole world, unless the gods were their foes. Throngs pressed to the city so that there were people and riches enough. After his city was finished Priam turned his thoughts to the Greeks and his dishonored sister. Filled with sadness he called his parliament about him. Many advised revenge, but finally they agreed to try peaceful means. They sent

Antenor to Thelamon to ask for the return of Esiona. But Thelamon sent him back with stout words. So the council was called again. Talk of war was stronger until the fearless Hector spoke. He called for peace, even though he was the most powerful warrior, more than equal to Greeks. For he knew that war would surely bring self-destruction. "All Europe belongs to Greece and that is a third of the whole world under heaven, while we are but a few folk. Better to leave than to begin what can not be finished. We have reason to curse and hate the Greeks, but before debating with those who are more mighty we must think of our own circumstances." Paris spoke next: "Strong thing it is to soffre wrong, / And suffre schame is more strong, / Bot we have suffred bothe tuo" (7377–7379). He reminded them of the failure of their effort for peace and also reminded them how ten have been known to defeat a hundred. Then he told them a dream which he had while hunting. He had pursued a great hart until he lost his way. When he had stopped to rest, sleep caught him and Mercury appeared to him in a vision. Mercury brought three goddesses—Minerva, Venus, and Juno; in his hand he carried a golden apple which was to be awarded to the fairest. Each goddess promised Paris a reward if he would choose her, but Venus promised the most—the fairest woman on earth, one living in Greece. So Paris gave the apple to Venus, and now was ready to claim his prize. The parliament considered Paris's tale and agreed that he should seek the woman. When Cassandra heard the decision for vengeance, she wept and warned them that Fortune's blind wheel would destroy them if they let Paris go. Helenus, her brother, also foresaw the doom. But men laughed at them. So Paris set out and chance brought him to an island where Helen had come to make sacrifice to Venus. When Paris learned of her presence at the temple he dressed himself in his finest clothes and went also to the temple. Helen, who had heard of his arrival, was eager to see him, and when she did, she was taken with his handsome and fresh manner and with the pleasance of his words. As far as her heart was concerned, she had been stolen away before he left the temple. That night Paris returned from his ship to the temple to find Helen at devotions, praying to Venus. He entered suddenly, went to the queen and seized her in his arms, then bore her to his ship. Up went the sail and the winds of Fortune soon brought them to Troy. All the city rejoiced in his return, except for Helenus and Cassandra, for they had seen in the shameful and slanderous act the destruction of Troy. The penalty for this sacrilege was total destruction (7590).

Achilles also died because he defiled the Temple of Apollo and took Polixena for his love. Similarly Troilus first loved Criseyde in a temple. All the world knows how he fared. His reward was betrayal to Diomede (7602).

Avarice has more forms than any other vice. Man must learn Largesse if he wishes to live in truth with God and the world. He must learn to act with measure. Avarice and Prodigality are the extremities of vice. Between them lie the virtues of Liberality and Largesse. They hold the middle way and bring much joy. It is better to give than to take. One should get on with what he has, not desire the goods of others. For as Seneca counsels: "Bot if thi good suffise / Unto the liking of thi wille, / Withdrawh thi lust and hold the stille, / And be to this good suffcant" (7736–7739). The rule of charity begins at home. But do not be a wastrel. In a world of prodigals, if you enrich twelve making yourself poor you will have little thanks. When a man has a full pack men say, "A good felawe is Jacke" (7752); but when he is poor and needy they pass him by. Some lovers waste their love prodigally (7791).

Amans says he is no prodigal. He has tasted in many places, but his heart is devoted to one only. Yet there his love seems wasted, for it brings no return. Genius advises Amans to be patient. No one can tell whether he has in fact lost or gained in love. Summer returns after winter. There is always hope. Amans thanks Genius for his kind advice and asks that his instruction continue with another of the seven sins (7844).]

Explicit Liber Quintus

INCIPIT LIBER SEXTUS

[The great original sin which has poisoned all men since Adam stems from Adam's tasting of the apple. It is Gluttony, whose branches are so numerous that Genius decides to touch on only two. The first branch is Drunkenness. Drunkenness is a wondrous vice: It can make a wise man foolish, yet turn a fool into a great clerk. The drunken man knows everything: he knows the sea, he knows the strand; he is a noble man of arms, though he has no strength left in his own. Drink makes a strong man feeble. He loses his wits so that he knows not true from false, day from night, one man from another. He forgets who he is or whether he is a man or beast. One moment he rages mad; the next he lies like a dead man, unable to move or speak. Thus he is often brought to bed to awaken the next day, complaining for more drink, arising half drunk to demand another cup for his dry mouth: "O, which a sorwe / It is a man be drinkeles!" (55-56). The cup is his pleasure and his disease. He serves the cup. It takes from him some cares in return for others. He weeps in joy and sings in sorrow. He drinks the wine, but at last the wine drinks him. It binds him fast and lays him drunk by the wall (75).

Lovers sometimes become so "adoted, and so bewhaped and assoted" (79-80) with love that their minds are those of drunken men. Like wine, love has such strength that none may withstand it. Love conquered wise Solomon and strong Samson. It captured knightly David and overcame Virgil and Aristotle. No wonder young men get drunk on love (111). Amans admits that he is drunk with love. He has become so turned outside of himself that he makes no sense to himself. He forgets all he knows and stands like a "mased man" (132). When he should play and have fun he sits alone and sulks like a clod who does not know

333

gentlemanly behavior, or like a stupid friar trying to do penance. And if he is supposed to dance and sing the hove dance and carols or do the "newefot" he cannot heave up his feet at all unless she is there, for without her his mirth is gone and his limbs are dull. Like a drunk who sinks witlessly into his stomach, so too he grows witless in lovesickness when she is away. But when she returns, he stares at her and his heart is so full of the gladness of her femininity and gentilesse that he could jump right through the wall, dancing and singing and leaping about all the while. He is drunk with the sight of her and in a paradise hotter than fire. No wine is half so sweet or potent. It is as if he slept in God's bosom. But when he awakens to cold reality, he is worse off than ever before, though his thirst is all the greater (305).

Genius advises Amans to consider well the effects which lovedrunkenness have on him, even though it is true that none can withstand love's intoxication entirely. Jupiter has in his cellar two tuns full of love's drink; one is joyous to drink from, the other bitter.[1] Cupid is butler of both, but he is blind and often serves amiss so that the most deserving receive of the bitter. It is clear from Amans's confession that he has drunk of the bitter. But through prayer there is still hope that his thirst may be satisfied (390). Remember the fate of Bacchus in the desert when he prayed to his father Jupiter that his woeful thirst might be staunched and that he and his host might find their way out of the desert to the country of their loves. Jupiter heard his prayer and sent a ram which spurned the ground, causing a fresh, clear spring to flow that they might allay their thirst. For this Bacchus erected a splendid temple on the spot (439).[2]

Lovers should therefore remember the fate of Bacchus and pray in their need for grace. Seldom does the dumb man get land. Words have power. Ask and pray early and late. Perhaps the butler will serve again, perchance this time from the sweet tun, which will make one sober. Another example of lovedrunkenness is Tristram, who drank the potion of love prepared by Brangwein to fall in love with Bele Isolde before King Mark married her (484).[3] But the story of Pirithous offers the best example of the ruinous effects of Drunkenness in love and illustrates why men should try to eschew the company of drunken men.[4] Pirithous fell in love with Ipotacie, of whose beauty all men spoke, and decided to marry her. He invited all his friends to his wedding feast and so served them wine aplenty that Bacchus and Venus together excited the centaurs to lovedrunkenness. They carried off violently the young wife despite their host, all of which brought much misfortune to many men and in more ways than in love alone (536).

A chronicle tells of Galba and Vitellus who were powerful men of Spain.[5] Both were gluttons and drunkards. Their Reason was no more capable than a blind man trying to thread a needle. In their drunkenness they oppressed all Spain. They defiled fair and ugly women alike, wives and maidens, until at last the land rose up against them and brought them to justice. To assuage their death sentence they had a great bowl filled with wine and drank themselves senseless; thus they were already half dead when the sentence was carried out (599).

Amans asks next to be instructed in the second aspect of Gluttony, which Genius calls Delicacy. The poor need not worry about this sin for it deals with pastries of paindemeine and varieties of wine. Delicacy lacks no delight which spicy meats or fancy drinks can give. That cook which satisfies man's need for sustenance alone will receive no thanks from Delicacy. His thanks are measured only by how well the cook serves his mouth. He seeks new tastes, and many the choices there must be before he is satisfied. So too the delicate in love cannot be satisfied with what he has. Even though he has the best wife or fairest love in all the land his heart falls on others whom he thinks more delicious. Though his Lady makes him good cheer she cannot offer him enough within the limits of honor. He must have surplus (686).

Amans says he is not guilty of Delicacy. If he had the wife of which Genius speaks he would ask for nothing more. As it is, he goes to bed fasting. If woe could feed a man's stomach then he would have more than enough. Still, he is a little bit delicate in that his hunger for love is fed with small satisfactions which are delicate indeed. One dainty which he feeds on insatiably is his Lady's looks. He takes such delight in this food that he needs no other. He feeds on the sight of her face, her eyes, her nose, cheeks, lips, and chin, her neck, her white hands, her round body, and small middle. And just as his eye is a lusty cook for his heart, so too his ear serves him love's delicate food. He dotes on the words of those who say she is wise, or that she is good, or of noble blood, or excellent bearing. Sometimes his ears feast his heart with words which she herself speaks, words full of truth and faith, delicacies finer than any Lombard could make. Her speech is truly a "restauratif" (859), like winds of the south. And if she sings he dines in Paradise itself. The romance of Ydoine and Amadas and others that tell of love in times past are also sweet. The joy of such stories that show that sorrow may not last forever he draws to memory. A third cook who serves him at night is called Thought, whose pots of love are ever boiling on the fire with fantasy and desire to be served to the heart at bedtime. Thought sets before him every sight and word of love he has heard or seen all day. Yet it is a feast of "would" and "wish," honey on the thorn. At best it keeps alive hope of a great feast which may come some day and arrest his hunger. Food of seeing, hearing, and thinking lacks taste or feel. He lives as the Plover does—on air. That does not seem much like gluttony (950).[6]

Genius agrees that Amans has indulged in "delices wonder smale" (954) but insists that if he did understand what being delicate really was he would not be so curious about it. If man's wisdom as books record it is to be followed, Delicacy of any sort should be eschewed, for it does grievance to the soul, as the story of Dives and Lazarus, which is no fable, illustrates.[7] Christ tells us that there was a rich man, a mighty lord of great estate, who was so delicate of his clothing that everyday he dressed himself in fine purple linen and ate and drank his fill as whim would have it. One day a poor leper came to his gate to beg food but could get nothing to stop his deadly hunger. The rich man, whose paunch was glutted, would not give even a crumb so that the poor man might live. Thus the leper lay starving and freezing at the gate. The hounds came from the hall and licked the wounds of his malady to offer some ease, but he was too far gone to escape death. When his soul passed from his body, the High God, whom nothing escapes, took him and placed him on high in Abraham's bosom. It befell that this rich man met with a sudden death at about the same time and went straight to hell. The fiend drew him into the eternal flames where he found pain enough. As he cast his eye about he saw Lazarus in heaven with Abraham. So he called out to the patriarch, "Send Lazarus down from thy seat that he might wet his finger in water and let fall a drop on my tongue to stop the great heat in which I burn." But Abraham replied, "My son, remember the great penance Lazarus did in the other life while you in jolly lust sought bodily delights. Because of your behavior then you get now the deadly pain of hell, while Lazarus enjoys heaven and everlasting joy. I shall not send Lazarus with a drop of water for none from this place ever enter hell, nor do any of you come hither." Then the rich man cried out again, "O Abraham, since Lazarus may not help me here I ask another favor. I have five brethren who dwell with my father. Send Lazarus to warn them how the world goes so that they might shun the pain I suffer." But the patriarch said, "Nay, for ever day your brothers have the opportunity to hear of Moses and the other prophets to learn what is best to do. If they will not obey now when living men show them the way, what good would the word of a dead man be?" So we see by Christ's own word the harm of Delicacy. He who denied the crumb was denied the drop of water. That man who is governor of the world's goods, if he is wise, will set no prize upon such things but will be generous. The delicate man acts as if everything were his. But man should feed his soul as well as his body. Still there are those who do not, as old examples show us (1150).

If you would learn to despise Delicacy consider Nero who unnaturally pampered his lusts until God cast him down. In seeking to know how his stomach fared he devised a subtle plan. He chose three men alike in age and complexion to himself and invited them to eat, drink, and play exactly as he did. Everyday they sat at his own table and ate the same food as he. But later the game was turned to earnest. After they had lived this way for a time Nero told one man, after a feast, to ride a courser about a field, whereupon that man was wondrously glad and went to prick and prance about. He told the second to lie upon his bed to sleep while the first rode. The third he told to walk about his chamber until the one who was riding returned. Then Nero had the three slain and their stomachs cut open to see whose food was best digested. The man who walked fared best, so Nero henceforth walked after his meals. Nero refrained from no bodily pleasure; he knew no abstinence. But above all earthly things he set his delight upon women. When the thirst of love seized him he spared neither wife nor maid. Because of Nero's drunken lusts, as long as there are books, men will read and sing forever of his depravity (1260).[8]

Delicacy and Drunkenness have made many a wiseman err, especially in love. The Senses know not Reason, but stand in the governance of Will, which waxes wild, seeking here and there with no respect for nature's law. Will tempts heaven, earth, and hell in its search for satisfaction. Who dares do anything that willful Love does not dare to do? Love bears no law and counts woe no more than weal, heat no more than cold, wet no more than dry, nor life more than death. He is blind and does marvels in his rage, until, like the blind steed Bayard, he falls into the ditch. There is no point which he refuses; he even uses witchcraft and sorcery to win his drury. Saturn was the founder of Sorcery.[9] Sorcery is divided into Geomance, whereby one makes magic through pricks on the sand; Ydromance, which concerns floods; Piromance, which concerns fire; and Aeremance which concerns the air. The lover tries all these crafts with his questions in his effort to win assent in love. These crafts have value in understanding nature if they are used with good intent. But the lover goes the other way. By Nigromance (black magic) he tries to make his incantation with hot subfumigation. He works on and on at the art called Spatula, whose author is Thosz the Greek and which is common among Pagans. He also knows Razel,

Solomon's Candarie and his Ydeac and Eutonye. He uses to his advantage the book and figure of Balamuz, the Seal of Ghenbal, the image of Thebith, and also Gibiere. Often he traces in the ground, while making invocations, Babilla with her seven sons, with Cernes both square and round. Full of information from the School of Honorius he pursues his way, sparing no sin. Like the Naturiens, who studied the stars, he seeks his love. He makes images, sculptures, writings, figures, calculations, and demonstrations. He keeps his hours of Astronomy for the inspection of his love. He would seek Hell and the Devil himself if he thought it would help (1357).

Amans says that he knows nothing of these arts, though there was a time when he would have tried anything to win his Lady. Genius warns him that there is no man who tries sorcery who does not regret it in the end. The Tale of Ulysses and Telegonus makes the point.[10]]

TALE OF ULYSSES AND TELEGONUS

Among hem whiche at Troie were,
Uluxes ate Siege there
Was on be name in special;
Of whom yit the memorial
Abit, for whyl ther is a mouth,
For evere his name schal be couth.
He was a worthi knyht and king
And clerk knowende of every thing;
He was a gret rethorien,
1400 He was a gret magicien;
Of Tullius the rethorique,
Of king Zorastes the magique,
Of Tholome thastronomie,
Of Plato the Philosophie,
Of Daniel the slepi dremes,
Of Neptune ek the water stremes,
Of Salomon and the proverbes,

Of Macer al the strengthe of herbes,
And the Phisique of Ypocras,
1410 And lich unto Pictagoras
Of Surgerie he knew the cures.
Bot somwhat of his aventures,
Which schal to mi matiere acorde,
To thee, mi Sone, I wol recorde.
　　　This king, of which thou hast herd
　　　　sein,
Fro Troie as he goth hom ayein
Be Schipe, he fond the See divers,
With many a wyndi storm revers.
Bot he thurgh wisdom that he schapeth
1420 Ful many a gret peril ascapeth,
Of whiche I thenke tellen on,
Hou that malgre the nedle and ston   [in spite of]
Wynddrive he was al soudeinly
Upon the strondes of Cilly,   [Sicily]
Wher that he moste abyde a whyle.
Tuo queenes weren in that yle
Calipsa named and Circes;
And whan they herde hou Uluxes
Is londed ther upon the ryve,   [shore]
1430 For him thei senden als so blive.
With him suche as he wolde he nam
And to the court to hem he cam.
Thes queenes were as tuo goddesses
Of Art magique Sorceresses,
That what lord comth to that rivage,   [landing place]
Thei make him love in such a rage
And upon hem assote so,
That thei wol have, er that he go,
Al that he hath of worldes good.
1440 Uluxes wel this understod,
Thei couthe moche, he couthe more;
Thei schape and caste ayein him sore

And wroghte many a soutil wyle,
Bot yit thei mihte him noght beguile.
Bot of the men of his navie
Thei tuo forschope a gret partie,   [those two transformed]
Mai non of hem withstonde here hestes;
Som part thei schopen into bestes,
Som part thei schopen into foules,
1450 To beres, tigres, Apes, oules,
Or elles be som other weie;
Ther myhte hem nothing desobeie,
Such craft thei hadde above kinde.
Bot that Art couthe thei noght finde,
Of which Uluxes was deceived,
That he ne hath hem alle weyved,   [refused]
And broght hem into such a rote,   [condition (ME 'route,' a
                                                     well-traveled way)]

That upon him thei bothe assote;
And thurgh the science of his art
1460 He tok of hem so wel his part,
That he begat Circes with childe.
He kepte him sobre and made hem wilde,
He sette himselve so above,
That with here good and with here love,
Who that therof be lief or loth,
Al quit into his Schip he goth.
Circes toswolle bothe sides
He lefte, and waiteth on the tydes,
And straght thurghout the salte fom
1470 He takth his cours and comth him hom,
Where as he fond Penolope;
A betre wif ther mai non be,
And yit ther ben ynowhe of goode.
Bot who hir goodschipe understode
Fro ferst that sche wifhode tok,
Hou many loves sche forsok
And hou sche bar hire al aboute,

Ther whiles that hire lord was oute,
He mihte make a gret avant   [boast]
1480 Amonges al the remenant
That sche was on of al the beste.
Wel myhte he sette his herte in reste,
This king, whan he hir fond in hele;
For as he couthe in wisdom dele,
So couthe sche in wommanhiede:
And whan sche syh withoute drede
Hire lord upon his oghne ground,
That he was come sauf and sound,
In al this world ne mihte be
1490 A gladdere womman than was sche.
  The fame, which mai noght ben hidd,
Thurghout the lond is sone kidd,
Here king is come hom ayein:
Ther mai noman the fulle sein,
Hou that thei weren alle glade,
So mochel joie of him thei made.
The presens every day be newed,
He was with yiftes al besnewed;
The poeple was of him so glad,
1500 That thogh non other man hem bad,
Taillage upon hemself thei sette, [taxation/themselves]
And as it were of pure dette
Thei yeve here goodes to the king:
This was a glad hom welcomyng.
Thus hath Uluxes what he wolde,
His wif was such as sche be scholde,
His poeple was to him sougit,
Him lacketh nothing of delit.
  Bot fortune is of such a sleyhte,
1510 That whan a man is most on heyhte,
Sche makth him rathest forto falle: [most quickly]
Ther wot noman what schal befalle,
The happes over mannes hed

Ben honged with a tendre thred.
That proved was on Uluxes;
For whan he was most in his pes,
Fortune gan to make him werre
And sette his welthe al out of herre.   [out of order]
Upon a dai as he was merie,
1520 As thogh ther mihte him nothing derie,   [harm]
Whan nyht was come, he goth to bedde,
With slep and bothe his yhen fedde.
And while he slepte, he mette a swevene: [dreamed/dream]
Him thoghte he syh a stature evene,
Which brihtere than the sonne schon;
A man it semeth was it non,
Bot yit it was as in figure
Most lich to mannyssh creature,
Bot as of beaute hevenelich
1530 It was most to an Angel lich:
And thus betwen angel and man
Beholden it this king began,
And such a lust tok of the sihte,
That fain he wolde, if that he mihte,
The forme of that figure embrace;
And goth him forth toward the place,
Wher he sih that ymage tho,
And takth it in his Armes tuo,
And it embraceth him ayein
1540 And to the king thus gan it sein:
"Uluxes, understond wel this,
The tokne of oure aqueintance is
Hierafterward to mochel tene: [sorrow]
The love that is ous betuene,
Of that we nou such joie make,
That on of ous the deth schal take,
Whan time comth of destine;
It may non other wise be."
Uluxes tho began to preie

1550 That this figure wolde him seie
What wyht he is that seith him so.
This wyht upon a spere tho
A pensel which was wel begon,   [banner]
Embrouded, scheweth him anon:
Thre fisshes alle of o colour
In manere as it were a tour
Upon the pensel were wroght.
Uluxes kneu this tokne noght,
And preith to wite in som partie
1560 What thing it myhte signefie,
"A signe it is," the wyht ansuerde,
"Of an Empire": and forth he ferde
Al sodeinly, whan he that seide.

Uluxes out of slep abreide,
And that was riht ayein the day,
That lengere slepen he ne may.
Men sein, a man hath knowleching
Save of himself of alle thing;
His oghne chance noman knoweth,
1570 Bot as fortune it on him throweth:
Was nevere yit so wys a clerk,
Which mihte knowe al goddes werk,
Ne the secret which god hath set
Ayein a man mai noght be let.
Uluxes, thogh that he be wys,
With al his wit in his avis,
The mor that he his swevene acompteth,
The lasse he wot what it amonteth:
For al his calculacion,
1580 He seth no demonstracion
At pleinly forto knowe an ende;
Bot natheles hou so it wende,
He dradde him of his oghne Sone.
That makth him wel the more astone,
And schop therfore anon withal,

So that withinne castel wall
Thelamachum his Sone he schette,
And upon him strong warde he sette.   [guard]
The sothe furthere he ne knew,   [truth]
1590 Til that fortune him overthreu;
Bot natheles for sikernesse,
Wher that he mihte wite and gesse
A place strengest in his lond,
Ther let he make of lym and sond
A strengthe where he wolde duelle;
Was nevere man yit herde telle
Of such an other as it was.
And forto strengthe him in that cas,
Of al his lond the sekereste   [most secure]
1600 Of servantz and the worthieste,
To kepen him withinne warde,
He sette his bodi forto warde;
And made such an ordinance,
For love ne for aqueintance,
That were it erly, were it late,
Thei scholde lete in ate gate
No maner man, what so betydde,
Bot if so were himself it bidde.

        Bot al that myhte him noght availe,
1610 For whom fortune wole assaile,
Ther mai be non such resistence,
Which mihte make a man defence;
Al that schal be mot falle algate.
This Circes, which I spak of late,
On whom Uluxes hath begete
A child, thogh he it have foryete,
Whan time com, as it was wone,   [custom]
Sche was delivered of a Sone,
Which cleped is Thelogonus.
1620 This child, whan he was bore thus,
Aboute his moder to ful age,

That he can reson and langage,
In good astat was drawe forth:
And whan he was so mochel worth
To stonden in a mannes stede,
Circes his moder hath him bede
That he schal to his fader go,
And tolde him al togedre tho
What man he was that him begat.
1630 And whan Thelogonus of that
Was war and hath ful knowleching
Hou that his fader was a king,
He preith his moder faire this,   [fairly]
To go wher that his fader is;
And sche him granteth that he schal,
And made him redi forth withal.
It was that time such usance,
That every man the conoiscance   [cognizance]
Of his contre bar in his hond,
1640 Whan he wente into strange lond;
And thus was every man therfore
Wel knowe, wher that he was bore:
For espiaile and mistrowinges   [espionage/suspicion]
They dede thanne suche thinges,
That every man mai other knowe.
So it befell that ilke throwe
Thelogonus as in this cas;
Of his contre the signe was
Thre fisshes, whiche he scholde bere
1650 Upon the penon of a spere:
And whan that he was thus arraied
And hath his harneis al assaied,
That he was redy everydel,
His moder bad him farewel,
And seide him that he scholde swithe   [strongly]
His fader griete a thousand sithe.
       Thelogonus his moder kiste

And tok his leve, and wher he wiste
His fader was, the weie nam,   [took]
1660 Til he unto Nachaie cam,
Which of that lond the chief Cite
Was cleped, and ther axeth he
Wher was the king and hou he ferde.
And whan that he the sothe herde,
Wher that the king Uluxes was,
Al one upon his hors gret pas   [horse's great pace]
He rod him forth, and in his hond
He bar the signal of his lond
With fisshes thre, as I have told;
1670 And thus he wente unto that hold,
Wher that his oghne fader duelleth.
The cause why he comth he telleth
Unto the kepers of the gate,
And wolde have comen in therate,
Bot schortli thei him seide nay:
And he als faire as evere he may
Besoghte and tolde hem ofte this,
Hou that the king his fader is;
Bot they with proude wordes grete
1680 Begunne to manace and threte,
Bot he go fro the gate faste,   [unless]
Thei wolde him take and sette faste.
Fro wordes unto strokes thus
Thei felle, and so Thelogonus
Was sore hurt and welnyh ded;
Bot with his scharpe speres hed
He makth defence, hou so it falle,
And wan the gate upon hem alle,
And hath slain of the beste fyve;
1690 And thei ascriden als so blyve   [cried out]
Thurghout the castell al aboute.
    On every syde men come oute,
Wherof the kinges herte afflihte,

And he with al the haste he mihte
A spere cauhte and out he goth,
As he that was nyh wod for wroth.
He sih the gates ful of blod,
Thelogonus and wher he stod
He sih also, bot he ne knew
1700 What man it was, and to him threw
His Spere, and he sterte out asyde.
Bot destine, which schal betide,
Befell that ilke time so,
Thelogonus knew nothing tho
What man it was that to him caste,
And while his oghne spere laste,
With al the signe therupon   [banner]
He caste unto the king anon,
And smot him with a dedly wounde.
1710 Uluxes fell anon to grounde;
Tho every man, "The king! the king!"
Began to crie, and of this thing
Thelogonus, which sih the cas,
On knes he fell and seide, "Helas!
I have min oghne fader slain:
Nou wolde I deie wonder fain,
Nou sle me who that evere wile,
For certes it is riht good skile."   [reason]
He crith, he wepth, he seith therfore,
1720 "Helas, that evere was I bore,
That this unhappi destine
So wofulli comth in be me!"
This king, which yit hath lif ynouh,
His herte ayein to him he drouh,
And to that vois an Ere he leide
And understod al that he seide,
And gan to speke, and seide on hih,
"Bring me this man." And whan he sih
Thelogonus, his thoght he sette

1730 Upon the swevene which he mette,   [dream/dreamed]
     And axeth that he myhte se
     His spere, on which the fisshes thre
     He sih upon a pensel wroght.
     Tho wiste he wel it faileth noght,
     And badd him that he telle scholde
     Fro whenne he cam and what he wolde.
          Thelogonus in sorghe and wo
     So as he mihte tolde tho
     Unto Uluxes al the cas,
1740 Hou that Circes his moder was,
     And so forth seide him everydel,
     Hou that his moder gret him wel,   [greets]
     And in what wise sche him sente.
     Tho wiste Uluxes what it mente,
     And tok him in hise Armes softe,
     And al bledende he kest him ofte,   [kissed]
     And seide, "Sone, whil I live,
     This infortune I thee foryive."
     After his other Sone in haste
1750 He sende, and he began him haste
     And cam unto his fader tyt.   [quickly]
     Bot whan he sih him in such plit,
     He wolde have ronne upon that other
     Anon, and slain his oghne brother,
     Ne hadde be that Uluxes
     Betwen hem made acord and pes,
     And to his heir Thelamachus
     He bad that he Thelogonus
     With al his pouer scholde kepe,
1760 Til he were of his woundes depe
     Al hol, and thanne he scholde him yive
     Lond wher upon he mihte live.
     Thelamachus, whan he this herde,
     Unto his fader he ansuerde
     And seide he wolde don his wille.

So duelle thei togedre stille,
These brethren, and the fader sterveth.   [dies]
    Lo, wherof Sorcerie serveth.
Thurgh Sorcerie his lust he wan,
1770 Thurgh Sorcerie his wo began,
Thurgh Sorcerie his love he ches,   [chose]
Thurgh Sorcerie his lif he les;   [lost]
The child was gete in Sorcerie,
The which dede al this felonie:
Thing which was ayein kynde wroght
Unkindeliche it was aboght;
The child his oghne fader slowh,
That was unkindeschipe ynowh.
Forthi tak hiede hou that it is,
1780 So forto winne love amis,
Which endeth al his joie in wo:
For of this Art I finde also,
That hath be do for loves sake,
Wherof thou miht ensample take,
A gret Cronique imperial,
Which evere into memorial
Among the men, hou so it wende,
Schal duelle to the worldes end.[11]

TALE OF NECTANABUS

ۀ The hihe creatour of thinges,
1790 Which is the king of alle kinges,
Ful many a wonder worldes chance
Let slyden under his suffrance;
Ther wot noman the cause why,
Bot he the which is almyhty.
And that was proved whilom thus,
Whan that the king Nectanabus,
Which hadde Egipte forto lede,—
Bot for he sih tofor the dede

Thurgh magique of his Sorcerie,
1800 Wherof he couthe a gret partie,
Hise enemys to him comende, [coming]
Fro whom he mihte him noght defende,
Out of his oghne lond he fledde
And in the wise as he him dredde
It fell, for al his wicchecraft,
So that Egipte him was beraft,
And he desguised fledde aweie
Be schipe, and hield the rihte weie
To Macedoine, wher that he
1810 Aryveth ate chief Cite.
Thre yomen of his chambre there
Al only forto serve him were,
The whiche he trusteth wonder wel,
For thei were trewe as eny stiel;
And hapneth that thei with him ladde
Part of the beste good he hadde.
Thei take logginge in the toun
After the disposicion
Wher as him thoghte best to duelle:
1820 He axeth thanne and herde telle
Hou that the king was oute go
Upon a werre he hadde tho;
But in that Cite thanne was
The queene, which Olimpias
Was hote, and with sollempnete
The feste of hir nativite,
As it befell, was thanne holde;
And for hire list to be beholde [desire]
And preised of the poeple aboute,
1830 Sche schop hir forto riden oute [prepared herself]
At after mete al openly.
Anon were alle men redy,
And that was in the monthe of Maii,
This lusti queene in good arrai

Was set upon a Mule whyt:
To sen it was a gret delit
The joie that the cite made;
With freisshe thinges and with glade
The noble toun was al behonged,
1840 And every wiht was sore alonged
To se this lusti ladi ryde.
Ther was gret merthe on alle syde;
Wher as sche passeth be the strete,
Ther was ful many a tymber bete
And many a maide carolende:
And thus thurghout the toun pleiende
This queene unto a pleine rod,
Wher that sche hoved and abod   [stayed/rested]
To se diverse game pleie,
1850 The lusti folk jouste and tourneie;
And so forth every other man,
Which pleie couthe, his pley began,
To plese with this noble queene.
    Nectanabus cam to the grene
Amonges othre and drouh him nyh.
Bot whan that he this ladi sih
And of hir beaute hiede tok,
He couthe noght withdrawe his lok
To se noght elles in the field,
1860 Bot stod and only hire behield.
Of his clothinge and of his gere
He was unlich alle othre there,
So that it hapneth ate laste,
The queene on him hire yhe caste,
And knew that he was strange anon:
Bot he behield hire evere in on
Withoute blenchinge of his chere.
Sche tok good hiede of his manere,
And wondreth why he dede so,
1870 And bad men scholde for him go.

He cam and dede hire reverence,
And sche him axeth in cilence
Fro whenne he cam and what he wolde
And he with sobre wordes tolde,
And seith, "Ma dame, a clerk I am,
To you and in message I cam,
The which I mai noght tellen hiere;
Bot if it liketh you to hiere,
It mot be seid al prively,
1880 Wher non schal be bot ye and I."
Thus for the time he tok his leve.
The dai goth forth til it was eve,
That every man mot lete his werk;
And sche thoghte evere upon this clerk,
What thing it is he wolde mene:
And in this wise abod the queene,
And passeth over thilke nyht,
Til it was on the morwe liht.
Sche sende for him, and he com,
1890 With his Astellabre he nom,   [astrolabe]
Which was of fin gold precious
With pointz and cercles merveilous;
And ek the hevenely figures
Wroght in a bok ful of peintures
He tok this ladi forto schewe,
And tolde of ech of hem be rewe   [by row (in order)]
The cours and the condicion.
And sche with gret affeccion   [fascination]
Sat stille and herde what he wolde:
1900 And thus whan he sih time, he tolde,
And feigneth with hise wordes wise
A tale, and seith in such a wise:
    "Ma dame, bot a while ago,
Wher I was in Egipte tho,
And radde in scole of this science,
It fell into mi conscience

That I unto the temple wente,
And ther with al myn hole entente
As I mi sacrifice dede,
1910 On of the goddes hath me bede
That I you warne prively,
So that ye make you redy,
And that ye be nothing agast;
For he such love hath to you cast,
That ye schul ben his oghne diere,
And he schal be your beddefiere,   [bed companion]
Til ye conceive and be with childe."
And with that word sche wax al mylde,
And somdel red becam for schame,
1920 And axeth him that goddes name,
Which so wol don hire compainie.
And he seide, "Amos of Lubie."
And sche seith, "That mai I noght lieve,   [believe]
Bot if I sihe a betre prieve."   [proof]
"Ma dame," quod Nectanabus,
"In tokne that it schal be thus,
This nyht for enformacion
Ye schul have an avision:
That Amos schal to you appiere,
1930 To schewe and teche in what manere
The thing schal afterward befalle.
Ye oghten wel aboven alle
To make joie of such a lord;
For whan ye ben of on acord,
He schal a Sone of you begete,
Which with his swerd schal winne and gete
The wyde world in lengthe and brede;
Alle erthli kinges schull him drede,
And in such wise, I you behote,   [promise]
1940 The god of erthe he schal be hote."   [called]
"If this be soth," tho quod the queene,
"This nyht, thou seist, it schal be sene.

And if it falle into mi grace,
Of god Amos that I pourchace
To take of him so gret worschipe,
I wol do thee such ladischipe,
Wherof thou schalt for everemo
Be riche." And he hir thonketh tho,
And tok his leve and forth he wente.
1950 Sche wiste litel what he mente,
For it was guile and Sorcerie,
Al that sche tok for Prophecie.
  Nectanabus thurghout the day,
Whan he cam hom wher as he lay,
His chambre be himselve tok,
And overtorneth many a bok,
And thurgh the craft of Artemage   [art magic]
Of wex he forgeth an ymage.
He loketh his equacions
1960 And ek the constellacions,
He loketh the conjunccions,
He loketh the recepcions,
His signe, his houre, his ascendent,
And drawth fortune of his assent:
The name of queene Olimpias
In thilke ymage write was
Amiddes in the front above.
And thus to winne his lust of love
Nectanabus this werk hath diht;   [prepared]
1970 And whan it cam withinne nyht,
That every wyht is falle aslepe,
He thoghte he wolde his time kepe,
As he which hath his houre apointed.
And thanne ferst he hath enoignted
With sondri herbes that figure,
And therupon he gan conjure,
So that thurgh his enchantement
This ladi, which was innocent

And wiste nothing of this guile,
1980 Mette, as sche slepte thilke while,   [dreamed]
Hou fro the hevene cam a lyht,
Which al hir chambre made lyht;
And as sche loketh to and fro,
Sche sih, hir thoghte, a dragoun tho,
Whos scherdes schynen as the Sonne,   [scales]
And hath his softe pas begonne   [steps]
With al the chiere that he may
Toward the bedd ther as sche lay,
Til he cam to the beddes side.
1990 And sche lai stille and nothing cride,
For he dede alle his thinges faire
And was courteis and debonaire:
And as he stod hire fasteby,
His forme he changeth sodeinly,
And the figure of man he nom,
To hire and into bedde he com,
And such thing there of love he wroghte,
Wherof, so as hire thanne thoghte,
Thurgh likinge of this god Amos
2000 With childe anon hire wombe aros,
And sche was wonder glad withal.
Nectanabus, which causeth al
Of this metrede the substance,   [dream-counsel]
Whan he sih time, his nigromance
He stinte and nothing more seide   [stopped]
Of his carecte, and sche abreide   [conjuration]
Out of hir slep, and lieveth wel
That it is soth thanne everydel
Of that this clerk hire hadde told,
2010 And was the gladdere manyfold
In hope of such a glad metrede,
Which after schal befalle in dede.
     Sche longeth sore after the dai,
That sche hir swevene telle mai

To this guilour in privete,
Which kneu it als so wel as sche:
And natheles on morwe sone
Sche lefte alle other thing to done,
And for him sende, and al the cas
2020 Sche tolde him pleinly as it was,
And seide hou thanne wel sche wiste
That sche his wordes mihte triste,   [trust]
For sche fond hire Avisioun
Riht after the condicion
Which he hire hadde told tofore;
And preide him hertely therfore
That he hire holde covenant
So forth of al the remenant,
That sche may thurgh his ordinance
2030 Toward the god do such plesance,
That sche wakende myhte him kepe
In such wise as sche mette aslepe.
And he, that couthe of guile ynouh,
Whan he this herde, of joie he louh,
And seith, "Ma dame, it schal be do.
Bot this I warne you therto:
This nyht, whan that he comth to pleie,
That ther be no lif in the weie   [nobody]
Bot I, that schal at his likinge
2040 Ordeine so for his cominge,
That ye ne schull noght of him faile.
For this, ma dame, I you consaile,
That ye it kepe so prive,   [secret]
That no wiht elles bot we thre
Have knowlechinge hou that it is;
For elles mihte it fare amis,
If ye dede oght that scholde him grieve."
And thus he makth hire to believe,
And feigneth under guile feith:
2050 Bot natheles al that he seith

Sche troweth; and ayein the nyht
Sche hath withinne hire chambre dyht,
Wher as this guilour faste by
Upon this god schal prively
Awaite, as he makth hire to wene: [believe]
And thus this noble gentil queene,
Whan sche most trusteth, was deceived.
    The nyht com, and the chambre is
    weyved, [vacated]
Nectanabus hath take his place,
2060 And whan he sih the time and space,
Thurgh the deceipte of his magique
He putte him out of mannes like, [likeness]
And of a dragoun tok the forme,
As he which wolde him al conforme
To that sche sih in swevene er this;
And thus to chambre come he is.
The queene lay abedde and sih,
And hopeth evere, as he com nyh,
That he god of Lubye were,
2070 So hath sche wel the lasse fere.
Bot for he wolde hire more assure,
Yit eft he changeth his figure,
And of a wether the liknesse [ram]
He tok, in signe of his noblesse
With large hornes for the nones:
Of fin gold and of riche stones
A corone on his hed he bar,
And soudeinly, er sche was war,
As he which alle guile can,
2080 His forme he torneth into a man,
And cam to bedde, and sche lai stille,
Wher as sche soffreth al his wille,
As sche which wende noght misdo.
Bot natheles it hapneth so,
Althogh sche were in part deceived,

Yit for al that sche hath conceived
The worthieste of alle kiththe,   [known men (kith)]
Which evere was tofore or siththe   [since]
Of conqueste and chivalerie;
2090 So that thurgh guile and Sorcerie
Ther was that noble knyht begunne,
Which al the world hath after wunne.
Thus fell the thing which falle scholde,
Nectanabus hath that he wolde
With guile he hath his love sped,   [advanced]
With guile he cam into the bed,
With guile he goth him out ayein:
He was a schrewed chamberlein,
So to beguile a worthi queene,
2100 And that on him was after seene.
Bot natheles the thing is do;
This false god was sone go,
With his deceipte and hield him clos,
Til morwe cam, that he aros.
        And tho, whan time and leisir was,
The queene tolde him al the cas,
As sche that guile non supposeth;
And of tuo pointz sche him opposeth.
On was, if that this god nomore
2110 Wol come ayein, and overmore,
Hou sche schal stonden in acord
With king Philippe hire oghne lord,
Whan he comth hom and seth hire grone.   [pregnant]
"Ma dame," he seith, "let me alone:
As for the god I undertake
That whan it liketh you to take
His compaignie at eny throwe,
If I a day tofore it knowe,
He schal be with you on the nyht;
2120 And he is wel of such a myht
To kepe you from alle blame.

Forthi conforte you, ma dame,
Ther schal non other cause be."
Thus tok he leve and forth goth he,
And tho began to forto muse
Hou he the queene mihte excuse
Toward the king of that is falle
And fond a craft amonges alle,
Thurgh which he hath a See foul daunted,   [sea fowl tamed]
2130   With his magique and so enchaunted,
That he flyh forth, whan it was nyht,
Unto the kinges tente riht,
Wher that he lay amidde his host:
And whanne he was aslepe most,
With that the See foul to him broghte
And othre charmes, whiche he wroghte
At hom withinne his chambre stille,
The king he torneth at his wille,
And makth him forto dreme and se
2140   The dragoun and the privete
Which was betuen him and the queene.
And over that he made him wene
In swevene, hou that the god Amos,
Whan he up fro the queene aros,
Tok forth a ring, wherinne a ston
Was set, and grave therupon
A Sonne, in which, whan he cam nyh,
A leoun with a swerd he sih;
And with that priente, as he tho mette.   [impression (OF *priendre*)]
2150   Upon the queenes wombe he sette
A Seal, and goth him forth his weie.
With that the swevene wente aweie,
And tho began the king awake
And sigheth for his wyves sake,
Wher as he lay withinne his tente,
And hath gret wonder what it mente.
      With that he hasteth him to ryse

Anon, and sende after the wise, [wise counselors]
Among the whiche ther was on,
2160 A clerc, his name is Amphion:
Whan he the kinges swevene herde,
What it betokneth he ansuerde,
And seith, "So siker as the lif,
A god hath leie be thi wif,
And gete a Sone, which schal winne
The world and al that is withinne.
As leon is the king of bestes,
So schal the world obeie his hestes,
Which with his swerd schal al be wonne,
2170 Als ferr as schyneth eny Sonne."
      The king was doubtif of this dom;
Bot natheles, whan that he com
Ayein into his oghne lond,
His wif with childe gret he fond.
He mihte noght himselve stiere,
That he ne made hire hevy chiere;
Bot he which couthe of alle sorwe,
Nectanabus, upon the morwe
Thurgh the deceipte and nigromance
2180 Tok of a dragoun the semblance,
And wher the king sat in his halle,
Com in rampende among hem alle [romping]
With such a noise and such a rore,
That thei agast were also sore
As thogh thei scholde deie anon.
And natheles he grieveth non,
Bot goth toward the deyss on hih; [seat of state]
And whan he cam the queene nyh,
He stinte his noise, and in his wise
2190 To hire he profreth his servise,
And leith his hed upon hire barm; [bosom]
And sche with goodly chiere hire arm
Aboute his necke ayeinward leide,

And thus the queene with him pleide
In sihte of alle men aboute.
And ate laste he gan to loute   [bow]
And obeissance unto hire make,
As he that wolde his leve take;
And sodeinly his lothly forme
2200   Into an Egle he gan transforme,
And flyh and sette him on a raile;
Wherof the king hath gret mervaile,
For there he pruneth him and piketh,
As doth an hauk whan him wel liketh,
And after that himself he schok,
Wherof that al the halle quok,
As it a terremote were;   [earthquake]
Thei seiden alle, god was there:
In such a res and forth he flyh.   [hurry (OE *raesan*, 'to
                                                  rush')]

2210   The king, which al this wonder syh,
Whan he cam to his chambre alone,
Unto the queene he made his mone
And of foryiveness hir preide;
For thanne he knew wel, as he seide,
Sche was with childe with a godd.
Thus was the king withoute rodd
Chastised, and the queene excused
Of that sche hadde ben accused.
And for the gretere evidence,
2220   Yit after that in the presence
Of king Philipp and othre mo,
Whan thei ride in the fieldes tho,
A Phesant cam before here yhe,
The which anon as thei hire syhe,
Fleende let an ey doun falle,   [egg]
And it tobrak tofore hem alle:
And as thei token therof kepe,
Thei syhe out of the schelle crepe

A litel Serpent on the ground,
2230 Which rampeth al aboute round,
And in ayein it wolde have wonne,
Bot for the brennynge of the Sonne
It mihte noght, and so it deide.
And therupon the clerkes seide,
"As the Serpent, whan it was oute,
Went enviroun the schelle aboute   [encompassing (adv.)]
And mihte noght torne in ayein,
So schal it fallen in certein:
This child the world schal environe,   [encompass]
2240 And above alle the corone
Him schal befalle, and in yong Age
He schal desire in his corage,
Whan al the world is in his hond,
To torn ayein into the lond
Wher he was bore, and in his weie
Homward he schal with puison deie."
     The king, which al this sih and herde,
Fro that dai forth, hou so it ferde,
His jalousie hath al foryete.
2250 Bot he which hath the child begete,
Nectanabus, in privete
The time of his nativite
Upon the constellacioun
Awaiteth, and relacion
Makth to the queene hou sche schal do,
And every houre apointeth so,
That no mynut therof was lore.
So that in due time is bore
This child, and forth with therupon
2260 Ther felle wondres many on
Of terremote universiel:
The Sonne tok colour of stiel
And loste his lyht, the wyndes blewe,
And manye strengthes overthrewe;   [strongholds]

The See his propre kinde changeth,
And al the world his forme strangeth;
The thonder with his fyri levene   [flash]
So cruel was upon the hevene,
That every erthli creature
2270 Tho thoghte his lif in aventure.
The tempeste ate laste cesseth,
The child is kept, his age encresseth,
And Alisandre his name is hote,
To whom Calistre and Aristote
To techen him Philosophie
Entenden, and Astronomie,
With othre thinges whiche he couthe
Also, to teche him in his youthe
Nectanabus tok upon honde.
2280   Bot every man mai understonde,
Of Sorcerie hou that it wende,
It wole himselve prove at ende,
And namely forto beguile
A lady, which withoute guile
Supposeth trouthe al that sche hiereth:
Bot often he that evele stiereth   [poorly steers]
His Schip is dreynt therinne amidde;
And in this cas riht so betidde.
Nectanabus upon a nyht,
2290 Whan it was fair and sterre lyht,
This yonge lord ladde up on hih
Above a tour, wher as he sih
The sterres suche as he acompteth,
And seith what ech of hem amonteth,
As thogh he knewe of alle thing;
Bot yit hath he no knowleching
What schal unto himself befalle.
Whan he hath told his wordes alle,
This yonge lord thanne him opposeth,
2300 And axeth if that he supposeth

What deth he schal himselve deie.
He seith, "Or fortune is aweie   [either]
And every sterre hath lost his wone,   [habit]
Or elles of myn oghne Sone
I schal be slain, I mai noght fle."
Thoghte Alisandre in privete,
"Hierof this olde dotard lieth":
And er that other oght aspieth,
Al sodeinliche his olde bones
2310 He schof over the wal at ones,
And seith him, "Ly doun there apart:
Wherof nou serveth al thin art?
Thou knewe alle othre mennes chance
And of thiself hast ignorance:
That thou hast seid amonges alle
Of thi persone, is noghte befalle,"
      Nectanabus, which hath his deth
Yit while him lasteth lif and breth,
To Alisandre he spak and seide
2320 That he with wrong blame on him leide;
Fro point to point and al the cas
He tolde, hou he his Sone was.
Tho he, which sory was ynowh,
Out of the dich his fader drouh,
And tolde his moder hou it ferde
In conseil; and whan sche it herde
And kneu the toknes whiche he tolde,
Sche nyste what sche seie scholde,
Bot stod abayssht as for the while
2330 Of his magique and al the guile.
Sche thoghte hou that sche was deceived,
That sche hath of a man conceived,
And wende a god it hadde be.
Bot natheles in such degre,
So as sche mihte hire honour save,
Sche schop the body was begrave.

       And thus Nectanabus aboghte
The Sorcerie which he wroghte:
Thogh he upon the creatures
2340 Thurgh his carectes and figures   [charms]
The maistrie and the pouer hadde,
His creatour to noght him ladde,
Ayein whos lawe his craft he useth,
Whan he for lust his god refuseth,
And tok him to the dieules craft.   [devil's]
Lo, what profit him is belaft:
That thing thurgh which he wende have
      stonde,
Ferst him exilede out of londe
Which was his oghne, and from a king
2350 Made him to ben an underling;
And siththen to deceive a queene,
That torneth him to mochel teene;   [vexation]
Thurgh lust of love he gat him hate,
That ende couthe he noght abate.
His olde sleyhtes whiche he caste,
Yonge Alisaundre hem overcaste,
His fader, which him misbegat,
He slouh, a gret mishap was that;
Bot for o mis an other mys
2360 Was yolde, and so fulofte it is;
Nectanabus his craft miswente,
So it misfell him er he wente.
I not what helpeth that clergie   [learning]
Which makth a man to do folie,
And nameliche of nigromance,
Which stant upon the mescreance.

[As further evidence of the futility of Sorcery, recall the fate of
Zoroaster, who was the first to practice magic.[12] Soon after his
birth he laughed, but that was a token of woe to follow. Despite
all his magic he was slain by a worthy king of Surrie. Saul too

forbade the practice of magic, yet he took counsel of the Phitonesse in Samaria. But it did him no good; he was slain the next day.[13] Man only harms himself by trying to know too much (2300).

Amans says that from this day forth he will eschew Sorcery. But he is curious about Genius's observations on Aristotle's teaching of Alexander and would have Genius explain further his teaching. So new a subject might ease the pain of love which he suffers with. Genius compliments him on his seeking after wisdom. He admits, however, that as a clerk of Venus he is not capable of knowing much about higher Philosophy (2440).]

Explicit Liber Sextus

INCIPIT LIBER SEPTIMUS

[Genius says he will speak of Aristotle's instruction of Alexander, although such matter lies outside the original intention of Venus's request that he be Love's confessor. But since Wisdom is to be sought above all else it too is ultimately important to lovers. So he will describe what Calistre and Aristotle wrote. Since learning is so diverse he will begin by rehearsing the nature of Philosophy which, according to Aristotle, has three divisions: Theorique, which deals with the Creator, creation, and first causes; Rhetorique, which deals with eloquence; and Practique, which involves the application of moral behavior.[1] Theorique has three divisions: Theology, the science whereby men discover evidence of the Trinity and its unity as well as the meaning of creation (61–135); Physics, the science of bodily things such as man, beast, herb, stone, fish, and fowl (136–144); and Mathematics, whose four subdivisions are Arithmetic, Music, Geometry, Astronomy (145–202).

Aristotle spoke also of the creation of the four elements out of the formless matter called "Ylem" (216). The first element is earth. It is the lowest of all and in form is round, substantial, strong, sad and sound, and sufficient to bear up all the rest. Like the fixed foot of the compass the earth stands at the center of creation and may not swerve aside. All things of the world desire to draw to that center according to the law of nature. Above the earth is water, the second element. Water encircles the earth, and though it is soft it often pierces the strength of the earth to flow in veins through it as blood does through man. Even in the highest hills men find streams of water, which proves that water is by nature higher than earth (253).

Air is the third element. No creature may live without it.

Creatures without air are like fish without water. Air is divided into three peripheries. The first periphery is lowest and engenders mist, dew, and hoar frost. From the second periphery, rain descends onto middle earth to temper it for seeds. Rain may be turned into snow or hail. The third periphery is the driest and highest and is chased sorely about by clouds until it lets fall fire and breaks the clouds with a great, fearful, cracking noise. Men see the fire and light before they hear the thunderstroke, which proves that sight is nearer to man than hearing.[2] In that place where lightning strikes there is no protection except God. It is from the third periphery of air that men see various forms of fire at night such as that which ignorant men call the firedrake or gliding stars. But Aristotle says such phenomena are neither star nor firedrake but rather impressions of diverse "exalacions" (330) upon cause and matter which have various names: "Assub" is the name for that which falls to ground and is congealed. Some say it is like a skipping goat and call it *Capra saliens* (347). Another form of night fire is "Eges" (351) which burns like a current of fire upon a cord when powder of sulfur is placed on it and ignited. Some speak of "Daaly" as the firedrake (367).

The fourth element is fire. It surrounds and permeates the other three, as we have seen, and is hot and dry.

The Creator has bestowed upon all nations of men four complexions which are related to the four elements. Corresponding to earth, which is cold and dry, is Melancholy. It is the "most ungoodlich and the werste" (404). It causes lack of will or strength in love at night. The man with this complexion is "Full of ymaginacion / Of dredes and of wrathful thoghtes" (410–411) and frets over nothing. Phlegm corresponds to water, which is moist and cold. It makes one forgetful, slow and weary of everything. The phlegmatic man is capable of acts of love but lacks appetite which normally accompanies such delight (413–420). The man who takes his nature from the air will be light and fair, for his complexion is blood. Of all there is none so good; he has both will and might to please and pay love its due. Where he undertakes love it is wrong to forsake (421–428). The complexion of fire is called Choler, whose property is hot and dry. It makes a man "enginous" (quick-witted), swift of foot, and wrathful. The choleric man is too foolhardy and contentious to think much of love. Though he promises well by day, at night he is not worth much (429–440).

Melancholy resides in the spleen, phlegm in the lungs, sanguinariness in the liver, and choler in the gall bladder. All four of these organs are servants to the heart, which is chief over all. The liver makes the heart love, the lungs give man his power of speech, the gall causes wretchedness, and the spleen causes laughter and play when uncleanness is away. Thus each has its function and is sustained and fed by the stomach, which is cook of the hall. Over all, the heart sits as a king in his empire to whom Reason is specially given for governance (441–489).

Thus Nature, in its foresight, has made man to live here on earth; but God has given man a Soul which no man fully understands, except that it has a form like unto God through which figure and likeness it is ennobled. But often the senses are blind and desire to serve only the body. One desires to serve hell, another heaven so that they are at odds unless the Soul have governance. Beasts easily serve their nature, but man must choose. To feast on the food of eternal life man must be deserving through good works (490–520).[3]

Let us consider next the principal divisions of the world, both land and water. The earth is divided into three parts: Asia, Africa, and Europe. These were settled by Noah's three sons after the flood. Asia lies to the East and was settled by Shem, the oldest son, who got the best and twice as much as the other two. Its western boundary is the Nile and the great sea, and it includes all of the Orient, even to the Gates of Paradise. To the West, Shem's brother Cham took Africa, and Japhet took Europe. Much of the land in the Occident is uninhabitable because of the cold, and there is desert in the Orient because of heat (521–586). The water also has various bounds which take their names from adjacent lands. The sea which has no "wane" is called Ocean, out of which come high floods. There is no little wellspring which does not take its beginning and, like a man who takes his breath according to nature, find its end in the great sea (587–600).

Aristotle speaks of a fifth element beyond the four which is called "orbis." It encloses all else, but to speak of it one must know the science of Astronomy, that part of Mathematics which is grounded in Theorique. For like an eagle which flies above all, so does this science fly above others (632). Astronomers say that temperature and the chances of the world which men call Fortune are influenced by the stars, whereby some men have health and others disease, some war and others peace. But divines say otherwise: If men are good and wise and pleasant toward God they need not fear the stars. For in the eyes of the Creator one man is worth more than all the stars. Yet the stars do influence creatures according to natural law and thus are worthy of attention. Astronomy is the study of the motions and locations of the stars, while Astrology is concerned with the effects of the stars on earth. The "orbis" of which old philosophers speak is the firmament in which the stars all stand, among which are the seven principal planets and the twelve signs of the Zodiac wherein the planets take their place (720). Beneath all others stands the moon, which controls the sea. It makes the tides and governs the growth of shellfish. All other stars shine of their own nature, but the moon is not bright of itself; it takes its light from the sun. The Almegest describes the faces of the moon and its shadows.[4] A man born under the power of the moon shall travel and seek strange lands. Its disposition is set upon the Germans and English, for they travel in every land. The second planet, which takes its place above the moon, is Mercury. Whoever is born under him will be studious of books and inquisitive in writing. He will be slow and lustless and love his ease. So he is not the worthiest, but yet he sets his heart somewhat on riches. The disposition of this planet is most strong in Burgoigne and France. Next to Mercury is Venus, who governs the nation of lovers, bringing some woe, some joy. She is for the most part soft and sweet, and the man born under her desires joy and mirth, gentilesse, courtesy, and debonair speech. He is so amorous that he knows no viciousness. The climate of her lechery is most common in Lombardy (721–814).

Next to the planet of love stands the bright sun, which hinders the night and furthers the day's light. He is the world's eye in which birds sing in the morning, fresh flowers grow, the high tree shades the ground, and which gladdens every man's heart. The sun is the head planet and sits in his seat nobly and richly. The wheels of his cart glisten with gold, and he is crowned with a circle of bright stones. In front are three stones which no person has on earth and which are called Licuchis, Astrices, and Ceramius. Behind there are three worthy stones too—Crystal, Adamant, and Ydiades. On the sides are set five more—the Smaragdine, Jasper, Heliotrope, Dendides, and Jacinctus. Such is the crown which shines forth as he travels the sky. Four horses pull his chariot: Eritheus, Acteos, Lampes, and Philogeus. So swift are they in the heaven that they circle the whole earth in twenty-four hours. As chief planet the sun reigns in the middle of the seven, with three planets beneath him and three above. Whoever is born in his constellation will be of good will and liberal, and enjoy the grace, thanks, and profit of his lord. The sun also gives man subtle wit to work in gold and wisdom in judging things which are costly. The place on earth where he reigns most in his wisdom is Greece (815–888).

The next planet to the sun is Mars, who controls the fortune of battles. In the old days conquerors honored this planet. The man born under its disposition will be fierce and foolhardy, desirous of war and strife. The climate he most commonly affects is that of the Holy Land, where there is no steadfast peace. Above Mars is the sixth planet, Jupiter the delicate, who causes peace and no debate. He is by nature soft, sweet, and temperate, a planet of delights. Man born into his regiment will be meek, patient, and fortunate as a merchant. He reigns especially over Egypt. He is so felicitous that there are no storms grievous to man or beast where he reigns, and the land is so honest that it is plenteous and never idle. The highest planet is Saturn, whose complexion is cold and who causes malice and cruelty to those born under his governance. All his works are grievous and enemies to man's health. His climate is in the Orient where he is most violent (889-946).[5]

Aristotle then taught Alexander the days of the week, the weeks of the month, and the months of the year. The days were named for the seven planets and the months assigned to the twelve heavenly signs of the Zodiac. The first is called Aries, who resembles a sheep. His figure is depicted with twelve stars whereof there are two in the womb, three in the head, and seven in the tail. He is hot and dry and the house of mighty Mars. The Creator of all nature began the world and made man under this constellation. If a man begins a work under this sign his operation should avail, for it offers good speed and felicity. The month of Aries is March when birds choose their mates, and every adder every snake, and when reptiles creep out again into the sun; it is the time when Ver begins. Taurus is the second sign and is shaped like a bull. He is dry and cold. Venus appertains to this house, somewhat discordantly. The stars which make the horns of the bull knit into the tail of Aries. There are eighteen stars in his breast and two more in his tail. His month is April, in which showers minister to flowers (947-1030).

Gemini is the third sign; it is figured as twin boys which stand naked. Their heads share two stars with the bull's tail, but they have five of their own for belly and also two in their feet. Lusty May is the month of Gemini, when every bird sings its lay, "And love of this pointure stingeth / After the lawes of nature / The youthe of every creature" (1048-1050). Cancer the crab with his sixteen stars, ten of which go before, two in the middle, and four behind, rules the fourth sign. He is moist and cold and is the house of the moon. June is the month of this sign. The fifth sign is called Leo and is shaped like a lion. His nature is hot and dry. The four stars of Cancer's end make up his head, and he has four more upon his breast and one in his tail. July is his month, in which men play many a game (1031-1080).

After Leo comes the sixth sign, Virgo, whose figure is a maid. She is the wealth and rising of lust and joy and is pleasing to

Mercury. She has plenty of stars: Leo lends her one which rests high upon her head, while five more form her womb and five others her feet. Her kindly disposition is cold and dry. Her month is August, when every field has corn aplenty and many a man plies his back. After Virgo comes Libra the scales, who sits in the seventh sign. He has three stars on top, two in the middle, and eight more beneath. He is hot and moist and thus is not loth to Venus who rests in his house often. Saturn also hies to this sign to be magnified. September is his month, when men pause to remember if any sore has been left behind which might be grievous to nature (1081–1120).

The eighth sign is Scorpio, the felonious Scorpion. He takes eight stars from Libra for his head and has three more for his middle and eight in his tail. His unbecoming nature is moist and cold. He is harmful and impairs Venus, although Mars repairs to his house. When they are together they make war. October is his month, which marks the beginning of winter. The ninth sign is called Sagittarius, whose figure is that of a monster with a bow in hand. The eight stars of Scorpio's tail form his head; eight more stand in his body, and seven others form his tail. He is hot and dry. His house is free to Jupiter, though he works great harm to Mercury. His month is November, when the leaf has lost its green and the plow oxen have been put in winter stalls, when fires burn in the hall and men drink wine and sing. The tenth sign, Capricorn the goat, is dry and cold. Saturn likes to sojourn in his house but the moon does not. Capricorn has three stars in his head, two in his body, and two in his tail. December is his month, when days are short and nights long (1121–1184).

The eleventh sign is Aquarius, who stands well in Saturn's grace but is outrageous to the sun. His shape is that of a man pouring water with both hands. He is moist and hot with two stars in his head, which he takes from Capricorn and, as Ptolemy says, twelve in his body and two at the bottom. Frosty cold January is his month, when Janus sits in his chair looking both ways, toward winter and toward the forthcoming year. From his dole comes the first primrose. The twelfth and last sign is called Pisces, which, as Scripture tells us, is two fishes. He is cold and moist with two stars from Aquarius in his head, two others in his middle, and twenty bright stars for the rest which are wondrous to see. The glorious Jupiter in accord with Venus dwells in this house. Pisces marks the month of February, when there is so much rain that floods rage across the land and fords become impassable (1185-1236).

These signs divide into four groups which have special influence on earth. The region around Antioch in the Orient is governed by Cancer, Virgo, and Leo. To the west, around Armenia, Capricorn, Pisces, and Aquarius govern. Southward, around Alexandria, Libra, Sagittarius, and Scorpio are most strong, while Constantinople is under the purview of Aries, Taurus, and Gemini. Thus was Alexander taught (1270). He was also instructed by Nectanabus in the meaning and power of the fifteen great stars, whereby men work many wonders.[6] The first star is Aldeboran, the clearest and greatest of them all. It is like Mars in condition and like Venus in complexion. The Carbuncle is its stone and its herb the Anabulla, which has great virtue. The second star is Clota or Pleiades, which is not without strength either. It is of the moon's condition and Mars's complexion. Its stone is Crystal and its herb Fennel. The third star is the clear, red Algol, whose nature is that of Saturn and complexion that of Jupiter. The Diamond is its stone and the black Eleborum its herb. The fourth star is Alhaiot, who takes its nature from Saturn and Jupiter and whose stone is Sapphire and herb Marrubium. Canis Major is the fifth magic star. Its nature is Venerien, its stone Beryl, its herb Saveine (1271-1354).

The sixth star is Canis Minor, who is Mercurial with martial complexion. Its stone is Agate, its herb the Primrose. The seventh is Arial, who has various natures. Its stone is the Gorgonza, its herb the fresh and green Celidoine. Ala Corvi is the eighth star. It does the will of Mars and Saturn. Its herb is Lapacia; its stone is Honochinus, through which men work great riot. The ninth star is fair Alaezel, whose proper nature accords with both Mercury and Venus. Its stone is the green Emerald, which is much praised, and its herb is Salge. The tenth star is Almareth, who, by the nature of Jupiter and Mars, influences life and death. Its stone is Jasper and its sovereign herb the Plantain. The eleventh star is Venenas, who takes its nature from Venus and the Moon. Adamant is its stone and Cicorea its herb. Alpheta is the twelfth star. It is governed by Scorpio. Its stone is the Topaz and its herb Rosemary. Cor Scorpionis is star thirteen. Its nature is given by Mars and Jupiter and its herb is Aristologie. The Sardis is its stone. The next to the last star is Potercadent, who is obedient to Mercury and Venus. Its stone is the Chrysolyte, its herb the Satureie. The last star is called the Tail of Scorpio. Its nature yields to Mercury and Saturn. Calcydon is its stone, Marjoram its herb (1355–1438).

The men who first set out to study Astronomy, the principal science for judging between weal or woe of natural things, were gracious and wise.[7] The first of them after Noah was Nembrot, who made a book called Megaster for his disciple Ychonithon. Another astronomer was Arachel, who wrote Abbategnyh. Ptolemy wrote the Almagest and Alfraganus a book called Chatemuz. Gebuz and Alpetragus also wrote astronomy books. Men say that Abraham and Moses were astronomers, though they did not write much about astronomy. Hermes, however, excelled all others. He identified many a star, as books still acknowledge. But there are many more stars in the heaven, a thousand and twenty-two which are bright enough for men to judge their nature and properties. But enough of Theorique. Aristotle also spoke of Rhetoric (1439–1506).

Man, above all other creatures, was given the word so that he might show, win or lose, what is in his heart. So should he, to whom God gave so great a gift, be the more honest and sure that he shifts not his words for wicked use. For Philosophy calls "word" the teacher of virtue. Rhetoric is the science proper to the reverence of words which are reasonable. Grammar and Logic both assist to make Rhetoric serviceable to men. Grammar deals with "congruite" (1531) of speech, while Logic deals with validity and is favored by philosophers. There is virtue in grass and stone, but books tell us that the word is virtuous above all earthly things. Because of the power of the word its deceit is great if it is misused. False rhetoric is much to be despised and feared. Ulysses used his eloquent and easy words to persuade Antenor to be guilty of treason and sell out Troy. Words beguile men, daunt wild beasts, enchant serpents, and heal wounds when other medicines fail. Sorcery depends on words. They can make friends of foes and foes of friends, peace from war and war from peace. The high God is appeased with words. The soft word stills the loud and supplies the want when goods fail. When words mingle with song the effect is even more pleasant (1507–1587).[8]

Tully's Rethorique explains how to pick the right word, make the appropriate construction, and pronounce plainly without "frounce" (1594). Read also the debate of Julius and Cithero with Cillene and Cato when they debated the treason of Cateline before parliament. Cillenus spoke first and proved openly Cateline's guilt and the justice of the death penalty. Cato agreed and showed that no punishment would be too strong for such an offense. But Julius with wise words knew how to excite the judges through his eloquence and set pity in their hearts to turn the sentence from death. The one side spoke plainly, the other used colors, and between them they dealt justly. Even so, with true rhetoric man may learn to justify his words in a dispute and thus knit a conclusion which will inform plain truth and abate the subtle tricks which every true man should expose (1588–1640).[9]

The third division of Philosophy which was explained to Alexander is called Practique. It deals with three matters pertinent to the governance of kings: Ethics, which is the science of virtue, personal and social morality, and everyday conduct such as manners; Economics, which teaches the king to rule his household; and Policy, which concerns the king's rule of his people both in war and peace. Thus this worthy young king was taught everything necessary for good rule and regiment. The Philosopher especially impressed upon him five points pertinent to policy in a worthy government.[10] Every man must be wise, but especially a king who leads people, for he may save or spill many men. His chief virtue must be Truth.]

Among the vertus on is chief,
And that is trouthe, which is lief   [dear]
To god and ek to man also.
And for it hath ben evere so,
Tawhte Aristotle, as he wel couthe,
To Alisandre, hou in his youthe
He scholde of trouthe thilke grace
1730 With al his hole herte embrace,
So that his word be trewe and plein,
Toward the world and so certein
That in him be no double speche:
For if men scholde trouthe seche
And founde it noght withinne a king,
It were an unsittende thing.   [unbecoming]
The word is tokne of that withinne,
Ther schal a worthi king beginne
To kepe his tunge and to be trewe,
1740 So schal his pris ben evere newe.   [praise (worth)]
Avise him every man tofore,
And be wel war, er he be swore,
For afterward it is to late,
If that he wole his word debate.

[The king's crown is a symbol of his power. The gold betokens his excellence whereby men should be reverent towards him. The stones have triple significance. First, they are hard and suggest his unvarying constancy. Second, they suggest his honesty, his truth in every promise. And third, their bright color which shines forth betokens the fame of his good name throughout the world. Moreover, the crown is circular as a sign of his kingdom over which he rules and keeps watch (1744–1782).

To illustrate that Truth is the king's most sovereign virtue

Genius tells the story of Darius, Sultan of Persia.[11] Darius continuously sought after wisdom. To three wisemen of his service, whose names were Arpaghes, Manachaz, and Zorobabel, he put the question: which is the strongest—wine, women, or the king? He gave them three days to prepare their answers and set a prize for the one who reasoned best. Arpaghes was first to argue, and he spoke in favor of the king: The king has power over man, the most noble of God's creatures. A king may spill, a king may save; he may make a lord of a knave or a knave of a lord. His power goes beyond law; he flies as a gentle falcon which no man may reclaim, yet he can tame whomever he pleases. Thus the king's might is strongest and of most value. But Manachaz argued for wine: Wine can take man's reason away. It can make a cripple to leap and the active man to be helpless, the blind to see and the bright-eyed to be dark. It makes the ignorant wise, the wise unwise; the coward it makes hardy and the avaricious generous. It improves the blood in which the soul rests. Thus Manachaz argued that wine was more mighty even than kings.

Zorobabel, for his part, argued in favor of women, for both the king and the wine drinker come from women. They also obey women in love, and to show the mastery of women in love he told how Apemen, daughter of Besazis, mastered the tyrant King Cyrus. With a mere look she made him debonaire and meek, and by the chin or cheek she lugged him wherever it pleased her. Now she joked, now she kissed, according to her desire. When she loured, he sighed, and when she was glad, he was glad. Men have no solace without women. Because of them men become knights and seek fame. They make a man fearful of shame and desirous of honor. A woman is man's remedy, his life, his death, his woe, his health. Their goodness is seen in the story of Alcestis. When the duke Admetus lay sick in bed and men awaited his death, Alcestis, his wife, went to the Temple of Minerva with a sacrifice to find out what might be done to recover her husband's health. She was told that if one would suffer the malady and die for him that he would live. So Alcestis gave Minerva great thanks and returned to her husband so that by her death he might be made whole. She entered the chamber and took her husband in both her arms and kissed him and told him what she knew. Soon this good wife was dead, and he quickly recovered. So one can see that next after God above, woman and her love is the mightiest power on earth. Thus Zorobabel argued, but in conclusion he said there was one thing stronger even than wine, women, or kings, and that is Truth itself. For he who is true will never rue it, nor suffer shame in the end. But he who is untrue will be scorned. There is no strength without Truth. And so Zorobabel was most commended and received the reward. And we may see by this story that every king's regime must be founded on Truth if his governance is to succeed (1783–1984).

The second point of policy that brings reverance to the king is Liberality. In the beginning the goods of the world were held in common, but as Fortune began to increase some men and as their lineages waxed great, common profit ceased. Every man advanced himself, so Envy was born, then debate, then wars, until no man could tell who was friend or foe. At last people chose kings who might restore order and protect them from covetousness.[12] So it sits well for a king to be in no way avaricious, but rather to set his heart upon Largesse towards himself and his people. It behooves a king to flee prodigality and to keep measure. Aristotle taught this to Alexander by example of the king of Chaldee, whose people were out of accord with him because he pillaged them. A good king should spend only his own goods and not those of his people. And his gifts should go to the deserving. The story of Julius and the poor knight illustrates the matter.[13] In Rome there was a worthy but poor knight who came before Julius in hopes of recovering his rights. Julius saw that he was a worthy knight but did nothing. So the knight cried out in anger, explaining how instead of buying a substitute he had fought by Julius's side in Africa and had been wounded. For that good effort he now receives not a single florin, nor even thanks. Julius knew that what he said was true, so he forgave his outrage and bestowed upon him enough goods to last him the rest of his life. Thus should every worthy king behave, rewarding those who are deserving. A king should also have discretion. King Antigonus, for example, when the poor Cinichus requested a large gift, refused because the gift requested was more worthy than the man. And when Cinichus then asked for a penny the king again refused, for so small a gift was unworthy of a king. A king must give judiciously. He must not give prodigally, for prodigality is the mother of poverty (1985–2176).

The king must especially be wary of flatterers. In their deceit flatterers sin against God, king, and society. There is no worse thing at court than flatterers who with feigned words make black into white and blue into green. To expose the ways of flattery men tell the story of Diogenes and Aristippus, two philosophers who went from Carthage to Athens to study.[14] There in time they surpassed all others in learning and became famous. At last they returned to Carthage. Diogenes cared little for worldly goods and dwelt at home beside a river and near a bridge; there he studied his philosophy and denied the world's pomp. But Aristippus put aside his books and went to court where he spoke many flattering words in order to please the prince. Thus he got honor and much wealth. One day in May, while Diogenes had gathered herbs from his garden and was washing them in the river, Aristippus came by, saw his old friend, and called out to him: "O Diogenes, there would be no need for you to sit there picking herbs if you had made yourself pleasing to the Prince." To which Diogenes replied: "O Aristippe, if you were pleased to pick herbs as I, there would be no need to purchase the king's thanks with flattery." So counseled Diogenes. Yet men receive well the example of Aristippus and say that office in court and gold in the coffer is now the best philosopher (2177–2327).[15]

The Romans did not spare truth with flattery but preferred plain and bare words. If an emperor had victory over his foe and returned to Rome in triumph he was assured of a triple honor. First he was placed in a chariot drawn by four white steeds. Then his prisoners marched along on either side while all the nobles of the land rode before and after. But in the chariot beside him rode a fool, who said: "Remember. For all this pomp and pride do not turn justice aside. Know thyself. Though you have had victory now, fortune may turn her wheel another day and overthrow you." Thus as the emperor stood openly in his glory he repressed his vanity. Hear also, on the authority of the Chronicle, how the emperor, after he was first enthroned, feasted in the palace, heard the minstrels sing his praises, and then received the masons who came for instructions on how to make his sepulchre. There was no flattery here to fool the prince. When flattery was uttered they were too discreet to be fooled, as a story of Caesar recorded in a Chronicle of Rome proves. Caesar received a man who fell down kneeling before him and so revered him as if he were a god that the whole court marveled. After a time the man arose, seated himself beside Caesar, and said: "If you who sit here are a god, then I have worshipped you aright. But if you are a man, as I am, then I may sit beside you, for we are of one nature." Caesar answered him and said: "O blind fool. If I am a god you do amiss to sit here beside me, and if I am a man you have been most foolish to revere me as a god." When the court heard how wisely Caesar answered they feared him all the more. None dared feign wise words, so nothing but truth and reason was brought to his ears (2328–2490).[16]

Flatterers know no love, only how to advance themselves. Thus kings are often deceived with their soft words. The king who bestows goods upon flatterers does harm to himself and to his kingdom, as many examples prove. In the Bible is the story of King Ahab who favored flatterers over men who spoke true. The Syrian King Benedab seized from Ahab the area of Israel called Ramoth Galaath. Ahab called Josaphat, King of Judah, to help him, for they had an alliance by marriage of Josaphat's son Joram to Ahab's daughter Godelie. Josaphat came and asked for counsel in the matter. Ahab called on Sedechie, a notorious flatterer, who came dressed up like a bull, ramped about thrusting his horns here and there, asserting that Benedab would fall before Ahab without resistance. Josaphat asked for further counsel, so Micaiah, a prophet whom Ahab hated and had thrown in prison, was summoned. Micaiah told how he saw in a vision the king surrounded with flatterers who advised him to go into the field against Benedab when the time was not right. He next saw the people of Israel scattered about the hills like sheep without a keeper. Then a voice said: "Go home to your house again until I have ordained better for you." When Micaiah finished, Sedechie rose in anger and struck him on the cheek, and the king had him cast again into prison. So Ahab ignored the truth and went into the field where Benedab killed him and dispersed his people.[17] A king does well to love those who speak true, for flattery is worth nothing (2491–2689).

The third point of policy in which Aristotle instructed Alexander is Justice.]

What is a lond wher men ben none?
What ben the men whiche are al one
Withoute a kinges governance?
What is a king in his ligance,   [rule]
Wher that ther is no lawe in londe?
2700 What is to take lawe on honde,
Bot if the jugges weren trewe?
These olde worldes with the newe
Who that wol take in evidence
Ther mai he se thexperience,
What thing it is to kepe lawe,
Thurgh which the wronges ben withdrawe
And rihtwisnesse stant commended,
Wherof the regnes ben amended.
For wher the lawe mai comune   [join]
2710 The lordes forth with the commune,   [commons]
Ech hath his propre duete;
And ek the kinges realte   [royalty]
Of bothe his worschipe underfongeth,   [receives]
To his astat as it belongeth,
Which of his hihe worthinesse

Hath to governe rihtwisnesse,
As he which schal the lawe guide.
And natheles upon som side
His pouer stant above the lawe,
2720 To yive bothe and to withdrawe
The forfet of a mannes lif;
But thinges whiche are excessif
Ayein the lawe, he schal noght do
For love ne for hate also.

    The myhtes of a king ben grete,
Bot yit a worthi king schal lete   [delay]
Of wrong to don, al that he myhte;
For he which schal the poeple ryhte,
It sit wel to his regalie
2730 That he himself ferst justefie
Towardes god in his degre:
For his astat is elles fre
Toward alle othre in his persone,
Save only to the god al one,
Which wol himself a king chastise,
Wher that non other mai suffise.
So were it good to taken hiede
That ferst a king his oghne dede
Betwen the vertu and the vice
2740 Redresce, and thanne of his justice
So sette in evene the balance
Towardes othre in governance,
That to the povere and to the riche
Hise lawes myhten stonde liche,
He schal excepte no persone.
Bot for he mai noght al him one
In sondri places do justice,
He schal of his real office   [royal]
With wys consideracion
2750 Ordeigne his deputacion
Of suche jugges as ben lerned,

So that his poeple be governed
Be hem that trewe ben and wise.
For if the lawe of covoitise
Be set upon a jugges hond,
Wo is the poeple of thilke lond,
For wrong mai noght himselven hyde:
Bot elles on that other side,
If lawe stonde with the riht,
2760 The poeple is glad and stant upriht.
Wher as the lawe is resonable,
The comun poeple stant menable,
And if the lawe torne amis,
The poeple also mistorned is.

[When Maximin made a man governor of a province he first inquired into the man's character to find out whether he was a good man or evil. Thus law in his reign held the right way. That was when the world stood upon the wise. In those days Gaius Fabricius, the Consul of Rome, when he was brought gold by the Samnites who hoped that he might favor them, tasted it, smelled it, and then said that he knew not what good it was. Better to rule men who have gold than to have gold and be ruled by those who gave it. So he turned them away, kept his liberty and dispensed justice equitably. Nowadays there are few such men. Nevertheless, law is made for peace, and to keep it is best. The just Emperor Conrad, to keep peace, had laws against disturbing order within his city. Nor would he make exceptions to the law for gold. Neither would the Praetorian Consul Carmidotirus, who made a law that no man, upon pain of death, should bear weapons in the council chamber. Once, when he came riding in from the fields, he forgot the law and entered the chamber still girded with his sword. The lords of the council sat silent until he discovered his error. "I have deserved the penalty of justice," he said, "Act quickly." But the twelve senators said that his error was no vice, for he had intended no malice; he was only guilty of a little sloth. But Carmidotirus would not burden his descendants with an unjust ancestor, so he slew himself to uphold the statute of his own law (2765–2888).[18]

Elsewhere we read of King Cambyses who found one of his judges to be lawless. He slew the man, flayed him, and upholstered his bench with his skin. He then sat the man's son upon the bench as the new judge, a man more mindful of justice than his father had been.[19] If judges fail the king must judge them and maintain the law. The good King Lycurgus was one who had good laws. When he saw how well they worked and the ease of common profit with which his people lived, he devised a wondrous scheme. He called his parliament to him, told them that his laws were sacred since they were given to him by Mercury himself. He then said he was going away for a time. But first the people must swear that during his absence they would break none of the laws. Thus they swore, and he left, never to return. Yet the Athenians, bound by oath, adhered to the law and to common profit (2889–3028).

Anyone who would adhere to the first laws should know the names of the first lawgivers. Moses was the first to bring law to the Hebrews, and Mercurius was the first lawgiver for the Egyptians. Neuma Pompilius brought law to the Trojans; Lycurgius to the Athenians. To the Greeks Foroneus gave law, and to the Romans it was Romulus. Kings ought to be led by law. The king who knows not his own laws nor enforces them is scandalous (3029–3102).[20]

In order to get the love of God and of his people, Alexander learned the fourth point of policy which is the virtue called Pity. The Highest Majesty was Himself guided by pity when he sent His Son to earth. And since our salvation rests on pity, we ought to have pity on our fellow men. Pity well befits a king. It makes him gracious and courteous. Blind justice spares no man. But in the land where pity fares, the king may never fail to love. Pity, through grace, confirms his reign in good estate.[21] Constantine said that he who is servant to Pity is worthy of being a lord. And Troian said that as emperor he would rather his people were obedient because of love instead of fear of law.[22]

For if a thing is done in doubt, often it turns out for the worse. But if a king is piteous he is the more gracious, so that much thrift occurs which otherwise would not.[23] Pity is a virtue in all men, but in none so much as in the king. Valerius Maximus tells the story of Codrus, king of Athens, who was told by Apollo that either he must die in battle or see his people defeated.[24] He had such pity that he chose to die for the sake of his people. Another story recounts how Pompeius fought long against the king of Armenia until at last he defeated him and led him prisoner to Rome. Pompeius saw the patience with which the Armenian king suffered his adversity and was moved to restore him to his throne, saying that it is better to make a king than to undo one. So the two who once warred ended in peace. Justice was kept, and Pompeius was commended. No king who ignores pity to be cruel may be excused. Cruelty is engendered from Tyranny, against whom God Himself is champion. God has always overpowered tyrants and redressed the grievances of the piteous king (3103–3266).

Many are the examples which illustrate the downfall of the cruel. There was the tyrant Leontius of Rome, who cruelly cut off the nose and lips of the merciful Justinian to make him loathsome to the people. But God ordained justice, and Tiberius overthrew Leontius and served him as he had served Justinian. King Therbellia of Bulgaria got Justinian out of prison and restored him to his throne.[25] A Chronicle tells also of Siculus, a king as cruel as the tempest, who slew in gladness whomever he might. One of his counselors was Berillus who thought to please the tyrant by making a bull of brass in which men might be burned to death. As the victims cried out in pain the bull with its gaping mouth would seem to bellow. As his reward Berillus was the first to be burned. Nor was there any man who complained for him.[26] This example shows how loathsome to men and God both cruel kings and cruel counselors are, and there are other examples besides. Dionysius, who fed men to his horses, was overthrown by Hercules to give his horses one last meal. Lichaon was another cruel man who met a just, pitiless death. He devoured his guests, ate up their bodies in his house. But the glorious Jupiter took vengeance upon this cruel king and transformed him into a wolf.[27] The vengeance of God above falls on men who lack pity. For he who has no tender love in the saving of a man's life shall be found guilty and receive no mercy when his time of need comes. Such is nature's law. The fierce lion will slay a man if he finds him in his way. But if that man falls on his face before the lion, as a sign of mercy and grace, the lion by nature will restrain his wrath as though he were a tame beast and turn away half ashamed rather than grieve the man. What then of the prince who would destroy a man who stands at his mercy? How shall he who behaves so unnaturally achieve grace? Books tell of a duke named Spertachus who was a cruel, bloodthirsty warrior. He killed whenever he could and spared no man. It happened by chance that he fell heir to the throne of Persia. As king, his tyrannies increased a thousandfold. But God shaped vengeance against his vice. Spertachus in his pride and rancor made war against Thameris, Queen of Marsagete, and captured her son, whom he had killed in his own presence. When the news of the son's violent death reached the mother's ear, she planned the king's downfall. She set a trap in a narrow pass and pretending to flee before the Persian king, drew him into the ambush. Her army struck him from all sides and two hundred thousand of his host were slain or taken. Nor did it help Spertachus to cry for mercy. Thameris took the blood of his slain princes to him in a vessel and said, "Lo, thus you may win the lust of your appetite. You delighted in blood. Drink your fill." Thus he found a strange mercy without grace (3267–3517).[28]

Pity is a great virtue when it is reasonable. There is an old saying which has some truth, however, that pity is cowardice. If a prince uses pity as an excuse to escape responsibility he does wrong. Pity should not exceed measure. Aristotle says a king should manifest honor and worthiness: if excessive pity interferes, justice suffers. A king who is fearful without a cause is like those in the fable who fled when they heard a mountain roaring in labor as it gave birth to a mouse. Horace told his prince that it would be better for him to be like Achilles and follow war than like Thersites who tried to avoid it: Achilles gained great fame.[29] And King Solomon said that there was a time for peace and a time for war. But the king should not seek war for glory, rather only to defend his lordship. Between the simplicity of pity and foolhardiness of cruelty stands true hardiness to which a king must address his heart. He must know when to war and when not to, and seek God's guidance (3518-3626).

The Bible tells the story of the noble duke Gideon, who fought under the guidance of God and won a great victory. It also tells the story of Saul and Agag. Saul showed mercy to King Agag against the advice of Samuel, who spoke God's word. Because of his indiscreet pity Saul lost his life and his kingdom.[30] Justice lies in the hands of the king; he must uphold it. If a man deserves death the king must see that the sentence is carried out. Again the Bible shows the way when it tells how David advised his son Solomon to have Joab slain. After inheriting the throne Solomon wisely followed his father's advice. Yet he showed no tyranny in his reign.[31] In Solomon one may see what is most necessary for a king to be worthy. God bade him choose the one thing he most desired and Solomon chose wisdom. Wisdom is mainly what a good king needs to keep a balance between justice and pity. A king must trust to himself and to God; he must rule in his own person and in good conscience (3627-3942).

A Chronicle tells the story of King Lucius of Rome who asked his Steward what men said about him.[32] The Steward, who was a flatterer who hoped to advance himself, said the people spoke well of the king, honored his name, and thought that he must be worthy since he maintained good counselors. But the Fool, who sat on a stool beside the fire playing with his bauble, laughed scornfully at them both, and said: "Sir King, if you were really wise you would not listen to bad counsel." The king marveled that the Fool spoke so wisely, and put away the vicious men about him and took the virtuous to him, amended wrongful laws, dispensed well the goods of the land, and no more oppressed the people. Then the king needed no more to worry about the clamor of his people (3942-4026).

Not all kings have been so wise. After Solomon's death Rehoboam received the crown.[33] The people with one voice asked him to release them from the debts which Solomon had placed them under, since the temple was all finished and there was no longer any need to pillage the people. Rehoboam thought over their request and called upon his counselors for advice. First he asked the old wise knights, who told him he should relax the taxes and win the hearts of the people. Then he asked the young men what he should do, and they told him it would be a shame not to keep the rights he got from his father. They advised him to tell the people outright that as long as he was king his littlest finger should be stronger than his father's whole body. If Solomon smote them with little rods, Rehoboam would smite them with scorpions. So the young king followed the advice of his young counselors. When the people heard of his malice and menace, they began to rave like the wild sea until he was fain to same himself. All but two of the twelve tribes left him and chose their own king, a poor knight named Jeroboam, and the nation ever after was divided. So we see that young counsel often does much harm (4027-4146).

Genius says he once found a book which raised the question of whether it is better to have a king himself be wise or have wise counsel? It is better to have wise counsel, for one man is more likely to err than several who are wise. If a king has wise counsel he will better be able to maintain the balance between harshness and pity. The Emperor Antonius said he would rather save one of his lieges than slay a thousand of his enemies, and this he learned from Cipio, his counselor.[34] Pity is the foundation of a king's reign, and if it is mingled with justice the reign will be stable (4147-4214).

The fifth point of policy which a king should adhere to is Chastity. The male is made for female, but Nature says man needs no more than one. When a man has a ready wife why should he seek in strange places to borrow another man's plow, especially when he knows his own equipment is good, while the worth of his neighbor's is unknown? So the Philosopher taught Alexander how he should govern his body with measure in order to overcome lust, especially since he is a king. A king has been anointed and sanctified like a prelate; he bears the dignity of the crown. Aristotle advised Alexander to frequent the company of many fair women, but not to beguile himself with them. For it is not women who beguile men but men themselves. A man starts musing on women in his imagination, blowing the fire within himself while the woman knows nothing about it. If a man drowns we do not blame the water, nor the gold if man covets it. Men begin the chase. Women flee and men pursue, especially these days. It is natural for men to love, but not to lose their wits in love. That is like frost in July, or heat in December, or wearing hose outside the shoe. Yet many princes have been guilty of such love and have misled themselves. Sardana Pallus, king of Assyria, burned so with lust that he seldom got out of bed to see how things went elsewhere. Instead he kissed and played, taught lasses to braid, weave purses, and thread pearls, until Barbarus the Prince of Mede overthrew his kingdom. King David had many loves also, but he avoided covetousness of the flesh and maintained his knighthood. He forgot not his lust for knightly arms while lying in his ladies' arms. When his country was in danger he was there with his army. Yet there are many who bought trouble by seeking ease. Cyrus, king of Persia, fought the Lydians but could not defeat them. So he made peace with them and they fell to fleshly lust. Then he pounced on them more suddenly than thunder and conquered them, though in truth it was their lechery which lost the land (4215–4405).[35]

The Bible tells how Amalech, a pagan king, could not defend his land against the worthy people of Israel until Balaam counseled him to send a group of beautiful women among the Hebrews.[36] Forth they went with grey eyes and bent brows, all well arrayed, and when they came among the Hebrews there was not one who did not catch as catch can to satisfy his lust. But for that they paid dear: When it came time for battle they were overthrown. So it went, until Phinees chopped off the heads of a couple of offenders and let them lie where all might see. Then the others prayed to God that their sins might be amended and He restored them with new grace. Thus it may be shown in many places how chastity accords with worthiness in men of arms. But especially the virtue must apply to the king if his land is to fare well. Solomon set his delight so much on women that the whole world still marvels how this man of wisdom could, because of fleshly lust, have turned to idolatry.[37] He took wives and concubines from among the Saracens. In his folly the Queen of Sidoyne led him sprawling before Astrathen, the goddess of her land. And the woman Moabite so delighted him that he devoured his wits and honored her god, Chamos. An Ammonite made him foolish too, so that he sacrificed incense to Moloch. Thus the wisest man was overthrown with blind lust, but he paid for it later. The prophet Achias Selonites warned him how his kingdom would be divided and Jeroboam rule ten parts of the twelve. And so it happened. A king must avoid the ignorance of lust. When nature has been satisfied that should be enough (4406–4573). Anthony was a voluptuary and for that he sorely paid. Of lechery another tale is told which you shall hear.[38]]

TALE OF TARQUIN, ARUNS, AND LUCRECE

So as these olde gestes sein,
The proude tirannyssh Romein
Tarquinus, which was thanne king
And wroghte many a wrongful thing,
Of Sones hadde manyon,
Among the whiche Arrons was on,
Lich to his fader of maneres;
4600 So that withinne a fewe yeres
With tresoun and with tirannie

Thei wonne of lond a gret partie,
And token hiede of no justice,
Which due was to here office
Upon the reule of governance
Bot al that evere was plesance
Unto the fleisshes lust thei toke.
And fell so, that thei undertoke
A werre, which was noght achieved,   [finished]
4610 Bot ofte time it hadde hem grieved,
Ayein a folk which thanne hihte
The Gabiens: and al be nyhte
This Arrons, whan he was at hom
In Rome, a prive place he nom
Withinne a chambre, and bet himselve   [beat]
And made him woundes ten or tuelve
Upon the bak, as it was sene;
And so forth with hise hurtes grene
In al the haste that he may
4620 He rod, and cam that other day
Unto Gabie the Cite,
And in he wente: and whan that he
Was knowe, anon the gates schette,
The lordes alle upon him sette
With drawe swerdes upon honde.
This Arrons wolde hem noght withstonde,
Bot seide, "I am hier at your wille,
Als lief it is that ye me spille,   [pleasing/destroy]
As if myn oghne fader dede."
4630 And forthwith in the same stede
He preide hem that thei wolde se
And schewede hem in what degre
His fader and hise brethren bothe,
Whiche, as he seide, weren wrothe,
Him hadde beten and reviled,
For evere and out of Rome exiled.
And thus he made hem to believe,

And seide, if that he myhte achieve
His pourpos, it schal wel be yolde,
4640 Be so that thei him helpe wolde.
　　　Whan that the lordes hadde sein
Hou wofully he was besein,
Thei token Pite of his grief;
Bot yit it was hem wonder lief　　　　　[pleasant]
That Rome him hadde exiled so.
These Gabiens be conseil tho
Upon the goddes made him swere,
That he to hem schal trouthe bere
And strengthen hem with al his myht;
4650 And thei also him have behiht
To helpen him in his querele.
Thei schopen thanne for his hele
That he was bathed and enoignt,
Til that he was in lusti point;
And what he wolde thanne he hadde,
That he al hol the cite ladde　　　　　　[led]
Riht as he wolde himself divise.
And thanne he thoghte him in what wise
He myhte his tirannie schewe;
4660 And to his conseil tok a schrewe,　　　[scoundrel]
Whom to his fader forth he sente
In his message, and he tho wente,
And preide his fader forto seie
Be his avis, and finde a weie,
Hou they the cite myhten winne,
Whil that he stod so wel therinne.
And whan the messager was come
To Rome, and hath in conseil nome
The king, it fell per chance so
4670 That thei were in a gardin tho,
This messager forth with the king.
And whanne he hadde told the thing
In what manere that it stod,

And that Tarquinus understod
Be the message hou that it ferde,
Anon he tok in honde a yerde,
And in the gardin as thei gon,
The lilie croppes on and on,   [blossoms (tops)]
Wher that thei weren sprongen oute,
4680 He smot of, as thei stode aboute,
And seide unto the messager:
"Lo, this thing, which I do nou hier,
Schal ben in stede of thin ansuere;
And in this wise as I me bere,
Thou schalt unto mi Sone telle."
And he no lengere wolde duelle,
Bot tok his leve and goth withal
Unto his lord, and told him al,
Hou that his fader hadde do.
4690 Whan Arrons herde him telle so,
Anon he wiste what it mente
And therto sette al his entente,
Til he thurgh fraude and tricherie
The Princes hefdes of Gabie   [heads]
Hath smiten of, and al was wonne:
His fader cam tofore the Sonne
Into the toun with the Romeins,
And tok and slowh the citezeins
Withoute reson or pite,
4700 That he ne spareth no degre.
And for the sped of his conqueste
He let do make a riche feste
With a sollempne Sacrifise
In Phebus temple; and in this wise
Whan the Romeins assembled were,
In presence of hem alle there,
Upon thalter whan al was diht
And that the fyres were alyht,
From under thalter sodeinly

4710 An hidous Serpent openly
Cam out and hath devoured al
The Sacrifice, and ek withal
The fyres queynt, and forth anon, [quenched]
So as he cam, so is he gon
Into the depe ground ayein.
And every man began to sein,
"Ha lord, what mai this signefie?"
And therupon thei preie and crie
To Phebus, that thei mihten knowe
4720 The cause: and he the same throwe
With gastly vois, that alle it herde,
The Romeins in this wise ansuerde,
And seide hou for the wikkidnesse
Of Pride and of unrihtwisnesse,
That Tarquin and his Sone hath do,
The Sacrifice is wasted so,
Which myhte noght ben acceptable
Upon such Senne abhominable.
And over that yit he hem wisseth, [informs]
4730 And seith that which of hem ferst kisseth
His moder, he schal take wrieche [vengeance]
Upon the wrong: and of that speche
Thei ben withinne here hertes glade,
Thogh thei outward no semblant made.
Ther was a knyht which Brutus hihte,
And he with al the haste he myhte
To grounde fell and therthe kiste,
Bot non of hem the cause wiste,
Bot wenden that he hadde sporned [tripped]
4740 Per chance, and so was overtorned.
Bot Brutus al an other mente;
For he knew wel in his entente
Hou therthe of every mannes kinde
Is Moder: bot thei weren blinde,
And sihen noght so fer as he.

Bot whan thei leften the Cite
And comen hom to Rome ayein,
Thanne every man which was Romein
And moder hath, to hire he bende
4750 And keste, and ech of hem thus wende
To be the ferste upon the chance,
Of Tarquin forto do vengance,
So as thei herden Phebus sein.

🙵 Bot every time hath his certein,
So moste it nedes thanne abide,
Til afterward upon a tyde
Tarquinus made unskilfully   [unreasonably]
A werre, which was fasteby
Ayein a toun with walles stronge
4760 Which Ardea was cleped longe,
And caste a Siege theraboute,
That ther mai noman passen oute.
So it befell upon a nyht,
Arrons, which hadde his souper diht,
A part of the chivalerie
With him to soupe in compaignie
Hath bede: and whan thei comen were
And seten at the souper there,
Among here othre wordes glade
4770 Arrons a gret spekinge made,
Who hadde tho the beste wif
Of Rome: and ther began a strif,
For Arrons seith he hath the beste.
So jangle thei withoute reste,
Til ate laste on Collatin,
A worthi knyht, and was cousin
To Arrons, seide him in this wise:
"It is," quod he, "of non emprise
To speke a word, bot of the dede,
4780 Therof it is to taken hiede.

Anon forthi this same tyde
Lep on thin hors and let ous ryde:
So mai we knowe bothe tuo
Unwarli what oure wyves do,
And that schal be a trewe assay."
This Arrons seith noght ones nay:
On horse bak anon thei lepte
In such manere, and nothing slepte,
Ridende forth til that thei come
4790 Al prively withinne Rome;
In strange place and doun thei lihte,
And take a chambre, and out of sihte
Thei be desguised for a throwe,
So that no lif hem scholde knowe.
And to the paleis ferst thei soghte,
To se what thing this ladi wroghte
Of which Arrons made his avant: [boast]
And thei hire sihe of glad semblant,
Al full of merthes and of bordes;   [jests]
4800 Bot among alle hire othre wordes
Sche spak noght of hire housebonde.
And whan thei hadde al understonde
Of thilke place what hem liste,
Thei gon hem forth, that non it wiste,
Beside thilke gate of bras,
Collacea which cleped was,
Where Collatin hath his duellinge.
Ther founden thei at hom sittinge
Lucrece his wif, al environed   [surrounded]
4810 With wommen, whiche are abandoned
To werche, and sche wroghte ek withal,
And bad hem haste, and seith, "It schal
Be for mi housebondes were,   [wearing]
Which with his swerd and with his spere
Lith at the Siege in gret desese.
And if it scholde him noght displese,

Nou wolde god I hadde him hiere;
For certes til that I mai hiere
Som good tidinge of his astat,
4820 Min herte is evere upon debat.
For so as alle men witnesse,
He is of such an hardiesse,
That he can noght himselve spare,
And that is al my moste care,
Whan thei the walles schulle assaile.
Bot if mi wisshes myhte availe,
I wolde it were a groundles pet,   [pit]
Be so the Siege were unknet,
And I myn housebonde sihe."
4830 With that the water in hire yhe
Aros, that sche ne myhte it stoppe,
And as men sen the dew bedroppe
The leves and the floures eke,
Riht so upon hire whyte cheke
The wofull salte teres felle.
Whan Collatin hath herd hire telle
The menynge of hire trewe herte,
Anon with that to hire he sterte,
And seide, "Lo, mi goode diere,
4840 Nou is he come to you hiere,
That ye most loven, as ye sein."
And sche with goodly chiere ayein
Beclipte him in hire armes smale,   [embraced]
And the colour, which erst was pale,
To Beaute thanne was restored,
So that it myhte noght be mored.   [increased]
      The kinges Sone, which was nyh,
And of this lady herde and syh
The thinges as thei ben befalle,
4850 The resoun of hise wittes alle
Hath lost; for love upon his part
Cam thanne, and of his fyri dart

With such a wounde him hath
    thurghsmite,
That he mot nedes fiele and wite
Of thilke blinde maladie,
To which no cure of Surgerie
Can helpe. Bot yit natheles
At thilke time he hield his pes,
That he no contienance made,
4860 Bot openly with wordes glade,
So as he couthe in his manere,
He spak and made frendly chiere,
Til it was time forto go.
And Collatin with him also
His leve tok, so that be nyhte
With al the haste that thei myhte
Thei riden to the Siege ayein.
Bot Arrons was so wo besein
With thoghtes whiche upon him runne,
4870 That he al be the brode Sunne
To bedde goth, noght forto reste,
Bot forto thenke upon the beste
And the faireste forth withal,
That evere he syh or evere schal,
So as him thoghte in his corage,
Where he pourtreieth hire ymage:
Ferst the fetures of hir face,
In which nature hadde alle grace
Of wommanly beaute beset,
4880 So that it myhte noght be bet;
And hou hir yelwe her was tresced
And hire atir so wel adresced,
And hou sche spak, and hou sche wroghte,   [worked]
And hou sche wepte, al this he thoghte,
That he foryeten hath no del,   [part]
Bot al it liketh him so wel,
That in the word nor in the dede

Hire lacketh noght of wommanhiede.
And thus this tirannysshe knyht
4890 Was soupled, bot noght half ariht,   [made supple]
For he non other hiede tok,
Bot that he myhte be som crok,
Althogh it were ayein hire wille,
The lustes of his fleissh fulfille;
Which love was noght resonable,
For where honour is remuable,   [unstable]
It oghte wel to ben avised.
Bot he, which hath his lust assised
With melled love and tirannie,   [mingled]
4900 Hath founde upon his tricherie
A weie which he thenkth to holde,
And seith, "Fortune unto the bolde
Is favorable forto helpe."
And thus withinne himself to yelpe,   [boast]
As he which was a wylde man,
Upon his treson he began:
And up he sterte, and forth he wente
On horsebak, bot his entente
Ther knew no wiht, and thus he nam
4910 The nexte weie, til he cam
Unto Collacea the gate
Of Rome, and it was somdiel late,
Riht evene upon the Sonne set,
As he which hadde schape his net
Hire innocence to betrappe.
And as it scholde tho mishappe,
Als priveliche as evere he myhte
He rod, and of his hors alyhte
Tofore Collatines In,
4920 And al frendliche he goth him in,
As he that was cousin of house.
And sche, which is the goode spouse,
Lucrece, whan that sche him sih,

With goodli chiere drowh him nyh,
As sche which al honour supposeth,
And him, so as sche dar, opposeth
Hou it stod of hire housebonde.
And he tho dede hire understonde
With tales feigned in his wise,
4930 Riht as he wolde himself devise,
Wherof he myhte hire herte glade,
That sche the betre chiere made,
Whan sche the glade wordes herde
Hou that hire housebonde ferde.
And thus the trouthe was deceived
With slih tresoun, which was received
To hire which mente alle goode;
For as the festes thanne stode,
His Souper was ryht wel arraied.
4940 Bot yit he hath no word assaied
To speke of love in no degre;
Bot with covert soubtilite
His frendly speches he affaiteth,   [contrives (adorns)]
And as the Tigre his time awaiteth
In hope forto cacche his preie.
Whan that the bordes were aweie
And thei have souped in the halle,
He seith that slep is on him falle,
And preith he moste go to bedde;
4950 And sche with alle haste spedde,
So as hire thoghte it was to done,
That every thing was redi sone.
Sche broghte him to his chambre tho
And tok hire leve, and forth is go
Into hire oghne chambre by,
As sche that wende certeinly
Have had a frend, and hadde a fo,
Wherof fell after mochel wo.
    This tirant, thogh he lyhe softe,

4960 Out of his bed aros fulofte,
And goth aboute, and leide his Ere
To herkne, til that alle were
To bedde gon and slepten faste.
And thanne upon himself he caste
A mantell, and his swerd al naked
He tok in honde; and sche unwaked
Abedde lay, but what sche mette,
Got wot; for he the Dore unschette
So prively that non it herde,
4970 The softe pas and forth he ferde
Unto the bed wher that sche slepte,
Al sodeinliche and in he crepte,
And hire in bothe his Armes tok.
With that this worthi wif awok,
Which thurgh tendresce of wommanhiede
Hire vois hath lost for pure drede,
That o word speke sche ne dar:
And ek he bad hir to be war,
For if sche made noise or cry,
4980 He seide, his swerd lay faste by
To slen hire and hire folk aboute.
And thus he broghte hire herte in doute,
That lich a Lomb whanne it is sesed
In wolves mouth, so was desesed
Lucrece, which he naked fond:
Wherof sche swounede in his hond,
And, as who seith, lay ded oppressed.
And he, which al him hadde adresced
To lust, tok thanne what him liste,
4990 And goth his wey, that non it wiste,
Into his oghne chambre ayein,
And clepede up his chamberlein,
And made him redi forto ryde.
And thus this lecherouse pride   [proud man]
To horse lepte and forth he rod;

And sche, which in hire bed abod,
Whan that sche wiste he was agon,
Sche clepede after liht anon
And up aros long er the day,
5000 And caste awey hire freissh aray,
As sche which hath the world forsake,
And tok upon the clothes blake:
And evere upon continuinge,
Riht as men sen a welle springe,
With yhen fulle of wofull teres,
Hire her hangende aboute hire Eres,   [hair]
Sche wepte, and noman wiste why.
Bot yit among full pitously
Sche preide that thei nolden drecche   [would not delay (OE *dreccan*, 'to vex')]

5010 Hire housebonde forto fecche
Forth with hire fader ek also.
        Thus be thei comen bothe tuo,
And Brutus cam with Collatin,
Which to Lucrece was cousin,
And in thei wenten alle thre
To chambre, wher thei myhten se
The wofulleste upon this Molde,   [earth]
Which wepte as sche to water scholde.
The chambre Dore anon was stoke,   [barred]
5020 Er thei have oght unto hire spoke;
Thei sihe hire clothes al desguised,
And hou sche hath hirself despised,
Hire her hangende unkemd aboute,   [unkempt]
Bot-natheles sche gan to loute   [bow]
And knele unto hire housebonde;
And he, which fain wolde understonde
The cause why sche ferde so,
With softe wordes axeth tho,
"What mai you be, mi goode swete?"
5030 And sche, which thoghte hirself unmete   [unworthy]

And the lest worth of wommen alle,
Hire wofull chiere let doun falle
For schame and couthe unnethes loke.   [could scarcely]
And thei therof good hiede toke,
And preiden hire in alle weie
That sche ne spare forto seie
Unto hir frendes what hire eileth,
Why sche so sore hirself beweileth,
And what the sothe wolde mene.
5040 And sche, which hath hire sorwes grene,
Hire wo to telle thanne assaieth,
Bot tendre schame hire word delaieth,
That sondri times as sche minte
To speke, upon the point sche stinte.
And thei hire bidden evere in on
To telle forth, and therupon,
Whan that sche sih sche moste nede,
Hire tale betwen schame and drede
Sche tolde, noght withoute peine.
5050 And he, which wolde hire wo restreigne,
Hire housebonde, a sory man,
Conforteth hire al that he can,
And swor, and ek hire fader bothe,
That thei with hire be noght wrothe
Of that is don ayein hire wille;
And preiden hire to be stille,
For thei to hire have al foryive.
Bot sche, which thoghte noght to live,
Of hem wol no foryivenesse,
5060 And seide, of thilke wickednesse
Which was unto hire bodi wroght,
Al were it so sche myhte it noght,   [even though she could not
                                              help it]

Nevere afterward the world ne schal
Reproeven hire; and forth withal,
Er eny man therof be war,

A naked swerd, the which sche bar
Withinne hire Mantel priveli,
Betwen hire hondes sodeinly
Sche tok, and thurgh hire herte it throng,
5070 And fell to grounde, and evere among,
Whan that sche fell, so as sche myhte,
Hire clothes with hire hand sche rihte,
That noman dounward fro the kne
Scholde eny thing of hire se:
Thus lay this wif honestely,
Althogh she deide wofully.
     Tho was no sorwe forto seke:
Hire housebonde, hire fader eke
Aswoune upon the bodi felle;
5080 Ther mai no mannes tunge telle
In which anguisshe that thei were.
Bot Brutus, which was with hem there,
Toward himself his herte kepte
And to Lucrece anon he lepte,
The blodi swerd and pulleth oute,
And swor the goddes al aboute
That he therof schal do vengance.
And sche tho made a contienance,
Hire dedlich yhe and ate laste
5090 In thonkinge as it were up caste,
And so behield him in the wise,
Whil sche to loke mai suffise.
And Brutus with a manlich herte
Hire housebonde hath mad up sterte
Forth with hire fader ek also
In alle haste, and seide hem tho
That thei anon withoute lette   [delay]
A Beere for the body fette;
Lucrece and therupon bledende
5100 He leide, and so forth out criende
He goth into the Market place

Of Rome: and in a litel space
Thurgh cry the cite was assembled,
And every mannes herte is trembled,
Whan thei the sothe herde of the cas.
And therupon the conseil was
Take of the grete and of the smale,
And Brutus tolde hem al the tale;
And thus cam into remembrance
5110 Of Senne the continuance,
Which Arrons hadde do tofore,
And ek, long time er he was bore,
Of that his fadre hadde do
The wrong cam into place tho;
So that the comun clamour tolde
The newe schame of Sennes olde.
And al the toun began to crie,
"Awey, awey the tirannie
Of lecherie and covoitise!"
5120 And ate laste in such a wise
The fader in the same while
Forth with his Sone thei exile,
And taken betre governance.
Bot yit an other remembrance
That rihtwisnesse and lecherie
Acorden noght in compaignie
With him that hath the lawe on honde,
That mai a man wel understonde,
As be a tale thou shalt wite,
5130 Of olde ensample as it is write.[39]

TALE OF VIRGINIA

✤ At Rome whan that Apius,
Whos other name is Claudius,
Was governour of the cite,
Ther fell a wonder thing to se

Touchende a gentil Maide, as thus,
Whom Livius Virginius
Begeten hadde upon his wif:
Men seiden that so fair a lif
As sche was noght in al the toun.
5140 This fame, which goth up and doun,
To Claudius cam in his Ere,
Wherof his thoght anon was there,
Which al his herte hath set afyre,
That he began the flour desire
Which longeth unto maydenhede,
And sende, if that he myhte spede
The blinde lustes of his wille.
Bot that thing mai he noght fulfille,
For sche stod upon Mariage;
5150 A worthi kniht of gret lignage,
Ilicius which thanne hihte,
Acorded in hire fader sihte
Was, that he scholde his douhter wedde.
Bot er the cause fully spedde,
Hire fader, which in Romanie
The ledinge of chivalerie
In governance hath undertake,
Upon a werre which was take
Goth out with al the strengthe he hadde
5160 Of men of Armes whiche he ladde:
So was the mariage left,
And stod upon acord til eft.
    The king, which herde telle of this,
Hou that this Maide ordeigned is
To Mariage, thoghte an other.
And hadde thilke time a brother,
Which Marchus Claudius was hote,
And was a man of such riote
Riht as the king himselve was:
5170 Thei tuo togedre upon this cas

In conseil founden out this weie,
That Marchus Claudius schal seie
Hou sche be weie of covenant
To his service appourtenant
Was hol, and to non other man;
And therupon he seith he can
In every point witnesse take,
So that sche schal it noght forsake.   [deny]
Whan that thei hadden schape so,
5180 After the lawe which was tho,
Whil that hir fader was absent,
Sche was somouned and assent   [sent for]
To come in presence of the king
And stonde in ansuere of this thing.
Hire frendes wisten alle wel
That it was falshed everydel,
And comen to the king and seiden,
Upon the comun lawe and preiden,
So as this noble worthi knyht
5190 Hir fader for the comun riht
In thilke time, as was befalle,
Lai for the profit of hem alle
Upon the wylde feldes armed,
That he ne scholde noght ben harmed
Ne schamed, whil that he were oute;
And thus thei preiden al aboute.
      For al the clamour that he herde,
The king upon his lust ansuerde,
And yaf hem only daies tuo
5200 Of respit; for he wende tho,
That in so schorte a time appiere
Hire fader mihte in no manere.
Bot as therof he was deceived;
For Livius hadde al conceived
The pourpos of the king tofore,
So that to Rome ayein therfore

In alle haste he cam ridende,
And lefte upon the field liggende
His host, til that he come ayein.
5210 And thus this worthi capitein
Appiereth redi at his day,
Wher al that evere reson may
Be lawe in audience he doth,
So that his dowhter upon soth
Of that Marchus hire hadde accused
He hath tofore the court excused.
     The king, which sih his pourpos faile,
And that no sleihte mihte availe,
Encombred of his lustes blinde
5220 The lawe torneth out of kinde,
And half in wraththe as thogh it were,
In presence of hem alle there
Deceived of concupiscence
Yaf for his brother the sentence,
And bad him that he scholde sese
This Maide and make him wel at ese;
Bot al withinne his oghne entente
He wiste hou that the cause wente,
Of that his brother hath the wyte   [blame]
5230 He was himselven forto wyte.   [to be censured]
Bot thus this maiden hadde wrong,
Which was upon the king along,
Bot ayein him was non Appel,   [appeal]
And that the fader wiste wel:
Wherof upon the tirannie,
That for the lust of Lecherie
His douhter scholde be deceived,
And that Ilicius was weyved
Untrewly fro the Mariage,
5240 Riht as a Leon in his rage,
Which of no drede set acompte
And not what pite scholde amounte,

A naked swerd he pulleth oute,
The which amonges al the route
He threste thurgh his dowhter side,
And al alowd this word he cride:
"Lo, take hire ther, thou wrongfull king,
For me is levere upon this thing   [more dear]
To be the fader of a Maide,
5250 Thogh sche be ded, than if men saide
That in hir lif sche were schamed
And I therof were evele named."
      Tho bad the king men scholde areste
His bodi, bot of thilke heste,
Lich to the chaced wylde bor,
The houndes whan he fieleth sor,
Tothroweth and goth forth his weie,
In such a wise forto seie
This worthi kniht with swerd on honde
5260 His weie made, and thei him wonde,   [avoid (turn aside from)]
That non of hem his strokes kepte;
And thus upon his hors he lepte,
And with his swerd droppende of blod,
The which withinne his douhter stod,
He cam ther as the pouer was
Of Rome, and tolde hem al the cas,
And seide hem that thei myhten liere   [learn]
Upon the wrong of his matiere,
That betre it were to redresce
5270 At hom the grete unrihtwisnesse,
Than forto werre in strange place
And lese at hom here oghne grace.
For thus stant every mannes lif
In jeupartie for his wif
Or for his dowhter, if thei be
Passende an other of beaute.
      Of this merveile which thei sihe
So apparant tofore here yhe,

Of that the king him hath misbore,
5280 Here othes thei have alle swore
That thei wol stonde be the riht.
And thus of on acord upriht
To Rome at ones hom ayein
Thei torne, and schortly forto sein,
This tirannye cam to mouthe,
And every man seith what he couthe,
So that the prive tricherie,
Which set was upon lecherie,
Cam openly to mannes Ere;
5290 And that broghte in the comun feere,
That every man the peril dradde
Of him that so hem overladde.
Forthi, er that it worse falle,
Thurgh comun conseil of hem alle
Thei have here wrongfull king deposed,
And hem in whom it was supposed
The conseil stod of his ledinge
Be lawe unto the dom thei bringe,   [judgment]
Wher thei receiven the penance
5300 That longeth to such governance.
And thus thunchaste was chastised,
Wherof thei myhte ben avised
That scholden afterward governe,
And be this evidence lerne,
Hou it is good a king eschuie
The lust of vice and vertu suie.

TALE OF TOBIAS AND SARA

❦ To make an ende in this partie,[40]
Which toucheth to the Policie
Of Chastite in special,
5310 As for conclusion final
That every lust is to eschue

Be gret ensample I mai argue:
Hou in Rages a toun of Mede
Ther was a Mayde, and as I rede,
Sarra sche hihte, and Raguel
Hir fader was; and so befell,
Of bodi bothe and of visage
Was non so fair of the lignage,
To seche among hem alle, as sche;
5320 Wherof the riche of the cite,
Of lusti folk that couden love,
Assoted were upon hire love,
And asken hire forto wedde.
On was which ate laste spedde,
Bot that was more for likinge,
To have his lust, than for weddinge,
As he withinne his herte caste,
Which him repenteth ate laste.
For so it fell the ferste nyht,
5330 That whanne he was to bedde dyht,
As he which nothing god besecheth
Bot al only hise lustes secheth,
Abedde er he was fully warm
And wolde have take hire in his Arm,
Asmod, which was a fend of helle,
And serveth, as the bokes telle,
To tempte a man of such a wise,
Was redy there, and thilke emprise,
Which he hath set upon delit,
5340 He vengeth thanne in such a plit,
That he his necke hath writhe atuo.
This yonge wif was sory tho,
Which wiste nothing what it mente;
And natheles yit thus it wente
Noght only of this ferste man,
Bot after, riht as he began,
Sexe othre of hire housebondes

Asmod hath take into hise bondes,
So that thei alle abedde deiden,
5350 Whan thei her hand toward hir leiden,
Noght for the lawe of Mariage,
Bot for that ilke fyri rage
In which that thei the lawe excede:
For who that wolde taken hiede
What after fell in this matiere,
Ther mihte he wel the sothe hiere.
Whan sche was wedded to Thobie,
And Raphael in compainie
Hath tawht him hou to ben honeste,
5360 Asmod wan noght at thilke feste,
And yit Thobie his wille hadde;
For he his lust so goodly ladde,
That bothe lawe and kinde is served,
Wherof he hath himself preserved,
That he fell noght in the sentence.

[Thus we learn of chastity in marriage. God has bound beasts only
to the law of nature, but to the creature man he has given
reason with which to modify natural urges and avoid lechery.
And so the wise philosopher taught Alexander, not only in chastity
but in all manner of honesty, so that as king he might, through
his praise of God, preserve himself and his people in peace, wealth,
honor, and health, both in this world and the other (5397).

Genius asks Amans if he has spoken enough about Aristotle's
lore. Amans says that he has and thanks him. Still, he is pre-
occupied with thoughts of love and asks Genius to speak more
on the subject so that he might amend his life. Genius says that
there is still more to be said, but that this will be the last of what
he has to say (5438).]

Explicit Liber Septimus

INCIPIT LIBER OCTAVUS

[God, who had no beginning, began all other things according to His will and pleasure. After He put away Lucifer and his followers, He made Adam and Eve and bade them increase and multiply. Their progeny was to equal the number of angels who fell with Satan from bliss. But it is well known how they sinned and were cast out of Paradise, filled with shame until nature reclaimed them both in love. First twin boys, Cain and Abel, were born, then two daughters, Calmana and Delbora. Cain married Calmana and Abel married Delbora, for in those first days there was no law against incest. Even in the Second Age, the Age of Noah, when the eight survivors on the Ark repopulated the earth, brothers married sisters. In the Third Age, the Age of Abraham, there were enough people on earth that sister and brother no longer married, although cousins still did. Rebecca was Isaac's cousin, and Jacob's two wives, by whom he engendered eight of the twelve patriarchs (the other four coming from his wives Bala and Zelpha), were his cousins. But now under Christian law, the Pope bids men not to marry second or third of kin. Yet some men ignore religion and kinship and behave as a cock among hens or a stallion in the fens, taking whatever is close at hand. Such delight is full of blame.

Amans says he has never been so wild a man that he desired sisters in love, neither his kin nor nuns. What good would come of it? Besides there is but one whom he loves. Genius says he is aware of the consistency with which Amans loves his Lady, but he continues to discuss the evils of incest, nevertheless. Incestuous love may seem sweet at first, but it always ends up sour. In Rome the Emperor Caligula bereft his three sisters of their virginity, then exiled them from the land. But God took vengeance and bereft

415

him of his life and empire. Thus, for a moment's pleasure he lost all that he desired. Amon also took his sister Thamar, until Absolom his brother slew him. The Bible tells further how Lot lay with his daughters after his wife had been turned into salt. Each of the daughters had sons from which two no-good nations, the false Moabites and the Ammonites, sprang up. Such love always leads to trouble and vengeance, as this story shows.[1]]

APOLLONIUS OF TYRE

Of a Cronique in daies gon,
The which is cleped Pantheon,
In loves cause I rede thus,
Hou that the grete Antiochus,
Of whom that Antioche tok
His ferste name, as seith the bok,
Was coupled to a noble queene,
And hadde a dowhter hem betwene:
Bot such fortune cam to honde,
280   That deth, which no king mai withstonde,
Bot every lif it mote obeie,
This worthi queene tok aweie.
The king, which made mochel mone,
Tho stod, as who seith, al him one   [alone by himself]
Withoute wif, bot natheles
His doghter, which was piereles
Of beaute, duelte aboute him stille.
Bot whanne a man hath welthe at wille,
The fleissh is frele and falleth ofte,
290   And that this maide tendre and softe,
Which in hire fadres chambres duelte,
Withinne a time wiste and felte:
For likinge and concupiscence
Withoute insihte of conscience
The fader so with lustes blente,

That he caste al his hole entente
His oghne doghter forto spille.
This king hath leisir at his wille
With strengthe, and whanne he time sih,
300   This yonge maiden he forlih: [lay with]
And sche was tendre and full of drede,
Sche couthe noght hir Maidenhede
Defende, and thus sche hath forlore
The flour which sche hath longe bore.
It helpeth noght althogh sche wepe,
For thei that scholde hir bodi kepe
Of wommen were absent as thanne;
And thus this maiden goth to manne,
The wylde fader thus devoureth
310   His oghne fleissh, which non socoureth,
And that was cause of mochel care.
Bot after this unkinde fare
Out of the chambre goth the king,
And sche lay stille, and of this thing,
Withinne hirself such sorghe made,
Ther was no wiht that mihte hir glade,
For feere of thilke horrible vice.
With that cam inne the Norrice
Which fro childhode hire hadde kept,
320   And axeth if sche hadde slept,
And why hire chiere was unglad.
Bot sche, which hath ben overlad
Of that sche myhte noght be wreke,   [avenged]
For schame couthe unethes speke;   [scarcely]
And natheles mercy sche preide
With wepende yhe and thus sche seide:
"Helas, mi Soster, waileway,
That evere I sih this ilke day!
Thing which mi bodi ferst begat
330   Into this world, onliche that
Mi worldes worschipe hath bereft."

With that sche swouneth now and eft,
And evere wissheth after deth,
So that welnyh hire lacketh breth.
That other, which hire wordes herde,
In confortinge of hire ansuerde,
To lette hire fadres fol desir   [hinder/foolish]
Sche wiste no recoverir:
Whan thing is do, ther is no bote,   [remedy]
340   So suffren thei that suffre mote;
Ther was non other which it wiste.
Thus hath this king al that him liste
Of his likinge and his plesance,
And laste in such continuance,
And such delit he tok therinne,
Him thoghte that it was no Sinne;
And sche dorste him nothing withseie.
     Bot fame, which goth every weie,
To sondry regnes al aboute
350   The grete beaute telleth oute
Of such a maide of hih parage: [rank]
So that for love of mariage
The worthi Princes come and sende,
As thei the whiche al honour wende,
And knewe nothing hou it stod.
The fader, whanne he understod,
That thei his dowhter thus besoghte,
With al his wit he caste and thoghte
Hou that he myhte finde a lette;   [hindrance]
360   And such a Statut thanne he sette,
And in this wise his lawe he taxeth,
That what man that his doghter axeth,
Bot if he couthe his question
Assoile upon suggestion   [solve]
Of certein thinges that befelle,
The whiche he wolde unto him telle,
He scholde in certein lese his hed.

And thus ther weren manye ded,
Here hevedes stondende on the gate,
370 Till ate laste longe and late,
For lacke of ansuere in the wise,
The remenant that weren wise
Eschuieden to make assay.

Til it befell upon a day
Appolinus the Prince of Tyr,
Which hath to love a gret desir,
As he which in his hihe mod
Was likende of his hote blod,
A yong, a freissh, a lusti knyht,
380 As he lai musende on a nyht
Of the tidinges whiche he herde,
He thoghte assaie hou that it ferde.
He was with worthi compainie
Arraied, and with good navie
To schipe he goth, the wynd him dryveth,
And seileth, til that he arryveth:
Sauf in the port of Antioche
He londeth, and goth to aproche
The kinges Court and his presence.
390 Of every naturel science,
Which eny clerk him couthe teche,
He couthe ynowh, and in his speche
Of wordes he was eloquent;
And whanne he sih the king present,
He preith he moste his dowhter have.
The king ayein began to crave,   [(OE *crafian*, 'to demand as right')]

And tolde him the condicion,
Hou ferst unto his question
He mote ansuere and faile noght,
400 Or with his heved it schal be boght:
And he him axeth what it was.

The king declareth him the cas

With sturne lok and sturdi chiere,
To him and seide in this manere:
"With felonie I am upbore,
I ete and have it noght forbore
Mi modres fleissh, whos housebonde
Mi fader forto seche I fonde,
Which is the Sone ek of my wif.
410 Hierof I am inquisitif;
And who that can mi tale save,
Al quyt he schal my doghter have;
Of his ansuere and if he faile,
He schal be ded withoute faile.
Forthi my Sone," quod the king,
"Be wel avised of this thing,
Which hath thi lif in jeupartie."
      Appolinus for his partie,
Whan he this question hath herd,
420 Unto the king he hath ansuerd
And hath rehersed on and on
The pointz, and seide therupon:
"The question which thou hast spoke,
If thou wolt that it be unloke,
It toucheth al the privete
Betwen thin oghne child and thee,
And stant al hol upon you tuo."
      The king was wonder sory tho,
And thoghte, if that he seide it oute,
430 Than were he schamed al aboute.
With slihe wordes and with felle   [sly/furious]
He seith, "Mi Sone, I schal thee telle,
Though that thou be of litel wit,
It is no gret merveile as yit,
Thin age mai it noght suffise:
Bot loke wel thou noght despise
Thin oghne lif, for of my grace
Of thretty daies fulle a space

I grante thee, to ben avised."
440   And thus with leve and time assised   [established]
This yonge Prince forth he wente,
And understod wel what it mente,
Withinne his herte as he was lered,   [learned]
That forto maken him afered
The king his time hath so deslaied.   [delayed]
Wherof he dradde and was esmaied,   [dismayed]
Of treson that he deie scholde,
For he the king his sothe tolde;
And sodeinly the nyhtes tyde,
450 That more wolde he noght abide,
Al prively his barge he hente
And hom ayein to Tyr he wente:
And in his oghne wit he seide
For drede, if he the king bewreide,
He knew so wel the kinges herte,
That deth ne scholde he noght asterte,   [escape]
The king him wolde so poursuie.
Bot he, that wolde his deth eschuie,
And knew al this tofor the hond,
460 Forsake he thoghte his oghne lond,
That there wolde he noght abyde;
For wel he knew that on som syde
This tirant of his felonie
Be som manere of tricherie
To grieve his bodi wol noght leve.
    Forthi withoute take leve,
Als priveliche as evere he myhte,
He goth him to the See by nyhte
In Schipes that be whete laden:
470 Here takel redy tho thei maden
And hale up Seil and forth thei fare.
Bot forto tellen of the care
That thei of Tyr begonne tho,
Whan that thei wiste he was ago,

It is a Pite forto hiere.
They losten lust, they losten chiere,
Thei toke upon hem such penaunce,
Ther was no song, ther was no daunce,
Bot every merthe and melodie
480 To hem was thanne a maladie;
For unlust of that aventure
Ther was noman which tok tonsure,
In doelful clothes thei hem clothe,
The bathes and the Stwes bothe
Thei schetten in be every weie;
There was no lif which leste pleie
Ne take of eny joie kepe,
Bot for here liege lord to wepe;
And every wyht seide as he couthe,
490 "Helas, the lusti flour of youthe,
Our Prince, oure heved, our governour,
Thurgh whom we stoden in honour,
Withoute the comun assent
Thus sodeinliche is fro ous went!"
Such was the clamour of hem alle.

Bot se we now what is befalle
Upon the ferste tale plein,
And torne we therto ayein.
Antiochus the grete Sire,
500 Which full of rancour and of ire
His herte berth, so as ye herde,
Of that this Prince of Tyr ansuerde,
He hadde a feloun bacheler,
Which was his prive consailer,
And Taliart be name he hihte:
The king a strong puison him dihte   [prepared]
Withinne a buiste and gold therto,   [box]
In alle haste and bad him go
Strawht unto Tyr, and for no cost
510 Ne spare he, til he hadde lost

The Prince which he wolde spille.   [destroy]
And whan the king hath seid his wille,
This Taliart in a Galeie
With alle haste he tok his weie:
The wynd was good, he saileth blyve,
Til he tok lond upon the ryve   [shore]
On Tyr, and forth with al anon
Into the Burgh he gan to gon,
And tok his In and bod a throwe.
520 Bot for he wolde noght be knowe,
Desguised thanne he goth him oute;
He sih the wepinge al aboute,
And axeth what the cause was,
And thei him tolden al the cas,
How sodeinli the Prince is go.
And whan he sih that it was so,
And that his labour was in vein,
Anon he torneth hom ayein,
And to the king, whan he cam nyh,
530 He tolde of that he herde and syh,
Hou that the Prince of Tyr is fled,
So was he come ayein unsped.
The king was sori for a while,
Bot whan he sih that with no wyle
He myhte achieve his crualte,
He stinte his wraththe and let him be.
    Bot over this now forto telle
Of aventures that befelle
Unto this Prince of whom I tolde,
540 He hath his rihte cours forth holde
Be Ston and nedle, til he cam
To Tharse, and there his lond he nam.
A Burgeis riche of gold and fee
Was thilke time in that cite,
Which cleped was Strangulio,
His wif was Dionise also:

This yonge Prince, as seith·the bok,
With hem his herbergage tok;
And it befell that Cite so
550 Before tyme and thanne also,
Thurgh strong famyne which hem ladde
Was non that eny whete hadde.
Appolinus, whan that he herde
The meschief, hou the cite ferde,
Al freliche of his oghne yifte
His whete, among hem forto schifte,
The which be Schipe he hadde broght,
He yaf, and tok of hem riht noght.
Bot sithen ferst this world began,
560 Was nevere yit to such a man
Mor joie mad than thei him made:
For thei were alle of him so glade,
That thei for evere in remembrance
Made a figure in resemblance
Of him, and in the comun place
Thei sette him up, so that his face
Mihte every maner man beholde,
So as the cite was beholde;
It was of latoun overgilt: [latten (copper-tin alloy)]
570 Thus hath he noght his yifte spilt.
        Upon a time with his route
This lord to pleie goth him oute,
And in his weie of Tyr he mette
A man, the which on knees him grette,
And Hellican be name he hihte,
Which preide his lord to have insihte
Upon himself, and seide him thus,
Hou that the grete Antiochus
Awaiteth if he mihte him spille.
580 That other thoghte and hield him stille,
And thonked him of his warnynge,
And bad him telle no tidinge,

Whan he to Tyr cam hom ayein,
That he in Tharse him hadde sein.
　　　Fortune hath evere be muable　　　　　　[mutable]
And mai no while stonde stable:
For now it hiheth, now it loweth,
Now stant upriht, now overthroweth,
Now full of blisse and now of bale,
590　As in the tellinge of mi tale
Hierafterward a man mai liere,
Which is gret routhe forto hiere.
This lord, which wolde don his beste,
Withinne himself hath litel reste,
And thoghte he wolde his place change
And seche a contre more strange.
Of Tharsiens his leve anon
He tok, and is to Schipe gon:
His cours he nam with Seil updrawe,
600　Where as fortune doth the lawe,
And scheweth, as I schal reherse,
How sche was to this lord diverse,
The which upon the See sche ferketh.　　　[conveys (OE *fercian*)]
The wynd aros, the weder derketh,
It blew and made such tempeste,
Non ancher mai the schip areste,
Which hath tobroken al his gere;
The Schipmen stode in such a feere,
Was non that myhte himself bestere,
610　Bot evere awaite upon the lere,　　　　　　[loss]
Whan that thei scholde drenche at ones.
Ther was ynowh withinne wones　　　　　　[possession]
Of wepinge and of sorghe tho;
This yonge king makth mochel wo
So forto se the Schip travaile:
Bot al that myhte him noght availe;
The mast tobrak, the Seil torof,　　　　　　[was riven to pieces]
The Schip upon the wawes drof,

Til that thei sihe a londes cooste.
620 Tho made avou the leste and moste,
Be so thei myhten come alonde;
Bot he which hath the See on honde,
Neptunus, wolde noght acorde,
Bot altobroke cable and corde,
Er thei to londe myhte aproche,
The Schip toclef upon a roche,
And al goth doun into the depe.
Bot he that alle thing mai kepe
Unto this lord was merciable,
630 And broghte him sauf upon a table,   [plank]
Which to the lond him hath upbore;
The remenant was al forlore,
Wherof he made mochel mone.
        Thus was this yonge lord him one,
Al naked in a povere plit:
His colour, which whilom was whyt,
Was thanne of water fade and pale,
And ek he was so sore acale   [a-cold]
That he wiste of himself no bote,
640 It halp him nothing forto mote   [to wish]
To gete ayein that he hath lore.
Bot sche which hath his deth forbore,
Fortune, thogh sche wol noght yelpe,   [boast]
Al sodeinly hath sent him helpe,
Whanne him thoghte alle grace aweie;
Ther cam a Fisshere in the weie,
And sih a man ther naked stonde,
And whan that he hath understonde
The cause, he hath of him gret routhe,
650 And onliche of his povere trouthe
Of suche clothes as he hadde
With gret Pite this lord he cladde.
And he him thonketh as he scholde,
And seith him that it schal be yolde,   [repaid]

If evere he gete his stat ayein,
And preide that he wolde him sein
If nyh were eny toun for him.
He seide, "Yee, Pentapolim,
Wher bothe king and queene duellen."
660 Whanne he this tale herde tellen,
He gladeth him and gan beseche
That he the weie him wolde teche;
And he him taghte; and forth he wente
And preide god with good entente
To sende him joie after his sorwe.
    It was noght passed yit Midmorwe,
Whan thiderward his weie he nam,
Wher sone upon the Non he cam.   [noon]
He eet such as he myhte gete,
670 And forth anon, whan he hadde ete,
He goth to se the toun aboute,
And cam ther as he fond a route   [company]
Of yonge lusti men withalle;
And as it scholde tho befalle,
That day was set of such assisse,
That thei scholde in the londes guise,
As he herde of the poeple seie,
Here comun game thanne pleie;
And crid was that thei scholden come
680 Unto the gamen alle and some
Of hem that ben delivere and wyhte,   [supple and nimble]
To do such maistrie as thei myhte.
Thei made hem naked as thei scholde,
For so that ilke game wolde,
As it was tho custume and us,   [use]
Amonges hem was no refus:
The flour of al the toun was there
And of the court also ther were,
And that was in a large place
690 Riht evene afore the kinges face,

Which Artestrathes thanne hihte.
The pley was pleid riht in his sihte,
And who most worthi was of dede
Receive he scholde a certein mede   [reward]
And in the cite bere a pris.
    Appolinus, which war and wys
Of every game couthe an ende,
He thoghte assaie, hou so it wende,
And fell among hem into game:
700 And there he wan him such a name,
So as the king himself acompteth
That he alle othre men surmonteth,
And bar the pris above hem alle.
The king bad that into his halle
At Souper time he schal be broght;
And he cam thanne and lefte it noght,   [did not neglect it]
Withoute compaignie al one:
Was non so semlich of persone,
Of visage and of limes bothe,
710 If that he hadde what to clothe.
At Soupertime natheles
The king amiddes al the pres
Let clepe him up among hem alle,
And bad his Mareschall of halle
To setten him in such degre
That he upon him myhte se.
The king was sone set and served,
And he, which hath his pris deserved
After the kinges oghne word,
720 Was mad beginne a Middel bord,
That bothe king and queene him sihe.
He sat and caste aboute his yhe
And sih the lordes in astat,
And with himself wax in debat
Thenkende what he hadde lore,   [lost]
And such a sorwe he tok therfore,

That he sat evere stille and thoghte,
As he which of no mete roghte.   [cared for no food]
    The king behield his hevynesse,
730 And of his grete gentillesse
His doghter, which was fair and good
And ate bord before him stod,
As it was thilke time usage,
He bad to gon on his message
And fonde forto make him glad.
And sche dede as hire fader bad,
And goth to him the softe pas
And axeth whenne and what he was,
And preith he scholde his thoghtes leve.
740 He seith, "Ma Dame, be your leve
Mi name is hote Appolinus,
And of mi richesse it is thus,
Upon the See I have it lore.
The contre wher as I was bore,
Wher that my lond is and mi rente,
I lefte at Tyr, whan that I wente:
The worschipe of this worldes aghte,   [possession (OE *agan* 'to own')]

Unto the god ther I betaghte."   [delivered]
And thus togedre as thei tuo speeke,
750 The teres runne be his cheeke.
The king, which therof tok good kepe,
Hath gret Pite to sen him wepe,
And for his doghter sende ayein,
And preide hir faire and gan to sein
That sche ne lengere wolde drecche,   [hesitate (OE *dreccan*)]
Bot that sche wolde anon forth fecche
Hire harpe and don al that sche can
To glade with that sory man.
760 And sche to don hir fader heste
Hir harpe fette, and in the feste
Upon a Chaier which thei fette

Hirself next to this man sche sette:
With harpe bothe and ek with mouthe
To him sche dede al that sche couthe
To make him chiere, and evere he siketh,   [sighs]
And sche him axeth hou him liketh.
"Ma dame, certes wel," he seide,
"Bot if ye the mesure pleide
Which, if you list, I schal you liere,   [teach]
770   It were a glad thing forto hiere."
"Ha, lieve sire," tho quod sche,
"Now tak the harpe and let me se
Of what mesure that ye mene."
Tho preith the king, tho preith the queene,
Forth with the lordes alle arewe,   [had pity]
That he som merthe wolde schewe;
He takth the Harpe and in his wise
He tempreth, and of such assise   [manner]
Singende he harpeth forth withal,
780   That as a vois celestial
Hem thoghte it souneth in here Ere,
As thogh that he an Angel were.
Thei gladen of his melodie,
Bot most of all the compainie
The kinges doghter, which it herde,
And thoghte ek hou that he ansuerde,
Whan that he was of hire opposed,   [questioned]
Withinne hir herte hath wel supposed
That he is of gret gentilesse.
790   Hise dedes ben therof witnesse
Forth with the wisdom of his lore;
It nedeth noght to seche more,
He myhte noght have such manere,
Of gentil blod bot if he were.
Whanne he hath harped al his fille,
The kinges heste to fulfille,
Awey goth dissh, awey goth cuppe,

Doun goth the bord, the cloth was uppe,
Thei risen and gon out of halle.
800   The king his chamberlein let calle,
And bad that he be alle weie
A chambre for this man pourveie,
Which nyh his oghne chambre be.
"It schal be do, mi lord," quod he.
Appolinus of whom I mene
Tho tok his leve of king and queene
And of the worthi Maide also,
Which preide unto hir fader tho,
That sche myhte of that yonge man
810 Of tho sciences whiche he can
His lore have; and in this wise
The king hir granteth his aprise,   [teaching]
So that himself therto assente.
Thus was acorded er thei wente,
That he with al that evere he may
This yonge faire freisshe May   [maiden]
Of that he couthe scholde enforme;
And full assented in this forme
Thei token leve as for that nyht.
820   And whanne it was amorwe lyht,
Unto this yonge man of Tyr
Of clothes and of good atir
With gold and Selver to despende
This worthi yonge lady sende:
And thus sche made him wel at ese,
And he with al that he can plese
Hire serveth wel and faire ayein.
He tawhte hir til sche was certein
Of Harpe, of Citole and of Rote,
830 With many a tun and many a note
Upon Musique, upon mesure,
And of hire Harpe the temprure
He tawhte hire ek, as he wel couthe.

Bot as men sein that frele is youthe,
With leisir and continuance
This Mayde fell upon a chance,
That love hath mad him a querele
Ayein hire youthe freissh and frele,
That malgre wher sche wole or noght,
840   Sche mot with al hire hertes thoght
To love and to his lawe obeie;
And that sche schal ful sore abeie.
For sche wot nevere what it is
Bot evere among sche fieleth this:
Thenkende upon this man of Tyr,
Hire herte is hot as eny fyr,
And otherwhile it is acale;   [a-cold]
Now is sche red, nou is sche pale
Riht after the condicion
850   Of hire ymaginacion;
Bot evere among hire thoghtes alle,
Sche thoghte, what so mai befalle,
Or that sche lawhe, or that sche wepe,
Sche wolde hire goode name kepe
For feere of wommanysshe schame.
Bot what in ernest and in game,
Sche stant for love in such a plit,
That sche hath lost al appetit
Of mete, of drinke, of nyhtes reste,
860   As sche that not what is the beste;
Bot forto thenken al hir fille
Sche hield hire ofte times stille
Withinne hir chambre, and goth noght
     oute:
The king was of hire lif in doute,
Which wiste nothing what it mente.
     Bot fell a time, as he out wente
To walke, of Princes Sones thre
Ther come and felle to his kne;

And ech of hem in sondri wise
870 Besoghte and profreth his servise,
So that he myhte·his doghter have.
The king, which wolde his honour save,
Seith sche is siek, and of that speche
Tho was no time to beseche;
Bot ech of hem do make a bille   [letter]
He bad, and wryte his oghne wille,
His name, his fader and his good;
And whan sche wiste hou that it stod,
And hadde here billes oversein,
880 Thei scholden have ansuere ayein.
Of this conseil thei weren glad,
And writen as the king hem bad,
And every man his oghne bok
Into the kinges hond betok,
And he it to his dowhter sende,
And preide hir forto make an ende
And wryte ayein hire oghne hond,
Riht as sche in hire herte fond.

    The billes weren wel received,
890 Bot sche hath alle here loves weyved,
And thoghte tho was time and space
To put hire in hir fader grace,
And wrot ayein and thus sche saide:
"The schame which is in a Maide
With speche dar noght ben unloke,
Bot in writinge it mai be spoke;
So wryte I to you, fader, thus:
Bot if I have Appolinus,
Of al this world, what so betyde,
900 I wol non other man abide.
And certes if I of him faile,
I wot riht wel withoute faile
Ye schull for me be dowhterles."
This lettre cam, and ther was press   [crowd]

Tofore the king, ther as he stod;
And whan that he it understod,
He yaf hem ansuer by and by,
Bot that was do so prively,
That non of othres conseil wiste.
910 Thei toke her leve, and wher hem liste
Thei wente forth upon here weie.
    The king ne wolde noght bewreie   [reveal]
The conseil for no maner hihe,   [haste]
Bot soffreth til he time sihe:
And whan that he to chambre is come,
He hath unto his conseil nome
This man of Tyr, and let him se
The lettre and al the privete,
The which his dowhter to him sente:
920 And he his kne to grounde bente
And thonketh him and hire also,
And er thei wenten thanne atuo,
With good herte and with good corage
Of full Love and full mariage
The king and he ben hol acorded.
And after, whanne it was recorded
Unto the dowhter hou it stod,
The yifte of al this worldes good
Ne scholde have mad hir half so blythe:
930 And forth withal the king als swithe,
For he wol have hire good assent,
Hath for the queene hir moder sent.
The queene is come, and whan sche herde
Of this matiere hou that it ferde,
Sche syh debat, sche syh desese,
Bot if sche wolde hir dowhter plese,
And is therto assented full.
Which is a dede wonderfull,
For noman knew the sothe cas
940 Bot he himself, what man he was;

And natheles, so as hem thoghte,
His dedes to the sothe wroghte
That he was come of gentil blod:
Him lacketh noght bot worldes good,
And as therof is no despeir,
For sche schal ben hire fader heir,
And he was able to governe.
Thus wol thei noght the love werne   [forbid]
Of him and hire in none wise,
950   Bot ther acorded thei divise
The day and time of Mariage.

     Wher love is lord of the corage,
Him thenketh longe er that he spede;
Bot ate laste unto the dede
The time is come, and in her wise
With gret offrende and sacrifise
Thei wedde and make a riche feste,
And every thing which was honeste
Withinnen house and ek withoute
960   It was so don, that al aboute
Of gret worshipe, of gret noblesse
Ther cride many a man largesse
Unto the lordes hihe and loude;
The knyhtes that ben yonge and proude,
Thei jouste ferst and after daunce.
The day is go, the nyhtes chaunce
Hath derked al the bryhte Sonne;
This lord, which hath his love wonne,
Is go to bedde with his wif,
970   Wher as thei ladde a lusti lif,
And that was after somdel sene,
For as thei pleiden hem betwene,
Thei gete a child betwen hem tuo,
To whom fell after mochel wo.

     Now have I told of the spousailes.
Bot forto speke of the mervailes

Whiche afterward to hem befelle,
It is a wonder forto telle.
It fell adai thei riden oute,
980   The king and queene and al the route,
To pleien hem upon the stronde,
Wher as thei sen toward the londe
A Schip sailende of gret array.
To knowe what it mene may,
Til it be come thei abide;
Than sen thei stonde on every side,
Endlong the schipes bord to schewe,
Of Penonceals a riche rewe.   [banners/row]
Thei axen when the schip is come:
990   Fro Tyr, anon ansuerde some,
And over this thei seiden more
The cause why thei comen fore
Was forto seche and forto finde
Appolinus, which was of kinde
Her liege lord: and he appiereth,
And of the tale which he hiereth
He was riht glad; for thei him tolde,
That for vengance, as god it wolde,
Antiochus, as men mai wite,
1000 With thondre and lyhthnynge is forsmite;
His doghter hath the same chaunce,
So be thei bothe in o balance.
"Forthi, oure liege lord, we seie
In name of al the lond, and preie,
That left al other thing to done,
It like you to come sone
And se youre oghne liege men
With othre that ben of youre ken,
That live in longinge and desir
1010 Til ye be come ayein to Tyr."
This tale after the king it hadde
Pentapolim al overspradde,

Ther was no joie forto seche;
For every man it hadde in speche
And seiden alle of on acord,
"A worthi king schal ben oure lord:
That thoghte ous ferst an hevinesse
Is schape ous now to gret gladnesse."
Thus goth the tidinge overal.
1020   Bot nede he mot, that nede schal:
Appolinus his leve tok,
To god and al the lond betok
With al the poeple long and brod,
That he no lenger there abod.
The king and queene sorwe made,
Bot yit somdiel thei weren glade
Of such thing as thei herden tho:
And thus betwen the wel and wo
To schip he goth, his wif with childe
1030 The which was evere meke and mylde
And wolde noght departe him fro,
Such love was betwen hem tuo.
Lichorida for hire office
Was take, which was a Norrice,
To wende with this yonge wif,
To whom was schape a woful lif.
Withinne a time, as it betidde,
Whan thei were in the See amidde,
Out of the North they sihe a cloude;
1040 The storm aros, the wyndes loude
Thei blewen many a dredful blast,
The welkne was al overcast,
The derke nyht the Sonne hath under,
Ther was a gret tempeste of thunder:
The Mone and ek the Sterres bothe
In blake cloudes thei hem clothe,
Wherof here brihte lok thei hyde.
This yonge ladi wepte and cride,

To whom no confort myhte availe;
1050 Of childe sche began travaile,
Wher sche lay in a Caban clos:
Hire woful lord fro hire aros,
And that was longe er eny morwe,
So that in anguisse and in sorwe
Sche was delivered al be nyhte
And ded in every mannes syhte;
Bot natheles for al this wo
A maide child was bore tho.
     Appolinus whan he this knew,
1060 For sorwe a swoune he overthrew,
That noman wiste in him no lif.
And whanne he wok, he seide, "Ha, wif,
Mi lust, mi joie, my desir,
Mi welthe and my recoverir,   [recovery]
Why schal I live, and thou schalt dye?
Ha, thou fortune, I thee deffie,
Nou hast thou do to me thi werste.
Ha, herte, why ne wolt thou berste,
That forth with hire I myhte passe?
1070 Mi peines weren wel the lasse."
In such wepinge and in such cry
His dede wif, which lay him by,
A thousend sithes he hire kiste;
Was nevere man that sih ne wiste
A sorwe unto his sorwe lich;
For evere among upon the lich   [corpse]
He fell swounende, as he that soghte
His oghne deth, which he besoghte
Unto the goddes alle above
1080 With many a pitous word of love;
Bot suche wordes as tho were
Yit herde nevere mannes Ere,
Bot only thilke whiche he seide.
The Maister Schipman cam and preide

With othre suche as be therinne,
And sein that he mai nothing winne
Ayein the deth, bot thei him rede,
He be wel war and tak hiede,
The See be weie of his nature
1090 Receive mai no creature
Withinne himself as forto holde,
The which is ded: forthi thei wolde,
As thei conseilen al aboute,
The dede body casten oute.
For betre it is, thei seiden alle,
That it of hire so befalle,
Than if thei scholden alle spille.
    The king, which understod here wille
And knew here conseil that was trewe,
1100 Began ayein his sorwe newe
With pitous herte, and thus to seie:
"It is al reson that ye preie.
I am," quod he, "bot on al one,
So wolde I noght for mi persone
Ther felle such adversite.
Bot whan it mai no betre be,
Doth thanne thus upon my word,
Let make a cofre strong of bord,
That it be ferm with led and pich."
1110 Anon was mad a cofre sich,
Al redy broght unto his hond;
And whanne he sih and redy fond
This cofre mad and wel enclowed,   [nailed]
The dede bodi was besowed   [sewn]
In cloth of gold and leid therinne.
And for he wolde unto hire winne
Upon som cooste a Sepulture,
Under hire heved in aventure
Of gold he leide Sommes grete
1120 And of jeueals a strong beyete   [great possession]

Forth with a lettre, and seide thus:
   "I, king of Tyr Appollinus,
Do alle maner men to wite,
That hiere and se this lettre write,
That helpeles withoute red
Hier lith a kinges doghter ded:
And who that happeth hir to finde
For charite take in his mynde,
And do so that sche be begrave
1130 With this tresor, which he schal have."
Thus whan the lettre was full spoke,
Thei haue anon the cofre stoke,   [shut]
And bounden it with yren faste,
That it may with the wawes laste,
And stoppen it be such a weie,
That it schal be withinne dreie,
So that no water myhte it grieve.
And thus in hope and good believe
Of that the corps schal wel aryve,
1140 Thei caste it over bord als blyve.   [quickly]
    The Schip forth on the wawes wente;
The prince hath changed his entente,
And seith he wol noght come at Tyr
As thanne, bot al his desir
Is ferst to seilen unto Tharse.
The wyndy Storm began to skarse,
The Sonne arist, the weder cliereth,
The Schipman which behinde stiereth,
Whan that he sih the wyndes saghte,   [at peace]
1150 Towardes Tharse his cours he straghte,
    Bot now to mi matiere ayein,
To telle as olde bokes sein,
This dede corps of which ye knowe
With wynd and water was forthrowe
Now hier, now ther, til ate laste
At Ephesim the See upcaste

The cofre and al that was therinne.
Of gret merveile now beginne
Mai hiere who that sitteth stille;
1160 That god wol save mai noght spille.
Riht as the corps was throwe alonde,
Ther cam walkende upon the stronde
A worthi clerc, a Surgien,
And ek a gret Phisicien,
Of al that lond the wisest on,
Which hihte Maister Cerymon;
Ther were of his disciples some.
This Maister to the Cofre is come,
He peiseth ther was somwhat in,   [feels by weight]
1170 And bad hem here it to his In,
And goth himselve forth withal.
Al that schal falle, falle schal;
They comen hom and tarie noght;
This Cofre is into chambre broght,
Which that thei finde faste stoke,
Bot thei with craft it have unloke.
Thei loken in, where as thei founde
A bodi ded, which was bewounde
In cloth of gold, as I seide er,
1180 The tresor ek thei founden ther
Forth with the lettre, which thei rede.
And tho thei token betre hiede;
Unsowed was the bodi sone,
And he, which knew what is to done,
This noble clerk, with alle haste
Began the veines forto taste,   [investigate]
And sih hire Age was of youthe,
And with the craftes whiche he couthe
He soghte and fond a signe of lif.
1190 With that this worthi kinges wif
Honestely thei token oute,
And maden fyres al aboute;

Thei leide hire on a couche softe,
And with a scheete warmed ofte
Hire colde brest began to hete,
Hire herte also to flacke and bete. [flutter]
This Maister hath hire every joignt
With certein oile and balsme enoignt,
And putte a liquour in hire mouth,
1200 Which is to fewe clerkes couth,
So that sche coevereth ate laste:
And ferst hire yhen up sche caste,
And whan sche more of strengthe cawhte,
Hire Armes bothe forth sche strawhte,
Hield up hire hond and pitously
Sche spak and seide, "Ha, wher am I?
Where is my lord, what world is this?"
As sche that wot noght hou it is.
Bot Cerymon the worthi leche [physician]
1210 Ansuerde anon upon hire speche
And seith, "Ma dame, yee ben hiere,
Where yee be sauf, as yee schal hiere
Hierafterward; forthi as nou
Mi conseil is, conforteth you:
For trusteth wel withoute faile,
Ther is nothing which schal you faile,
That oghte of reson to be do."
Thus passen thei a day or tuo;
Thei speke of noght as for an ende,
1220 Til sche began somdiel amende,
And wiste hireselven what sche mente.
  Tho forto knowe hire hol entente,
This Maister axeth al the cas,
Hou sche cam there and what sche was.
"Hou I cam hiere wot I noght,"
Quod sche, "bot wel I am bethoght
Of othre thinges al aboute":
Fro point to point and tolde him oute

Als ferforthli as sche it wiste.
1230 And he hire tolde hou in a kiste   [chest]
    The See hire threw upon the lond,
    And what tresor with hire he fond,
    Which was al redy at hire wille,
    As he that schop him to fulfille   [prepared himself]
    With al his myht what thing he scholde.
    Sche thonketh him that he so wolde,
    And al hire herte sche discloseth,
    And seith him wel that sche supposeth
    Hire lord be dreint, hir child also;
1240 So sih sche noght bot alle wo.
    Wherof as to the world nomore
    Ne wol sche torne, and preith therfore
    That in som temple of the Cite,
    To kepe and holde hir chastete,
    Sche mihte among the wommen duelle.
    Whan he this tale hir herde telle,
    He was riht glad, and made hire knowen
    That he a dowhter of his owen
    Hath, which he wol unto hir yive
1250 To serve, whil thei bothe live,
    In stede of that which sche hath lost;
    Al only at his oghne cost
    Sche schal be rendred forth with hire.   [delivered]
    She seith, "Grant mercy, lieve sire,   [dear]
    God quite it you, ther I ne may."
    And thus thei drive forth the day,
    Til time com that sche was hol;
    And tho thei take her conseil hol,
    To schape upon good ordinance
1260 And make a worthi pourveance
    Ayein the day whan thei be veiled.
    And thus, whan that thei be conseiled,
    In blake clothes thei hem clothe,
    This lady and the dowhter bothe,

And yolde hem to religion.
The feste and the profession
After the reule of that degre
Was mad with gret solempnete,
Where as Diane is seintefied;
1270 Thus stant this lady justefied
In ordre wher sche thenkth to duelle.
  Bot now ayeinward forto telle
In what plit that hire lord stod inne:
He seileth, til that he may winne
The havene of Tharse, as I seide er;
And whanne he was aryved ther,
And it was thurgh the Cite knowe,
Men myhte se withinne a throwe,
As who seith, al the toun at ones,
1280 That come ayein him for the nones,
To yiven him the reverence,
So glad thei were of his presence:
And thogh he were in his corage
Desesed, yit with glad visage
He made hem chiere, and to his In,
Wher he whilom sojourned in,
He goth him straght and was resceived.
And whan the presse of poeple is weived,
He takth his hoste unto him tho,
1290 And seith, "Mi frend Strangulio,
Lo, thus and thus it is befalle,
And thou thiself art on of alle,
Forth with thi wif, whiche I most triste.
Forthi, if it you bothe liste,
My doghter Thaise be youre leve
I thenke schal with you beleve
As for a time; and thus I preie,
That sche be kept be alle weie,
And whan sche hath of age more,
1300 That sche be set to bokes lore.

And this avou to god I make,
That I schal nevere for hir sake
Mi berd for no likinge schave,
Til it befalle that I have
In covenable time of age
Beset hire unto mariage."
Thus thei acorde, and al is wel,
And forto resten him somdel,
As for a while he ther sojorneth,
1310 And thanne he takth his leve and torneth
To Schipe, and goth him hom to Tyr,
Wher every man with gret desir
Awaiteth upon his comynge.
Bot whan the Schip com in seilinge,
And thei perceiven it is he,
Was nevere yit in no cite
Such joie mad as thei tho made;
His herte also began to glade
Of that he sih the poeple glad.
1320 Lo, thus fortune his hap hath lad;
In sondri wise he was travailed,
Bot hou so evere he be assailed,
His latere ende schal be good.
        And forto speke hou that it stod
Of Thaise his doghter, wher sche duelleth,
In Tharse, as the Cronique telleth,
Sche was wel kept, sche was wel loked,
Sche was wel tawht, sche was wel boked,
So wel sche spedde hir in hire youthe
1330 That sche of every wisdom couthe,
That forto seche in every lond
So wys an other noman fond,
Ne so wel tawht at mannes yhe.
Bot wo worthe evere fals envie!
For it befell that time so,
A dowhter hath Strangulio,

The which was cleped Philotenne:
Bot fame, which wole evere renne,
Cam al day to hir moder Ere,
1340 And seith, wher evere hir doghter were
With Thayse set in eny place,
The comun vois, the comun grace
Was al upon that other Maide,
And of hir doghter noman saide.
Who wroth but Dionise thanne?
Hire thoghte a thousend yer til whanne
Sche myhte ben of Thaise wreke   [avenged]
Of that sche herde folk so speke.
And fell that ilke same tyde,
1350 That ded was trewe Lychoride,
Which hadde be servant to Thaise,
So that sche was the worse at aise,   [ease]
For sche hath thanne no servise
Bot only thurgh his Dionise,
Which was hire dedlich Anemie
Thurgh pure treson and envie.
Sche, that of alle sorwe can,
Tho spak unto hire bondeman,
Which cleped was Theophilus,
1360 And made him swere in conseil thus,
That he such time as sche him sette
Schal come Thaise forto fette,
And lede hire oute of alle sihte,
Wher as noman hire helpe myhte,
Upon the Stronde nyh the See,
And there he schal this maiden sle.
This cherles herte is in a traunce,
As he which drad him of vengance
Whan time comth an other day;
1370 Bot yit dorste he noght seie nay,
Bot swor and seide he schal fulfille

Hire hestes at hire oghne wille.
    The treson and the time is schape,
So fell it that this cherles knape   [knave]
Hath lad this maiden ther he wolde
Upon the Stronde, and what sche scholde
Sche was adrad; and he out breide   [drew]
A rusti swerd and to hir seide,
"Thou schalt be ded." "Helas!" quod sche,
1380 "Why schal I so?" "Lo thus," quod he,
"Mi ladi Dionise hath bede,
Thou schalt be moerdred in this stede."   [place]
This Maiden tho for feere schryhte,   [shrieked]
And for the love of god almyhte
Sche preith that for a litel stounde
Sche myhte knele upon the grounde,
Toward the hevene forto crave,
Hire wofull Soule if sche mai save:
And with this noise and with this cry,
1390 Out of a barge faste by,
Which hidd was ther on Scomerfare,   [piracy]
Men sterten out and weren ware
Of this feloun, and he to go,
And sche began to crie tho,
"Ha, mercy, help for goddes sake!"
Into the barge thei hire take,
As thieves scholde, and forth thei wente.
Upon the See the wynd hem hente,
And malgre wher thei wolde or non,
1400 Tofor the weder forth thei gon,
Ther halp no Seil, ther halp non Ore,
Forstormed and forblowen sore
In gret peril so forth thei dryve,
Til ate laste thei aryve
At Mitelene the Cite.
In havene sauf and whan thei be,

The Maister Schipman made him boun,   [ready]
And goth him out into the toun,
And profreth Thaise forto selle.
1410 On Leonin it herde telle,
Which Maister of the bordel was,
And bad him gon a redy pas
To fetten hire, and forth he wente,
And Thaise out of his barge he hente,
And to this bordeller hir solde.
And he, that be hire body wolde
Take avantage, let do crye,
That what man wolde his lecherie
Attempte upon hire maidenhede,
1420 Lei doun the gold and he schal spede.
And thus whan he hath crid it oute
In syhte of al the poeple aboute,
He ladde hire to the bordel tho.
    No wonder is thogh sche be wo:
Clos in a chambre be hireselve,
Ech after other ten or tuelve
Of yonge men to hire in wente;
Bot such a grace god hire sente,
That for the sorwe which sche made
1430 Was non of hem which pouer hade
To don hire eny vileinie.
This Leonin let evere aspie,
And waiteth after gret beyete;
Bot al for noght, sche was forlete,
That mo men wolde ther noght come.
Whan he therof hath hiede nome,
And knew that sche was yit a maide,
Unto his oghne man he saide,
That he with strengthe ayein hire leve
1440 Tho scholde hir maidenhod bereve.
This man goth in, bot so it ferde
Whan he hire wofull pleintes herde

And he therof hath take kepe,
Him liste betre forto wepe
Than don oght elles to the game.
And thus sche kepte hirself fro schame,
And kneleth doun to therthe and preide
Unto this man, and thus sche seide:
"If so be that thi maister wolde
1450 That I his gold encresce scholde,
It mai noght falle be this weie:
Bot soffre me to go mi weie
Out of this hous wher I am inne,
And I schal make him forto winne
In som place elles of the toun,
Be so it be religioun,
Wher that honeste wommen duelle.
And thus thou myht thi maister telle,
That whanne I have a chambre there,
1460 Let him do crie ay wyde where,
What lord that hath his doghter diere,
And is in will that sche schal liere
Of such a Scole that is trewe,
I schal hire teche of thinges newe,
Which as non other womman can
In al this lond." And tho this man
Hire tale hath herd, he goth ayein,
And tolde unto his maister plein
That sche hath seid; and therupon,
1470 Whan than he sih beyete non   [gain]
At the bordel be cause of hire,
He bad his man to gon and spire   [inquire for]
A place wher sche myhte abyde,
That he mai winne upon som side
Be that sche can: bot ate leste
Thus was sche sauf fro this tempeste.
　　He hath hire fro the bordel take,
Bot that was noght for goddes sake,

Bot for the lucre, as sche him tolde.
1480 Now comen tho that comen wolde
Of wommen in her lusty youthe,
To hiere and se what thing sche couthe:
Sche can the wisdom of a clerk,
Sche can of every lusti werk
Which to a gentil womman longeth,
And some of hem sche underfongeth
To the Citole and to the Harpe,
And whom it liketh forto carpe
Proverbes and demandes slyhe,
1490 An other such thei nevere syhe,
Which that science so wel tawhte:
Wherof sche grete yiftes cawhte,
That sche to Leonin hath wonne;
And thus hire name is so begonne
Of sondri thinges that she techeth,
That al the lond unto hir secheth
Of yonge wommen forto liere.

Nou lete we this maiden hiere,
And speke of Dionise ayein
1500 And of Theophile the vilein,
Of whiche I spak of nou tofore.
Whan Thaise scholde have be forlore,
This false cherl to his lady
Whan he cam hom, al prively
He seith, "Ma Dame, slain I have
This maide Thaise, and is begrave
In prive place, as ye me biede.   [commanded]
Forthi, ma dame, taketh hiede
And kep conseil, hou so it stonde."
1510 This fend, which this hath understonde,
Was glad, and weneth it be soth:
Now herkne, hierafter hou sche doth.
Sche wepth, sche sorweth, sche
     compleigneth,

And of sieknesse which sche feigneth
Sche seith that Taise sodeinly
Be nyhte is ded, "as sche and I
Togedre lyhen nyh my lord."
Sche was a womman of record, [note]
And al is lieved that sche seith; [believed]
1520 And forto yive a more feith,
Hire housebonde and ek sche bothe
In blake clothes thei hem clothe,
And made a gret enterrement;
And for the poeple schal be blent, [blinded]
Of Thaise as for the remembrance,
After the real olde usance [royal]
A tumbe of latoun noble and riche
With an ymage unto hir liche [body]
Liggende above therupon
1530 Thei made and sette it up anon.
Hire Epitaffe of good assisse
Was write aboute, and in this wise
It spak: "O yee that this beholde,
Lo, hier lith sche, the which was holde
The faireste and the flour of alle,
Whos name Thaïsis men calle.
The king of Tyr Appolinus
Hire fader was: now lith sche thus.
Fourtiene yer sche was of Age,
1540 Whan deth hir tok to his viage." [journey]
          Thus was this false treson hidd,
Which afterward was wyde kidd, [known]
As be the tale a man schal hiere.
Bot forto clare mi matiere, [declare]
To Try I thenke torne ayein,
And telle as the Croniqes sein.
Whan that the king was comen hom,
And hath left in the salte fom
His wif, which he mai noght foryete,

1550 For he som cónfort wolde gete,
 He let somoune a parlement,
 To which the lordes were asent;   [summoned]
 And of the time he hath ben oute,
 He seth the thinges al aboute,
 And told hem ek hou he hath fare,
 Whil he was out of londe fare;
 And preide hem alle to abyde,
 For he wolde at the same tyde
 Do schape for his wyves mynde,   [memory]
1560 As he that wol noght ben unkinde.
 Solempne was that ilke office,
 And riche was the sacrifice,
 The feste reali was holde: [royally]
 And therto was he wel beholde;
 For such a wif as he hadde on
 In thilke daies was ther non.
   Whan this was do, thanne he him thoghte
 Upon his doghter, and besoghte
 Suche of his lordes as he wolde,
1570 That thei with him to Tharse scholde,
 To fette his doghter Taise there:
 And thei anon al redy were,
 To schip they gon and forth thei wente,
 Til thei the havene of Tharse hente.
 They londe and faile of that thei seche
 Be coverture and sleyhte of speche:
 This false man Strangulio,
 And Dionise his wif also,
 That he the betre trowe myhte,   [believe (trust)]
1580 Thei ladden him to have a sihte
 Wher that hir tombe was arraied.
 The lasse yit he was mispaied,   [displeased]
 And natheles, so as he dorste,
 He curseth and seith al the worste
 Unto fortune, as to the blinde,

Which can no seker weie finde:
For sche him neweth evere among,
And medleth sorwe with his song.
Bot sithe it mai no betre be,
1590   He thonketh god and forth goth he
Seilende toward Tyr ayein.
Bot sodeinly the wynd and reyn
Begonne upon the See debate,
So that he soffre mot algate
The lawe which Neptune ordeigneth;
Wherof fulofte time he pleigneth,
And hield him wel the more esmaied   [dismayed]
Of that he hath tofore assaied.   [endured]
So that for pure sorwe and care,
1600 Of that he seth his world so fare,
The reste he lefte of his Caban,
That for the conseil of noman
Ayein therinne he nolde come,
Bot hath benethe his place nome,
Wher he wepende al one lay,
Ther as he sih no lyht of day.
And thus tofor the wynd thei dryve,
Til longe and late thei aryve
With gret distresce, as it was sene,
1610 Upon this toun of Mitelene,
Which was a noble cite tho.
And hapneth thilke time so,
The lordes bothe and the comune
The hihe festes of Neptune
Upon the stronde at the rivage,
As it was custumme and usage,
Sollempneliche thei besihe.   [attended to]
    When thei this strange vessel syhe
Come in, and hath his Seil avaled,   [lowered]
1620 The toun therof hath spoke and taled.
The lord which of the cite was,

Whos name is Athenagoras,
Was there, and seide he wolde se
What Schip it is, and who thei be
That ben therinne: and after sone,
Whan that he sih it was to done,
His barge was for him arraied,
And he goth forth and hath assaied.
He fond the Schip of gret Array,
1630 Bot what thing it amonte may,
He seth thei maden hevy chiere,
Bot wel him thenkth be the manere
That thei be worthi men of blod,
And axeth of hem hou it stod;
And thei him tellen al the cas,
Hou that here lord fordrive was   [desperately driven]
And what a sorwe that he made,
Of which ther mai noman him glade.
He preith that he here lord mai se,
1640 Bot thei him tolde it mai noght be,
For he lith in so derk a place,
That ther may no wiht sen his face:
Bot for al that, thogh hem be loth,
He fond the ladre and doun he goth,
And to him spak, bot non ansuere
Ayein of him ne mihte he bere
For oght that he can don or sein;
And thus he goth him up ayein.
        Tho was ther spoke in many wise
1650 Amonges hem that weren wise,
Now this, now that, bot ate laste
The wisdom of the toun this caste,
That yonge Taise were asent.
For if ther be amendement
To glade with this woful king,
Sche can so moche of every thing,
That sche schal gladen him anon.

A Messager for hire is gon,
And sche cam with hire Harpe on honde,
1660 And seide hem that sche wolde fonde
Be alle weies that sche can,
To glade with this sory man.
Bot what he was sche wiste noght,
Bot al the Schip hire hath besoght
That sche hire wit on him despende,
In aunter if he myhte amende,
And sein it schal be wel aquit.
Whan sche hath understonden it,
Sche goth hir doun, ther as he lay,
1670 Wher that sche harpeth many a lay
And lich an Angel sang withal;
Bot he nomore than the wal
Tok hiede of eny thing he herde.
And whan sche sih that he so ferde,
Sche falleth with him into wordes,
And telleth him of sondri bordes,   [tales]
And axeth him demandes strange,
Wherof sche made his herte change,
And to hire speche his Ere he leide
1680 And hath merveile of that sche seide.
For in proverbe and in probleme
Sche spak, and bad he scholde deme
In many soubtil question:
Bot he for no suggestioun
Which toward him sche couthe stere,
He wolde noght o word ansuere,
Bot as a madd man ate laste
His heved wepende awey he caste,
And half in wraththe he bad hire go.
1690 Bot yit sche wolde noght do so,
And in the derke forth sche goth,
Til sche him toucheth, and he wroth,
And after hire with his hond

He smot: and thus whan sche him fond
Desesed, courtaisly sche saide,
"Avoi, mi lord, I am a Maide;
And if ye wiste what I am,
And out of what lignage I cam,
Ye wolde noght be so salvage."
1700   With that he sobreth his corage
And put awey his hevy chiere.
Bot of hem tuo a man mai liere
What is to be so sibb of blod:
Non wiste of other hou it stod,
And yit the fader ate laste
His herte upon this maide caste,
That he hire loveth kindly,
And yit he wiste nevere why.
Bot al was knowe er that thei wente;
1710 For god, which wot here hol entente,   [their]
Here hertes bothe anon descloseth.
This king unto this maide opposeth,
And axeth ferst what was hire name,
And wher sche lerned al this game,
And of what ken that sche was come.   [kin]
And sche, that hath hise wordes nome,
Ansuerth and seith, "My name is Thaise,
That was som time wel at aise:
In Tharse I was forthdrawe and fed,
1720 Ther lerned I, til I was sped,
Of that I can. Mi fader eke
I not wher that I scholde him seke;
He was a king, men tolde me:
Mi Moder dreint was in the See."
Fro point to point al sche him tolde,
That sche hath longe in herte holde,
And nevere dorste make hir mone
Bot only to this lord al one,
To whom hire herte can noght hele,   [conceal]

1730 Torne it to wo, torne it to wele,
    Torne it to good, torne it to harm.
    And he tho toke hire in his arm,
    Bot such a joie as he tho made
    Was nevere sen; thus be thei glade,
    That sory hadden be toforn.
    For this day forth fortune hath sworn
    To sette him upward on the whiel;
    So goth the world, now wo, now wel:
    This king hath founde newe grace,
1740 So that out of his derke place
    He goth him up into the liht,
    And with him cam that swete wiht,
    His doghter Thaise, and forth anon
    Thei bothe into the Caban gon
    Which was ordeigned for the king,
    And ther he dede of al his thing,   [put off]
    And was arraied realy.
       And out he cam al openly,
    Wher Athenagoras he fond,
1750 The which was lord of al the lond:
    He preith the king to come and se
    His castell bothe and his cite,
    And thus thei gon forth alle in fiere,   [all together]
    This king, this lord, this maiden diere.
    This lord tho made hem riche feste
    With every thing which was honeste,
    To plese with this worthi king,
    Ther lacketh him no maner thing:
    Bot yit for al his noble array
1760 Wifles he was into that day,
    As he that yit was of yong Age;
    So fell ther into his corage
    The lusti wo, the glade peine
    Of love, which noman restreigne
    Yit nevere myhte as nou tofore.

This lord thenkth al his world forlore,
Bot if the king wol don him grace;
He waiteth time, he waiteth place,
Him thoghte his herte wol tobreke,
1770 Til he mai to this maide speke
And to hir fader ek also
For mariage: and it fell so,
That al was do riht as he thoghte,
His pourpos to an ende he broghte,
Sche weddeth him as for hire lord;
Thus be thei alle of on acord.
    Whan al was do riht as thei wolde,
The king unto his Sone tolde
Of Tharse thilke traiterie,
1780 And seide hou in his compaignie
His doghter and himselven eke
Schull go vengance forto seke.
The Schipes were redy sone,
And whan thei sihe it was to done,
Withoute lette of eny wente
With Seil updrawe forth thei wente
Towardes Tharse upon the tyde.
Bot he that wot what schal betide,
The hihe god, which wolde him kepe,
1790 Whan that this king was faste aslepe,
Be nyhtes time he hath him bede
To seile into an other stede:
To Ephesim he bad him drawe,
And as it was that time lawe,
He schal do there his sacrifise;
And ek he bad in alle wise
That in the temple amonges alle
His fortune, as it is befalle,
Touchende his doghter and his wif
1800 He schal beknowe upon his lif.
The king of this Avisioun

Hath gret ymaginacioun,
What thing it signefie may;
And natheles, whan it is day,
He bad caste Ancher and abod;
And whil that he on Ancher rod,
The wynd, which was tofore strange,
Upon the point began to change,
And torneth thider as it scholde.
1810 Tho knew he wel that god it wolde,
And bad the Maister make him yare,
Tofor the wynd for he wol fare
To Ephesim, and so he dede.
And whanne he cam unto the stede
Where as he scholde londe, he londeth
With al the haste he may, and fondeth
To schapen him be such a wise,
That he may be the morwe arise
And don after the mandement
1820 Of him which hath him thider sent.
And in the wise that he thoghte,
Upon the morwe so he wroghte;
His doghter and his Sone he nom,
And forth unto the temple he com
With a gret route in compaignie,
Hise yiftes forto sacrifie.
The citezeins tho herden seie
Of such a king that cam to preie
Unto Diane the godesse,
1830 And left al other besinesse,
Thei comen thider forto se
The king and the solempnete.
    With worthi knyhtes environed
The king himself hath abandoned
Into the temple in good entente.
The dore is up, and he in wente,
Wher as with gret devocioun

Of holi contemplacioun
Withinne his herte he made his schrifte;
1840   And after that a riche yifte
He offreth with gret reverence,
And there in open Audience
Of hem that stoden thanne aboute,
He tolde hem and declareth oute
His hap, such as him is befalle,
Ther was nothing foryete of alle.
His wif, as it was goddes grace,
Which was professed in the place,
As sche that was Abbesse there,
1850   Unto his tale hath leid hire Ere:
Sche knew the vois and the visage,
For pure joie as in a rage
Sche strawhte unto him al at ones,
And fell aswoune upon the stones,
Wherof the temple flor was paved.
Sche was anon with water laved,   [washed]
Til sche cam to hirself ayein,
And thanne sche began to sein:
"Ha, blessed be the hihe sonde,
1860   That I mai se myn housebonde,
That whilom he and I were on!"
The king with that knew hire anon,
And tok hire in his Arm and kiste;
And al the toun thus sone it wiste.
Tho was ther joie manyfold,
For every man this tale hath told
As for miracle, and were glade,
Bot nevere man such joie made
As doth the king, which hath his wif.
1870   And whan men herde hou that hir lif
Was saved, and be whom it was,
Thei wondren alle of such a cas:
Thurgh al the Lond aros the speche

Of Maister Cerymon the leche   [physician]
And of the cure which he dede.
The king himself tho hath him bede,
And ek this queene forth with him,
That he the toun of Ephesim
Wol leve and go wher as thei be,
1880 For nevere man of his degre
Hath do to hem so mochel good;
And he his profit understod,
And granteth with him forto wende.
And thus thei maden there an ende,
And token leve and gon to Schipe
With al the hole felaschipe.
    This king, which nou hath his desir,
Seith he wol holde his cours to Tyr.
Thei hadden wynd at wille tho,
1890 With topseilcole and forth they go,
And striken nevere, til thei come
To Tyr, where as thei havene nome,
And londen hem with mochel blisse.
Tho was ther many a mowth to kisse,
Echon welcometh other hom,
Bot whan the queen to londe com,
And Thaise hir doghter be hir side,
The joie which was thilke tyde
Ther mai no mannes tunge telle:
1900 Thei seiden alle, "Hier comth the welle
Of alle wommannysshe grace."
The king hath take his real place,
The queene is into chambre go:
Ther was gret feste arraied tho;
Whan time was, thei gon to mete,   [dinner]
Alle olde sorwes ben foryete,
And gladen hem with joies newe:
The descoloured pale hewe
Is now become a rody cheke,

1910 Ther was no merthe forto seke,
Bot every man hath that he wolde.
　　　The king, as he well couthe and scholde,
Makth to his poeple riht good chiere;
And after sone, as thou schalt hiere,
A parlement he hath sommoned,
Wher he his doghter hath coroned
Forth with the lord of Mitelene,
That on is king, that other queene:
And thus the fadres ordinance
1920 This lond hath set in governance,
And seide thanne he wolde wende
To Tharse, forto make an ende
Of that his doghter was betraied.
Therof were alle men wel paied,　　　　　[pleased]
And seide hou it was forto done:
The Schipes weren redi sone,
And strong pouer with him he tok;
Up to the Sky he caste his lok,
And syh the wynd was covenable.
1930　　　Thei hale up Ancher with the cable,
The Seil on hih, the Stiere in honde,
And seilen, til thei come alonde
At Tharse nyh to the cite;
And whan thei wisten it was he,
The toun hath don him reverence.
He telleth hem the violence,
Which the tretour Strangulio
And Dionise him hadde do
Touchende his dowhter, as yee herde;
1940 And whan thei wiste hou that it ferde,
As he which pes and love soghte,
Unto the toun this he besoghte,
To don him riht in juggement.
Anon thei were bothe asent
With strengthe of men, and comen sone,

And as hem thoghte it was to done,
Atteint thei were be the lawe   [convicted]
And diemed forto honge and drawe,
And brent and with the wynd toblowe,
1950 That al the world it myhte knowe:
And upon this condicion
The dom in execucion
Was put anon withoute faile.
And every man hath gret mervaile,
Which herde tellen of this chance,
And thonketh goddes pourveance,
Which doth mercy forth with justice.
Slain is the moerdrer and moerdrice
Thurgh verray trowthe of rihtwisnesse,
1960 And thurgh mercy sauf is simplesse
Of hire whom mercy preserveth;
Thus hath he wel that wel deserveth.
     Whan al this thing is don and ended,
This king, which loved was and frended,
A lettre hath, which cam to him
Be Schipe fro Pentapolim,
Be which the lond hath to him write,
That he wolde understonde and wite
Hou in good mynde and in good pes
1970 Ded is the king Artestrates,
Wherof thei alle of on acord
Him preiden, as here liege lord,
That he the lettre wel conceive
And come his regne to receive,
Which god hath yove him and fortune;
And thus besoghte the commune
Forth with the grete lordes alle.
This king sih how it was befalle,
Fro Tharse and in prosperite
1980 He tok his leve of that Cite
And goth him into Schipe ayein:

The wynd was good, the See was plein,
Hem nedeth noght a Riff to slake,
Til thei Pentapolim have take.
The lond, which herde of that tidinge,
Was wonder glad of his cominge;
He resteth him a day or tuo
And tok his conseil to him tho,
And sette a time of Parlement,
1990 Wher al the lond of on assent
Forth with his wif hath him corouned,
Wher alle goode him was fuisouned.   [provided in abundance]
Lo, what it is to be wel grounded:
For he hath ferst his love founded
Honesteliche as forto wedde,
Honesteliche his love he spedde
And hadde children with his wif
And as him liste he ladde his lif;
And in ensample his lif was write,
2000 That alle lovers myhten wite
How ate laste it schal be sene
Of love what thei wolden mene.
For se now on that other side,
Antiochus with al his Pride,
Which sette his love unkindely,
His ende he hadde al sodeinly,
Set ayein kinde upon vengance,
And for his lust hath his penance.

[And so we see that it is best to love properly. Although Fortune
is not stable, yet sometimes it is favorable to those who are true
in love. Love which is unnatural always brings sorrow. Love
should accord with reason; otherwise, it becomes bestial and dis-
honest (2009–2028). Amans thanks Genius for his instructions,
but still expresses uncertainty over what he should do. He is
reasonable in all things except his love and that is what bothers
him most. He has thought carefully how to beseech her love,

but with one syllable, no, she overthrows a thousand of his words. He asks Genius what he thinks he should do (2059). So Genius turns from his role as moral confessor to offer direct advice. Take love where it may not fail. The present course of Amans offers no profit and thus is unwise. The more a stock is burnt the more it turns to ashes; the toe which trips often sends the head flying. Love is blind and sees not where it is going. Heed good counsel, for it more than anything helps a king, and every man has a kingdom to justify and that is his own judgment. If he misrules that kingdom he misrules himself, and that is worse than loss of ship and oar. For a man who is not himself is less than a shell without pearls. Even if one ruled the whole world but possessed not himself, all would be vain. Therefore, before you fall beyond recovery, leave blind love, withdraw, and set your heart under the law of reason instead of will. Remember the examples you have heard (2060–2148).

Amans accuses Genius of treating his love as if it were a game. A man's health may not be likened to a hart. It is easy, he says, for Genius to make his pronouncements, because he is not the one afflicted. He does not feel what Amans feels. The deer which goes free knows nothing of the ox's labors. Amans asks Genius to be a good priest and present a supplication to Cupid and Venus and return with a good answer. He then describes a debate which arose between him and Genius.[2] His reason could follow Genius's argument, but his will is opposed. Never has a man been able to act under such circumstances. Love and Reason must be of one governance. Amans says that he finally spoke debonairly to Genius, made peace, and got him to agree to present his appeal, providing that it was in writing. So Amans sat upon a green, and full of love's fantasy wrote with tears instead of ink this complaint.]

The wofull peine of loves maladie,
Ayein the which mai no phisique availe,
Min herte hath so bewhaped with sotie,   [befuddled with folly]
2220 That wher so that I reste or I travaile,

I finde it evere redy to assaile
Mi resoun, which that can him noght de-
    fende:
Thus seche I help, wherof I mihte
    amende.

Ferst to Nature if that I me compleigne,
Ther finde I hou that every creature
Som time ayer hath love in his demeine,
So that the litel wrenne in his mesure
Hath yit of kinde a love under his cure;
And I bot on desire, of which I misse:
2230 And thus, bot I, hath every kinde his
    blisse.

The resoun of my wit it overpasseth,
Of that Nature techeth me the weie
To love, and yit no certein sche compasseth
Hou I schal spede, and thus betwen the
    tweie
I stonde, and not if I schal live or deie.   [know not whether]
For thogh reson ayein my will debate,
I mai noght fle, that I ne love algate.

Upon miself it thilke tale come,
Hou whilom Pan, which is the god of
    kinde,
2240 With love wrastlede and was overcome:
For evere I wrastle and evere I am behinde,
That I no strengthe in al min herte finde,
Wherof that I mai stonden eny throwe;
So fer mi wit with love is overthrowe.

Whom nedeth help, he mot his helpe
    crave,
Or helpeles he schal his nede spille:

Pleinly thurghsoght my wittes alle I have,
Bot non of hem can helpe after mi wille;
And als so wel I mihte sitte stille,
2250 As preie unto mi lady eny helpe:
Thus wot I noght wherof miself to helpe.

Unto the grete Jove and if I bidde,
To do me grace of thilke swete tunne,
Which under keie in his celier amidde
Lith couched, that fortune is overrunne,
Bot of the bitter cuppe I have begunne,
I not hou ofte, and thus finde I no game;
For evere I axe and evere it is the same.

I se the world stonde evere upon eschange,
2260 Nou wyndes loude, and nou the weder
        softe;
I mai sen ek the grete mone change,   [moon]
And thing which nou is lowe is eft alofte;
The dredfull werres into pes fulofte
Thei torne; and evere is Danger in o place,
Which wol noght change his will to do
        me grace.

Bot upon this the grete clerc Ovide,
Of love whan he makth his remembrance,
He seith ther is the blinde god Cupide,
The which hath love under his govern-
        ance,
2270 And in his hond with many a fyri lance
He woundeth ofte, ther he wol noght hele;
And that somdiel is cause of mi querele.

Ovide ek seith that love to parforne
Stant in the hond of Venus the goddesse,
Bot whan sche takth hir conseil with Sat-
        orne,

Ther is no grace, and in that time, I gesse,
Began mi love, of which myn hevynesse
Is now and evere schal, bot if I spede:
So wot I noght miself what is to rede.

2280　Forthi to you, Cupide and Venus bothe,
With al myn hertes obeissance I preie,
If ye were ate ferste time wrothe,
Whan I began to love, as I you seie,
Nou stynt, and do thilke infortune aweie,
So that Danger, which stant of retenue
With my ladi, his place mai remue.

O thou Cupide, god of loves lawe,
That with thi Dart brennende hast set
　　　afyre
Min herte, do that wounde be withdrawe,
2290　Or yif me Salve such as I desire:
For Service in thi Court withouten hyre
To me, which evere yit have kept thin
　　　heste,
Mai nevere be to loves lawe honeste.

O thou, gentile Venus, loves queene,
Withoute gult thou dost on me thi wreche;
Thou wost my peine is evere aliche grene
For love, and yit I mai it noght areche:
This wold I for my laste word beseche,
That thou mi love aquite as I deserve,
2300　Or elles do me pleinly forto sterve.

Whanne I this Supplicacioun
With good deliberacioun,
In such a wise as ye nou wite,
Hadde after min entente write
Unto Cupide and to Venus,

This Prest which hihte Genius
It tok on honde to presente,
On my message and forth he wente
To Venus, forto wite hire wille.
2310 And I bod in the place stille,
And was there bot a litel while,
Noght full the montance of a Mile,
Whan I behield and sodeinly
I sih wher Venus stod me by.
So as I myhte, under a tre
To grounde I fell upon mi kne,
And preide hire forto do me grace:
Sche caste hire chiere upon mi face,
And as it were halvinge a game
2320 Sche axeth me what is mi name.
"Ma dame," I seide, "John Gower."
"Now John," quod sche, "in my pouer
Thou most as of thi love stonde;
For I thi bille have understonde,
In which to Cupide and to me
Somdiel thou hast compleigned thee,
And somdiel to Nature also.
Bot that schal stonde among you tuo,
For therof have I noght to done;
2330 For Nature is under the Mone
Maistresse of every lives kinde,
Bot if so be that sche mai finde
Som holy man that wol withdrawe
His kindly lust ayein hir lawe;
Bot sielde whanne it falleth so,
For fewe men ther ben of tho,
Bot of these othre ynowe be,
Whiche of here oghne nycete
Ayein Nature and hire office
2340 Deliten hem in sondri vice,
Wherof that sche fulofte hath pleigned,

And ek my Court it hath desdeigned
And evere schal; for it receiveth
Non such that kinde so deceiveth.
For al onliche of gentil love
Mi court stant alle courtz above
And takth noght into retenue
Bot thing which is to kinde due,
For elles it schal be refused.
2350 Wherof I holde thee excused,
For it is manye daies gon,
That thou amonges hem were on
Which of my court hast ben withholde;
So that the more I am beholde
Of thi desese to commune,
And to remue that fortune,
Which manye daies hath the grieved.
Bot if my conseil mai be lieved,
Thou schalt ben esed er thou go
2360 Of thilke unsely jolif wo,
Wherof thou seist thin herte is fyred:
Bot as of that thou hast desired
After the sentence of thi bille,
Thou most therof don at my wille,
And I therof me wole avise.
For be thou hol, it schal suffise:
Mi medicine is noght to sieke
For thee and for suche olde sieke,
Noght al per chance as ye it wolden,
2370 Bot so as ye be reson scholden,
Acordant unto loves kinde.
For in the plit which I thee finde,
So as mi court it hath awarded,
Thou schalt be duely rewarded;
And if thou woldest more crave,
It is no riht that thou it have."

Venus, which stant withoute lawe[3]
In noncertein, bot as men drawe
Of Rageman upon the chance,[4]
2380 Sche leith no peis in the balance,   [weight]
Bot as hir lyketh forto weie;
The trewe man fulofte aweie
Sche put, which hath hir grace bede,
And set an untrewe in his stede.
Lo, thus blindly the world sche diemeth
In loves cause, as tome siemeth:
I not what othre men wol sein,
Bot I algate am so besein,
And stonde as on amonges alle
2390 Which am out of hir grace falle:
It nedeth take no witnesse,
For sche which seid is the goddesse,
To whether part of love it wende,
Hath sett me for a final ende
The point wherto that I schal holde.
For whan sche hath me wel beholde,
Halvynge of scorn, sche seide thus:
"Thou wost wel that I am Venus,
Which al only my lustes seche;
2400 And wel I wot, thogh thou beseche
Mi love, lustes ben ther none,
Whiche I mai take in thi persone;
For loves lust and lockes hore
In chambre acorden neveremore,
And thogh thou feigne a yong corage,
It scheweth wel be the visage
That olde grisel is no fole: [old gray nag/foal]
There ben fulmanye yeres stole
With thee and with suche othre mo,
2410 That outward feignen youthe so
And ben withinne of pore assay.

Min herte wolde and I ne may
Is noght beloved nou adayes;
Er thou make eny suche assaies
To love, and faile upon the fet,
Betre is to make a beau retret;
For thogh thou myhtest love atteigne,
Yit were it bot an ydel peine,
Whan that thou art noght sufficant
2420 To holde love his covenant.
Forthi tak hom thin herte ayein,
That thou travaile noght in vein,
Wherof my Court may be deceived.
I wot and have it wel conceived,
Hou that thi will is good ynowh;
Bot mor behoveth to the plowh,
Wherof the lacketh, as I trowe:
So sitte it wel that thou beknowe
Thi fieble astat, er thou beginne
2430 Thing wher thou miht non ende winne.
What bargain scholde a man assaie,
Whan that him lacketh forto paie?
Mi Sone, if thou be well bethoght,
This toucheth thee; foryet it noght:
The thing is torned into was;
That which was whilom grene gras,
Is welked hey at time now.   [sun-dried hay]
Forthi mi conseil is that thou
Remembre wel hou thou art old."
2440   Whan Venus hath hir tale told,
And I bethoght was al aboute,
Tho wiste I wel withoute doute,
That ther was no recoverir;
And as a man the blase of fyr
With water quencheth, so ferd I;
A cold me cawhte sodeinly,
For sorwe that myn herte made

Mi dedly face pale and fade
Becam, and swoune I fell to grounde.
2450 And as I lay the same stounde, [time]
Ne fully quik ne fully ded,
Me thoghte I sih tofor myn hed
Cupide with his bowe bent,
And lich unto a Parlement,
Which were ordeigned for the nones,
With him cam al the world at ones
Of gentil folk that whilom were
Lovers, I sih hem alle there
Forth with Cupide in sondri routes.
2460 Min yhe and as I caste aboutes,
To knowe among hem who was who,
   I sih wher lusty Youthe tho,
As he which was a Capitein,
Tofore alle othre upon the plein
Stod with his route wel begon,
Here hevedes kempt, and therupon
Garlandes noght of o colour,
Some of the lef, some of the flour,
And some of grete Perles were;
2470 The newe guise of Beawme there,[5] [Bohemia]
With sondri thinges wel devised,
I sih, wherof thei ben queintised.
It was al lust that thei with ferde,
Ther was no song that I ne herde,
Which unto love was touchende;
Of Pan and al that was likende
As in Pipinge of melodie
Was herd in thilke compaignie
So lowde, that on every side
2480 It thoghte as al the hevene cride
In such acord and such a soun
Of bombard and of clarion
With Cornemuse and Schallemele, [bagpipe/shawm]

That it was half a mannes hele   [health]
So glad a noise forto hiere.
And as me thoghte, in this manere
Al freissh I syh hem springe and dance,
And do to love her entendance
After the lust of youthes heste.
2490 Ther was ynowh of joie and feste,
For evere among thei laghe and pleie,
And putten care out of the weie,
That he with hem ne sat ne stod.
And overthis I understod,
So as myn Ere it myhte areche,
The moste matiere of her speche
Was al of knyhthod and of Armes,
And what it is to ligge in armes
With love, whanne it is achieved.
2500   Ther was Tristram, which was believed
With bele Ysolde, and Lancelot
Stod with Gunnore, and Galahot
With his ladi, and as me thoghte,
I syh wher Jason with him broghte
His love, which that Creusa hihte,
And Hercules, which mochel myhte,
Was ther berende his grete Mace,
And most of alle in thilke place
He peyneth him to make chiere
2510 With Eolen, which was him diere.
    Theseüs, thogh he were untrewe
To love, as alle wommen knewe,
Yit was he there natheles
With Phedra, whom to love he ches:
Of Grece ek ther was Thelamon,
Which fro the king Lamenedon
At Troie his doghter refte aweie,
Eseonen, as for his preie,
Which take was whan Jason cam

2520 Fro Colchos, and the Cite nam
In vengance of the ferste hate;
That made hem after to debate,
Whan Priamus the newe toun
Hath mad. And in avisioun
  Me thoghte that I sih also
Ector forth with his brethren tuo;
Himself stod with Pantaselee,
And next to him I myhte se,
Wher Paris stod with faire Eleine,
2530 Which was his joie sovereine;
And Troilus stod with Criseïde,
Bot evere among, althogh he pleide,
Be semblant he was hevy chiered,
For Diomede, as him was liered,   [taught]
Cleymeth to ben his parconner.   [partner]
And thus full many a bacheler,
A thousend mo than I can sein,
With Yowthe I sih ther wel besein
Forth with here loves glade and blithe.
2540   And some I sih whiche ofte sithe
Compleignen hem in other wise;
Among the whiche I sih Narcise
And Piramus, that sory were.
The worthy Grek also was there,
Achilles, which for love deide:
Agamenon ek, as men seide,
And Menelay the king also
I syh, with many an other mo,
Which hadde be fortuned sore
In loves cause.
2550   And overmore
Of wommen in the same cas,
With hem I sih wher Dido was,
Forsake which was with Enee;
And Phillis ek I myhte see,

Whom Demephon deceived hadde;
And Adriagne hir sorwe ladde,
For Theseüs hir Soster tok
And hire unkindely forsok.
I sih ther ek among the press
2560 Compleignende upon Hercules
His ferste love Deyanire,
Which sette him afterward afyre:
Medea was there ek and pleigneth
Upon Jason, for that he feigneth,
Withoute cause and tok a newe;
Sche seide, "Fy on alle untrewe!"
I sih there ek Deÿdamie,
Which hadde lost the compaignie
Of Achilles, whan Diomede
2570 To Troie him fette upon the nede.
  Among these othre upon the grene
I syh also the wofull queene
Cleopatras, which in a Cave
With Serpentz hath hirself begrave
Alquik, and so sche was totore,
For sorwe of that sche hadde lore
Antonye, which hir love hath be:
And forth with hire I sih Tisbee,
Which on the scharpe swerdes point
2580 For love deide in sory point;
And as myn Ere it myhte knowe,
She seide, "Wo worthe alle slowe!"
The pleignte of Progne and Philomene
Ther herde I what it wolde mene,
How Tereüs of his untrouthe
Undede hem bothe, and that was routhe;
And next to hem I sih Canace,
Which for Machaire hir fader grace
Hath lost, and deide in wofull plit.
2590 And as I sih in my spirit,

Me thoghte amonges othre thus
The doghter of king Priamus,
Polixena, whom Pirrus slowh,
Was there and made sorwe ynowh,
As sche which deide gulteles
For love, and yit was loveles.
  And forto take the desport,
I sih there some of other port,
And that was Circes and Calipse,
2600 That cowthen do the Mone eclipse,
Of men and change the liknesses,
Of Artmagique Sorceresses;
Thei hielde in honde manyon,
To love wher thei wolde or non.
  Bot above alle that ther were
Of wommen I sih foure there,
Whos name I herde most comended:
Be hem the Court stod al amended;
For wher thei comen in presence,
2610 Men deden hem the reverence,
As thogh they hadden be goddesses,
Of al this world or Emperesses.
And as me thoghte, an Ere I leide,
And herde hou that these othre seide,
"Lo, these ben the foure wyves,
Whos feith was proeved in her lyves:
For in essample of alle goode
With Mariage so thei stode,
That fame, which no gret thing hydeth,
2620 Yit in Cronique of hem abydeth."
  Penolope that on was hote,
Whom many a knyht hath loved hote,
Whil that hire lord Ulixes lay
Full many a yer and many a day
Upon the grete Siege of Troie:
Bot sche, which hath no worldes joie

Bot only of hire housebonde,
Whil that hir lord was out of londe,
So wel hath kept hir wommanhiede,
2630 That al the world therof tok hiede,
And nameliche of hem in Grece.

That other womman was Lucrece,
Wif to the Romain Collatin;
And sche constreigned of Tarquin
To thing which was ayein hir wille,
Sche wolde noght hirselven stille,
Bot deide only for drede of schame
In keping of hire goode name,
As sche which was on of the beste.
2640 The thridde wif was hote Alceste,
Which whanne Ametus scholde dye
Upon his grete maladye,
Sche preide unto the goddes so,
That sche receyveth al the wo
And deide hirself to yive him lif:
Lo, if this were a noble wif.

The ferthe wif which I ther sih,
I herde of hem that were nyh
Hou sche was cleped Alcione,
2650 Which to Seyix hir lord al one
And to nomo hir body kepte;
And whan sche sih him dreynt, sche lepte
Into the wawes where he swam,
And there a Sefoul sche becam,
And with hire wenges him bespradde
For love which to him sche hadde.

Lo, these foure were tho
Whiche I sih, as me thoghte tho,
Among the grete compaignie
2660 Which Love hadde forto guye:
Bot Youthe, which in special
Of Loves Court was Mareschal,

So besy was upon his lay,
That he non hiede where I lay
Hath take. And thanne, as I behield,
Me thoghte I sih upon the field,
Where Elde cam a softe pas
Toward Venus, ther as sche was.
With him gret compaignie he ladde,
2670 Bot noght so manye as Youthe hadde:
The moste part were of gret Age,
And that was sene in the visage,
And noght forthi, so as thei myhte,
Thei made hem yongly to the sihte:
Bot yit herde I no pipe there
To make noise in mannes Ere,
Bot the Musette I myhte knowe,
For olde men which souneth lowe,
With Harpe and Lute and with Citole.
2680 The hovedance and the Carole,
In such a wise as love hath bede,
A softe pas thei dance and trede;
And with the wommen otherwhile
With sobre chier among thei smyle,
For laghtre was ther non on hyh.
And natheles full wel I syh
That thei the more queinte it made
For love, in whom thei weren glade.
        And there me thoghte I myhte se
2690 The king David with Bersabee,
And Salomon was noght withoute;
Passende an hundred on a route
Of wyves and of Concubines,
Juesses bothe and Sarazines,
To him I sih alle entendant:
I not if he was sufficant,
Bot natheles for al his wit
He was attached with that writ

Which love with his hond enseleth,
2700 Fro whom non erthly man appeleth.
And overthis, as for a wonder,
With his leon which he put under,
With Dalida Sampson I knew,
Whos love his strengthe al overthrew.

I syh there Aristotle also,
Whom that the queene of Grece so
Hath bridled, that in thilke time
Sche made him such a Silogime,
That he foryat al his logique;
2710 Ther was non art of his Practique,
Thurgh which it mihte ben excluded
That he ne was fully concluded
To love, and dede his obeissance.
And ek Virgile of aqueintance
I sih, wher he the Maiden preide,
Which was the doghter, as men seide,
Of themperour whilom of Rome;
Sortes and Plato with him come,
So dede Ovide the Poete.[6]
2720 I thoghte thanne how love is swete,
Which hath so wise men reclamed,
And was miself the lasse aschamed,
Or forto lese or forto winne
In the meschief that I was inne:
And thus I lay in hope of grace.

And whan thei comen to the place
Wher Venus stod and I was falle,
These olde men with o vois alle
To Venus preiden for my sake.
2730 And sche, that myhte noght forsake
So gret a clamour as was there,
Let Pite come into hire Ere;
And forth withal unto Cupide
Sche preith that he upon his side

Me wolde thurgh his grace sende
Som confort, that I myhte amende,
Upon the cas which is befalle.
And thus for me thei preiden alle
Of hem that weren olde aboute,
2740 And ek some of the yonge route,
Of gentilesse and pure trouthe
I herde hem telle it was gret routhe,
That I withouten help so ferde.
And thus me thoghte I lay and herde.

❦ Cupido, which may hurte and hele
In loves cause, as for myn hele
Upon the point which him was preid
Cam with Venus, wher I was leid
Swounende upon the grene gras.
2750 And, as me thoghte, anon ther was
On every side so gret presse,   [crowd]
That every lif began to presse,
I wot noght wel hou many score,
Suche as I spak of now tofore,
Lovers, that comen to beholde,
Bot most of hem that weren olde:
Thei stoden there at thilke tyde,
To se what ende schal betyde
Upon the cure of my sotie.   [folly]
2760 Tho myhte I hiere gret partie
Spekende, and ech his oghne avis
Hath told, on that, an other this:
Bot among alle this I herde,
Thei weren wo that I so ferde,
And seiden that for no riote
An old man scholde noght assote;
For as thei tolden redely,
Ther is in him no cause why,
Bot if he wolde himself benyce;

2770 So were he wel the more nyce.
And thus desputen some of tho,
And some seiden nothing so,
Bot that the wylde loves rage
In mannes lif forberth non Age;
Whil ther is oyle forto fyre,
The lampe is lyhtly set afyre,
And is fulhard er it be queynt,
Bot only if it be som seint,
Which god preserveth of his grace.
2780 And thus me thoghte, in sondri place
Of hem that walken up and doun
Ther was diverse opinioun:
And for a while so it laste,
Til that Cupide to the laste,
Forth with his moder full avised,
Hath determined and devised
Unto what point he wol descende.
And al this time I was liggende
Upon the ground tofore his yhen,
2790 And thei that my desese syhen
Supposen noght I scholde live;
Bot he, which wolde thanne yive
His grace, so as it mai be,
This blinde god which mai noght se,
Hath groped til that he me fond;
And as he pitte forth his hond
Upon my body, wher I lay,
Me thoghte a fyri Lancegay,
Which whilom thurgh myn herte he caste,
2800 He pulleth oute, and also faste
As this was do, Cupide nam
His weie, I not where he becam,
And so dede al the remenant
Which unto him was entendant,
Of hem that in Avision

I hadde a revelacion,
So as I tolde now tofore.
　　　Bot Venus wente noght therfore,
Ne Genius, whiche thilke time
2810 Abiden bothe faste byme.
And sche which mai the hertes bynde
In loves cause and ek unbinde,
Er I out of mi trance aros,
Venus, which hield a boiste clos,　　　　　[box]
And wolde noght I scholde deie,
Tok out mor cold than eny keie
An oignement, and in such point
Sche hath my wounded herte enoignt,
My temples and my Reins also.　　　　　[kidneys (L. *renes*)]
2820 And forth withal sche tok me tho
A wonder Mirour forto holde,
In which sche bad me to beholde
And taken hiede of that I syhe;
Wherinne anon myn hertes yhe
I caste, and sih my colour fade,
Myn yhen dymme and al unglade,
Mi chiekes thinne, and al my face
With Elde I myhte se deface,
So riveled and so wo besein,
2830 That ther was nothing full ne plein,
I syh also myn heres hore.
Mi will was tho to se nomore
Outwith, for ther was no plesance;
And thanne into my remembrance
I drowh myn olde daies passed,
And as reson it hath compassed,
I made a liknesse of miselve
Unto the sondri Monthes twelve,
Wherof the yeer in his astat
2840 Is mad, and stant upon debat,
That lich til other non acordeth.

For who the times wel recordeth,
And thanne at Marche if he beginne,
Whan that the lusti yeer comth inne,
Til Augst be passed and Septembre,
The myhty youthe he may remembre
In which the yeer hath his deduit   [delight]
Of gras, of lef, of flour, of fruit,
Of corn and of the wyny grape.
2850 And afterward the time is schape
To frost, to Snow, to Wind, to Rein,
Til eft that Mars be come ayein:
The Wynter wol no Somer knowe,
The grene lef is overthrowe,
The clothed erthe is thanne bare,
Despuiled is the Somerfare,
That erst was hete is thanne chele.
     And thus thenkende thoghtes fele,   [many]
I was out of mi swoune affraied,
2860 Wherof I sih my wittes straied,
And gan to clepe hem hom ayein.
And whan Resoun it herde sein
That loves rage was aweie,
He cam to me the rihte weie,
And hath remued the sotie
Of thilke unwise fantasie,
Wherof that I was wont to pleigne,
So that of thilke fyri peine
I was mad sobre and hol ynowh.
2870   Venus behield me than and lowh,   [laughed]
And axeth, as it were a game,
What love was. And I for schame
Ne wiste what I scholde ansuere;
And natheles I gan to swere
That be my trouthe I knew him noght;
So ferr it was out of mi thoght,
Riht as it hadde nevere be.

"Mi goode Sone," tho quod sche,
"Now at this time I lieve it wel,   [believe]
2880 So goth the fortune of my whiel;
Forthi mi conseil is thou leve."
     "Ma dame," I seide, "be your leve,
Ye witen wel, and so wot I,
That I am unbehovely   [unfit]
Your Court fro this day forth to serve:
And for I may no thonk deserve,
And also for I am refused,
I preie you to ben excused.
And natheles as for the laste,
2890 Whil that my wittes with me laste,
Touchende mi confession
I axe an absolucion
Of Genius, er that I go."
The Prest anon was redy tho,
And seide, "Sone, as of thi schrifte
Thou hast ful pardoun and foryifte;
Foryet it thou, and so wol I."
     "Min holi fader, grant mercy,"
Quod I to him, and to the queene
2900 I fell on knes upon the grene,
And tok my leve forto wende.
Bot sche, that wolde make an ende,
As therto which I was most able,
A Peire of Bedes blak as Sable
Sche tok and heng my necke aboute;
Upon the gaudes al without
Was write of gold, *Por reposer.*
"Lo," thus sche seide, "John Gower,
Now thou art ate laste cast,
2910 This have I for thin ese cast,
That thou nomore of love sieche.
Bot my will is that thou besieche
And preie hierafter for the pes,

And that thou make a plein reles
To love, which takth litel hiede
Of olde men upon the nede,
Whan that the lustes ben aweie:
Forthi to thee nys bot o weie,
In which let reson be thi guide:
2920 For he may sone himself misguide,
That seth noght the peril tofore.
Mi Sone, be wel war therfore,
And kep the sentence of my lore
And tarie thou mi Court nomore,
Bot go ther vertu moral duelleth,
Wher ben thi bokes, as men telleth,
Whiche of long time thou hast write.
For this I do thee well to wite,
If thou thin hele wolt pourchace,
2930 Thou miht noght make suite and chace,
Wher that the game is nought pernable;   [proper to be taken (OF *prendre*, 'to take')]

It were a thing unresonable,
A man to be so overseie.   [imprudent]
Forthi tak hiede of that I seie;
For in the lawe of my comune
We be noght schape to comune,
Thiself and I, nevere after this.
Now have y seid al that ther is
Of love as for thi final ende:
2940 Adieu, for y mot fro the wende." [7]
And with that word al sodeinly,
Enclosid in a sterred sky,
Venus, which is the qweene of love,
Was take in to hire place above,
More wiste y nought wher sche becam.
And thus my leve of hire y nam,
And forth with al the same tide
Hire prest, which wolde nought abide,

Or be me lief or be me loth,
2950 Out of my sighte forth he goth,
And y was left with outen helpe.
So wiste I nought wher of to yelpe,
Bot only that y hadde lore
My time, and was sori ther fore.
And thus bewhapid in my thought,
Whan al was turnyd in to nought,
I stod amasid for a while,
And in my self y gan to smyle
Thenkende uppon the bedis blake,
2960 And how they weren me betake,   [given to me]
For that y schulde bidde and preie.
And whanne y sigh non othre weie
Bot only that y was refusid,
Unto the lif which y hadde usid
I thoughte nevere torne ayein:
And in this wise, soth to seyn,
Homward a softe pas y wente,
Wher that with al myn hol entente
Uppon the point that y am schryve   [confessed]
2970 I thenke bidde whil y live.   [to pray]

> Parce precor, Criste, populus quo gaudeat iste;
> Anglia ne triste subeat, rex summe, resiste.
> Corrige quosque status, fragiles absolue reatus;
> Vnde deo gratus vigeat locus iste beatus.[8]

He which withinne daies sevene
This large world forth with the hevene
Of his eternal providence
Hath mad, and thilke intelligence
In mannys soule resonable
Hath schape to be perdurable,   [eternal]
Wherof the man of his feture
Above alle erthli creature

Aftir the soule is immortal
2980 To thilke lord in special,
As he which is of alle thinges
The creatour, and of the kinges
Hath the fortunes uppon honde,
His grace and mercy forto fonde
Uppon my bare knes y preie,
That he this lond in siker weie
Wol sette uppon good governance.
For if men takyn remembrance
What is to live in unite,
2990 Ther ys no staat in his degree
That noughte to desire pes,
With outen which, it is no les,
To seche and loke in to the laste,
Ther may no worldes joye laste.
    Ferst forto loke the Clergie,
Hem oughte wel to justefie
Thing which belongith to here cure,
As forto praie and to procure
Oure pes toward the hevene above,
3000 And ek to sette reste and love
Among ous on this erthe hiere.
For if they wroughte in this manere
Aftir the reule of charite,
I hope that men schuldyn se
This lond amende.
              And ovyr this,
To seche and loke how that it is
Touchende of the chevalerie,
Which forto loke, in som partie
Is worthi forto be comendid,
3010 And in som part to ben amendid,
That of here large retenue
The lond is ful of maintenue,
Which causith that the comune right

In fewe contrees stant upright.
Extorcioun, contekt, ravine
Withholde ben of that covyne,
Aldai men hierin gret compleignte
Of the desease, of the constreignte,
Wher of the poeple is sore oppressid:
3020 God graunte it mote be redressid.
For of knyghthode thordre wolde
That thei defende and kepe scholde
The comun right and the fraunchise
Of holy cherche in alle wise,
So that no wikke man it dere,   [injure]
And ther fore servith scheld and spere:
Bot for it goth now other weie,
Oure grace goth the more aweie.

    And forto lokyn ovyrmore,
3030 Wher of the poeple pleigneth sore,
Toward the lawis of oure lond,
Men sein that trouthe hath broke his bond
And with brocage is goon aweie,
So that no man can se the weie
Wher forto fynde rightwisnesse.

    And if men sechin sikernesse   [certitude]
Uppon the lucre of marchandie,
Compassement and tricherie
Of singuler profit to wynne,
3040 Men seyn, is cause of mochil synne,
And namely of divisioun,
Which many a noble worthi toun
Fro welthe and fro prosperite
Hath brought to gret adversite.
So were it good to ben al on,
For mechil grace ther uppon
Unto the Citees schulde falle,
Which myghte availle to ous alle,
If these astatz amendid were,

3050 So that the vertus stodyn there
      And that the vices were aweie:
      Me thenkth y dorste thanne seie,
      This londis grace schulde arise.
         Bot yit to loke in othre wise,
      Ther is a stat, as ye schul hiere,
      Above alle othre on erthe hiere,
      Which hath the lond in his balance:
      To him belongith the leiance
      Of Clerk, of knyght, of man of lawe;
3060 Undir his hond al is forth drawe
      The marchant and the laborer;
      So stant it al in his power
      Or forto spille or forto save.
      Bot though that he such power have,
      And that his myghtes ben so large,
      He hath hem nought withouten charge,
      To which that every king ys swore:
      So were it good that he ther fore
      First un to rightwisnesse entende,
3070 Wherof that he hym self amende
      Toward his god and leve vice,
      Which is the chief of his office;
      And aftir al the remenant
      He schal uppon his covenant
      Governe and lede in such a wise,
      So that ther be no tirandise,
      Wherof that he his poeple grieve,
      Or ellis may he nought achieve
      That longith to his regalie.
3080 For if a kyng wol justifie
      His lond and hem that beth withynne,
      First at hym self he mot begynne,
      To kepe and reule his owne astat,
      That in hym self be no debat
      Toward his god: for othre wise

Ther may non erthly kyng suffise
Of his kyngdom the folk to lede,
Bot he the kyng of hevene drede.
For what kyng sett hym uppon pride
3090 And takth his lust on every side
And wil nought go the righte weie,
Though god his grace caste aweie
No wondir is, for ate laste
He schal wel wite it mai nought laste,
The pompe which he secheth here.
Bot what kyng that with humble chere
Aftir the lawe of god eschuieth
The vices, and the vertus suieth,   [follows]
His grace schal be suffisant
3100 To governe al the remenant
Which longith to his duite;
So that in his prosperite
The poeple schal nought ben oppressid,
Wherof his name schal be blessid,
For evere and be memorial.
          And now to speke as in final,
Touchende that y undirtok
In englesch forto make a book
Which stant betwene ernest and game,
3110 I have it maad as thilke same
Which axe forto ben excusid,
And that my bok be nought refusid
Of lered men, whan thei it se,
For lak of curiosite:
For thilke scole of eloquence
Belongith nought to my science,
Uppon the forme of rethoriqe
My wordis forto peinte and pike,
As Tullius som tyme wrot.
3120 Bot this y knowe and this y wot,
That y have do my trewe peyne

With rude wordis and with pleyne,
In al that evere y couthe and myghte,
This bok to write as y behighte,   [promised]
So as siknesse it soffre wolde;
And also for to my daies olde,
That y am feble and impotent,
I wot nought how the world ys went.
So preye y to my lordis alle
3130   Now in myn age, how so befalle,
That y mot stonden in here grace:
For though me lacke to purchace
Here worthi thonk as by decerte,
Yit the symplesse of my poverte
Desireth forto do plesance
To hem undir whos governance
I hope siker to abide.

     But now uppon my laste tide
That y this book have maad and write,
3140   My muse doth me forto wite,
And seith it schal be for my beste
Fro this day forth to take reste,
That y nomore of love make,   [write about]
Which many an herte hath overtake,
And ovyrturnyd as the blynde
Fro reson in to lawe of kynde;
Wher as the wisdom goth aweie
And can nought se the ryhte weie
How to governe his oghne estat,
3150   Bot everydai stant in debat
Withinne him self, and can nought leve.
And thus forthy my final leve
I take now for evere more,
Withoute makynge any more,
Of love and of his dedly hele,
Which no phisicien can hele.
For his nature is so divers,

That it hath evere som travers
Or of to moche or of to lite,
3160 That pleinly mai noman delite,
Bot if him faile or that or this.
Bot thilke love which that is
Withinne a mannes herte affermed,
And stant of charite confermed,
Such love is goodly forto have,
Such love mai the bodi save,
Such love mai the soule amende,
The hyhe god such love ous sende
Forthwith the remenant of grace;
3170 So that above in thilke place
Wher resteth love and alle pes,
Oure joie mai ben endeles.

Explicit iste liber, qui transeat, obsecro liber
Vt sine liuore vigeat lectoris in ore.
Qui sedet in scannis celi det vt ista Iohannis
Perpetuis annis stet pagina grata Britannis,
Derbeie Comiti, recolunt quem laude periti,
Vade liber purus, sub eo requiesce futurus.[9]

NOTES

Notes to the Prologue

[1] Sluggishness, dullness of perception, little leisure, and scant application, all these plead extenuation for me, least of poets, for inditing somewhat slight themes.

In that tongue spoken on the Island of Brutus, and aided by the English Muse, I shall offer my songs. It has not, therefore, been my intention to cover over with pretty words a lack of inner substance in my verses; and may a vicious expounder of them never discover the gold that lies hidden there. (F.W.L.)

[2] Gower completed his first version of the *Confessio Amantis* during or prior to 1390, the fourteenth year of King Richard II's reign. Although portions of the poem may have been written six or seven years earlier, when Chaucer was working on *Troilus* and beginning the *Legend of Good Women,* the Prologue and conclusion of the *Confessio Amantis* must have been written last, in that they refer to the later date. In the first version, lines 24–92* of the Prologue tell how the poet, while rowing on the Thames "Under the toun of newe Troye, / Which tok of Brut his ferste joye" (37–38 *), came upon King Richard's boat. The King bade Gower to come aboard the royal barge and, among other things, suggested that he write "som newe thing" which the King himself might peruse. The poet says he agreed to undertake the task, despite his ill health, and that his book has been written "for king Richardes sake"; it will offer "wisdom to the wise / And pley to hem that lust to pleye" (84–85*).

By 1392, the sixteenth year of Richard's reign, Gower had

---

* Indicates lines of the first or second recension omitted by Gower in his final 1392 edition of the poem, which our selection follows.

apparently become disenchanted with Richard's behavior as king, perhaps because of the king's harsh treatment of the officials of the City of London early in that year. He rewrote the beginning of the poem which tells of the king's commissioning of the poem and also the end of the poem in which he had praised Richard's worthiness (see notes 7 and 8 to Book VIII). In the revised version (1392), which our selection from the poem follows, Gower shifts his concern from the welfare of the throne to the welfare of the State of England (24 ff.). That he sees hope for England residing in a man like Henry of Lancaster (see Prol. 81–92 and the Latin postscript to Book VIII), even as much as seven years before Henry would become king, is indeed clairvoyant. (See Macaulay, *Works of John Gower* (Oxford, 1901), II, cxxvii–clxx, for a description of most of the known MSS and an account of the revisions; see John Fisher, *John Gower* (New York, 1964), pp. 116–127, for discussion of the revisions in their historical setting.)

[3] Although the allusion to the poet's illness enhances the Prologue's theme of the degenerating world and thus anticipates the conclusion to the poem where the poet rejects mundane love because of his decrepitude, biographers generally agree that Gower was in fact in ill health during his later years. He had retired from public life some fifteen years earlier and was now over sixty years old.

[4] Macaulay suggests that in lines 77 ff. Gower alludes to Book VII, which deals with the instruction of great men. He glosses the lines to read: "I shall make a discourse also with regard to those who are in power, marking the distinction between the virtues and the vices which belong to their office" (II.459). Gower may mean, however, that in writing about love which has upset so many men he will "in this wyse" (that is, in the mode of courtly romance) consider virtues and vices which have general significance to men of all times.

[5] Gower prefaces his discussion of the present state of England with a twelve-line Latin epigram on the peaceful virtues of former times:

Present fortune has forsaken the blessed past and overturns ancient ways. In former times, when a man's looks declared his thought, concord and love gave birth to peace. In those days a single-colored light shown in the laws; in those days the ways were filled with justice. But now concealed hate paints a face of love. Beneath feigned peace, a call to arms is covered. The law acts like a chameleon, fickle and varied; new kingdoms, thus new laws. Times that once were most sound are thus dissolved throughout the world, their centers not at rest. (A.G.)

The sentiment is commonplace. (Cf. Chaucer's *The Former Age* and *Lak of Stedfastnesse,* both of which are strongly Boethian.)

[6] Gower is alluding to the recurrent wars with France, Spain, and Scotland. A three-year truce had been made with France and Scotland in 1389,but, because of profiteering, it was not maintained. An attempt for a truce with Spain in the same year failed. Not until 1396, when Richard married the daughter of the king of France, was a firm truce established with the French.

[7] Gower prefaces his discussion of the present state of the Church (193 ff.) with a ten-line Latin stanza on ecclesiastical corruption:

The laws which old Moses and new John himself cherished are of yesterday, scarcely cherished by the present day. Thus, the former church, finely wrought by double virtue, is now, with both paths in neglect, become more pale. Once, in keeping with Christ's words, the sword shrank from the way of blood and was returned to Peter's sheath of peace. But now avarice brandishes a sword, drenched with continuous bloodshed, while the sacred law grows cool. The shepherd is a wolf; the father an enemy. Death is compassionate; the giver, an object of prey. The world's peace is fear. (A.G.)

[8] Simon Magus (Acts 8:9–24) was a Samaritan sorcerer who offered money to Peter for instruction in the imparting of the Holy Ghost by laying on of hands. His name became synonymous with ecclesiastical corruption.

[9] The Lombards were so notorious as bankers, moneylenders, and pawnbrokers that their name came to denote such behavior in both Old French and Middle English (OED). Langland links Lombards and Jews to exemplify avarice in *Piers Plowman*

(B V.242), and in (C V.191–194) he yokes merchants, "mytrede bisshopes," Lombards, and Jews as enemies of Conscience. Lombard bankers were often employed as intermediaries in church and state transactions. (Cf. King Richard's dispute with London when city officials would not lend revenue to the king but would lend to Lombards.) Macaulay notes that the letter referred to in line 209 is the papal provision, or perhaps the letter of request addressed to the pope in favor of a particular person (II.461). Gower makes a similar complaint in *Vox Clamantis,* III.1375 ff. (cf. *Confessio,* II.2093 ff.).

[10] Positive law refers to any law which is arbitrarily instituted; it is customarily classified as distinct from divine law and natural law. Under its jurisdiction fell the selling of indulgences, pardons, trentals, and the like. Chaucer satirizes abuse of such laws in the "Friar's Tale," the "Summoner's Tale," and the "Pardoner's Tale." See also *Piers Plowman* (B VII.168–194) and *Vox Clamantis* (III.227 ff.).

[11] Macaulay (II.461–462) notes: "The allusion is to the circumstances of the campaign of the Bishop of Norwich in 1385; cf. *Vox Clam.* iii.373 (margin), and see Froissart (ed. Lettenhove [Brussels, 1870]), vol.x.p.207."

[12] Gregory the Great, in his well-known *Regula Pastoralis,* I.8, 9 (*PL,* LXXVI, 1128).

[13] The allusion is to Mount Etna which Gower uses here and elsewhere as a metaphor for Envy (cf. *Conf. Am.* II.20, 163, 2837; V.1289). He most likely takes the figure from Ovid, *Metam.* XIII.868.

[14] Gower refers to the papal dispute between Clement VII at Avignon and Boniface IX at Rome, both of whom claimed the allegiance of Christendom. He sees the schism in the head of the church as responsible for schismatic heresies such as Lollardry throughout the clergy.

[15] Gower introduces his discussion of the Commons (Prol. 499 ff.) with a six-line Latin stanza:

The commons (*vulgaris populus*), oppressed by the king's law, will lie prostrate until a gentle lamb takes up the burden. If it raises its head and gives free reign to its own law, insofar as it is willful it is like a tiger. Fire and the lordly flood are a pair which knows no piety; but the wrath of the mob is more violent still.   (A.G.)

The discussion of man's personal responsibility regardless of Fortune's whims is Boethian in concept. (Cf. Boethius's discussion of Fortune in Book II of the *Consolatio*, especially *prosae* 1 and 4.)

[16] Gower introduces his account of Nebuchadnezzar's dream with a six-line Latin stanza on the inconstancy of the world:

Now prosperous, now adverse, the unclean world, in its devious way, deceives all kinds. The world turns on the event as dice fall by chance when a greedy hand throws hastily in play. Like man's image, the world's seasons vary, and nothing stands firm except the love of God.   (A.G.)

Macaulay observes that the vision of Nebuchadnezzar is made the subject of an illustration in those MSS which have miniatures at or near the beginning of the *Confessio*. Gower's account of the vision is based on Daniel 2:19–45, though Gower expands Daniel's commentary anachronistically (633–821) in order to comment on the decadence of contemporary history. (Cf. *Vox Clam.* lib. VII, where he uses the same device.)

[17] Ll. 745 ff. "It is hardly necessary to point out that our author's history is here incorrect. Charlemagne was not called in against the Emperor Leo, who died in the year before he was born, but against the Lombards by Adrian I, and then against the rebellious citizens of Rome by Leo III, on which latter occasion he received the imperial crown" (Macaulay, II, 464). Gower is following Brunetto Latini's account in the *Trésor*.

[18] Macaulay sees an allusion here to St. Paul, I Cor. 10:11–12, though more likely the apostle referred to is St. John in Revelation, where Babylon is the apocalyptic emblem of the fallen world. (Cf. Prol. 883, "Thende of the world," and the apocalyptic overtones of the various references to the world divided against itself

in wars, especially 883–904 and 1029–1044.) Throughout his later years, because of the turmoil of national and international affairs, Gower seems to have identified closely with the Book of Revelation. In *Vox Clamantis* he sees its author as his own namesake and likens his role as prophet crying in the wilderness to that of St. John of the Apocalypse. Cf. *Vox Clam.* I. prol. 55–58.

[19] *Moralia* VI.16 (*PL*, LXXV, 740). Gregory is commenting on Job 5:10, where he gives the *sensus mysticus* of *universa* as "man." That man is a microcosm was one of Gower's favorite conceptions. (Cf. *Mirour de l'Omme* 26869 ff. and *Vox Clamantis* VII.639 ff.)

[20] Gower's theory of death and the corruptibility of mixed elements is in agreement with medical theories of his day. Averroes, following Aristotle's thesis that all living things consist of mixtures of the primal elements, argues that if bodies were one and the same there would be no contrariety corrupting them. But unlike stones, which have one nature and are permanent, the body is composed of various natures and thus decays. (*Avicennae Cantica cum Averrois Commentariis*, I.19. See Fox, *Medieval Sciences in the Works of Gower* [Princeton, 1931], p. 34.) Plato explains this idea of corruptibility fully in *Timaeus*, 81c–82b. The *Timaeus* was the one platonic dialogue that was known and honored in the Latin West during the Middle Ages and, unlike Averroes, it is readily available to interested students. Although Gower probably did not know the *Timaeus* first hand, he certainly knew of it.

[21] See Ovid, *Fasti*, II.83 ff., though the story was well known and may be found in collections of Latin moralized tales such as those described in the *British Museum Catalogue of Romances* and in some versions of the *Gesta Romanorum* (for example Oesterley, cap. 148). Gower ignores that part of the story which deals with the dolphin and concentrates on Arion the peacemaker to create an effect appropriately reminiscent of the peaceable kingdom in Isaiah 11:1–10. See *Vox Clamantis* I.i.1–124, for a description of what England might be like if it were to find its Arion.

Notes to Book One

[1] Created love subjects the world to the Laws of Nature, and incites all to be of one mind in being wild. Love seems to be the Prince of this world, and no matter what their estate, rich or poor, all are in need of him. Love and Fortune are equally matched: the one lures blind folk into snares, and both have their wheels. Love is health that is a sickness, a stillness without quiet, a truancy that is faithful, a peace that is all war, a refreshing wound, a sweet evil. (F.W.L.)

[2] Line 93 is preceded by an eight-line Latin epigram on the Lover's circumstance:

I do not have the strength of Samson, nor Hercules's prowess in arms, but I, like both of them, am vanquished by as great a love. Amidst uncertainties, experience is the teacher of those who would know what path to take. A patrol spreads out to explore for dangers; its captain, stationed behind, follows later, lest he be felled with them. Therefore I bend my course to write openly of the calamities (*casus*) in which Venus has snared me—a lover, an example for the world. (A.G.)

[3] The originals behind Gower's Genius may be found in Jean de Meun's *Roman de la Rose* and Alanus de Insulis's *De Planctu Naturae,* where Genius is presented as a creative agent, a priest, and an intermediary between man and Nature. (See Introduction.)

[4] Line 203 is preceded by a four-line Latin epigram which may be translated as follows:

Whether confession to Genius is the medicine of health for the disease Venus herself has brought, I shall try to discover. The body is cured and made healthy, even of sword wounds, yet rarely does the wound of love have a physician. (A.G.)

[5] Line 289 is preceded by an eight-line Latin epigram which may be translated as follows:

'Sight and fragile hearing are the mind's doors. No vicious hand can close them. They are a wide path, a road for the enemy to the heart's chamber whereby he enters and in the entrance steals a precious coin. These beginnings my confessor Genius provides me with, even while my remorseful life is in the extreme of malady. Insofar as the speech of one half dead can confess, I will now, with fearful tongue, speak sensible words. (A.G.)

[6] See *Timaeus* 45b–47e for Plato's explanation of why the eye is man's principal sense organ and the ear next in importance. These two senses enable man to perceive the numbers, motions, harmonies, and rhythms of the universe, whereby the soul is illuminated. The other three senses he ignores entirely as agencies for illuminating the soul, although later (61d–68d) he discusses all five senses as part of man's physical mechanism for understanding physical phenomena. Plato's premises constitute one basis for medieval preoccupations with vision and harmony (see note 5). They also explain why Genius exorcises only these two of the Lover's five senses. They are the doors to his soul, which Genius hopes to restore.

[7] Cf. Ovid, *Metam*. III.130–259. Gower omits from the story Acteon's companions and his friendly gesture of giving them the rest of the day off, the account of Diana's disrobing, the efforts of the nymphs to hide their mistress from the eyes of the intruder, the throwing of the water on Acteon, the catalog of hounds, Acteon's efforts to speak, and the debate of the gods on the justice of Diana's revenge; he adds the detail of Acteon's pride (341). Ovid puts the blame on Fortune, but Gower implies that Acteon might have turned his eye away had he chosen to (366). The conventional romance description of his entering the forest (352–360) suggests why he did not; he enters the *hortus conclusus* and does not get out. Amans fares better, thanks to Genius.

[8] Cf. Ovid, *Metam*. IV.772–803. Gower is apparently using additional sources, however. He names Medusa's sisters, as Ovid

does not, though he calls Stheno, "Stellibon," and Euryale he calls "Suriale." Moreover he confuses the story of the Graeae, who share one tooth and one eye, with the story of the Gorgons. Macaulay (II.468) notes that this confusion appears in Boccaccio, *Geneologiæ Deorum Gentilium*, X.10, which Gower may have known. Whether Gower follows Boccaccio or not, the mingling of the two stories is fortuitous for Gower's purpose in demonstrating the evil of "misloke" and the wisdom of looking well.

⁹ The legend of the "Aspidis" derives from Psalm 57:5, which speaks of "the deaf asp that stoppeth her ears." Augustine in his commentary on the Psalm explains how the serpent can stop two ears with one tail; his suggestion is followed by Isidore in *Etym.* XII.4, though neither mention the carbuncle. That detail may come from the legendary jewel in the toad's head, or perhaps from Brunetto Latini's *Trésor*, as Macaulay (II.468) suggests, though serpents were commonly supposed to carry treasures. Cf. the jewel-bearing serpent in the *Tale of Adrian and Bardus* (*Conf. Am.* V.5060 ff.), or the serpent who carries a jewel of health in his mouth in the English *Gesta Romanorum* (cap. VII).

¹⁰ Gower here follows Guido di Colonna, *Hist. Troiana*, lib. 32. Benôit tells the story in *Roman de Troie*, but he does not include all the details which Gower includes, though *Vat. Myth.* II (101) does.

¹¹ The story of Mundus and Paulina is historical and is told by Josephus, *Ant.* XVIII. Hegesippus, II.4, follows Josephus, who in turn is followed by Vincent of Beauvais, *Spec. Hist.* VII.4, any of which may have been Gower's source. The story is told in verse by Godfrey of Viterbo, *Pantheon* XV, but Macaulay says this version was certainly not Gower's source (II.470).

¹² Just as the eye is the most important sense organ for human revelation (see Book I, note 6), so too it is the principal sense organ for guiding reason. Augustine's three steps toward virtue (*visio, contemplatio, actio*) mark also the three steps toward sin. In both instances the process begins with the eye's response to beauty. The

process is one, though the ends are different. Cf. all cupidinous lovers who are first struck through the eye by Cupid's arrow.

[13] The story of the Trojan Horse is found in Dictys V.II, 12; Benôit, 25620 ff.; and Guido, *Hist. Troiana* XXX (*Gest Hist.* XXIX.11846 ff.), all of which Gower may have known. The name Epius appears to come from Virgil through Benôit (as opposed to Apius in Guido) as does the account of the destruction of Neptune's gates. Guido and his translators (not Dictys or Benôit) describe the horse as made of brass.

[14] The "Tale of Florent" is apparently based on the same source as Chaucer's "Wife of Bath's Tale," a source which joins folk motifs of the loathly lady transformed through love and the answering of a riddle to save one's life. (See Stith Thompson, *Motif Index of Folk-Literature*, D 732.) A similar story is found in *The Weddynge of Sir Gawene and Dame Ragnell*. (See B. J. Whiting, in *Sources and Analogues of Chaucer's Canterbury Tales*, pp. 223–268.) Macaulay notes Shakespeare's allusion to Gower's version of the story in *Taming of the Shrew*, I.ii.69.

[15] The story of Capaneus's presumption was a favorite exemplum of medieval writers. Cf. Chaucer, *Anel.* 59; *Troilus* V.1504. His story is told in Statius, *Thebaid* III.598 ff.; IV.165 ff.; VI.731 ff.; and X. *passim*, especially 738 to end). Statius is probably Gower's main source, though the story is mentioned in varying degrees of completeness in Hyginus, *Fabularum Liber* LXVIII, LXX, LXXI; Bocc. *Gen.* IX.36; and Ovid, *Metam.* IX.404.

[16] Versions of the *Trump of Death* occur in the Latin *Gesta Romanorum* (cap. CXLIII) and *Vita Barlaam et Josaphat*, cap.vi (*PL*, LXXIV, 462).

[17] Cf. Ovid, *Metam.* III.344–510; also Bocc. *Gen.* VII.59. Gower alters the conclusion.

[18] The popular story of Albinus and Rosemund is first told by Paulus Diaconus, *Gest. Langob.* II.28. See also Godfrey of Viterbo, *Pantheon*, XXIII.5–6.

[19] Based on Daniel 4.1–34 (Dan. 4:4–37—King James). The story was a popular exemplum of pride (cf. *Vox Clam.* VII; *Mirour*, 1885–1895; and Chaucer's "Monk's Tale," VII.2143–2182).

[20] No source for the "Tale of Three Questions" has yet been discovered.

Notes to Book Two

[1] Cf. Ovid, *Metam.* XIII.738–897.

[2] From the widely known Fables of Avianus.

[3] Chaucer's Man of Law also tells the "Tale of Constance." (See Margaret Schlauch's discussion in *Sources and Analogues*, pp. 155–206.) Although both Gower's and Chaucer's poems are derived from Nicholas Trivet's *Anglo-Norman Chronicle*, Gower's version was apparently written earlier than Chaucer's. Macaulay enumerates Gower's variations from his original (II.482–484). An analogue of the story of Constance, which includes a moral commentary, may be found in the English *Gesta Romanorum* (cap. lxix).

[4] From several sources, including Justin, *Epitome*, lib.xxxii; Valerius Maximus, *Mem.* I.5.3; Orosius, IV.20; and perhaps Vincent of Beauvais, *Spec. Hist.* V.65 ff. See Macaulay (II.487) for discussion.

[5] Cf. Ovid, *Metam.* IX.8–272. See also Hyginus, *Fab.* XXXVI; *Vat. Myth.* I (58); Ovid, *Heroides* IX; and Bocc. *Gen.* IX.17.

[6] Gower's story of Geta and Amphitrion is based on the legend of Hercules's conception. (See *Metam.* VI.112; Hyg. *Fab.* XXIX; *Vat. Myth.* I (50), where Zeus lies with Alcmene disguised as Amphitrion, her husband.) Gower substitutes Amphitrion for the supplanter; where he gets Geta is not known.

[7] A source for the "Tale of the False Bachelor" is not known.

[8] Gower might have found accounts of Boniface's corruption of the papacy in various Chronicles, including those of Rishanger,

Hidgen, and Walsingham. See Macaulay's discussion (II.490–491) of both historical and legendary materials on Boniface.

[9] Abbot Joachim's warning has not been identified. Accounts of Joab's treachery and Achitophel's death occur in II Kings 3:6–39; 16:20–17:23 (II Sam. 3:6–39; 16:20–17:23, King James). The reference to Seneca in line 3095 is based on Dante, *Inf.* XIII.64. Cf. *Mirour de l'Omme*, 3831 ff.

[10] Based on the *Legenda Aurea*.

Notes to Book Three

[1] Cf. Ovid, *Heroides* XI. Gower softens the story and appeals to the reader's sympathy for Canacee by adding her speech to her father and her letter to her brother. To heighten the pathos and focus on the father's cruel anger he places the death of the child, bathed in the mother's blood, after the mother's death. Cf. Chaucer's witty allusion to this "wikke ensample" in *Cant. Tales* II (B) 77–80. Lydgate retells Gower's version in his *Fall of Princes*.

[2] Macaulay notes: "Gower's view is that there is nothing naturally immoral about an incestuous marriage, but that it is made wrong by the 'lex positiva' of the Church. This position he makes clear at the beginning of the eighth book, by showing that in the first ages of the world such marriages must have been sanctioned by divine authority, and that the idea of kinship as a bar to marriage had grown up gradually, cousins being allowed to marry among the Jews, though brother and sister might not, and that finally the Church had ordered,

That non schal wedden of his ken
Ne the seconde ne the thridde.   VIII.147 f.

If attacked by Chaucer with regard to the subject of this story, he would no doubt defend himself by arguing that the vice with which it dealt was not against nature, and that the erring brother and sister were in truth far more deserving of sympathy than the father who took such cruel vengeance" (II.493).

[3] The details for the story of Tiresias and the Snakes occur in *Metam*. III.324–327; Hyg. *Fab*. LXXV; and *Vat. Myth*. I (16), all of which Gower probably knew.

[4] Chaucer's Jankyn puts his chiding Wife of Bath in her place with the same story [III(D)727–732]. He learned the story from Jerome, *Adv. Jov*. I.48 (*PL*, XXIII, 278), from whence Gower may also have learned it, though the story was a commonplace epitome of patience.

[5] A continuation of the account cited in note 3 above.

[6] Chaucer's Manciple also tells a version of this tale. It is a story often told by medieval authors; e.g. Ovid, *Metam*. II.531–632; *Ovide Moralisé*; Machaut, *Le Livre du Voir Dit*, 7773–8110; *Seven Sages of Rome*, 2193–2292; and various allusions in *Roman de la Rose*. (See James Work, in *Sources and Analogues*, pp. 699–722.)

[7] Cf. Ovid, *Fasti*, II.585–616.

[8] The story of Nauplius's revenge occurs in Benôit, *Roman de Troie*, 27671–27930; Guido, XXXII; *Gest Hist*. XXXII.12552–12704; Hyg. *Fab*. CXVI; and *Vat. Myth*. II (201). Gower appears to have followed more than one source.

[9] A favorite medieval tale. Cf. Vincent of Beauvais, *Spec. Hist*. III.68 ff.; Latin *Gesta Romanorum* (cap. CLXXXIII); Walter Burley, *De Vita Philosophorum*, cap. I. The messenger and the tun on the axeltree are apparently Gower's additions to the story.

[10] Chaucer also tells the story in *Legend of Good Women*. The story is based on Ovid, *Metam*. IV.55–166. Of the two, Chaucer follows the authority more closely. For a comparison of the two Middle English accounts with Ovid see Macaulay (II.497–498).

[11] Cf. Ovid, *Metam*. I.452–567.

[12] Gower's story of Athemas (Acamas) and Demephon is based chiefly on *Roman de Troie*, 28147 ff., though it is found also in Dictys and Guido.

[13] Gower's most direct source for the story of Orestes seems to be Benôit, *Roman de Troie* 28047–28112; 28285–28412; 28469–28533. This is one of the few instances in which Gower's story, with its conflict of religious and political obligations, is longer than his author's.

[14] The story of Alexander and the Pirate was popular; for example, Augustine, *Civ. Dei*, IV.4; the Latin *Gesta Romanorum* (cap. CXLVI); Jofroi of Waterford's *Secretum Secretorum*.

[15] Gower apparently follows Benôit, 6519–6612, though the story also occurs in Dares, XVI, and Guido, XIII (cf. *Gest Hist.* XIII. 5225 ff.).

Notes to Book Four

[1] From Ovid, *Heroides* VII. Cf. Chaucer's *Hous of Fame*, 219–432; *Legend of Good Women*, 924–1367; and Jean de Meun's *Rom. de la Rose*, 13173 ff.

[2] Gower's version of Ulysses' return vaguely follows *Heroides* I, though the story is so common and here so brief that he probably wrote from memory.

[3] Many apocryphal stories of magic grew around the reputations of Robert Grosseteste and Roger Bacon and their experiments. Cf. Robert Greene's play, *Friar Bacon and Friar Bungay*, which offers a more elaborate version of the story of the talking head of brass: the head talked, but the experimenter slept through his success.

[4] Matt. 25:1–13.

[5] Cf. Ovid, *Metam.* X.243–297, and Jean de Meun, *Roman de la Rose*, 20817–21210.

[6] The story of Iphis is from Ovid, *Metam.* IX.666–797. The account of the ring of oblivion, which follows, is perhaps based on Peter Comestor's commentary on *Exodus* VI (*PL*, CXCVIII, 1144).

[7] The tale of Phyllis was well known. Cf. *Roman de la Rose,* 13211 ff., and Chaucer, *Legend of Good Women,* 2394–2561. Gower's version seems to be derived from Ovid, *Heroides* II, and *Rem. Am.* 591–604, though he might also have consulted works such as Hyg. *Fab.* LIX; *Vat. Myth.* I (159), II (214); or Bocc. *Gen.* X.52, XI.25. Gower alters several details (for example, he reverses Demophon's itinerary so that he is on his way to Troy instead of returning). Gower may have been the first to translate "amygdalus" as "fillibert," thereby creating the pun. Lydgate follows Gower's suggestion in *Temple of Glas,* 88.

[8] Cf. Ovid, *Metam.* II.1–328. See also Hyg. *Fab.* CLIV; *Vat Myth.* II(57); and Bocc. *Gen.* VII.41. Macaulay notes (II.504): "The moral drawn by Gower from the story of Phaeton is against going too low, that is abandoning the higher concerns of love owing to slothful negligence. The next story is against aiming too high and neglecting the due claims of service."

[9] Cf. Ovid, *Metam.* VIII.183–259, though the story was common. Cf. *Conf. Am.* V.5286.

[10] No specific source is known for this tale, though stories of punishment for aloof ladies are common in medieval literature. Cf. W. A. Neilson, "Purgatory of Cruel Beauties," *Romania,* XXIX (1900), 85–93.

[11] From Judges 11.

[12] Cf. Hyg. *Fab.* XCV, and Ovid, *Metam.* XIII.39, though both name Palamedes, son of Nauplius, as the exposer of Ulysses. Gower also adds the foxes to pull the plow instead of the horse and oxen of Hyginus.

[13] Cf. Ovid, *Heroides* XIII.

[14] From I Kings 27–31 (I Sam. 27–31, King James).

[15] Cf. Statius, *Achilleid,* II.110–128, for the education of Ulysses by Chiron.

[16] Cf. Ovid, *Metam.* IX.1–97, though Gower seems to be loosely following some other source which accounts for the pillars of brass and the ancestry of Mercury.

[17] Cf. Benôit, *Roman de Troie*, 24309 ff. and 25767 ff.

[18] Genius's discussion of gentilesse (2204–2319) is Boethian in origin. Cf. Chaucer's "Gentillesse," as well as the discussion of the subject in the "Wife of Bath's Tale" and the "Franklin's Tale"; Dante, *Convivio*, IV.10; *Roman de la Rose*, 18607–18946; and Gower's *Mirour*, 23389.

[19] I John 3:14. "He who does not love abides in death."

[20] Job 5:7.

[21] That man must labor is one of the primary conditions of post-lapsarian existence (Gen. 3:17–19). Each man must reclaim Paradise for himself, and that effort involves mental as well as physical cultivation. (Cf. *Parl. of Fowles*, 15–28, and Chaucer's Canon's Yeoman's philosophy of labor.) Many of the founders of the various arts, industries and sciences which Genius enumerates are found in Godfrey of Viterbo's *Pantheon*, though not all occur there. See Macaulay, II.508–511.

[22] On the basis of this phrase Macaulay concludes that Gower supposed Tullius and Cicero to be two different persons (II.510). The line might conceivably be glossed: "Tully with the name of Cicero," although the verb (*writen*) which the phrase governs is plural. Gower does not always maintain subject-verb agreement, however.

[23] From Ovid, *Metam*. XI.266–748. Cf. *Book of the Duchess*, 62–220, and the storm scene in *Vox Clamantis*, I.1663–1694.

[24] Inspired perhaps by Ovid's *Amores*, I.13.39–40, though there the situation is reversed, with Aurora invoking the steeds of night. The prayer is apparently original for the most part with Gower. Saturn's metal is lead; it is thus associated with dullness and slowness. Cephalus would have the sun residing under Saturn's influence in order that it might be slow getting up.

[25] Cf. Ovid, *Metam*. I.588–721.

[26] Cf. Ovid, *Metam*. XIV.698–761. Gower reverses the social rank of the lover and his mistress. In Ovid, Anaxarete is high born while the youth is low born. Ovid's lady feels no remorse; she is

simply turned into a stone as she sees the funeral pass by her window.

Notes to Book Five

[1] Cf. Ovid, *Metam.* XI.85–145. Midas's debate over the three choices is Gower's addition to the traditional story.

[2] The story of Tantalus was well known: for example, Hyg. *Fab.* LXXXII; Fulg. II.18; *Vat. Myth.* II (102); Bocc. *Gen.* XII.1. Ovid alludes to the story several times, though he never tells it fully.

[3] Cf. Jean de Meun's jealous husband in *Roman de la Rose,* 8455–9492. Both writers associate jealousy with Avarice.

[4] Loosely based on Ovid, *Ars Am.* II.561–592.

[5] Gower's principal authority in his discussion of the Chaldean and Egyptian religions is *Vita Barlaam et Josaphat,* XXVII (*PL,* LXXIII, 548). That work also includes lore on the Greek gods, though they were better known, and Gower's generalizations about them are by no means restricted to this single source. (For a succinct discussion of the history behind such catalogues of classical deities as Gower's, see Jean Seznec, *The Survival of the Pagan Gods,* New York, 1953, Chapter 1.) The observations by Dindimus to Alexander at the end of the discussion could be drawn from any number of versions (Latin, Old French, Middle English) of the ever-popular history of Alexander.

In my paraphrase I have followed Gower's spelling of the Egyptian deities. *Orus* apparently refers to Horus the Elder, while *Orayn* would be Horus the Child. *Isirus* is, of course, Osiris, and *Typhon* is Seth. I have used modern spelling for the Greek deities except in those instances when I have not been able to identify the character. For example, when Gower calls the father of Ilia, *Mynitor,* the reference is clearly to Numitor; so too his *Ypolitus* is Hippotas, and his *Sibeles* is Cybele. In such instances I have used the modern form. *Philerem,* the mother of Jupiter, I leave, however. Gower may be referring to Philyra, the mother of Chiron by Saturn, though no known classical authority relates her to Jupiter. Of the two pits of Hell which Pluto swears by, *Stige* must be Styx, but I have not been able to identify *Segne*.

[6] *In I Reg.* VIII.7 (*PL*, LXXIX, 222).

[7] A similar version of this story is found in *Roman des Sept Sages*, though it was popular and occurs in various forms in the Latin moralized tales (for example, Latin *Gesta Romanorum*, clxxxvi).

[8] The "Tale of the Two Coffers" is similar to that told by Boccaccio, *Decam.* X.i. Variations of the story are found in such collections of moral tales as *Vita Barlaam et Josaphat*, cap. vi (*PL*, LXXIV, 462); Vincent of Beauvais, *Spec. Hist.* XV.10; *Legenda Aurea*; and English *Gesta Romanorum* (cap. LXVI). Cf. Shakespeare's *Merchant of Venice*.

[9] A story similar to that of the two pasties occurs in the Latin *Gesta Romanorum*, cap. cix.

[10] Based on *Roman des Sept Sages*.

[11] Told fully in Statius, *Achilleid*, I.198–960. Condensed versions occur in collections of moralized tales (for example, Latin *Gesta Romanorum*, cap. clvi).

[12] Gower's story of Medea draws both from Benôit's *Roman de Troie*, 715–2078, and Ovid's *Metam.* VII.1–424. Macaulay discusses Gower's use of Benôit (III.497). Cf. Chaucer's version of the Medea story in *Legend of Good Women*, 1500–1679.

[13] The story of Phrixus and Helen occurs without much variation of detail in Hyg. *Fab.* II–III; *Vat. Myth.* I (23), II (134); Bocc. *Gen.* XIII.67; and Ovid, *Fasti*, III.851–876.

[14] Cf., *Metam.* III.359 ff. Gower modifies the story considerably.

[15] Founded on the *Comoedia Babionis*, a Latin elegiac poem in a quasi-dramatic form which was popular in the fourteenth century. See *Early Mysteries and Other Latin Poems of the 12th & 13th Centuries*, ed. Th. Wright (London, 1838), p. 65.

[16] The "Tale of Adrian and Bardus" is Eastern in origin. It occurs near the end of the *Speculum Stultorum* and a variation of it is told by Richard I in Matthew Paris's *Historia Major* (entry for 1195).

[17] The story of Ariadne is told in Ovid, *Metam*. VIII.169, and Hyg. *Fab*. XL–XLIII, though Gower is not following either source closely. Cf. Chaucer's *Legend of Good Women*, 1886–2227.

[18] Gower's story of Tereus comes loosely from Ovid, *Metam*. VI.424–674. Cf. Chaucer's *Legend of Good Women*, 2228–2393, and *Troilus and Criseyde*, II.64–73.

[19] Cf. Ovid, *Metam*. II.568–588.

[20] Cf. Ovid, *Metam*. II.409–507, where she is named *virgo Nonacrina*, and *Fasti*, II.155–192, where she is called Callisto.

[21] Cf. *Mirour*, 17119 ff., where the saying is attributed to Jerome. Valerius does speak of a man named Spurina (*Mem*. IV.5) who destroys the beauty of his face to protect his virginity. Cf. *Mirour*, 18301 ff. The subsequent reference to the Apocalypse is Rev. 14:4. The account of Valentinian's virginity occurs in *Epistola Valerii ad Rufinum*, where the Emperor is said to be *octogenarius*.

[22] Not Chaucer's Criseyde, but Briseis. Cf. *Heroides* III.

[23] Cf. Ovid, *Metam*. IV.190–270.

[24] Cf. Ovid, *Fasti*, II.303–358.

[25] In some manuscripts of the *Confessio* about 200 additional lines on sacrilege follow line 6980 and include the "Tale of Lucius and the Statue," a tale told also in *Mirour de l'Omme*, 7093–7128, and which is to be found in various fourteenth century Latin and Middle English story books (cf. English *Gesta Romanorum*, cap. LXVIII). The story may be summarized as follows: Before Rome was Christian, Caesar made a statue of Apollo, gorgeously adorned with a gold beard, a gold mantle, and a fine carbuncle ring. It happened that a famous clerk named Lucius, a courtier of wit and amusement, squandered all his goods and fell into poverty. To make up for his losses he robbed the statue of its ring, mantle, and beard. The king was informed of the desecration, and Lucius

was discovered in possession of the loot. When questioned about the robbery Lucius replied: "When I beheld the god, his hand was outstretched, offering me the ring, which I took in appreciation of his largesse. Moreover, in gratitude, I removed the cold heavy gold mantle which so encumbered his shoulders—a garment too cold for winter and too heavy for summer. Then, as I looked at him, I saw his large beard and remembered that his father, who stood there before him, was a beardless youth. So I removed the beard that he might be like his father. Therefore I ask to be excused of the charges against me." See how men lighten their consciences with sacrilege!

[26] From Benôit, *Rom. de Troie,* 3845–3928; 4167–4936. See also Dares, VII–X, and Guido, VI–VII.

Notes to Book Six

[1] Cf. *Rom. de la Rose,* 6813 ff., and Chaucer's Wife of Bath [III(D)170], who delights in assuming Cupid's role as butler of the tuns to serve sweet or bitter as she pleases.

[2] The story of Bacchus's return from war and the miraculous fountain in the desert occurs in Hyg. *Poet. Astr.* II.20, under the heading "Aries," and in *Vat. Myth.* I (121).

[3] The Tristan story was very popular. For a full account of the drinking of the love potion see Gottfried von Strassburg's *Tristan.*

[4] Cf. Ovid, *Metam.* XII.210 ff.

[5] No source has been identified for this story.

[6] Compare the three dainties of Amans to the three gifts— *Douz Penser* (sweet thought), *Douz Parler* (sweet speech), and *Douz Regart* (sweet sight)—which Cupid gives to the lover to assuage his pain in *Roman de la Rose* (2643–2764).

[7] Luke 16:19–31.

[8] Whether the raconteur be Chaucer, Jean de Meun, Boethius, or a marketplace storyteller, tales about Nero's atrocities and

follies offered the medieval imagination almost endless moral pleasure. Terence Tiller notes that this particular episode is also told of Frederick II Hohenstaufen. (Penguin edition of *Confessio,* p. 228.)

[9] Gower's principal source here seems to be Albertus Magnus(?), *Speculum Astronomiae.* Fox notes that *spatula* is the art of divination from the shoulderblades of animals and that *cernes* are circles of peripheral figures used in magic. The "School of Honorius" apparently refers to those who took an oath in order to gain possession of *Liber Sacratus* which Honorius supposedly wrote. See Macaulay, III.515–516, for identification of the various magicians, and Fox, pp. 141 ff., for a discussion of Gower's knowledge of magic.

[10] The story of Ulysses and Telegonus is told by Dictys, VI.14, 15; and Benôit, *Rom. de Troie,* 28701–28825, 29815–30300; and *Gest Hist.* XXXIV.13208–13253, XXXVI.13802–13989.

[11] Because he was Alexander's teacher and a magician too, Nectanabus was another favorite character in popular medieval literature. Gower may be working from the Anglo-Norman *Roman de toute Chevalerie,* the Latin *Historia Alexandri de Preliis,* Valerius's *Res Gestae Alexandri,* or some version of the *Alexandreis* by Gaultier de Châtillon.

[12] Cf. Pliny, *Nat. Hist.* VII.15, and Augustine, *De Civ. Dei,* XXI.14.

[13] I Kings 27–31 (I Sam. 27–31, King James).

Notes to Book Seven

[1] Gower did not, of course, know Aristotle first hand. Genius's account of Aristotle's division of Philosophy into *Théorique, Réthorique,* and *Practique* is based mainly on Brunetto Latini's *Trésor.*

[2] A further proof of the pre-eminence of sight over the other senses. See Book I, note 6.

[3] Cf. *Vox Clamantis* II.217–348, where Gower discusses the relationship between men, animals, and morality.

[4] Gower is not actually following Ptolemy's *Almagest,* though that work certainly underlay the sources he was working with. Part of his material may have been gleaned from Brunetto Latini's *Trésor,* part from Vincent of Beauvais's *Speculum Naturale* and from Fulgentius's *Mythologicon,* part from redactions of Martianus Capella's *De Nuptiis Philologiae et Mercurii,* and part from astronomical lists and treatises such as the *Speculum Astronomiae* (variously ascribed to Roger Bacon and Albertus Magnus) and the writings of Alchandrus. (See Fox, pp. 65–83.)

[5] The association of planets with man's elemental character was maintained on the best authority, though usually the writers were careful to maintain free will too. (For example, John of Salisbury, *Polycraticus,* 2.18–19; Herman of Dalmatia's translation of Albumazar, *Introductorium in Astronomiam,* which became the basis for Aquinas's views on astrology in *Summa Theologiae*; and the *Speculum Astronomiae.* Medieval theory of planetary influence may be ultimately traced back through Ptolemy to the *Timaeus,* where the planets are viewed as instruments of time.) Theories of planetary influence provided a convenient means for characterizing men and circumstances and are thus commonly alluded to in medieval literature. Cf. Chaucer's use of Saturn as a malignant influence beyond which there is only Higher Love in the "Knight's Tale," and *Vox Clamantis,* II.221 ff., where we are told that God will hold the heavens in check and make Saturn pleasing if men become willing to observe His precepts.

[6] Gower's discussion of the Universe moves from earth, through the planets, to the fixed stars which occupy the eighth sphere and are immutable. That the fixed stars are fifteen in number perhaps suggests through number symbolism the conjoining of heaven and earth, eternity and temporality. (Cf. Hugh of St. Victor's discussion of the number fifteen in *De Arca Noe Morali,* III.16.) Because of their permanence (and thus potency) more magicians than Nectanabus based wonder working calculations on

them. (Cf. Chaucer's "tregetour" in the "Franklin's Tale," F.1280.) Gower's account of the fifteen stars with their respective herbs and stones is taken from *Liber Hermetis de XV Stellis et de XV Lapidibus et de XV Herbis, XV Figuris, etc.* Vincent of Beauvais observes (*Speculum Naturale*, 16.53) that every herb on earth has a star in the sky which is concerned for it and causes it to grow.

[7] Here Gower seems to be following Albertus Magnus's *De libris licitis et illicitis*, the *Speculum Astronomiae*, and, perhaps, Michael Scot's *Introductio Astrologiae*.

[8] Since Christ himself is God's Word, the Second Person being the *expression* of the First Person, abuse of language is a sin against Truth. Gower follows the Platonic-Aristotelian tradition in which truth (not simply persuasion) is a fundamental requisite of Rhetoric. Words used for persuasion, regardless of truth, are false rhetoric.

[9] Rather than Tully, Gower is following Brunetto Latini in the *Trésor*, which also uses the Roman Senate's discussion of the fate of Catiline as a model of right use of Rhetoric.

[10] The five points of policy which Genius outlines here follow vaguely the model of kingly instruction in the *Secretum Secretorum*. There the recommended virtues are liberality, wisdom, chastity, mercy, truth, and also justice. In the *Secretum*, Aristotle is less systematic than Genius is. This portion of the *Confessio* is pointedly directed towards the English throne. Cf. George R. Coffman, "John Gower, Mentor for Royalty: Richard II," *PMLA*, LXIX (1954), 953–964; and, George Hamilton, "Some Sources of the Seventh Book of Gower's *Confessio Amantis*," *MP* (1912), 323–346.

[11] The story of the three counselors is based on III Esdras 3:4. Gower has added Zorobabel's illustrative account of Alcestis. (Cf. Chaucer's use of Alcestis as the model of virtue in his *Legend of Good Women*.) A variation of the story occurs in the Latin *Gesta Romanorum*, cap. cclviii.

[12] Cf. *Roman de la Rose*, 9603–9636, 18545–18606; and *Piers Plowman* (B.Pro. 113, 132–138, 141–142), where kings are also

looked on, not as part of the original order, but rather as an expediency, a necessary evil which resulted from the fall.

[13] The account of the King of Chaldee's prodigality may be found in the *Secretum Secretorum*. The story of Julius and the Poor Knight, which comes next, is based ultimately on Seneca, *De Beneficiis*, V.24, though it is retold in the Latin *Gesta Romanorum*, cap. lxxxvii. The story of King Antigonus, which follows, may originate with Brunetto Latini's *Trésor*, though there the story is an example of hypocritical excuses.

[14] Based on an anecdote told by Valerius Maximus, *Mem.* IV.3.

[15] In four MSS of the second recension, line 2328 is followed by twelve lines which cite Dante's rebuff of a flatterer.

[16] Of these accounts of the Roman Triumphal processions Macaulay (III.530) notes: "The Roman Triumph as here related was a commonplace of preachers and moralists, cf. Bromyard, *Summa Praedicantium*, T.v.36." See also the Latin *Gesta Romanorum*, cap. xxx. Precisely which "Chronicle" Genius speaks of is not known. Hoccleve's *Regement of Princes* mentions the custom of masons visiting the Emperor to plan his sepulcher; a marginal note there refers the reader to *Vita Johannis Eleemosynarii*. That custom is also described in Jofroi's *Secretum Secretorum*.

[17] III Kings 22 (I Kings 22, King James).

[18] The account of Maximin is found in Godfrey of Viterbo, *Speculum Regum*, while the accounts of Gaius Fabricius, Emperor Conrad, and Consul Carmidotirus are based on Valerius Maximus, *Facta et Dicta Memorabilia*.

[19] The story of Cambyses and his judge, first told by Herodotus (V.25), was popular with medieval audiences. Macaulay (III.531) notes its reoccurance in Valerius Maximus, *Mem.* VI.3; the Latin *Gesta Romanorum*, cap. xxix; Hoccleve's *Regement of Princes*. The story of Lycurgus, which follows, was another oft repeated story. Cf. Latin *Gesta Romanorum*, cap. clxix.

[20] The list of lawgivers is based on the *Trésor*.

[21] Three MSS of the second recension include about thirty additional lines which cite James the Apostle, Cassiodorus, Tully, and Alexander on the importance of pity in kings.

[22] See the story of Constantine and Sylvester (*Conf. Am.* II.3187 ff.) for a further exemplum of Constantine's pity. An account of Troian may be found in Godfrey of Viterbo, *Spec. Reg.* II.14.

[23] Six MSS of the second recension follow line 3162 with the "Tale of the Jew and the Pagan" (based on the *Secretum Secretorum*), which may be summarized as follows: To exemplify Pity, Aristotle told King Alexander how two men met one hot summer in the wilderness between Cairo and Babylon. One asked the other about his faith. The other said he was a Pagan whose law bade him to be gracious, debonair, and to love all men alike, whether they be rich or poor. The first man then said he was a Jew who by his law would be a true fellow to no man unless he be another Jew. For if the fellow were not a Jew, he might take both life and goods from him. The Pagan marveled at so strange a law. As they traveled on under the hot sun, the Jew, who was on foot, schemed how he might ride. So he said to the Pagan, who rode upon an ass to which he had tied all his goods: "If your law is as you say you are beholden to me in my weariness and distress to let me ride a mile or two that I might rest my body." The Pagan, who would not displease his companion, saw his plight and in pity let him ride full soft. On they went, chatting away about this and that until at last the Pagan could go no further. When he asked the Jew to let him ride again, the Jew hastened on ahead, saying: "You upheld your law by giving me succor; now I will do my duty according to the law of Jewry: 'Thin asse schal go forth with me / With al thi good, which I have sesed; / And that I wot thou art desed, / I am riht glad and noght mispaid.'" The deserted Pagan knelt on the ground, raised his hands to heaven, and prayed: "O highest Trust, who loves righteousness, I beseech with humble heart that you see and judge this quarrel. Mercy or vengeance I leave to your judgment." So he went on "with drery

chiere," hoping to catch sight of the Jew, but without success until nightfall. Then from the highway he at last beheld the Jew, lying all bloody in a valley, slain by a lion. Looking about he found his ass nearby, still in harness, safe and sound. See how the piteous man deserves pity, as Aristotle bears witness. Pity is the source of all virtue, and God will repress under foot its enemies. (See Ruth Ames, "The Source and the Significance of 'The Jew and the Pagan,' " *Mediaeval Studies*, XIX (1957), 37–47.)

24 Both stories of Codrus and Pompeius may be found in Valerius Maximus, *Mem.* V. The story of Codrus also occurs in the Latin *Gesta Romanorum*, cap. xli, and Jofroi's *Secretum Secretorum*.

25 Macaulay (III.532) notes: "Justinian II is described by Gibbon as a cruel tyrant, whose deposition by Leontius was fully deserved, and who, when restored by the help of Terbelis, took a ferocious vengeance on his opponents: 'during the six years of his new reign, he considered the axe, the cord, and the rack as the only instruments of royalty.' Nothing apparently could be less appropriate than the epithet 'pietous,' which Gower bestows upon him."

26 Gower apparently read the story in Godfrey of Viterbo's *Pantheon*, where Barillus is the name given to Perillus, as in the *Confessio*, though the story was a favorite (cf. Latin *Gesta Romanorum*, cap. XLVIII).

27 The tyrant Dionysius has been confused with Diomedes, whom Hercules overthrew. The story of Lycoan may be found in *Metam*. I.221–243.

28 The story of Spartachus occurs in Justin, *Epitome*, I.8, and Orosius, *Hist*. II.7. Macaulay (III.532) suggests that the names in Gower's account apparently come from Peter Comestor (*PL*, CXCVIII, 1471).

29 The reference should be to Juvenal, *Sat*. VIII.269 ff., instead of Horace. The following reference to Solomon is to Ecclesiastes 3:8.

[30] For Gideon's story see Judges 7; the story of Saul and Agag occurs in I Kings 15 (I Sam. 15, King James).

[31] For David's advice to Solomon and Solomon's wisdom in following it, see III Kings 2–12.

[32] Gower's "Chronicle" is Godfrey of Viterbo's *Pantheon*.

[33] III Kings 12. Notice that throughout this portion of the poem, where his criticism of the king and his counsel becomes most pointed, Gower makes extensive use of Biblical sources; his argument rests on the highest authority, of which there can be no dispute.

[34] The king is Antoninus Pius, whose story Gower probably knew from Godfrey of Viterbo's *Pantheon*.

[35] The story of Sardanapulus occurs in Godfrey of Viterbo's *Pantheon*, where the conqueror Arbaces is referred to as Barbatus. The account of Cyrus's conquest over the Lydians occurs in Herodotus and in Justin, *Epit.* 1.7, though in those versions Cyrus's corruption of the Lydians takes place after he has had to put down (successfully) a revolt.

[36] Numbers 24–25, where the Pagan King is Balak, not Amalech.

[37] Cf. III Kings 11.

[38] The story is much enlarged from Ovid, *Fasti*, II.687–852. Cf. Chaucer's *Legend of Good Women*, 1680–1885; Latin *Gesta Romanorum*, cap. CXXXV; and Shakespeare's *Rape of Lucrece*.

[39] Like the "Rape of Lucrece," the "Tale of Virginia" was very popular. The original version occurs in Livy. Jean de Meun includes it in *Roman de la Rose*, Boccaccio includes it in *De Mulieribus Claris*, and Chaucer includes it in the *Canterbury Tales* as the "Physician's Tale." Boccaccio and Chaucer cite Livy as their sources, though in fact they follow Jean de Meun. Gower follows Livy or perhaps Pierre Berçuire's Old French translation of Livy.

[40] From the Book of Tobias, 6–8.

Notes to Book Eight

[1] The "Tale of Apollonius" was popular and appears in English before Gower in an Old English translation. It occurs in the *Pantheon*, which Gower used frequently, though his version includes many details not to be found in Godfrey, and in the Latin *Gesta Romanoroum*, cap. CLIII. The eleventh-century Latin prose version, *Historia Apollonii Tyrii*, a version which Godfrey used as his source, was most likely known by Gower. It includes details found in Gower which do not occur in Godfrey. (See Macaulay's discussion, III.536–538.) Shakespeare's *Pericles*, in which "Gower" is the commentator, is based only in part on Gower's version of the story.

[2] Here Gower shifts his narrative point of view from that of a dramatic dialogue to that of an onlooking narrator (still first person). The shift in tone anticipates the Lover's new perspective which will enable him to disengage himself from his venial infatuation so that his love-wound might be healed.

[3] Line 2377 is preceded by a ten-line epigram on the perfecting of desire:

Whoever desires what he is unable to have, wastes his time; where there is no possibility of fulfillment, even wishing is unhealthy. The work of summer is not for grey hair; when the heat is gone, winter takes over. Nature does not give May's gifts to December. Mud cannot consort with flowers, nor can the decrepit pleasures of old men blossom into—what Venus herself seeks—a young man's compliance.   (A.G.)

[4] See Macaulay's note (III.544–545) for a discussion of Rageman, a dice game the play of which apparently involved women and verses. Cf. Skeat, *Piers the Plowman*, II, 10 (note 73) and 238 (note 122).

[5] Richard II's new queen was, of course, Anne of Bohemia; thus Bohemian fashions were the current rage.

[6] Macaulay notes, regarding *Sortes*: "Perhaps it stands for the well-known 'Sortes Sanctorum' (Virgilianae, etc.), personified here as a magician, and even figuring, in company with Virgil and the rest, as an elderly lover." (III.547) The term may be, however, merely a corruption of "Socrates." Cf. *Piers Plowman*, B. XII.269, and Skeat's discussion of the name in *Piers the Plowman*, II, 187.

[7] In the first recension of the *Confessio* (1390), lines 2941*–2957* dedicate the poem to Gower's friend Geoffrey Chaucer: [Venus is speaking to Amans]

' And gret wel Chaucer whan ye mete,
As mi disciple and mi poete:
For in the floures of his youthe
In sondri wise, as he wel couthe,
Of Ditees and of songes glade,
The whiche he for mi sake made,
The lond fulfild is overal:
Whereof to him in special
Above alle othre I am most holde.
2950* For thi now in hise daies olde
Thow schalt him telle this message,
That he upon his latere age,
To sette an ende of alle his werk,
As he which is myn owne clerk,
Do make his testament of love,
As thou hast do thi schrifte above,
So that mi Court it mai recorde.'

In the Fairfax Manuscript, lines 2938 to the end of Book VIII are written in a different hand. The new scribe uses slightly different orthography. Particularly noticeable is *y* for the pronoun *I*, and *i* or *y* for *e* in inflections.

[8] Spare, I beg, O Christ, this people's joy; resist England's grievous demise, O highest king. Set right all conditions and ranks, set free those weakly accused; then this land, pleasing to God, will grow strong and blessed.   (A.G.)

In the first recension, Gower began this concluding section with a prayer for Richard, which was followed by 144 lines praising the king, "In whom hath evere yit be founde / Justice medled with pite, / Largesce forth with charite." He commends Richard for not being cruel in retaliation against his enemies and for remaining stable and sun-bright during times of trouble: "Althogh the weder be despeired, / The hed planete is not to wite [blame]." He then presents his book to the king and, after confessing his allegiance, bids farewell to earthly love in order to contemplate the peace of heaven.

[9] This book is finished, and wherever it may go, I beg that it may without shame find favor in the reader's mouth. May he who sits on the throne of Heaven grant that this book of John's remain pleasing to the Britains forever. Go, simple (*purus*) book, to the Count of Derby, whom learned men praise, and you will find refuge with him.   (F. W. L.)

SELECTED BIBLIOGRAPHY
FOR THE NOTES

Benôit de Sainte-Maure. *Le Roman de Troie*, ed. Léopold Constans. 6 vols. Société des Anciens Textes Français. Paris, 1904–1912.

Boccaccio, Giovanni. *Genealogie Deorum Gentilium Libri*, ed. Vincenzo Romano, 2 vols. Scrittori D'Italia, n. 200–201. Luglio, 1951.

Boethius. *Consolatio Philosophiae*, ed. H. F. Stewart. (Loeb Classic), Cambridge, Mass., 1918.

Brunetto Latini. *Li Livres dou Trésor*, ed. Francis J. Carmody. Berkeley, 1948.

Chaucer, Geoffrey. *The Works of Geoffrey Chaucer*, ed. F. N. Robinson. 2d Edition. Cambridge, Mass., 1957.

Dares Phrygius. *De Excidio Troiae Historia*, ed. F. Meister. Leipzig, 1873.

Dictys Cretensis. *Ephemeridos Belli Troiani*, ed. F. Meister. Leipzig, 1872.

Gest Hystoriale of the Destruction of Troy, eds. G. A. Panton and David Donaldson. Early English Text Society, Nos. 39 and 56. London, 1879.

Gesta Romanorum: Early English Versions, ed. Sidney J. H. Herrtage. EETS ex. ser. 33. London, 1879.

Gesta Romanorum (Latin), ed. Hermann Oesterley. Berlin, 1872.

Godfrey of Viterbo. *Pantheon*, ed. George Waitz. *Monumenta Germaniae Historica: Scriptores* (Hanover, 1872), XXII, 107–307.

———. *Speculum Regum*, ed. G. Waitz. *MGH:S.* XXII, 21–93.

Gower, John. *The Works of John Gower*, ed. G. C. Macaulay. 4 vols. Oxford, 1901. (Vol. I: French Works; Vols. II–III: English Works; Vol. IV: Latin Works.)

Guido de Columnis. *Historia Destructionis Troiae*, ed. Nathaniel E. Griffin. Cambridge, Mass., 1936.

Guillaume de Lorris et Jean de Meun. *Le Roman de la Rose*, ed. Ernest Langlois. 5 vols. SATS. Paris, 1914–1924.

Hyginus, C. Julius. "Fabularum Liber; Poeticon Astronomicon," in *Mythographi Latini*. Amsterdam, 1681.

Langland, William. *Piers the Plowman*, ed. W. W. Skeat. 2 vols. Oxford, 1886.

"Mythographi Vaticani," in *Scriptores Rerum Mythicarum*, ed. Georgius Henricus Bode. 2 vols. [Göttingen], 1834.

Ovid. *Fasti*, ed. Sir James G. Frazer. 5 vols. London, 1929.

————. *Heroides* and *Amores*, ed. Grant Showerman. (Loeb Classic), Cambridge, Mass., 1914.

————. *Metamorphoses*, ed. Frank J. Miller. 2 vols. (Loeb Classics), Cambridge, Mass., 1921.

Secreta Secretorum: Three Prose Versions, ed. Robert Steele. 2 vols. EETS ex. 74–75. London, 1898.

Sources and Analogues of Chaucer's Canterbury Tales, eds. W. F. Bryan and G. Dempster. Chicago, 1941.

Statius. *Silvae, Thebaid, Achilleid*, ed. J. H. Mozley. 2 vols. (Loeb Classics), London, 1928.

Vincent of Beauvais. *Speculum Maius: Naturale, Doctrinale, Morale, Historiale*. Graz, Austria, 1964–1965.

NOTE: Migne's *Patrologia Latina* is abbreviated *PL* in the notes; works therein are cited by volume and column number. All biblical references are based on the Douay translation of the Vulgate, with occasional cross references to the King James translation.